DUNDEE CITY COUNCIL

CENTRAL LIBRARY

REFERENCE SERVICES

FOR REFERENCE ONLY

History of Universities

VOLUME XXV/2

2011

History of Universities is published bi-annually

Editor:
Mordechai Feingold (California Institute of Technology)

Managing Editor:
Jane Finucane (Trinity College, University of Glamorgan)

Editorial Board:
R. D. Anderson (University of Edinburgh)
L. W. Brockliss (Magdalen College, Oxford)
C. Toniolo Fascione (University of Rome, Tor Vergata)
W. Frihoff (Vrije Universiteit, Amsterdam)
N. Hammerstein (University of Frankfurt)
D. Julia (Institut Universitaire, Européen, Florence)
M. Nelissen (Leuven)
H. de Ridder-Symoens (Ghent)
S. Rothblatt (University of California, Berkeley)
N. G. Siraisi (Hunter College, New York)

A leaflet 'Notes to OUP Authors' is available on request from the editor.

To set up a standing order for History of Universities contact Standing Orders, Oxford University Press, North Kettering Business Park, Hipwell Road, Kettering, Northamptonshire, NN14 1UA
Email: StandingOrders.uk@oup.com
Tel: 01536 452640

History of Universities

VOLUME XXV/2
2011

OXFORD
UNIVERSITY PRESS

OXFORD
UNIVERSITY PRESS

Great Clarendon Street, Oxford OX2 6DP

Oxford University Press is a department of the University of Oxford.
It furthers the University's objective of excellence in research, scholarship,
and education by publishing worldwide in

Oxford New York

Auckland Cape Town Dar es Salaam Hong Kong Karachi
Kuala Lumpur Madrid Melbourne Mexico City Nairobi
New Delhi Shanghai Taipei Toronto

With offices in

Argentina Austria Brazil Chile Czech Republic France Greece
Guatemala Hungary Italy Japan Poland Portugal Singapore
South Korea Switzerland Thailand Turkey Ukraine Vietnam

Oxford is a registered trade mark of Oxford University Press
in the UK and in certain other countries

Published in the United States
by Oxford University Press Inc., New York

British Library Cataloguing in Publication Data
Data available

Library of Congress Cataloging in Publication Data
Data available

Typeset by SPI Publishers Services, Pondicherry, India
Printed in Great Britain
on acid-free paper by
MPG Books Group, Bodmin and King's Lynn

ISBN 978-0-19-969404-4

1 3 5 7 9 10 8 6 4 2

Contents

The Viterban *Studium* of the sixteenth century: an educational experiment of the Italian Renaissance

Marta Materni

In September 1546, Bartolomeo Appoggio da Macerata, representative of Pope Paul III in the *Patrimonium of San Pietro* in Tuscia the Papal States,[1] is registered in the *Libro delle Riforme* of the commune of Viterbo. This decree authorized the foundation of a *Studium litterarium* in the city. Humanist culture had already penetrated Viterbo in the previous century, the *Quattrocento*, and the existing evidence permits us to identify four significant dates illustrating the development.

First, in 1454, Giovanni of Gallese prior of the church of Sancta Maria Nuova and *profexor grammatice atque rethorice*, was appointed public schoolmaster in a letter which includes the following phrase: 'Concedentes tibi et tuis qui te auditori undecumque oriundi fuerint scholaribus omnium immunitatum, prerogativarum, securitatum et exceptionum privilegia quae magistris et scholaribus urbis Romae et ceterarum urbium regiarum in quibus generalia liberalium artium Studia vigere consueverunt.'[2] Viterbo's Statute of 1250–1 already made reference to the *Autentica Habita*; the wording of this letter of appointment further epitomizes the attitude of Viterbo's civic world towards education.

Second, the 1469 Statute includes an article regulating public lectures in Law and Medicine, financed by the commune. Third, in December 1494, when Charles VIII stayed in Viterbo, the *magister ludi* Tommaso Veltrellini welcomed him with an oration from which I quote this passage:

Et quantum regium putamus et celeberrimis virtutibus convenire, non solum civitates conservare, verum etiam moribus, institutisque bonarum artium augere. Nec ob aliam causam Octavium, Caesarem Augustum appellatum legimus, ceterosque tanto nomine ornatos, nisi quod rempublicam humanis comodis, equo iure, legibus et doctrina amplificaverint. Nam P. Emilius, devicto Perse Macedonum rege, copia librorum in Urbem advecta, ex qua litterarum studium

Rome florere cepit; maximam gloriam sibi paravit Albinum quoque anglicum legimus, Caroli Magni eruditorem, ingenio et honestate morum et studio philosophie prestantissimum, Perusie per eumdem imperatorem prepositum, initia Perusini Studii, quod adhuc durat et floret, prebisse, ob hanc rem nomen illius inmortale factum est. Potentissime Rex, hoc idem hec Vetulonia civitas Viterbiensis expectat, hoc idem hic Herculeus, Trossolus populus rogat, hoc idem hic Senatus consultus, senes, juvenes, adolescentes orant: ut hec civitas Tuo regio officio, Tua regia munificentia, liberalitate et gratitudine, quibus et aliis amplissimis virtutibus memoriam maiestatis Tue facias sempiternam, ornetur, et Studio liberalium artium, jurisque canonici et civilis augeatur: quod opus sanctum et divinum ad comune omnium comodum et emolumentum est, cum et doctrinarum exercitia viros nobilitent pariter et illustrent.[3]

Finally, in 1495, Charles's request was repeated and sent forward to the Pope: [we supplicate] quod eius sancta maiestas sua regia munificentia operari dignetur quod in dicta civitate Viterbii Studium erigatur instar Studii Perusini, pro cuius substentatione et manutentione aliqua competens dos fiat, attento quod alias Studium predictum redderetur frustratorum cum maxime salaria legentium aliunde et ex redditibus dicte communitatis solvi non possent cum illi ad alios usus sint destinati pro necessitatibus dicte civitatis.[4]

There is notable evidence too outside the official documentation, as in a letter addressed to the Council by *ser* Andrea Giovenali da Corneto, dated 1536:

Considerando l'amore che porto alla vostra città donne ho imparato quelle poche littere che so et cossì questi nostri figlioli sotto el vestro mastro grammaticale fanno el medesimo, cognioscendo la presente oportunità che la santità di nostro signore ab antiquo [...] et considerato el fervente amore che porta ad questa città, ho preso animo che con facilità sua santità donarìa la mità del subsidio apostolico ogni anno ad questa comunità per fondare qui uno Studio a perpetua sua gloria et ad utilità della sua excelsa et illustrissima casa et del suo stato et per utilità di questa città e de tutti provinciali li quali et con denari et con littere aricharìano et nobilitarìano dicta città, della quale de vostri senza l'altri ne surgeriano tanti litterati che in quella patria de Roma sarìano sublevati a grandi dignità et varie, et perché reconosco dentro in questo Studio un mirabile utile della fede apostolica que multi prelati et loro nepoti et parenti [...] ibi farìano studiare et instruere qui. Mostrata et apertoli questa porta sanza dubio ho certissimo et faranno conto sua santità et la sede apostolica perché levano alla sede apostolica questa mità del subsidio nolli importa un dramma, [...] Pio II ne donò a Cornetani ducati 150 per el maestro della scola et el medico, et perché quest'opera è tanto utile et onorevole alla città anchora ne sonno modi da trovare del publico 200 ducati più con poca sua lesione, et un altro modo expugniato el primo ne sequirà per ingrandire detto Studio, perché le opere bone da Dio et da cieli sono sempre favorite. Interea presento a vostre magnifiche signorie esaminino bene questa intenzione et non se lassino perdere la presente occasione perché in manibus vestris est dictus et pontifex et si la manigiate colla vostra solita prudentia so certissimo el disegno sortiscerà effetto, che quando in altro tempo se reservasse, persa la presente occasione, in altri se trovarìa difficoltà.'[5]

The word *Studium*, which seems to unite a number of aspirations, emerges regularly in Viterbo's documentation. For the sixteenth century, it seems to refer to a concrete reality. With the present study I hope to trace the vicissitudes of that *Studium* throughout the sixteenth century, sifting through the rhetorical pomp of the sources in order to identify the limits and effective realities of the institution, and emphasizing how its experience corresponds with a widespread historical trend involving many Italian communities.[6]

The commune's set of *Libro delle Riforme* is the most significant source for this investigation. Complementary sources are the *Bollettari*, the *Lettere ai Superiori*, the *Lettere diverse*, the *Ricordi dei Priori*, edited material on parchment, the fifteenth-century city chronicle of Niccolò della Tuccia and the Sacchi family's *Ricordi*.[7]

What Grendler describes as 'the third Wave' of the Italian university foundations began in the middle of the sixteenth century, after a hiatus of almost a hundred years: these were the foundation of the High Renaissance.[8] During this period the institution and strengthening of a *Studium* often worked to compensate for a territory's decline in importance or loss of autonomy: 'New foundations abounded, established in settlements on the peripheries or in the new capitals of regional States. This trend was especially evident in provincial cities'.[9]

The Viterban experience fits neatly into this historical trend and can be explained with reference to the shared context. An awareness of similar experiences all over Italian territories must surely have had a strong influence on the city government's resolutions on intellectual affairs, and on the ambitions of the professional *élite*.[10] In particular, the fact that the Viterban initiatives to found a *Studium* appeared more frequently in the 1540's suggests that the foundation of Macerata university in 1540, by the same Paul III[11] who gave Viterbo its Papal brief, stimulated Viterban ambitions. In any case, the Papal States had the highest number of university foundations in Renaissance Italy, with the establishment of the Macerata *Studium* in 1540, Fermo in 1585 and Ferrara in 1598; and, we can add, with all the provisos to be mentioned later, Viterbo, in 1546.

A summary of Macerata's endeavours will reveal useful parallels with the Viterban experience. The municipal government campaigned for and created the *Studium*; its institution was preceded by pedagogical activity incorporating a municipal Latin school and some occasional lectures in law. 1548 was the first turning point: Leo X allowed the college of *legisti* to award academic degrees. Between 1534 and 1539, numerous attempts were made to gain Papal permission for the foundation of a *Studium*; meanwhile, in 1536, the commune started to pay a salary to a lecturer in the *Institutes* of Justinian. Finally, in July 1540, Paul III issued a bull of foundation for the Macerata *Studium*.

The commune aimed to create a small legal university which would guarantee students from the Marche an administrative career. Initially, there were nine lecturers, two of whom were *legisti* from Siena. The subjects were law (ordinary and extraordinary), the *Institutes*, canon law, medicine, logic, moral philosophy; and lather Latin and Greek literature. Later again, law predominated and there was never more than one lecturer for medicine; in some years, he was even absent.[12] The evolution of the Viterban *Studium* would be analogous but with one essential difference: it was never licensed to award degrees.[13]

Early references to higher education

Viterbo's Statute of 1250–1 was not chronologically the first, but it was surely first in importance and symbolic value. It included two articles devoted to *scolares*, inspired by Frederick I's *Autentica Habita*.[14] These are the earliest references in Viterbo's documentation to higher education:

Sectio III. Rub.[ca] 83. De scolaribus. Scolares causa studii Viterbium venientes tam ipsi quam nuntii eorum in personis et rebus salvi sint et securi in eundo et redeundo et stando. Et eos et res eorum potestas salvare et mantenere atque defendere teneatur a cunctis. Et illud idem dicimus in doctoribus et magistris nisi essent publici inimici aut exbanditi Viterbii. Rub.[ca] 84. De scolarium libertate. Item statuimus quod omnes scolares forenses in causis civilibus coram suis doctoribus et magistris debeant conveniri, et de omnibus exactionibus, exercitibus, angariis et perangariis sint exempti. Si vero aliquis magister veniret Viterbium ad regendum de omnibus exercitibus, cavalcamento, datiis, angariis et perangariis sit immunis.[15]

The articles thus guaranteed personal security to foreign students and teachers, established exceptions to this guarantee, and finally announced the *privilegium fori* for *scolares* involved in *causis civilis*. Without other supporting evidence it is only possible to speculate about the categories of teaching and students to which these rules applied: the references to *doctores* and *magistri* are the only evidence that higher education was at issue here.

This first use to *Autentica Habita* is elaborated in a text with more direct links to Viterbo, Article 73 of Book IV of the 1469 Statute, entitled *De salario docentium publice in scolis et de eorum exemptione*, which reveals that Viterbo offered public lectures in law and medicine.[16] The annual series of lectures in law was dedicated to the *Codicem vel Digestum novum vel vetus*, and the lecturer must complete a full analysis of the selected text by the end of the year; otherwise would forego the salary of 40 *libre*, which was paid by the commune in two instalments: at Christmas and at Easter. There are ambiguities in the language applied to these teachers: in the second part of the article the term *doctor* is employed, with the specification that *quilibet doctor* would be paid only on condition he had *ad minus duos scolares*; earlier however there was a reference to *docentes* who, in addition to having students, must also be *sufficientes*. The use of this adjective, which signifies personal competence rather than possession of a doctoral degree, may mean that possession of degree was not at this time an indispensable condition for teaching in the civic context. In addition to lecturers in medicine and law, the commune financed the activity of *doctores grammaticae et dictaminis*: they were not more than four in number, received a salary of twenty-five *libre* and had a schoolhouse reserved for their use. This form of instruction in letters would eventually be embodied in the institutional figure, omnipresent in the *Libri delle Riforme* of the sixteenth century: the *preceptor publicus* or *magister ludi litterarii*.

The above article and another dealing with student subsidies bear witness to cultural effervescence marking both the restoration of civic peace in the Papal States after a series of inner conflicts, and a renewal of economic well-being, which is confirmed by the city chronicles. Iuzzo, in 1471, noted that 'la nostra città si veniva integrando di omini. Aveva molti studenti, e molti in corte a Roma'[17]; and Niccolò della Tuccia, in 1472, related that, thanks to political stability alone 'Viterbo migliorava la sua condizione infinitamente, e cresceva in popoli, e teneva li studi di grammatica e loica e altre scienze'.[18]

Student Grants

Besides undertaking to assure provision of teaching approaching, or rather preparing students for university level, the commune created a coherent system of grants for students aspiring to continue as far as the *privilegium doctoratus*. The grant was linked at first to a particular area of study, then to the condition of being a *studens pauper*.[19]

The Statute of 1469

The Statute of 1469 contains the first formal reference to this grant[20] in the sources consulted. As already observed, this Statute surpassed the provisions made in 1250–1 by a more complex system of public lectures now officially codified.

The *Libro IV Rub.*[ca] *157* is indeed entitled 'Quod provideatur per Commune studentibus in iure civili':[21] humanist rhetoric and practical necessities combine in its first lines, where the iniative is justified 'pro honore, statu et commodo civitatis et subventione iurium', but also by the shortage of jurists and lawyers which has resulted from the city's mid-century wars. At this stage, therefore, the condition for the allocation of the grant was the choice by 'quilibet civis et habitator civitatis' to study 'ius civile Bononie vel alibi ubi sit Studium generale': it was no longer necessary for the candidate to be *studens pauper*. The grant amounted to twenty golden *fiorini*, paid in two instalments over three years: at the beginning of October and at Easter. For their part, students must testify to the commune annually[22] that they were attending lectures in law with a *doctor* ('habita fide quod talis studens audivit iura a doctore'). However it was only later that beneficiaries of the grant were expressly charged with completing their studies and achieving the *privilegium* on pain of returning twice the value of the whole grant.

The *Libri delle Riforme* reveal that other grants existed at this time for those higher studies. The first type is attested in the brief of Sixtus IV, presented to the city on 6 January 1475 by Pietro Paolo Passerino, 'homo virtuosus et bone litterature'.[23] Passerino was prior of the collegiate chapter of the church of S. Stefano and frequently delivered public orations before the Pope.[24] The papal brief invited the commune to grant this favourite of his what was described as the usual sum of 25 *fiorini* allocated to students of letters: 'ex vestra antiqua et laudabile consuetudine soletis concives vestros litterarum studiis operam dantes et in illis maxime commendatos in eorum subventione de 25 florenis auri auxilio iuvare et sublevare'.

It is not clear whether the grant of 4 March 1475,[25] to 'venerabilis et religiosus pater magister Iacobus Ambrosii de Viterbio sacre teologie professor, ordinis fratrum Heremitarum Sancti Augustini', is of the same type. Here too, Sixtus IV intervened, asking the commune to pay the sum of 25 *ducati* to Iacopo ('per vos pro subsidio gradus sumendi assignatam'), because he was ill; the sum had not been claimed earlier, but was now necessary.[26] The *Capitoli dello Studente* of 1582 (see below) mentions a grant of 25 *ducati* 'per vigor dello Statuto' assigned to graduates who had studied at their own expense: this must be the grant requested for Ambrosio, but it is not certain that Passerino's payment was made on the same basis.

The *Bollettari* and the *Riforme* attest to situations involving a sum of 36 *ducati*: in August 1528, 36 *ducati* were assigned 'pro subventione studii' to 'eximius artium et medicine doctor magister Iacobus ser Ambrosii'; in April 1532, to 'eruditus iuvenis magister Antonius Ioannes Turchus artium et medicine professor';[27] in September 1545, to 'magistro Francisco e magistro Cesare Bussi per causa del loro dottorato come in la patente';[28] in November 1546, to 'eruditum iuvenem dominum Faustum quondam Petri Pauli Sacchi civem nostrum ac iuris utriusque professorem';[29] in June 1547, to 'eruditum iuvenem Paulum Dionitii iuris utriusque professorem'.[30] The fact that men already holding the doctoral degree were awarded grants 'pro subventione studii' can be explained only if this was a repayment of costs incurred during studies; but the *Bollettari* records only the date when these sums were allocated.

Besides the contribution of thirty-six *ducati* to graduates' outlay on their studies, another type of grant is attested: payment of a sum of eighteen *scudi* to young people still studying. The *Bollettario* records the completion in June 1453 of payment of eighteen *scudi*, 'che la nostra comunità per vigore delli Statuti è solita dare a dicti studenti'. The student in question was Cesare Pollione, who was studying *in iure civili* in Bologna,[31] and would graduate *in utroque iure* in 1548. The name of Fausto Sacchi reappears in the *Riforme*: he received thirty-six *ducati* in November 1546, then a further eighteen *scudi* on 27 May 1547,[32] as 'subventio sui studii iuxta formam Satuti': a sum obtained from the tax *super panetteria*. But these payments seem to have been two instalments of the same grant.

Finally, in 1582, it was declared that student Ascanio Delicato, would qualify for one of the newly established grants on condition he renounce the sum of '18 scudi soliti darsi prima [before the revision of the *Capitoli*] dalla comunità per vigore dello Statuto.'[33]

But besides these statutory provisions, there were of course cases of private 'charity'.[34] On 25 May 1562[35] Pacifico Peronio, formerly an official in the chancellery, produced Giovanni Botonto's will before the General Council. The will decreed that 'heredes teneantur in perpetuum manutenere in publicis Studiis tres studentes de Viterbio'; if the heirs defaulted, the burden was to be transferred to the hospital of San Salvatore *in Urbe*: the *instrumentum* (that is the copy of the will) is delivered to the Council and ratified.[36]

Niccolò della Tuccia's civic chronicle confirms that many of Viterbo's young men undertook university studies. He noted for 1472, in the context of a general civic revival incorporating introduction of higher-level teaching, that 'insino al dì d'oggi erano assai giovani tornati a Viterbo con onore, dottori di legge civile, e assai giovani dotti in scienze; e ancora in corte di Roma vi erano assai li quali stavano in casa de' signori cardinali per migliorare la loro condizione'.[37]

Sacchi's *Ricordi* note further that, in 1477, the Servite Domenico Maltempi died and 'contavasi essere in Fiorenza stato avvelenato per invidia, che era valentissimo, e erano di molti maestri Viterbesi a quelli tempi valentissimi; anco molti dottori di legge e medici'.[38]

The 1582 *Capitoli dello studente*

The *Capitoli dello studente* are inserted in the 1582 *Libri delle Riforme*. This document was prepared by Pietro Pollione, *legum doctor*, and was dated 3 February 1582.[39] The original was solemnly deposited 'in capsa sigilli magnifice communitatis Viterbii'. On 18 March[40] the *Capitoli* were presented to the legate of the Papal States in Rome; on 22 July[41] the public announcement was promulgated, printed[42] and put on display in the city. The *Capitoli dello studente*, with additions made in 1604 and 1627, were also inserted into the 1649 Statute (*Lib. III, Rub.*[ca] *XIII*).

The subvention, funded through a tax on vegetables ('li ortaggi di tutta la Viterbese'), comprised 6 *scudi* a month over four years; it was to be paid only to native Viterban students, of all ranks ('nobili e ignobili'), unable to maintain themselves at their own expense ('non possano spendere il ben dell'ingegno che Nostro Signore gli ha dato'). As before, necessity and idealisme were united. In establishing the grant, the community represented itself as 'piissima et amantissima mater erga filios pauperes'; the objective being 'riempire la città di huomini letterati et virtuosi',[43] but with a preference for law graduates[44] who were 'di grandissimo giovamento et ornamento alla comunità'. This preference, combined with the fact that provisions for funding were actually made for a limited period and confined to the education of twelve students, suggests that Viterbo was suffering a shortage of the professionals required for the ever more complex needs of its developing political structures. The commune had therefore decided to invest public money in training its staff. In this regard, the tone of the public proclamation speaks volumes. If an individual was prevented from studying, 'n'è seguito particolare et publico danno'. To prevent this damage to private and public well-being, the commune had decided to invest 100 *scudi* in twelve young men 'acciò poi a loro stessi et alla città ne risulti splendore, utilità et ornamento.'

The provisions for twelve students to be sent *ad Studium*, to any public institution, no at a rate of no more than three per year so that the city would not suffer the loss of too many young people at once. The ratio of *legisti* to *artisti* must be two to one. Candidates for the grant must prove themselves suitable (*idonei*) by undergoing a public examination, after which the award winners were chosen by drawing lots. The examination took place before the vice-legate, the priori, law and medicine graduates, citizens, and, in the case of candidates hoping to study medicine or philosophy, teachers from the various monasteries. A potential *legista* was assigned his *punctus* by the lawyer of the commune; an *artista* received his *punctus* from a clergy man, usually a Dominican from the Monastery of Santa Maria in Gradi[45] or the Franciscan teaching brother.[46] Twenty-four hours later, the candidate would give a public recitation of the *punctus*.[47] At examinations, he would declaim an *oratiuncula*, recite the *punctus*, and respond to questions posed by graduates or lecturers in attendance.[48] If he passed the exam, he was declared 'sufficiens et valde habilis ad maiora studia destinandus', 'dignus et sufficiens' or simply *idoneus*.[49] Subsequently, when he left Viterbo for his chosen *Studium*, the student would produce his guarantors at a public ceremony.[50]

The existence of this examination accounts for the third absolute condition which candidates for financial support had to fulfil: two years' prior attendance at the public lectures on logic and *Institutes*. Hence these lectures can be described as pre-university preparatory courses. They maintained this function until the seventeenth century.

Candidates who obtained the grant must study for four years without interruption, returning home only 'per cause urgenti e necessarie', on pain of losing the subvention. If they had such urgent cause for return, they were advised to inform the legate and the priori in advance.[51] They must send the commune written testimony, from their *doctores*, every July, that they were dedicating themselves 'alli studi et tenere buona vita né essere discoli et dishonesti'. They must undertake the graduate not only from their own *Studia* but also from colleges of *doctores*: a problem at the time was the existence of multiple routes to qualification.[52] After graduating, they must 'fare l'entrata' (for which we have several testimonies in the *Libri delle Riforme*, discussed below), display the *privilegium*[53] in public and, after two months, 'tenere conclusioni pubbliche'. In practice, these obligations were all fulfilled on the same occasion. Students who completed their studies 'sumptibus magnifice communitatis' were not of course entitled to the bonus of 25 *ducati* awarded to those who had studied at their own expense.

The rule that only three students per year must receive this subvention was contravened immediately. Already on 21 October 1582,[54] on the occasion of the first competition, the legate, Cardinal Farnese, ordered that all four of that year's applicant, all judged *idonei*, should be sent to their chosen *Studia*. In 1586,[55] it was objected that the system might produce discontent both because of the limited number of places offered and because of economic discrimination. Then commune decided[56] that the 1586 cohort would be the last, and that the money set aside for the grade would be diverted to a *Studium* for Viterbo ('allo Studio da farsi in questa città come cosa molto più utile et di molto maggior honore et grandezza alla città nostra et anche in maggior commodo ai cittadini'). The commune would continue meanwhile to support the four students 'già a Studio [. . .] nel modo consueto, ma intanto si cerchi di eriggere in Viterbo lo Studio e subito eretto e dato principio cessi la provisione delli studenti quali si ritroveranno fuori'. The vice-legate, the *conservatori*, and four citizens to be elected would have the authority to deal with the legalities ('hanno autorità di fare capitoli, provisioni et ordini').

On 8th January 1587,[57] the Council sent a letter to the vice-legate asking him to plead with the Pope, on the basis that 'è tutto pronto e altro non manca salvo l'autorità di poter dottorare come nelli altri Studi pubblici.' But this was the umpteenth unsuccessful attempt to obtain licence to award degrees, and the grant system was continued. Another attempt to change the situation came in 1589. Following the advice of the Governor, the commune resolved to ask that six places at the Perugian Sapienza Vecchia or Nuova should be reserved for Viterbo's students: 'È nata qualche difficoltà nel mandare tanto numero di studenti che ora sono a spese del pubblico et monsignor illustrissimo Governatore ha proposto che seria molto meglio di comperare tanti beni et assegnarli per haver sei luoghi della Sapienza di Perugia, il che seria di maggior frutto et manco spesa essa per la comunità'.[58] On 20 October the Council decided to send Giovanni Battista Nino to Perugia to obtain information.[59] On his return 'exhibuit illustribus dominis Conservatoribus quedam capitula facta, ut asseruit per deputatos seu superstites Sapientiae Novae super emptione sex locorum dictae Sapientiae, ad effectum illa videndi et super eius discutendi, asserens quod brevi ab illismet scribetur summa quam oportebit erogare indicta emptione'.[60] Unfortunately the discussion cannot be traced in Council records after this point, as it was delegated to a committee 'super studentibus et locis Sapientiae Perusii', consisting of Giovan Battista Nino, Onorato di ser Matteo, and Pietro Cordellio.

On 3 October of the same year,[61] the vice-legate ordered, on the legate's wishes, thtat the number of students to be funded at external *Studia* must be increased again to twelve. This is the only indication we have that the number was at some stage reduced. The limited number of grants, and the condition that their beneficiaries must be *studentes pauperes* made the system a constant cause of dissatisfaction for citizens. In the 1592 *Riforme* we find in fact evidence of a controversy as to whether a third student who had passed the examination should be sent *ad Studium* ('Perché fra i cittadini deve servirsi l'equità talmente che uno non sia di meglio o peggiore condizione d'altro, si propone alle Signorie vostre se il temperamento usato con m. Lucio Bussi et m. Ottavio Faiani debba osservarsi con m. Pierotto Mosti, acciò la parzialità non sia causa di guastare così nobili instituta degli studenti').[62] Payments to the students are last recorded in the *Bollettario* for 1592; the list of the year's expenditure includes '432 scudi, studenti per numero sei l'anno', but corresponding information is not provided in the following years.

There follows the text of the 1582 *Capitoli dello Studente*:

Ordini e costitutioni da osservarsi attorno al decreto del publico et general Consiglio sopra li dodeci studenti da mantenersi in perpetuo in Studio dalla magnifica comunità di Viterbo fatti dall'illustrissimo et reverendissimo monsignor Vicelegato, magnifici domini Priori et quattro cittadini spetialmente deputati.

In prima, ch'el numero di detti studenti sia prefinito et determinato di dodeci in tutto fra legisti et artisti quali debbino esser Viterbesi, et questa qualità d'esser Viterbesi s'habbi da intendere secundo lo statuto che parla di questa materia. Et perché si è considerato che mandando detti dodeci studenti tutti in una volta potrebbe apportar pregiuditio in varii et diversi modi alli giovani che alla giornata verranno, per questo s'ordina che ogni anno uno debba mandare tre e non più. Et per essere li dottori di legge di grandissimo giovamento et ornamento alla comunità piace che delli tre che si mandaranno due siano legisti et uno artista. Ma perché sì laudabile instituto è stato introdotto per riempire la città di huomini litterati et virtuosi, il che può anche provenire da persone di bassa conditione, si statutisce che tanto nobili quanto ignobili, purché siano Viterbesi come di sopra, siano admessi nel numero di detti studenti indifferentemente, servato però il modo et forma infrascritta: cioè che debbino havere atteso due anni in Viterbo ad Instituta o Logica, et quando alcuno vorrà essere imbossolato debba presentarsi davanti monsignor Vicelegato et magnifici signori Priori dalli quali, o vero da un deputato da loro, gli sarà assignato un punto quale egli il giorno seguente nella medesima hora che gli fu assignato debba recitare davanti li sopraditti signori et anco in presentia delli signori dottori et scolari, et inoltre gli sia argumentato sopra i testuali ad effetto di far prova se sia atto alli studii più alti. Quali giovani, doppo che saranno stati esaminati, si saranno admessi per idonei debbino imbossolarsi in due bossole, cioè in una i legisti et nell'altra gli artisti, et poi nel tempo congruo se ne cavino tre persone secondo la distintione detta di sopra; quale estrattione debba farsi insieme con quella del magistrato et altri officiali che si suol fare attorno al fin di giugno.

Item, che quelli che saranno estratti possino andare a studiare in quel Studio che a loro parerà purché sia publico, dove potranno commorare anni quattro et non più a spese della comunità.

Item, si ordina et statuisce per provisione di detti studenti scudi sei di moneta <al> mese per ciasche studente indifferentemente per li detti quattr'anni. Et dicti danari da spendersi per detto uso siano fondati et debbino cavarsi dalli hortaggi di tutta la Viterbese [...].

Item, che li detti anni gratis s'intendino correnti et continui et non spezzati, o vero utili..

Item, saranno forzati quelli che vorranno essere in detto numero dare idonea sigurtà di ritornare dottorati in Studio publico dal collegio di dottori et non da persona privilegiata in camera, et mancando per qual si voglia caso o causa, escecto di morte naturale e non accidentale per caso fortuito et ancora per infermità incurabile, di restituire così i denari che hanno havuto.

Et quia non negligentibus sed impotentibus subveniant, per questo si prohibisce che nessun ricco di beni patrimoniali o frutti di benefici o che da qual si voglia modo possa da se stesso mantenersi nello Studio possa esser admesso in detto numero ma solo quelli che per parenti non possano spendere il talento del ingegno che Nostro Signore Dio gli ha dato, della quale habilità o inhabilità, ricchezza o povertà, debba starsi alla dichiaratione di monsignor Vicelegato, magnifici signori Priori et congregatione pro tempore. Et volendo similmente provedere quanto sia possibile che quelli che anderanno a studiare venghino a perfetione, si è risoluto che durante il detto quatriennio non possino tornare nella patria se non per causa urgente et necessaria qual debba esser allegata a monsignor Vice-legato, signori Priori et congregatione inanzi che venghino, et essendo la lor causa approvata et admessa possino venire et delli sopradetti non gli corra la provisione per quel tempo che staranno in Viterbo, et non di meno s'intenda correre il tempo delli quattr'anni; et che ogn'anno del mese di luglio siano dicti scolari obligati mandar fede dal dottore che odiranno d'attendere alli studii et tener buona vita né essere discoli et dishonesti.

Item, saranno obligati quando torneranno dottorati far l'entrata et mostrare il privilegio publico del dottorato secondo l'ordine fin qui osservato dalli signori dottori, et fra dui mesi doppo il loro dottorato tenere conclusioni publiche in Viterbo, et di questo debbono darne sigurtà avanti la partita loro che contra-venendo restituiranno tutto quello che havranno dalla magnifica comunità ricevuto.

Sed quia in uno gravatus in alio est relevandus, vogliamo che quelli che con questa provisione studieranno et doctoreranno non possino domandare ne debba darseli li 25 ducati quali per vigore dello statuto soglion darsi alli dottori o medici che a sue spese si siano dottorati quando fanno l'entrata. Datum Romae, in palatio cancellerie apostolice nostre solite residentie, sub anno 1582, die vero IX mensis martii, pontificatus sanctissimi domini nostri domini Gregorii papae XIII anno decimo. Alexander cardinalis Farnesius legatus. Loco + sigilli. Fran-ciscus Linus secretarius. Original dictorum capitulorum fuit repositus in capsa sigilli magnifice communitatis Viterbii, adquod habeatur relatio'.[63]

The Capitoli in the 1649 Statute

In 1582 it seemed that the new initiative recorded in the *Capitoli*, which was to fund only a specific number of students, would be temporary. However, as the city proved unable to establish a *Studium* of its own

empowered to grant the relevant qualifications, the initiative quickly
became a custom with Viterban students still obliged to undertake this
short-ranging *peregrinatio*.[64]
The *Liber III Rub.*[ca] *XIII* of the Statute, 'Quod provideatur per
Commune studentibus in iuri civili', reproduces the 1469 text along
with an *additio* of 1604 and a revised version of the 1582 *Capitoli*.
The 1604 *additio* inserted in the Statute a letter from the Papal
congregation *de Bono Regimine* (the *Buon Governo*), signed by Cardinal
Aldobrandino and dated 7 July. This letter referred to Cardinal Farnese's
decree and approved the decision to fund 'quattro gioveni nativi di dicto
luogo' with the sum of ten *scudi* monthly for four years. However, the
Congregation imposed a condition: two of the four students must be
clerics and the bishop must control their selection.
In response, the new 1604 *Capitoli* established that grants of six *scudi*
monthly (not ten as in the letter) to be offered to four youths – two
clerics and two laymens – for four years. All must be 'Viterbese nativi et
di padre nativo tanto nobili quanto ignobili e di bassa condizione, purché
siano Viterbesi'. The text of the *Capitoli* reproduced that of 1582, with
some elaborations:

1) The clerics must study Theology or *in utroque iure*;[65] while one of
the laymen must study medicine and the other *in utroque iure*: 'e non
essendo tra li dicti due laici alcuno sufficiente per studiare in medicina,
si debba servare dicto luogo e provisione per il primo sufficiente che
vorrà andare, e il medesimo si intenda per il legista'.
2) Those wishing to be funded to study theology or medicine must
attend lectures in logic in preparation for their studies in natural philosophy; those wishing to study law must prepare for the examination by
familiarizing themselves with the *Institutes*; they should be 'atti ad udire
gli ordinari e di questo ne abbiano fede giurata da loro dottori; a caso che
da quelli non la potessero havere, per essere assenti o morti o in altro
modo impediti, si debbano esporre all'esame et alla relazione giurata de'
signori esaminatori si habbia a dare fide'. The reference to this exam
and the specifications that 'quelli, i quali saranno estratti o eletti, debbano
il giorno presentarsi' and 'gli sarà deputato un punto' – shows that the
mechanism of recruitment was now more complicated. There were two
rounds to the selection process, the recitation of the *punctus* now a formal
test rather than a substantial one. The examination of the *punctus* was held
before the bishop and the *conservatori* for clerics; and before the vice-
legate and the *conservatori* for laymen.

3) It was specified that the *punctus* must be one paragraph of the *Instituta* for the *legista*, and one paragraph from *Predicabili o Predicamenti* for students of theology or medicine.

4) The condition that beneficiaries of the grant must earn doctoral rank was now subject to further regulations; not only must the *privilegium doctoratus* be granted by both a public *Studium* and a doctoral college; it was specified that it must not be awarded by a 'persona privilegiata in Camera'.

5) The economic conditions qualifying candidates to apply for the grant were established. They must not be in a position to fund their own studies: 'nessuno ricco di beni patrimoniali o frutto di benefici, o che in qualsivoglia modo possa mantenersi allo studio, debba essere ammesso in detto numero; ma solo quelli che, per povertà, non possono compire il corso dello studio; della quale povertà, o ricchezza, debba starsi alla dichiarazione di monsignor Vescovo e delli signori Conservatori per li due clerici, e di monsignor Vicelegato e di detti signori Conservatori per li due laici'.

6) Finally, it was specified that students might return home without permission where there was danger of death, and that they must account for return before the *conservatori*: 'periculum est in mora, purché ritornati vadano ad allegare la causa della loro venuta avanti li detti signori Conservatori'.

The 1546 foundation

At the end of 1546 a *Studium litterarium* was officially founded in Viterbo, thanks to a papal privilege. Although they had not held university chairs, Viterbo's preceptors had been teaching above elementary level for almost three centuries, and had succeeded in attracting foreign students. The foundation of the *Studium* was their crowning achievement. It followed at least fifty years of requests to royal and papal authority.

On September 1546 Pope Paul III received the following request: 'Si notifica a Vostra Santità essersi pensato di dare un principio ad uno Studio e per adesso havere solo quattro lectori, tutti Viterbesi, con salario di scudi cento fra tutti, et più e meno secondo la deliberatione del generale Conseglio'.[66] Already, these few lines reveal some fundamental peculiarities of the Viterban university experience: 1) a rudimentary form of *Studium* pre-dated the papal privilege and its institutionalization was now requestes; 2) the number of lecturers is reduced and would later decrease further as the university was restructured in line with its new aspirations; 3) all lecturers were citizens: this clause became an explicit rule when the *Studium* was refounded in the 1560s, at which stage it was required that lecturers should be Viterban natives. This is a manifestation of cultural and professional parochialism,[67] confirmed in the statutes by the articles devoted to the organization of doctors' and jurists' colleges, from which foreigners were excluded. The cultural and professional urban elite emphasized its own honourable rank and used the institution to project its own privileged social status; 4) salaries were very low:[68] in fact, the publicus preceptor's salary was always 100 *scudi* at least and represented the sum of all the lecturers' salaries. He was evidently the real protagonist of municipal intellectual life. When the *Studium* was re-founded in 1566, the legate Cardinal Farnese deplored the fact that salaries were so low, in fact, hardly fitting. This is further proof that teaching at the Viterban *Studium* was not a profitable professional activity, but the expression of privileged social and cultural status;[69] 5) the fundamental role of the *general Conseglio* and then of the local council was already made clear: the *Studium* was a 'creature' of the commune which was entirely responsible for its management; in this connection, the fact that the *Studium*'s classrooms were situated below the Palazzo dei Priori is significant: 'locus legentium et schole[70] dicti litterari Studii sint et esse debeant ubi ad presens exercetur esecutoria et ubi sunt tam publice quam secreti carceres tam a dextris quam a sinistris subtus palatium magnificorum dominorum Priorum';[71] this is where the public school would be placed.

The request continues: 'si supplica a Vostra Beatitudine si contenti concedere a tal principiato Studio qualche privilegio et massimamente di havere autorità di doctorare in qual sia facoltà'. There were thus two main requests. The first was to grant privileges which would facilitate the institutionalization of the *Studium*. In the event, the relevant privileges were limited to authorization to reinstate a tax which had fallen into disuse and which was now used to fund the *Studium*. The second and more important request was for permission to award degrees. This was the grand vision which animated this cultural initiative. The request was for *qualsia facoltà*, which would have made the Viterban *Studium* a

Studium generale. This primary ambition seems however to have been disappointed: the Papal brief in fact regulated lectures and salaries, but did not mention permission to award degrees.[72] The request was repeated in January 1547, a sure sign that it had not succeeded; indeed, it was never to be granted:

Si supplica Vostra Beatitudine che essendosi dato questo principio di Studio altre volte a Vostra Santità ragionato et detto, et acciò dal principio habbia di bene in meglio ad ampliasse si supplica Vostra Beatitudine si contenti concedere a tal principiato Studio ampli privilegi come in le altre pleclare città di studio, et massimamente di haver autorità di doctorare in qual sia facoltà.[73]

The fact that the Viterban *Studium* could not award degrees may explain why information about graduations is absent from the *Libri delle Riforme*, while the same texts commemorate the solemn and glorious homecoming of graduates from other Italian *Studia*; it also explains the coexistence of legislation concerning, on the one hand, grants to study further afield and on the other hand, public lectures in law and medicine in the city itself. There is further evidence that this request was rejected: in the public proclamation of 24 October, the Pope granted 'che sempre et in perpetuo li sia lecito et permesso in dicta città havere et tenere il dicto litterario Studio, et in qual sia facoltà pubblicamente lectori condurre, salariare et fare legere':[74] but again with no mention of permission award degrees. The city's appeal to the Pope for the right to award degrees was repeated again in 1587, as yet another attempt was made to found a *Studium* for Viterbo.[75]

The definition of the Viterban *Studium* as *Studium litterarium* needs some investigation. This adjective does not appear much in the sources for university-level institutions of this period, but as Bellomo emphasizes, 'apart from the regular selection, we find terms which are less familiar, either because they have been excluded, correctly, from the more rigorous historiography, or because they are not yet well known or accepted'.[76] Having situated the Viterban definition within this heterogeneous group of less familiar terms, we must determine what the expression means. Is it a term describing type of teaching? Viterbo did in fact possess a deeply rooted humanist culture, or, more precisely a culture linked to the *humanae litterae*. The public proclamation announcing the foundation of the *Studium*[77] emphasized that it would be 'di generale satisfatione di tutti litterati et amatori di littere'. And, as demonstrated above with regard to Pietro Paolo Passerino, Viterbo's students in literary subjects received a subsidy. Actual teaching in Viterbo at this higher level, however, was in all instances centred on civil law and logic or philosophy. Moreover, the public elementary school continued to exist alongside the *Studium*: it was the public schoolmaster there who delivered a regular Renaissance curriculum, founded positively on the *humanae litterae*; and it was he alone who introduced a literary element to the new born *Studium*, being entrusted with a lecture on Cicero.

We must therefore seek to explain the nomenclature with reference to institutional factors. The most significant parallel for this expression is in the letter of foundation issued by Innocent IV for the *Studium Curiae*.[78] The version of this letter edited by Denifle corresponds to Bibliothèque de Grenoble ms. 72: 'providimus quod ibidem de cetero regatur Studium litterarum'. The noun, 'littera', is used here, whereas Viterbo's institution is described, more precisely, with the adjective. In the later version preserved in the *Liber Sextus*, the term is abandoned in favour of 'Studium iuris divini et umani, canonici videlicet et civilis'. The document later specifies that the *Studium litterarum* will enjoy privileges identical to those provided 'in scolis ubi regitur Studium generale'. Evidently the two expressions, *litterarum* and *generale*, correspond with different institutional realities. To be more precise, as Paravicini emphasizes, 'Innocenzo IV could justify the grant to the *Studium Curiae* of a *Studium generale*'s privileges only [by trying to] disguise its circumstances with the term *Studium*'. What then distinguished the *Studium Curiae* or *Studium litterarum* from a *Studium generale*? Probably the same feature which characterizes the Viterban *Studium*: the lack of degree-granting powers. 'From an institutional perspective, the *Studium Curiae* had the features of a *Studium generale* [. . .] but the absolute lack of information concerning the award of degrees by the *Studium Curiae* may not result from the paucity of sources alone'.

The papal brief was copied into the *Libri delle Riforme* under the date 13 October 1546:

Decretum et ordinatum extitit ut in civitate Viterbii erigatur litterarium Studium pro decoro et utilitate civitatis predicte, et sic elapsis diebus per magnificos dominos Priores et non nullos cives fuit ad sanctum dominum nostrum supplicatum et a sanctitate sua obtentum. Solim igitur restat providere scutos centum pro salario quatuor doctorum qui in huiusmodi principio in dicto Studio legent, videlicet: pro Logica et Instituta scutos 40, et pro Philosophia et Ordinaria legum lectione scutos 60. Et quia tale opus magnificus dominus Locumtenens prefatus multum laudavit et ad illud executioni demandandum exhortavit, et ad effectum

predictum infrascrittum decretum ordinavit perpetuis futuris temporibus dura-
turum. Cuius decreti tenor talis est, videlicet. In Dei nomine amen. Cupientes
nos Bartholomeus Appogius de Macerata utriusque legum doctor Advocatus
Curie generalis Provincie Marchie et ad presens pro reverendissimo domino
nostro Paulo tertio pontifice maximo nobilissime civitatis Viterbii totiusque
provinciae Locumtenens generalis, ut optimum dicet gubernare provincie et
civitati predicte omni quo possumus paterno affectu consulere, ipsasque con-
dignis omnibus quibus possumus honoribus ac dignitatibus decorare et insignire
pro ipsarum cuiuslibet earundemque posterorum perpetuis futuris temporibus
ornamentis pariter et emolumentis, presenti nostro decreto sancimus quatenus in
hac nobilissima civitate Viterbiensi, anno quolibet ac tempore solite prout in
aliis Italie Studiis fieri solet, legi debeant in scholis per dicte civitatis universi-
tates eligende et deputande per legum doctores et phisicos eiusdem quatuor
lectiones. Una videlicet super Institutionibus et altera super Ordinariis iuris
civilis et similiter una in Logica et altera in Philosophia. Declarantes salarium
Institutiones et Logicam profitentium fore et esse scutorum viginti pro quolibet,
Ordinaria vero iuris civilis et Philosophie legentium scutorum triginta, de bimestre in bimestrem eisdem solvendum. Et quia premissa omnia ut supra statuta
sancti domini nostri collata de eiusdem consensu et voluntate sancita fuerunt,
idcirco percipimus et mandamus Prioribus et universitati predicte Viterbiensi
quo facilius predicta omnia debite executioni demandent et modum reperiant
unum merces predicta eisdem solvenda statutis ut supra temporibus valeat
reperiri sub penis arbitrio nostro imponendis etc. Declarantes post modum fieri
et ordinari debere per nos et universitatem predictam seu ab ipsa eligendi
homines, capitula et alia que necessaria esse videbitur pro premissorum omnium
manutensione et perpetua defensione, ad laudem altissimam domini nostri Iesu
Christi eiusque gloriosissimae Virginis matris Marie ac divi Laurenti capitis et
ducis predicte civitatis Viterbii pariter et sanctorum Hilarii et Valentini quorum
corpora hac in civitate requiescunt. Bartholomeus Appogius locumtenens qui
sua manu subscripsit.[79]

The document institutionalizes lectures in four disciplines only – 'super
Institutionibus,[80] super ordinariis iuris civilis,[81] in logica [and] in philosophia'. It stipulates that these subjects should be taught by *legum
doctores* and *phisici* according to schedules customary at Italian *Studia*.
Public lectures therefore seem to be the *Studium*'s only authorized
activity. The papal brief established salaries, confirming the total of
100 *scudi* already announced by the commune: 30 *scudi* for the lecturers
in *ordinaria iuris civilis* and *philosophia*, 20 *scudi* for teachers of the
Institutiones and *logica*. Dates of payment were also established: *de
bimestrem in bimestrem*. Finally, the University was granted the responsibility, and thus also the freedom, of arranging its own internal affairs.[82]

The *Studium*'s foundation was promulgated on 24 October 1564:[83]

Il molto magnifico et eccellentissimo signor magistro Bartholomeo Appogio di Macerata della magnifica città di Viterbo et provincia del Patrimonio per la santità di nostro signor general Lochotenente et li magnifici signori Priori et Conservatori del populo di dicta magnifica città di Viterbo havendo per spetial commissione, ordine, et decreto del publico et general Conseglio di dicta magnifica città il dì 5 del mese di settembre prossimo passato, tutti unitamente supplicato, et humilmente alla santita di nostro signore Paulo dignissimo papa tertio domandato che, per universal bene di dicta magnifica città di Viterbo, sua gloria, esaltatione et universale comodità di tutto lo stato ecclesiastico et altri luoghi vicini et non vicini, et generale satisfatione di tutti litterati et amatori di littere et virtù, che in dicta magnifica città si concieda gratia, comodità, licentia, facultà et privilegio di erigere et principiare un nuovo litterario Studio. Et il prefato signore sancto nostro in Viterbo et a dicta molta istanzia et requisitione di dicti magnifici signori et loro publico et generale Conseglio, paternamente et con sua solita benignità, pietà, clementia et bonità concesse a dicti magnifici signori, populo et comunità di Viterbo che sempre et in perpetuo li sia lecito et permesso in dicta città havere et tenere il dicto litterario Studio, et in qualsia facultà publicamente lectori condurre, salariare et fare legere, offerendone scilicet per esecutione di tal cosa amplissime gratie et privilegii. Et però li prefati magnifici et illustrissimi signori volendo tanto honorevil et degna inpresa di dicto litterario Studio eseguire, per il presente loro publico bandito a tutti e singoli di qualsia luogho, città, terra o castello tanto dello stato ecclesiastico quanto a qual sia principe, signore o repubblica subietto o non subietto, se intima, se bandisce et notifica che in dicta magnifica città di Viterbo si è novamente eretto et principiato il dicto nuovo litterario Studio, dove publicamente per huomini et lettori granni et famosi et litterati si legerando in principio di Studio, cioè in la prima settimana di novembre del presente anno 1546, tutte le infrascritte lectioni: un solito ordinario in Iure civili della mattina et la sera la Instituta; item un altro ordinario in Philosophia la mattina et la sera la Logica; item in Humanità la Rectorica di Cicerone. Et tali sopradicte lectioni secundo che in li altri famosi Studii si costuma continuatamente et in publico si legerando, et però si eshorta ciaschuno a venire in dicta città di Viterbo ad abitare, che chi alli dicti litterarii Studii attenderà, goderà et haverà tutte gratie, privilegii et esentioni dal dicto sanctissimo Signor nostro per la causa alla dicta magnifica comunità concessi et più ampliamente secundo in li altri luoghi et Studii soliti concedersi. Domenicus Nellus Auditor et Locumtenens.[84]

The announcement follows a sequence of rhetorical *topoi*, common in documentation relating to acts of foundation: 1) the *Studium* would bring glory to its city and, most importantly, assure citizens' welfare;

2) citizens were invited to spread the news; 3) the lecturers' fame was announced;[85] 4) young students were encouraged to come to Viterbo. These and other rhetorical *topoi* appear too in the *patentes littere* sent to the lecturers on 1 December 1546. The letters patent refer to the glory of the city; build an image of a city governed by wise men (a leitmotif recurring in the *patentes litterae* addressed to the public schoolteachers), and describe the advantages which a local *Studium* will bring to the citizens, whose education will be useful to the entire community.

Magnifici domini Priores et Conservatores populi civitatis Viterbii de consensu legum doctoris generalis Locumtenentis Patrimonii mandarunt mihi Cancellario infrascritto ut efficerem patentes litteras quatuor lectoribus in dicto publico litterario Studio cum salario in eis specificato, et quod dictas patentes faciam sub datis 11 novembris proximi decursi, in quo die dictum litterarium Studium initium habuit. Cuius commisionis vigore infrascrittas patentes effeci et lectoribus sigillo Communis segnatas ac manu prelibati magnifici domini Locumtenentis subscripti effectualiter dedi et tradidi. Quarum patentium tenor talis est, videlicet. Bartholomeus Appogius de Macerata iuris utriusque doctor Provincie Patrimonii ac civitatis Viterbii pro Sanctissimo Domino Nostro papa ac reverendissimo domino Legato generalis locumtenens, Priores et Conservatores populi civitatis Viterbii ac quatuor infrascritti super conservatione litterarii Studii Viterbiensis vigore publici et generalis Consilii specialiter electi et deputati. Cum sanctus dominus noster Paulus divina providentia dignus papa tertius hanc suam civitatem veluti precipuam ac dilectissimam patriam intimo complectato affectu eamque semper insignire et decorare intendat inter alias dignitates ad eiusdem civitatis ac suorum civium presentium et futurorum et omnium quorum utilitatem, comodum et honorem, nuper gratiosus concessit, voluit et instituit, quemadmodum plures Italie urbes litterario Studio clariores et nobiliores existant pariter et ista Etrurie vetustissima et Provincie Patrimonii caput litterario Studio atque Gymnasio omnino prorsus litteratis generibus pollens perpetuo gaudere ac florere possit et debeat potestatemque debuit eligendi et ordinandi doctores sive lectores tam in iure ure canonico et civile quam in medicina, philosophia ceterisque liberalibus artibus eisque mercedes et emolumenta ad nostrum nostrisque Communis libitum designandi atque solvendi. Nos autem cognoscentes quantum utilitatis, honoris et glorie perpetuis futuris temporibus hec allatura sit santissima institutio, eo precipue quod non recte nisi a sapientibus viris civitates gubernari possunt, voluimus ut omnibus hic liber ad litteraria studia pateat aditus et continus audiere et adiscere possit in esse comoditas, ut non solum sibi, parentibus et patrie sed Sancte Romane Ecclesie universisque populis commodo pariter et ornamento existant. Nos qui te magistrum Iacobum Sacchum artium medicine doctorem eximium esse cognoscimus et tue vite ac morum probitas, virtutum merita ac dictarum artium medicine et philosophie excellentia inducunt ut te meritis et favoribus prosequamur, decrevimus propterea te virum moribus et litteris prestantissimum in nostri Communis et publici nostri litterarii Studii tam philosophie quam artium medicine lectorem ad annum a presentium dato incohandum et ut sequitur prospere finiendum eligendum, nominandum et deputandum prout per presentes, cum salario scutorum quinquaginta de iuliis decem anno quolibet aliisque honoribus et oneribus in aliis Italie Studiis solitis et consuetis harum serie et presentium tenore eligimus, nominamus et deputamus mandantes propria quibuscumque nostri Communis gabellariis et presertim gabelle nostre mercature vini conduttoribus ut dictam summam pro rata de tertiara in tertiariam tibi integram persolvant. Quam sic solutam in eorum computis admitti volumus et mandamus et hoc tam vigore nostri publici et generalis consilii ac eiusdem decretorum et auctoritate ut supra nobis attributa etc. in quorum fidem. Fuerunt similiter concesse patentes littere domino Francesco Bussio iuris utriusque doctori sub dicto tenore pro scutis triginta tantum pro uno anno. Fuerunt etiam date et traddite patentes littere magistro Antonio del Turco artium medicine doctori eximio et in dicto litterario Studio in logica sive dialetica lectori pro scutis viginta pro dicto anno. Nec non dominus Iohannes Valerio Canapina iuris utriusque doctor ac in dicto litterario Studio Instituta sive Institutiones lector patentes litteras sub dicto tenore habuit cum salario scutorum viginti pro uno anno. Et similiter fuerunt concesse patentes lictere Iohanni Baptiste alias Zazarone pro bidello cum salario carlinos viginti mense quolibet [. . .] Quod dicti quatuor sapientes ut supra electi una cum magnifico domino Locumtenente et magnificis dominis Prioribus autoritatem habeant undecumque et qualitercumque ex introitibus Communis minus dannosis pro salario lectorum pecunias inveniendi et persolvendi.[86]

As was invariably the case in this period, the commune's first problem was the funding of the new institution. On 18 October 1546,[87] a diplomatic mission composed of Iacopo Sacchi, *doctor in medicina*, and Cesare Bussi and Antonio Gentile, both *doctores in lege*, petitioned the Pope for permission to levy a tax on the wine-trade, reserving the revenues for the *Studium*. The same arrangement was in place for the *Studium Urbis* and Macerata University:[88]

Item supplicarete a sua Beatitudine che, per supplire alle necessarie spese dello già principiato Studio, noi et nostra comunità hanno risoluto imponere una non dannosa impositione et gabella, ansi solita, utile, e per le ragioni a voi notissime necessaria, supra la mercantia del vino; per il che suppliarete sua Beatitudine li piaccia et si contenti non ostante qual sia cosa in contrario concederne licentia et autorità di possere dicta impositione et gabella solum per causa de mercantia de vino imporre, acciò ogni esactione di tal cosa sia et se intenda alle necessarie spese di dicto già principiato Studio integramente applicata.

On 5 November 1546,[89] the General Council received notification of papal approval: this was finally promulgated on 6 January 1547.[90]

The second step after finding funding was the election of the *conservatori*, on 20 October 1546.[91] The *conservatori* were to remain in office for only four months, and, having made the necessary preliminary arrangements, were to see the university's official activities inaugurated. Their remit was comprehensive, incorporating such pedagogical concerns as the appointment of lecturers, and the practical questions of arranging payment of salaries, and sitting and furnishing classrooms[92] ('autoritatem tam lectores eligendi quam eisdem salaria costituendi, locum et scholas eligendi, cathedras et banchas coeficiendi facere, et ex introitibus communitatis pro eiusdem necessariis occurrentiis et predictis conficiendi pecunias undecumque et qualitercumque inveniendi, et omnia alia et singula in premissis faciendi que circa ea necessaria et oportuna esse cognoverint'). These names were: Ottaviano degli Spiriti, Agostino Almadiani, Paolino Tignosino *legum doctor*, and Michele Florenzolo *legum doctor*.

Lecturing hours and the initial selection of lecturers were supplied in the public announcement.[93] For *ius civile*, Innocenzo Ugonio *legum doctor* was the first choice. If he declined the position, either Nicola Malagriccia *legum doctor* or Francesco Bussi *iuris utriusque doctor* was to be substituted: in the event, Francesco Bussi was appointed with an annual salary of thirty *scudi* and lectures in the morning (*de mane*). Iacopo Sacchi *phisicus*[94] was selected for *philosophia*, with a salary of thirty *scudi* and lectures to be given *de mane*. For *logica*, the first choice was Prospero *phisicus*, to be paid a salary of twenty *scudi*, and to lecture in the evenings (*de sero*). If he declined the position, it was to be offered to another not specified: the appointment was Antonio Turco *phisicus*. It was stipulated that lecturers in the *Instituta* must be recent graduates ('aliquis ex his novitiis doctor'),[95] as if to ensure that the new blood would be on display, bolstering the institution's reputation. This practice would be reinforced in the 1566 refoundation. The salary was to be twenty *scudi*, with lectures given *de sero*. Giovanni Valerio di Francesco of Canepina, *iuris utriusque doctor*, was appointed to this position. Finally, the public schoolmaster was to give lectures in the *Studium* on Ciceronian rhetoric. It is worth noting that his salary would be one hundred *scudi*.

All those named in the announcement were prominent in Viterban politics, Innocenzo Ugonio in particular. His voice dominated proceedings in the General Council at this time, and was still more loudly heard in later years. He was usually the first to intervene in debates after the agenda had been announced, and often succeeded in imposing his will.

He had a higher profile than even Iacopo Sacchi. Sacchi was a man very much in love with his city, and a member of a prominent family, but his activities had however been confined mostly to the Roman court until he became *protomedicus*.

As the new wine tax had yet to be introduced, the lecturers were at first paid from the commune's existing revenues: 'pro quibus scutos centum reperiendos et habendos dicti omnes unanimes decreverunt ut omnes braviorum cursus hactenus soliti penitus amoventur excepto bravio dive Virginis de Quercu de mense tamen septembris et dictorum braviorum pecunie applicentur dictis salariis, residuum vero usque ad dictam summam centum scutorum quod inveniantur et habeantur ex introitibus Communis'.

The institution was at first situated 'subtus palatium magnificorum dominorum Priorum', but the commune would discuss on January 1547 plans for a new magisterial palace (*Palazzo del Podestà*), part of which would house the *Studium*.[96]

The *Studium*'s inauguration ceremonies took place between 7 and 24 November. On 7 November,[97] the inaugural mass was celebrated in the Cathedral of San Lorenzo, in the presence of the *Luogotenente*, the *Priori* and *aliis doctores*: this confirms that the *doctores* formed a visible social group easily identifiable and always present in important moments of Viterbo's public life. On this occasion and over the following days the lecturers or their representatives delivered orations: the inaugural oration was declaimed by Giovanni Francesco, son of Innocenzo Ugonio (7 November);[98] Francesco Bussi delivered his *principium*,[99] which was attended by an unnamed 'eximius iuris utriusque doctor dominus', who undertook to engage in a disputation with Bussi (11 November); Antonio Turco gave an oration[100] before an audience including 'excellentissimus philosophie professor et dominus doctor Antonius de Mirandola' (12 November); Iacopo Sacchi performed[101] in the presence of 'dominus Reginaldus Polus Sacre Romane Ecclesie diaconus cardinalis et dicte civitatis Viterbii et Provincie Patrimonii dignissimus Legatus' (15 November); and events culminated with the *principium* of Giovanni Valerio son of Francesco of Canepina, lecturer in *Institutiones Iustiniani imperatoris* (24 November).[102]

On 1 December 1546,[103] letters patent were officially dispatched to the lecturers appointed; they set the salaries and days of payment, with a contract valid for one year.[104] The salaries offered in the latter patent are not entirely consistent with those announced earlier: an instance of economic restructuring. Iacopo Sacchi, lecturer in philosophy and medicine was now offered fifty *scudi*; Francesco Bussi, lecture in civil law, thirty *scudi*; Antonio Turco, lecturer in logic and dialectics, twenty *scudi*; and Giovanni Valerio of Canepina, lecturer in the *Instituta sive Institutiones*, twenty *scudi*. At the same time a beadle was appointed: Giovanni Battista *alias Zazarone*, with an annual salary of eighteen *scudi*.

The records in the *Bollettario* of payments made during the *Studium*'s second year of activity reveal changes in personnel: in November 1547,[105] there were still four lecturers but 'magister Ysach ebreo' had replaced Antonio Turco, lecturer in Logic. The lecturer in the *Instituta*, Giovanni of Canepina, was mentioned for the last time in February 1548.

There are gaps in the *Libri delle Riforme*, but one fact stands out: references to the *Studium* became more and more rare, then disappeared altogether, while the attention and the care dedicated to the choice of the public schoolteacher intensified. Viterbo, which was after all a provincial town, was perhaps not a suitable setting for an educational institution more advanced than the elementary school, which was probably all it could maintain. Provisions recorded on 1 December 1548[106] reveal that the *Studium* had by then ceased to operate ('non perseveratio Studii'). Payment of lecturers' salaries had now been suspended, and it was determined that proceeds from the wine tax established to finance these salaries would be diverted to help fund the building of the new magisterial palace ('sed reservetur gabella super mercatura vini ut applicata intelligatur litterario Studio et publico Gymnasio his elapsis annis in hac civitate nostra incepto [...] et quia ad presens salaria lectorum in dicto Studio non solventur id circo pecunie dicte gabelle mercature vini debent exponi in fabrica et pro fabrica huius palatii'). The commune's *Bollettario* confirms this fact: in September 1548 the three lecturers had received payment of the 'ultima terziaria [and] ogni resto'.[107]

On 19 March 1556,[108] the Council discussed a proposal to institute courses in logica and the *Institutiones* for *adolescentes*, with a guaranteed salary for the lecturers: this demonstrates that no account was taken of the *Studium* ten years after its foundation ('pro institutione adolescentium fuit alius prepositum quod bonum esset ut legerent lectiones logices et Institutiones, et lectoribus aliquod salarium constituetur'). The courses were entrusted to public officials, who were awarded a pay rise: the commune's lawyer, and the doctor employed at the town hospital.

An entry for 10 June 1559 mentions a teacher of logic,[109] Br Lucasanto
of Rieti, a Franciscan of the Roman Province, who besides preaching,
lectured daily on the Pauline espistles and gave lessons in logic and
philosophy. As his courses also attracted foreign students ('multi studentes forienses concurrerint'), the Council resolved to make payment to
the learned friar 'pro honore civitatis'.

The *Libri delle Riforme* make no further reference to a *Studium* or the
lectures until 1566.

The 1566 re-foundation

After a silence of almost twenty years, the word *Studium* reappears in
the 1565–7 *Libro delle Riforme*. The new endeavour seems to have been
presented as a re-foundation. Rhetoric aside, however, it was far from
matching the ambition which marked the 1546 foundation even apart
from its failed aspiration of granting degrees. The 1566 project seems in
fact to have produced a return to the previous custom of funding public
chairs for the elementary teaching of law and logic. It was intended that
these courses would be delivered within a quasi-university framework,
but the reality was much more limited. The new *Studium* was restricted
too by competition from a public school which, thanks to the *preceptor*,
was Viterbo's real intellectual centre, and from new forms of intellectual
associations such as the *Academia smarritorum*, instieud a few months
before the re-foundation.

In the surviving documentation at least, the attempt to renew the *Studium*
appears abruptly: during the session of 25 March 1566, on the initiative of
Iacopo Sacchi, *prothomedicus* of the Papal Court. The language is ambiguous, referring not to founding a *Studium* but to the institution of courses.
The reference is to the *Institutiones*, so that the level of the teaching must
not be advanced, which confirms the introductory quality of these *lettioni*.
Salaries were the same as in 1546, and were considered very low. Finally,
as in 1546, the municipal authorities were to have a fundamental role in
managing the life of this institution in its early days; again four *conservatori* were appointed for the *Studium*:

Vedendo i signori che nela città nostra ogni dì più crescono i giovani desiderosi
di letture e di virtù, parendoci non sol bene ma debito di aiutarli, hanno pensato
acciò più facilmente e più brevemente possino venire a qualche grado che saria

bona cosa dar loro comodità d'udire in Viterbo la lezione d'Instituta e dela Logica, e però parendoli che in ogni modo debbano instituire le dette dui letioni, non volendosi risolvere da loro hanno voluto che vi si proponga in questo Consiglio avvertendovi che ciò sarà grandissimo benificio a la città e non costarà se non 48 scudi l'anno dei quali se ne trovano già scudi vigintiquattro che si davano a certi altri li quali gli si levano, però la spesa sarà quasi niente et l'utilità infinita. Consigliate dunque. Dominus Iacobus Sacchus ascendens consulendo dixit: io laudo quanto si è proposto et anco monsignor Vicelegato et signori Priori che l'hanno fatto proporre e tanto più quanto che l'illustrissimo e reverendissimo Legato nostro è di questa mente e vuole che si facci né si guardi a li danari ma si piglino perciò dove si potrà et si ordini chi ha da leggere e dove, e si pare che si piglino i giovani a leggere e si cavino per bossolo per sei mesi o per tre, o altrimenti si come meglio parerà a monsignor Vicelegato e signori Priori e dui huomini sopra di ciò da elegersi i quali habbino ogni authorità insieme, come di sopra, sopra la detta cosa e di fare tutti li ordini che si convengono ma leggasi in publico. Dominus Anselmus Ninus etiam ascendens in summa consulens confirmavit dictum Iacobi addendendo che per trovare i danari si debba mettere due o tre più per cento sopra la gabella delle bestie vive. Capitaneus Bernardinus Chisius etiam ascendens consulens dixit che per trovar danari li parerebbe che si dovesse levare il salario al advocato et procuratore de la comunità perioché sono benefitiati dalla comunità e sono essenti di gabelle, et si un dottore viene dottorato tira dalla comunità ducati 25. Dominicus Casata surgens consulens dixit che per trovar danari si potria fare pagare la gabella a forestieri che lavorano nela Viterbese et ne estraggano il grano. Dominus Ludovicus Veltrius ascendens consulens dixit che in ogni modo si debbano fare le dette lettioni et li trovino li denari ancor fino a la summa di 50 scudi, e per trovarli si facci un publico bando che tutti i forestieri che non habitano in Viterbo et hanno terreni nela Viterbese debbano venire a fare catasto e pagar intanto per soma di sementa fra un certo termine. Et cum nemo aliud dicere vellet, placuit dicto reverendissimo Vicelegato et Prioribus poni ad partitum consilium dicti domini Iacobi infrascritto tamen modo, videlicet: che onninamente si istituischino e leghino le due lettioni una de Instituta e l'altra di Logica con salario di scudi 24 per lettore per anno, et si legga in quei lochi e con quelli ordini e per quelli lettori che pareranno a monsignor Vicelegato et signori Priori e quattro huomini sopra di ciò da eleggersi da esso.[110]

Iacopo Sacchi's proposal came to fruition slowly, with the first concrete results coming on 2nd November,[111] following months of discussion: 'cumque deinde, tam coram illustrissimo ac reverendissimo domino Legato quam coram reverendissimo domino Andrea Recuperato Vicelegato prefato, fuerunt desuper et per dictos dominos deputatos et per magnificos dominos Priores et Conservatores, bimestribus preteritis, facta plura et diversa colloquia, ratiocinationes et discussiones'. On this occasion the names of the 'deputati agli affari dello Studio' were given: Gabriele Tignosino (perhaps a relative of the 1546 *conservatore* Paolino Tignosino?), Ascanio Salimbene *legum doctor*, Anselmo Nino, and Domenico Poggi.

The November session produced a decree specifying the limits and functions of this new (if pre-existing) institution: 'decretum fuerit quod in hac civitate duae lectiones, altera Institutionum et altera Logices, omnino legere deberent pro erudiendis iuvenibus, et ut sic aliquantulum introducti ad Gymnasia publica deinde se conferentes facilius, commodius et cum multo minori impensa ad doctoratus apicem pervenire queant.' That is, courses were to supply introductory instruction in the two subjects of young men wishing to obtain degrees, for which of course they would have to study elsewhere (again, as in 1546).

On this occasion the *conservatori* appointed two lecturers: their own Ascanio Salimbene for the *Institutiones* and Giovanni Turco *artium et medicine doctor* (perhaps, a relative of Antonio Turco *artium et medicine doctor*, appointed lecturer in 1546?). These lecturers were not prominent members of the council as had been the case for those appointed at the original foundation.

Some fundamental details of institutional life were established and noted in the so-called 'decreta et statuta': 1) Lecture hours were established: they must take place daily 'ut in publicis fieri solet Studiis', logic 'de mane', *Institutiones* 'de sero'; 2) Rigorous supervision of the lecturers' work was ensured: a fine was to be levied on lecturers who did not teach as scheduled, with the revenue reserved for the *Studium* (first mention under this name here) ('et ut in legendo sint magis solliciti et diligentes voluerunt quod quicumque ipsorum sine legittima causa legere defecerit perdat de suo onorario seu provisione pro singula lectione iulios tres commodo Studii applicandos'); the beadle was to monitor lecturers' fulfilment of their duties ('etiam bidellus teneatur sic deficientes apuntare et suae apuntationi credatur'). Such provisions, which had been totally lacking in 1546, imply a drive to formalize and conform with university practices in an effort to compensate for the lack of real university privileges. This was not a *Studium* in the strict sense of the word, but a public institution imitating a conventional *Studium*'s organization; 3) Lecturers' salaries were fixed at twenty-four *scudi* for the lecturer in the *Institutiones* and twenty-nine for the lecturer in logic; 4) Giovanni Battista Tollerono was appointed beadle, with a salary of six *scudi*, and his duties outlined: 'qui scolarum curam habeat, illas tempore debito aperiat et claudat, campanam pulset, denuntianda in scholis denuntiet, et alias faciat quae bidelli in Studiis publicis facere soliti sunt'; 5) salaries, as in 1546, would be financed through a tax, in this case it was described as the chestnut tax, the 'gabella dicta la castagnaria'; 6) Days were indicated for annual payment, in three instalments: on Christmas Eve, on the first day of Lent, and on Easter; on these occasions fines due for non-attendance would be calculated; 7) Finally, lecturers' contracts would be issued annually, and, most importantly, the task of public lecturing was reserved to recent graduates, 'doctores iuniores' ('et singulo quoque anno novissimi doctores tam iuris quam artium intelligantur, et sint electi, creati et deputati lectores pro uno anno'), as in 1546 for the lecturer in the *Institutiones*. Lecturers had to fulfil two conditions: they must be of Viterban origin with degrees obtained through examination at a public *Studium*.

The development of the Viterban Studium

The *Studium* solemnly re-founded in 1566 ceased activity again after a few years, at least so far as its university ambitions were concerned. It returned gradually to its starting-point: the funding of public lectures by graduate professors, a custom which stabilized and endured into the next century, as the seventeenth-century statutes show. It is thus evident that, unlike for example Macerata, Viterbo could never offer higher-level teaching beyond this introductory level, probably because sufficient internal demand simply did not exist. Who was likely to attend a new *Studium* so close to the more prestigious centre of Rome, Siena, and Perugia?

The *Studium* seems to have been fully operational still in 1569: Ascanio Salimbene 'lector Institutionum' and Giovanni Turco 'lector logicae' delivered their inaugural lecturers at the *Palazzo dei Priori* on 20 and 21 October.[112] It was surely a positive sign that the beadle and the lecturer in logic had their salaries increased on 22 November,[113] from eight to ten *scudi* and from thirty to forty *scudi* respectively. The latter was noted to have earned this increase because: 'satis elaborat in legendo logicam, et in Gymnasio et in domi, et bene inseruit in legendo'.[114] This date saw another reference to the *conservatori* of the *Studium*: Domenico Poggi, Anselmo Nini, Gabriele Tignosino, and Camillo Finiziano, who were mentioned again in November 1570,[115] when Cardinal

Farnese appointed the three lecturers: Ascanio Salimbene *arcipresbitero* of San Sisto church for the *Institutiones*, Giovanni Turco for logic, and Francisco Scotto, public schoolteacher, for rhetoric. But the first difficulties had begun to appear by 1571.[116] On 24 September the *deputati super Studio* Gabriele Tignosino, Domenico Poggi, Camillo Finiziano, and Anselmo Nini met with Legate Alessandro Farnese and the Vicelegate in Farnese's private chamber in Viterbo, 'ut Studium in civitate Viterbii inceptum conservetur'. Lecturer in logic Giovanni Turco had his pay reduced from thirty to twenty-five *scudi* because 'paucos discipulos habet et parum elaborat'; but on 26 September his position was confirmed for three years. Muzio Bussi legum doctor was nominated to fill the vacant position of lecturer in the *Institutes*, with an annual salary of twenty-five *scudi*, very much reduced compared with the sixty *scudi* of 1566. Evidently the position was no longer regarded as sufficiently profitable: Muzio declined and Giovanni Battista Fustino *legum doctor* was appointed instead.[117] Agostino Colaldo[118] was appointed beadle in the place of Tommasino of Grisedia on 7 august 1574,[119] demonstrating that the *Studium*, in spite of its defects, still functions as, or at least was perceived as, a university.

In the sources for the following years, however, the word *Studium* gradually disappears. There is a return to the custom of delivering public lectures, when named, was dubbed a *Gymnasium*, as was the school were the *publicus preceptor*, the elementary teacher, worked: a single institution appears to have been operating on two levels. The *Bollettario* for 1578 still registered'58 scudi per lo Studio' amongst its outgoings for the year, but the documentation in the *Riforme* shows that the institution existed by then only in name. The section devoted to the students' grants even included a suggestion, made in 1586, that a sum of money should be reserved for student maintenance, to attempt 'di eriggere in Viterbo lo Studio come cosa molto più utile et di molto maggior honore et grandezze alla città nostra et anche in maggior commodo ai cittadini',[120] an indication that less tan twenty years after the refoundation, the 1566 Viterban *Studium* had been forgotten.

The *Libri delle Riforme* and the commune's *Bollettarii*, despite chronological gaps, allow us to trace the history of these public lectures through to the end of the century, giving both the lecturers' names and their subjects: [121]

1) 1574–75. *I.*: Pietro Pollioni; *L.*: Francesco Scotto; *C.*: Agostino Colaldo[122]

2) 1575–76. *I.*: Pietro Pollioni;[123] *L.*: Francesco Scotto; *C.*: Agostino Colaldo[124]

3) 1576–77. *I.*: Pietro Pollioni; *L./P.*: Pietro Paolo Sacchi;[125] *C.*: Agostino Colaldo[126]

4) 1577–78. *I.*: Pietro Pollioni;[127] *L./D.*: Pietro Paolo Sacchi; *C.*: Agostino Colaldo[128]

5) 1578–79. *I.*: Pietro Pollioni; *L./D.*: Pietro Paolo Sacchi; *C.*: Agostino Colaldo[129]

6) 1579–80. *I.*: Pietro Pollioni; *L./D.*: Pietro Paolo Sacchi; *C.*: Agostino Colaldo[130]

7) 1582–83. *I.*: Pietro Pollioni;[131] *P.*: Pietro Paolo Sacchi;[132] *D./L.*: Giovanni Battista degli Speroni[133]

8) 1583–84. *I.*: Pietro Pollioni;[134] *P.*: Pietro Paolo Sacchi; *D.*: Giovanni Battista degli Speroni[135]

9) 1584–85. *I.*: Pietro Pollioni; *P.*: Pietro Paolo Sacchi; *D.*: Giovanni Battista degli Speroni[136]

10) 1585–86. *I.*: Pietro Pollioni;[137] *P.*: Pietro Paolo Sacchi[138]

11) 1586–87. *I.*: Pietro Pollioni; *P.*: Pietro Paolo Sacchi[139]

12) 1589–90. *I.*: Pietro Pollioni; *P.*: Pietro Paolo Sacchi; *C.*: Agostino Colaldo[140]

13) 1591–92. *I.*: Pietro Pollioni; *P.*: Nicola Torellini; *C.*: Agostino Colaldo[141]

A final notable aspect of Viterbo's engagement with the world of universities is a particular ceremony, perfectly balanced between private and public contexts, mentioned frequently in the *Libri delle Riforme* from the middle of the sixteenth century. The individual and private fact of earning the degree led to a general celebration involving the highest civic officials and the town's *doctores*, and featuring public display of the *privilegium doctoratus*.[142]

The ceremony's structure[143] remained constant over the years. The new graduate processed with *doctores* and citizens ('associatus quam plurimis doctoribus et civibus') from his own home ('domus sue solitae habitationis') or, in some cases, from a religious house,[144] to the palace of the *Priori*. Received by the *Priori* 'in pede scalarum', he was led into the presence of the Vicelegate and delivered his *privilegium* to the chancellor of the commune, who read it aloud to the municipal authorities, the representatives of the Papal States, the assembled citizens, the *doctores*, and to teachers from the monasteries if the degree was in medicine or philosophy. The new graduate delivered a public oration,[145] and received the congratulations of the other *doctores*. The procession escorted him home, where a solemn banquet (*ientaculum*) was sometimes held.

Conclusion

It has been observed that the sixteenth century witnessed a flourishing of provincial universities, and Viterbo's experiences are entirely consistent with this historical phenomenon. The late medieval period is considered a time of decline and fossilization for the university, with the institution's early splendour and the intellectual vivacity a distant memory. This decline was counteracted with the reorganization of large traditional universities during the modern era. At the same time, university qualifications became more and more necessary to a professional career in the modern world. Employment need no longer depend on an individual's private ties if such an external, universally recognized, and reputedly objective measure existed. We could say that a sort of 'licentia ubique praticandi' replaced the old 'licentia ubique docendi'.

Nevertheless and paradoxically, the qualification itself often lost in content, and specific degrees did not necessarily guarantee relevant employment. As more students graduated, the degree was transformed from an intellectual to an honorary qualification. Hence the insistence, in Viterbo's documentation, that the degree must be assigned 'in Studio publico' by a college of *doctores*. *Doctores* were necessary because the increasing bureaucratization of the political machine and of daily life created ever more frequent demands for specific professional qualities; yet, because contemporaries were aware that the mechanism by which the university certified learning had altered, they required confirmation that the *doctores* on whom they relied were authentic, that the qualification correspond with real knowledge.

However, the Viterban case is of interest for study of the history of ideas as well as that of institutions. Viterbo represents an urban reality in which intellectual matters were of primary concern. Turning points in the town's educational endeavours mirror reflect its political development, and correspond with the moments of the commune's greatest achievements. The *Authentica Habita*, as observed above, coincided with the Statute of 1250–1; more complex rules concerning public lectures appeared in the Statute of 1469, in harmony with a trend witnessed all over Italian territories. A system of grant for university studies was maintained throughout the period, culminating in the elaboration of the *Capitoli dello studente* in 1582. Furthermore, the *Consiglio dei Quaranta* regularly deliberated on the appointment of teachers to the *publicum Gymnasium*, establishing sub-committees which included prominent council members, themselves usually *doctores*.

The public elementary school seems to have been a real source of civic pride. Sixteenth-century Viterbo's most ambitious educational project, the attempt to found a *Studium generale*, started with the expansion of the public school's prerogatives. Massimo Miglio identified 1454 as 'the moment when Viterbo showed the most acute consciousness of the function of teaching, expressed through the desire to connect with the tradition of the *Studia generalia* and through the reference to the nearby Roman University'.[146] The appeal to Charles VIII reveals the other reference point for the ambitions of Viterbo's political and cultural elite, that is, the Perugian *Studium*, which with Siena was the favourite destination of young Viterban students.

There was also a desire to convert the system of public lectures funded by the commune into an authentic university institution which could award degrees; this would have assured the city's prestige, allowed its *doctores* to advertise their distinction, and given Viterbo an advantage over the majority of Italian communes. But the project was destined to fail, and not only because, as was often the case in Italy, the commune could not support its cost. The rapid disappearance of the *Studium* from the *Libri delle Riforme* in the years following its foundation and re-foundation suggest that it was a quasi-university without students. This demonstrates that it was not popular demand which drove the *Studium*. Viterbans were attracted still to the *Studia* of Perugia and Siena, and also to Padua and Rome. The project was an aspiration of Viterbo's *doctores*, who had resolved to reproduce at home the atmosphere they had experienced while studying further afield.

Caught between the theory and the reality of a university institution, this small social group of civic professionals was still tantalized by the vision of teaching from a *cathedra*.

34 *History of Universities*

Dottoranda di Ricerca dell'Università di Roma "La Sapienza"
Dipartimento di Studi Europei, Americani e Interculturali

REFERENCES

1. On the *Patrimonium* see Joselita Raspi Serra and Caterina Laganara Fabiano, *Economia e territorio. Il Patrimonio Beati Petri nella* Tuscia (Naples, 1987).
2. Quoted in Massimo Miglio, 'Cultura umanistica a Viterbo nella seconda metà del Quattrocento', in Giuseppe Lombardi and Teresa Sampieri (eds), *Cultura umanistica a Viterbo: per il V centenario della stampa a Viterbo (1488–1988) (Viterbo, 12 novembre 1988)* (Viterbo, 1991), 11–46.
3. Quoted in Cesare Pinzi, 'Carlo VIII a Viterbo', in *Bollettino Storico Archeologico Viterbese*, 1 (1908), 36–9.
4. Viterbo, Biblioteca Comunale degli Ardenti, Archivio storico preunitario, *Libri delle Riforme* (R.), 25, 158v.
5. Viterbo, Biblioteca Comunale degli Ardenti, Archivio storico preunitario, IV AO II 21bis, *Lettere diverse*, doc. 138.
6. Robert Black has researched similar phenomena in Arezzo, discovering long-forgotten documents from which he has been able to reconstruct the story of a veritable city *Studium* active during the Renaissance. See Robert Black, 'The Studio Aretino in the fifteenth and early sixteenth centuries', *History of Universities*, 5 (1985), 55–82; and Robert Black, *Studio e scuola in Arezzo durante il Medioevo e il Rinascimento. I documenti d'archivio fino al 1530* (Arezzo, 1996).
7. On these city chronicles see Massimo Miglio, 'Cronisti viterbesi del secolo XV', *Biblioteca e società. Rivista del Consorzio per la gestione delle Biblioteche di Viterbo*, 6 (1984), 73–5, and Giuseppe Lombardi, 'Cronache e libri di famiglia: il caso di Viterbo', in *Saggi* (Rome, 2003), 199–210; for a description of these documents see Marta Materni, 'Riformanze consiliari e bollettarii come fonti per lo studio delle popolazioni studentesche nella prima età moderna', *Annali di storia delle Università italiane*, 12 (2008), 357–85.
8. The first stage was marked by the foundations in Bologna, Padua, Naples, Siena, Rome, and Perugia; the second, extending from the foundation of the University of Florence to the foundation of the University of Catania, coincided with the first century of the Renaissance; the third lasted from 1540 to 1601 and featured university foundations in Macerata, Messina, Urbino, Salerno, and Parma (Richard L. Kagan, 'Le università in Italia, 1500–1700', *Società e storia*, 28 (1985), 275–317). The Renaissance produced institutions which have been conceptualized as 'provincial universities' (Piero Del Negro, 'Il principe e l'università in Italia dal XV secolo all'età napoleonica', in Gian Paolo Brizzi and Angelo Varni (eds), *L'università in Italia fra età moderna e contemporanea. Aspetti e momenti* (Bologna, 1991), 12–27) and 'minor universities' (Gian Paolo Brizzi, 'Le università minori in

Italia in età moderna', in Andrea Romano (ed.), *Università in Europa. Le istituzioni universitarie dal Medio Evo ai nostri giorni. Strutture, organizzazione, funzionamento* (Messina, 1995), 287–96). Brizzi explains: 'I wish to use the concept of minor universities to cover [institutions] offering higher level teaching which fulfilled at least part of the educational remit of the principal universities, and likewise ratifying the course of studies by issuing of academic degrees. In most cases these were formally established *Studia generalia*: the difference with the major universities [. . .] was in the internal organization and in the *modus operandi*' (287).

9. See Del Negro, 'Il principe'.

10. Ibid.: '[For some cases, when the communal magistrates intervened on behalf of the institution or when a *Studium* was restored,] it is possible to discover by reading between the lines clear signs of the pressure exerced by professional groups with academic credentials, particularly jurists. [Jurists were] the most influential because of their very close relationship with government bureucracy in some circumstances and with the town councils and éilites in others' (21).

11. On his pontificate see Ludwig von Pastor, *Paolo III (1534–1549), (Storia dei papi dalla fine del Medioevo, Vol. V*, Rome, 1924); for his interventions in aid of the Sapienza college in Rome see Giovanna Falcone, 'La Sapienza e i suoi studenti', in Paolo Cherubini (ed.), *Roma e lo Studium Urbis. Spazio urbano e cultura dal Quattro al Seicento* (Rome, 1989).

12. Antonio Marongiu, 'L'Università di Macerata nel periodo delle origini', *Annali dell'Università di Macerata*, 17 (1948), 3–73; for the sources see *Studium generale. Atti dello Studium generale Maceratese dal 1541 al 1551*, ed. Sandro Serangeli (Turin, 1998); *Studium generale. Atti dello Studium generale Maceratese dal 1551 al 1579*, ed. Sandro Serangeli (Turin, 1999); *Gli Statuta dell'antica università di Macerata (1540–1824)*, ed. Sandro Serangeli, Lorella Ramadù-Mariani and Raffaella Zambuto (Turin, 2006).

13. An analogous case of a university which lacked the authority to award degrees, at least for a period, was another Renaissance *Studium*: Messina. The university was solemnly inaugurated in 1596 after almost 160 years of attempts by the commune: in 1548, with the Jesuits' collaboration, the commune created a quasi-university institution but there was strong opposition from the Catania *Studium* which was determined to maintain its monopoly within Sicily: so Messina was permitted to pay lecturers and offer teaching within a university framework, but could not award degrees. Finally in 1590, in return for a huge donation, the Commune obtained the power to award degrees from Spanish *Camera*. This privilege was later conceded through a papal bull. See Michele Catalano, 'L'Università di Catania nel Rinascimento', in *Storia della Università di Catania dalle origini ai giorni nostri* (Catania, 1934), 3–98; Mario Scaduto, 'Le origini dell'Università di Messina', *Archivum Historicum Societatis Iesus*, 17 (1948), 102–59; Rosario Moscheo, 'Istruzione superiore e autonomia locale

nella Sicilia moderna: apertura e sviluppi dello *Studium* Urbis Messane (1590–1641)', *Archivio Storico Messinese*, 59 (1991), 75–221.

14. See Antonio Marongiu, 'La Costituzione *Habita* di Federico I: problemi e discussioni', *Clio*, 1 (1965), 1–24; Id., 'Alle origini dell'Università (laCostituzione *Habita* di Federico Barbarossa)', *Rivista giuridica della scuola*, 5 (1966), 313–20; and Walter Ullmann, 'The medieval interpretation of Frederick's Authentic *Habita*', in Walter Ullmann (ed.), *Scolarship and Politics in the Middle Ages* (London, 1978), 101–36. Another example for the reception of the *Autentica Habita* in the thirteenth-century documents is Perugia in 1275 (Luigi Tarulli, 'Documenti per la storia della medicina in Perugia (dalle epoche più remote al '400)', *Bollettino della Regia Deputazione di Storia Patria per l'Umbria*, 25 (1922), 159–90). The question of teaching in this period requires attention, ad needs to be placed in the context of statutes which 'generally rather late, pay little attention to elementary teaching and to the connected problems. The instructions contained in the Bassano statutes of 1259, in the article entitled *De magistro scolis*, are unique: they testify to the advanced educational agenda of the Venetian hinterland'. (Giovanna Petti Balbi, 'Istituzioni cittadine e servizi scolastici nell'Italia centro-settentrionale fra XIII e XV sec.', in *Città e servizi sociali nell'Italia dei secoli XII–XV. Atti del XII Convegno Internazionale di Studi (Pistoia, 9–12 ottobre 1987)* (Pistoia, 1990), 21–48).

15. *Cronache e statuti della città di Viterbo*, ed. Ignazio Ciampi (Florence, 1872).

16. From the sixteenth century, publicly funded lectures were a common feature of Italian communes, many of which aspired to establish university. The appointment of a lecturer in a university subject could indicate the wish to introduce higher education in the institutional form of the *Studium*. Consider the experiences of Lucca between the fourteenth and sixteenth century, Genoa in the fourteenth century, and Vicenza in the fourteenth and fifteenth centuries. See Jonathan Davies, 'A Paper University? The Studio Lucchese, 1369–1487', in Hilde De Ridder-Symoens (ed.), *Universities in Early Modern Europe (1500–1800) (A History of the University in Europe, Vol. II*, Cambridge, 1991), 262–306; Giovanna Petti Balbi, *L'insegnamento nella Liguria medievale: scuole, maestri, libri* (Genoa, 1979), 107–13; Vincenzo Sansonetti, 'Le pubbliche scuole in Vicenza durante il Medioevo e l'Umanesimo', *Aevum*, 26 (1952), 156–79. There is one case very similar to Viterbo's: Piacenza's. In Piacenza public lectures were established by 1500; the *Collegio dei Notari* sought in 1509 and gained in 1518 the official establishment of a chair for instruction in the *Institutes*. These lectures took place at *Collegio dei Notari*, beside the commune's palace, then were transferred to the college of the Doctors and Judges from 1565. There was a strong emphasis on the local (as in the Viterban case): the lecturer had to be a graduate, native to Piacenza, and the appointment (as in Viterbo) was the prerogative of the general city council. Lecturer were added in scripture (1513) and humanities (1527), and a professor of logic was appointed in

1540; but by the end of the next decade only a lecturer in the *Institutes* remained (a trajectory similar to Viterbo's) (Emilio Nasalli Rocca, 'Le cattedre di istituzioni legali nelle città italiane con particolare riguardo a Piacenza', *Rivista di storia del diritto italiano*, 21 (1948), 211–30).

17. *Cronache e statuti*, 110.

18. Ibid.

19. On the problems of interpretation presented by the term *studens pauper* see Antonio I. Pini, 'Scolari ricchi e scolari poveri tra Medioevo ed età moderna', in Gian Paolo Brizzi and Jacques Verger (eds), *Le università dell'Europa. Gli uomini e i luoghi. Secoli XII–XVIII* (Milan, 1993), 157–89; he emphasizes that in the Middle Ages *pauper* meant: 'an individual not having sufficient means in relation to his social status or his established aims'. The author also examines the phenomenon of public subsidization of study costs. On poor university students, see also Jacques Paquet, 'L'universitaire "pauvre" au Moyen Age: problèmes, documentations, question de méthode', in Jacques Paquet and Jozef Ijsewijn (eds), *Les universités à la fin du Moyen Age* (Louvain, 1978), 329–425.

On the value of university studies see Jacques Verger, *Gli uomini di cultura nel Medioevo* (Bologna, 1999), 85: 'Certainly, until the end of the Middle Ages, university studies and degrees offered to young men of humble origins, most remarkably [...] But it is also true that in some families, above all those of medics and civil servants, university studies were already a habitual custom through which the sons succeeded the fathers, assuring the continuity of the familial vocation. It is also probable that amongst the established elites – old noble families and, in some cases, mercantile dynasties beset by uncertainty in times of crisis – university studies allowed young men to maintain their social status by giving them access to the ranks of "men of culture" '.

20. An analogous initiative is recorded for Lucca where, from 1340–50, grants from three to over ten *fiorini* were established, funding studies for a period of up to six years. Later, in 1599, Lucca like Viterbo announced that a particular number of students would receive grants (twenty-nine, as against Viterbo's total of twelve announced in 1582). See Paul F. Grendler, *La scuola nel Rinascimento italiano* (Rome, 1991), 24.

21. *Lo statuto del Comune di Viterbo del 1469*, ed. Corrado Buzzi (Roma, 2004), 368.

22. More information on these letters was recorded in 1583, in R. 67, 25v: 'Che le fedi che hanno da mandare li studenti ogn'anno conforme alli capitoli debbino essere sigillate con li sigilli delli lettori che odano in Studio e sottoscritte da loro'.

23. R. 19, 162v.

24. For the relationship between this Pope and the world of Humanism see Egmont Lee, *Sixtus IV and Men of Letters* (Rome, 1978). On Pietro Paolo Passerino see also John W. O'Malley, *Praise and Blame in Renaissance Rome. Rhetoric, Doctrin and Reform in the Sacrated Orators of the Papal*

Court, c. 1450–1521 (Durham, 1979), 252: ms. Roma, Bibl. Angelica, 246, ff. 252r-263r, is a transcription of an oration delivered by Passerino in 1481.
25. R. 19, 186r.
26. The following sums were probably distributed on the same basis as this award of 25 *ducati*: the sum that the *Priori*, in 1476, ordered to *Vice-cancelliere* to pay a citizen committed to the 'studium legum et iuris civilis pro studio suo et doctoratu' in Rome (quoted in Giuseppe Lombardi, 'Tre biblioteche viterbesi del XV secolo', in Lombardi (ed.), *Saggi*, 309–36); and the 26 *ducati* paid to Anselmo di ser Giovan Battista dei Nini 'eruditus adulescens [. . .] per gli studi', registered in the *Bollettario del Comune* (Bo.) 1524 in October 1530.
27. Viterbo, Biblioteca Comunale degli Ardenti, Archivio storico preunitario, II F 2 20, *Bollettario del Comune* (Bo.) 1524, August 1528: 'Tibi eximio artium et medicine doctori magistro Iacobo ser Ambrosii salutem. Quam diu et fere semper consuevit respublica virtutum sectatores non solum dignis prosegui laudibus verum etiam pro ipsius rei publice viribus summis meritis decorare et in eorum cum evenerit subvenire necessitatibus, ne igitur a nostrorum tam laudabili maiorum instituto discedamus duximus te magistrum Iacobum antedictum pluribus decoratum virtutibus aliquibus muneribus et gratis onestare, ut tuo exemplo alii ad similia fiant promptiores et audaciores; idcirco iuxta nostrum solitum nostrisque Communis solitam et laudabilem consuetudinem pro tui subventione studii te antedictum magistrum Iacobum physicum nostris Communis ducatorum triginta sex ad Lta facimus et harum serie constituimus creditorum etc. mandantes etc.'.
   April 1532: 'Exierunt etiam patentes littere in favorem eruditi iuvenis magistri Antonii Ioannis Turchii artium et medicine professoris et sectatoris pro summa et quantitate ducatorum triginta sex ad Lta iuxta solitum, et hoc pro subventione sui studii'. Antonio Turco would be appointed lecturer at the *Studium* in 1546 (see below).
28. Bo. 1545–48.
29. Bo. 1545.
30. Ibid.
31. Bo. 1542, June 1543: 'Allo erudito giovane Cesari Polione studente in Bologna in iure civili scuti nove de iulii dece per scudo et per lui a Lutiano Polione suo tiano, quali sonno per resto delli scudi diece et otto che la nostra communità per vigore delli Statuti è solita dare a dicti studenti, atteso ancora che in forma ha prestata cautione che in evento che non si fesse dottore de restituirli alla communità come ne è rogato il nostro cancelliere, et ancora di consenso del reverendissimo signor Vicelegato nostro'.
32. R. 44, 54v.
33. R. 67, 20r: 'Et che il magistro Ascanio figlio di magistro Leonardo Delicati il quale ha ricevuti li 18 scudi soliti darsi per prima dalla communità per vigore dello Statuto, debba restituirli in termine di 18 mesi, cioè uno scudo il mese, et per quo effecto durante detti 18 mesi segli faccia la bolletta di scudi cinque solamente il mese et scud'uno si ritenga per tal conto per la

communità, et da 18 mesi in là se gli faccia di sei scudi come agli altri'. The sum was in fact paid in 1578, as can be deduced from Bo. 1575 and 1578.

34. Sixteenth-century Roman cases are cited in, 'La Sapienza, in 41–8.
35. R. 55, 112v.
36. Lombardi cites in *Tre biblioteche*, 311, the will of Vittore Vittori (1504), which offers evidence of a grant paid to a member of the same family: in relation to Vittore's sister's dowry, it was specified that 6 *ducati* had already been delivered to the husband, Domenico *del fu* Sigismondo from Canino, Viterban citizen, to resolve some difficulties he had experienced when 'accessit ad Studium civitatis Senensis'.
37. *Cronache e statuti*, 110.
38. Ibid., 146.
39. R. 64, 118r.
40. R. 64, 128r.
41. R. 64, 145r.
42. The printed version of the proclamation is quoted in Attilio Carosi, *Librai cartai e tipografi in Viterbo e nella Provincia del Patrimonio di S. Pietro in Tuscia nei secoli XV e XVI* (Viterbo, 1988); the text of the proclamation is in Viterbo, Biblioteca Comunale degli Ardenti, Archivio storico preunitario, IV AP 4 34, *Bandi 1522–50*, doc. 274.
43. R. 64, 146r.
44. Paul F. Grendler, *The Universities of the Italian Renaissance* (Baltimore, 2001), 473: 'Demand [for law graduates] was high, because Italy and the rest of Europe had become societies in which the credential of a law degree mattered more than in the past. The increased demand probably originated with governement. Italian and European states seem to have been expanding their jurisdiction and, therefore, needed more trained personnel with law degrees. The call for legal traininig may have started at the top.' The ideal cultural preparation for the highest state officials would include a degree in civil law along with humanist training. The professional pre-eminence of the jurists also implies a cultural pre-eminence (Verger, *Gli uomini*, 41–2): 'Although the theologians and the medics appear to us today to have been the original thinkers among men of learning, law was sureley the most significant discipline of all the possible components of medieval learned culture. This applies too if we think only in terms of the numbers involved, or of social kudos. The last centuries of the Middle Age were for the jurists a golden age which in many countries continued throughout the years of the *ancien régime* and beyond [...] Throughout the West, at the end of the Middle Ages, the learned man was often a juris'.
45. Although it was one of the biggest monasteries of Lazio – perhaps even in central Italy – there are not detailed studies of this Dominican foundation. This may be due in part to the fact that the sources are now difficult to assemble, being dispersed over several centres. Some indications

concerning the institution's intellectual activity and its library are in Massimo Miglio, *Santa Maria in Gradi* (Viterbo, 1996).

46. On 26 July, the Council decided upon the composition of the board of examiners (R. 67, 18v): 'Furono deputati per esaminatori di detti studenti, cioè a quelli che vorranno attendere alle leggi, il sopradetto Auditore et altri dottori di Viterbo, et a quelli che vorranno attendere alla filosofia, il reverendo padre lettore di Santa Maria in Grado et il reverendo padre lettore di San Francesco, con intervento ancora di altri medici et dottori di tal professione'.

47. We have some examples of the assigned *puncti*: on 17 August 1582 (R. 64, 152v) the *punctus* assigned to Rosio Malagriccia for law was *ff. his quos nunquam fin. De heredibus instituendis* (*Inst.*, Lib. II, Tit. XIV); on 22 August 1585 (R. 65, 138r), the *punctus* assigned to Cesare Crivellato for logic was *in capite De accidenti, videlicet accidens est quod adest et abest propter subiecti corruptionem* (*Isag.*, V.1); on 23 October 1585 (R. 65, 146r), Paolo Caparozio was assigned, for logic, *in capite De proprio* (*Isag.*, IV); on the same day and again for logic, Giovanni Foglia was assigned *in capite De specie, species est quod de pluribus et differentibus numero predicatum ad effectum* (*Isag.*, II.4); on 7 November 1588 (R. 66, 129r), Cesare Ilario Brigidi was assigned, for theology, *in capite De differentia videlicet differentia est quae predicatur de pluribus differentibus specie in eo quod quale cum omnibus suis distinctionibus et divisionibus* (*Isag.*, III.10); on 5 January 1589 (R. 66, 146r), Muzio Liberato was assigned, for law, *qui tutores in testamento dari possint* (*Inst.*, Lib. I, Tit. XIV); on 28 October 1590 (R. 68, 80r), Giuseppe Architetto was assigned, for law, *in principio Institutae De adoptionibus* (*Inst.*, Lib. I, Tit. XI); on 12 August 1591 (R. 68, 158r), Ottavio Faiano was assigned, for logic, *in capitulo De differentia* (*Isag.*, III); on the same day (R. 68, 158v), Perozio Mustio was assigned, for law, *in 55 Institutae De capitis diminutione* (*Inst.*, Lib. I, Tit. XVI).

48. R. 64, 128r (1582): 'Et inoltre gli sia argomentato sopra i testuali ad effetto di far prova se sia atto alli studi più alti'; R. 64, 146v (1582): 'Punctum legit et recitavit, argumentis eorundem patrum lectorum et aliorum doctorum sibi factis acute et subtiliter respondendo'; R. 68, 80r (1590): 'Recitavit et enodavit punctum divisiones tituli assignando, dubia solvendo et notabilia demonstrando'.

49. The formalities characterizing this examination were clearly inspired by the graduation ceremony, on which see Giorgio Cencetti, 'La laurea nelle università medievali', in Roberto Ferrara, Gianfranco Orlandelli, and Augusto Vasina (eds), *Giorgio Cencetti. Lo Studio di Bologna. Aspetti, momenti e problemi: 1935–1970* (Bologna, 1989), 77–94. For a description of examinations held in Siena during the sixteenth century see Giovanni Minnucci and Leo Košuta, *Lo Studio di Siena nei secoli XIV–XVI. Documenti e notizie biografiche* (Milan, 1989), pp. xiii–xiv.

50. On 28 October (R. 67, 20r) it was declared: 'Non siano admessi né si possino accettare per sigurtà li padri di essi studenti ma altre persone idonee a sodisfazione sempre delli signori Priori pro tempore'. We have records of the presentation of guarantors for 1590: (R. 68, 78r) Bernardino Paulonio guarantor for Arcangelo Iuzzanti; (R. 68, 78v) Evangelista Peio for Muzio Liberato; (R. 68, 80v) Paolo Architetto for Giuseppe Architetto; and for 1591: (R. 68, 162v) Paolino Tignosino for Cesare Tignosino; (R. 68, 181v), Leonardo Spadario for Ottavio Faiano; (R. 68, 182v), Valerio Bussio for Lucio Bussio.

51. 1589 saw one instance of a return authorized by the *Priori*. This is recorded in R. 66, 219v: 'Magnificus dominus capitaneus Iulius de Brigidis exhibuit et presentavit magnificis dominis Conservatoribus fidem licentiae concessae reverendo domino Cesare eius filio redeundi in patriam iustis de causis, subscriptam a quatuor dominis Conservatoribus bimestris preteritis'. In the same year, as recorded in R. 67, 64v, measures were taken to prevent students from returning home without permission: 'Che quanto alle bollette degli studenti che sono stati in Viterbo senza licenza che si osservino li capitoli sopra ciò fatti, et si ritenghino li denari et si faccino rimettere'. Bo. 1590 (September 1591) refers again to Cesare Brigidi: 'Scudi sei per messer Cesare suo figliuolo studente in Roma che ha domandato licenza di venire per il presente mese'.

52. The same Viterban sources testify to one of the various other mechanism for obtaining a degree, the *privilegium* granted by imperial authority. Niccolò della Tuccia *Cronaca* notes that Emperor Frederik III exercised this privilege and granted doctorates to Viterban citizens when he stopped at the city on his way to Rome in 1469 ('fe' de Viterbesi dottori e conti palatini'). For 1594, R. 70, 232v registers the public exhibition of Francesco Mentebona's *privilegium doctoratum*, granted in Padua by a *conte palatino*. For more examples, concerning different locations, see Elda Martellozzo Forin, 'Conti palatini e lauree conferite per privilegio: l'esempio padovano del sec. XV', *Annali di storia delle Università italiane*, 3 (1999), 79–119; and Carla Penuti, 'Collegi professionali di giureconsulti con prerogativa di addottorare in area estense e romagnola', in Gian Paolo Brizzi and Jacques Verger (eds), *Le università minori in Europa (secoli XV–XIX). Convegno internazionale di Studi* (Catanzaro, 1998), 337–52. For the problem of the degrees awarded by professional colleges or *conti palatini*, see Grendler, *The Universities*, 183–6; and Ad Tervoort, *The iter italicum and the Northern Netherlands: Dutch students at Italian Universities and their role in the Netherlands' society (1426–1575)* (Leiden, 2005). According to Tervoort, it was Emperors Charles IV and Sigismund who first gave the *conti palatini* the right to award degrees.

53. A physical description of the *privilegium* is given in entries for 1582 (R. 63, 13v): 'In carta pergamina cum sigillo appenso et manu publici notarii publicatum'; 1593 (R. 70, 174r): 'Doctoratus privilegium in quodam libello carte pergamine descriptum'; 1594 (R. 70. 232v): 'In carta pergamina descriptum et duobus sigillis appensione munitum'.

54. R. 64, 161v.
55. R. 67, 46v.
56. R. 65, 227v.
57. Viterbo, Biblioteca Comunale degli Ardenti, Archivio storico preunitario, IV AP 1 1, *Letterario del Comune* (Let.) 1585, 65v.
58. Let. 1585, 65v.
59. R. 66, 214r; Let. 1585, 259r.
60. R. 66, 219v.
61. R. 66, 43v: 'Illustrissimus dominus Vicelegatus, de ordine illustrissimi et reverendissimi domini Legati et vigore litterarum sibi a prefato illustrissimo ut asseruit trasmissarum, auxit numerum studentium qui volunt ad Studia publica sumptibus communitatis usque ad numerum duodecim prout erant ante reductionem alias factam per dominum illustrissimum'.
62. R. 70, 27r.
63. R. 64 128r.
64. For the development of student mobility, and the connections between this phenomenon and the increasingly regional character of fourteenth- and fifteenth-century universities, see Jacques Verger, 'Peregrinatio Academica', in Brizzi and Verger (eds), *Università dell'Europa*, 107–35. On the composition of the student body in the modern period, see also Maria Rosa Di Simone, 'Per una storia delle università europee: consistenza e composizione del corpo studentesco dal '500 al '700', *Clio*, 12–13 (1986), 349–88. As emphasized in Maria Teresa Guerrini (ed.), *Qui voluerit in iure promoveri . . . : i dottori in diritto nello Studio di Bologna (1501–1796)* (Bologna, 2005)), it is necessary to distinguish precisely between the phenomenon of straightforward student mobility, which saw students travel from their places of origin to locations with *Studia*, and the *peregrinatio academica*, the custom of attending several *Studia*, very common for example among the North European students who journeyed through the various Italian university centres. Particular sources for the study of this second phenomenon are the *Libri Amicorum*: that is, the travel books in which students collected the dedications of teachers and acquaintances encountered during this sort of *Grand Tour* (Gian Paolo Brizzi, 'Una fonte per la storia degli studenti: i *libri amicorum*', in Francesco Piovani and Luciana Sitran-Rea (eds), *Studenti, università, città nella storia padovana. Atti del Convegno (Padova, 6–8 febbraio 1998)* (Trieste, 2001), 389–402). Unfortunately, it was principally German students who produced such documents, and Italian equivalents are very rare. On student mobility in Italy, see Gian Paolo Brizzi, 'ASFE: una banca dati per lo studio della mobilità universitaria e per un onomasticon dei laureati in Italia nell'età moderna', *Annali di storia delle università italiane*, 8 (2004), 449–53, in which he describes the ASFE database project, named after the expression used by Frederik II in the *Habita, Amore Studii Facti Exules*. The members of the FIRB research project, *Percorsi tra le università storiche europee*, have adopted this database in order to register information concerning the presence of students

and graduates in Bologna, Pavia, Padua, Pisa, and Siena: 'The structure of the database should make it possible to assemble all information concernig a particular individual, who will potentially have numerous contacts with the multiple universities operating in the peninsula'. The project originated in the Bolognese context from the plan elaborated by Brizzi, *La storia sui muri*, that is, the initiative of creating a registry of the students' family crests on the walls of the *Arhiginnasio*: 'Since [this material] provides a record only for those students who were not citizens [. . .], it provides direct evidence of manner in which the ancient universities could contribute to the construction of the European cultural identity, as did such institutions and associations as the humanistic societies and learned academies' (451).

Sandro Serangeli and Laura Marconi (ed.s), *I laureati dell'antica Università di Macerata, 1541–1824. In appendice: La matricola degli studenti marchigiani a Perugia, 1511–1720 e un piccolo esempio di* migratio *accademica fra le università di Perugia e Macerata* (Turin, 2003), incorporates an appendix edited by Marconi which provides examples of *peregrinatio* from the *Studia* of Perugia and Macerata. Furthermore, a new sort of *peregrinatio* from *Studium* to *Studium* appeared in the late middle ages: the custom of moving to a smaller university which specialized in an easier or cheaper route to the degree, based on more or less rigorous training. Ferrara might, for example, be chosen over Bologna for this advantage.

65. Ennio Cortese, 'Legisti, canonisti e feudisti: la formazione di un ceto medievale', in *Università e società*, 195–284, emphasizes the fact that a new theory of law evolved from the end of twelfth century: it would eventually entail the replacement of specialists in either one of civil or canon law with the *doctor in utroque iure*. This convergence of the two legal branches was encouraged above all by the canonists, who welcomed the new attention to decretals and the general renewal of Roman law.

66. R. 43, 200r (5 September 1546).

67. In Perugia, for example, contracts were granted only to members of the Perugian college of *doctors*, but these men did not have to be natives of the city. Because of the parochialism which characterizes this period, it was often necessar to have attended the university at which one aspired to lecture, a situation which produced some true dynasties of lecturers. But in Viterbo, where it was never possible to award degrees, only citizenship or at most Viterban origin was required. On the tendency of late medieval universities towards regional particularism see Verger, *Gli uomini*, 83–5.

68. Florence offers an example of conflict between political institutions and lecturers over the salaries to be paid at a *Studium*. See Armando F. Verde, 'Vita universitaria nello Studio della Repubblica Fiorentina alla fine del Quattrocento', in *Università e società nei secoli XII–XVI. Atti del IX Convegno Internazionale* (Pistoia, 1982), 495. On salaries see also Gaines Post, 'Master's Salaries and Student-Fees in the Mediaeval Universities', *Speculum*, 7 (1932), 181–98.

69. On the other hand, the *Studium's* lecturers were totally immersed in the political life of the city, and clearly supported themselves through their other duties. In the case of Viterbo then, we see the reverse of the more common scenario according to which the lecturer supplemented his salary through his professional activities: jurists by providing *consilia* to the commune, doctors by operating as courtly physicians, humanists by becoming tutors to great families. The Viterban case does not comply with Grendler's observation that, despite these distractions, 'the majority [of lecturers] devote[d] their professional lives to university teaching'; see Grendler, *Universities*, 161. See also Mario Ascheri, '*Consilium sapientis*, perizia medica e *res iudicata*: diritto di dottori e istituzioni comunali', in Stephan Kuttner and Kennet Pennington (eds), *Proceedings of the Fifth International Congress of Medieval Canon Law (Salamanca, 21–25 September 1976)* (Vatican City, 1980), 534–79.

70. The term *in scholis* referred to the physical locations where lectures were delivered in the university. See Alfonso Maierù, 'Gli atti scolastici nelle Università italiane', in Luciano Gargan and Oronzo Limone (eds), *Luoghi e metodi di insegnamento nell'Italia medioevale (secoli XII–XIV). Atti del Convegno Internazionale di studi (Lecce-Otranto, 6–8 ottobre 1986)* (Lecce, 1989), 249–87.

71. R. 43, 216r. See R. 43, 131v: 'in platea Communis subtus scolam publicam'.

72. Ermini notes that the privilege of teaching and the *facultas doctorandi* were often, but not invariably, granted in combination. In Perugia the two privileges were in fact awarded at different times: Giuseppe Ermini, *Storia dell'università di Perugia* (2 vols., Florence, 1971), i, 28.

73. R. 44, 45r. In Bo. 1545, October 1547, there is a record of a payment 'a Pietro Famiglio per ire a Roma per causa dello Studio'. However, as the *Letterario* for that year have not been preserved, it is impossible to identify Famiglio's mission.

74. R. 43, 217r.

75. Let. 1585, 65v. The 1587 request suggests that papal permission was been granted but never exploited: 'Che altre volte la medesima facoltà ne fu concessa dalla santa memoria di Paolo terzo, se bene non ne fu fatta espeditione'.

76. Manlio Bellomo, 'Scuole giuridiche e università studentesche in Italia', in Gargan and Limone (eds), *Luoghi e metodi*, 121–52, 123.

77. R. 43, 217r.

78. Agostino Paravicini Bagliani, 'La fondazione dello *Studium curiae*: una rilettura critica', in Gargan and Limone (eds), *Luoghi e metodi*, 59–81.

79. R. 43, 211r.

80. On the importance and the geographical distribution of such teaching during the period in question, see Emilio Nasalli Rocca, 'Le cattedre di istituzioni legali nelle città italiane con particolare riguardo a Piacenza', *Rivista di storia del diritto italiano*, 21 (1948), 211–30, 211: 'In the context of the history of teaching and of legal studies, we have noted the existence of a

particular chair, above all for the period beginning in the sixteenth and seventeenth centuries and extending to the end of the seventeenth century [...]: the chair in the legal or imperial Institutes *"cesaree" (Instituta)'*. Outside universities, the subject was taught in cities which had no *Studium* at that stage of their existence. This trend is exemplified very precisely by Viterbo: in fact, when the *Studium* ceased activity, the commune continue to pay an annual salary to a public lecturer in the *Institutes*. Such lecturerships, insofar as they often existed to compensate for the lack of an actual university, present an interpretative problem: 'Should we classify [the instruction] as intellectual, of the type which characterizes very high university culture [...], an introduction to advanced Roman Law starting from the study of the other sections of Justinian's legislature [...]; or was this elementary instruction with practical aims, serving the bourgeois culture?' Rocca favours the second interpretation but tempers it by noting that university experience has always been informed by the local civic mindset. In the Viterban case, an introduction to university studies was one of the acknowledged aims of these courses, even if it was not their exclusive function.

The contente of these lectures (although faithfully linked to Justinian's text) 'may perhaps have contributed, inadvertently, [...] to the formulation, to the creation of the commom law [...] in fact, the aim of such courses was not so much to explain texts in slavish conformity to Justinian's *Institutes* as to provide definitions of concepts and institutions informing the legal training of the citizens. [...] This chair was very useful to the advancement of the legal culture and its influence in civic society' (213–6).

81. Two of the three available categories of lecturer are listed here: Perugia's *condotte*, which are contemporary, mention *ordinaristi*, i.e. the lecturers in civil or canon law who are required to interpret the text; and *istituzionalisti*, i.e. those lower down on the professional scale. The third category, not present here, was that of the *satrordinaristi* required to read without commenting. Usually the *ordinarista* had the privilege of teaching in his own home during holydays or on feast deays, while others could teach only at the university. See Maierù, 'Gli atti scolastici', 259–68.

82. For contrast, see the Paul III's bull of foundation for the Macerata *Studium*. This document features a formula analogous to Viterbo's, but in this case the term is 'corrected' later in the text when the institution is described as a *Studium generale*: 'Nobis fuit humiliter supplicatum [...] ut in ipsa civitate literarum studium incrementum suscipat, opportune providere de benignitate apostolica dignaremus [...] Nos igitur, attendentes quod ex literarum studio, tam publica quam privata spiritualia et temporalia comoda proveniunt [...] huiusmodi supplicationibus inclinati, in eadem civitate Maceratensi perpetuis futuris temporibus Generale Studium cuiuscumque facultatis et scientie licet cum cathedris facultatum earumdem ac potestate et facultate doctorandi seu magistrandi, nec non rectorie et aliis pro illius prospero et felici redimine necessariis facultatibus et officiis, ita ut in ibi

Generale Studium in qualibet licita facultatibus perpetuo habeatur et vigeat, auctoritate apostolica tenore presentium erigimus et instituimus'. (*Gli Statuta dell'antica università*, 53)

83.	On 6 November (R. 43, 227r) the Vice legate and the *Priori* ordered that a public announcement should be printed (now ms. 414). This is a symptom of modernity. The connection between the modern cultural word and printing is so strong that the *Studium* was allocated its own print shop, in the charge of Antonio Blado and Pier Matteo Tesoro. Carosi examines Viterban printers of the fifteenth and sixteenth centuries, and provides the transcription from the *Libri delle Riforme* of the commune's ordinance entrusting the shop to the two printers: *Librai, cartai e tipografi*, 50. The most significant passage reads: 'Havendo noi et nostra comunità in questi prossimi passati giorni ottenuta gratia dalla Santirà di N.S. di erigere, principiare et in perpetuum, etc., continuare in questa città di Viterbo un nuovo letterario studio e per manutenzione del quale di continuo havere, et tenere, condurre, et salariare famosi et eccellenti doctori et considerando noi al gran concurso de' studenti, altre persone letterate che in questa città concorreranno [e] perché voi et ciasch'un di voi per comodità di dicto novo, eretto et principiato studio volete in questa città di Viterbo erigere et principiare il bel et onorevole esercitio della stampa in dicta città non più esercitato'. The connection between *Studium* and printer recurred witht the 1566 refoundation: on the initiative and intercession of Giovanni of Canepina, governor of Foligno (lecturer in the *Institutes* at the 1546 *Studium*) and Ascanio Salimbene (lecturer in the refounded *Studium*), the commune persuaded printer Agostino Coraldi to move from Foligno to Viterbo, and granted him licence to print in Viterbo on 27 December 1567. The words of Giovanni of Canepina are significant: 'certamente con lo Studio va accompagnata la stampa'. Like the public school and later the *Studium*, the printshop was also 'in platea Communis'.

84.	R. 43, 217r.

85.	The gap between reality and rhetoric is widest here: aspiring lecturers would in fact have to be Viterban natives.

86.	R. 43, 237r.

87.	R. 43, 214r.

88.	On Rome, see David S. Chambers, '*Studium Urbis* and *gabella Studii*: the University of Rome in the Fifteenth Century', in Cecil H. Clough (ed.), *Cultural Aspects of the Italian Renaissance. Essays in Honour of Paul Oskar Kristeller* (Manchester and New York, 1976), 68–110; and Maria Cristina Dorati da Empoli, 'I lettori dello studio e i maestri di grammatica a Roma da Sisto IV ad Alessandro VI', *Rassegna degli Archivi di Stato*, 40 (1980), 98–147. The expression 'gabella vini forensis ad minutum' or 'gabella Studii' was first attested under Pope Paolo III, and established definitively by Eugene IV for the Roman *Studium* in 1431.

89.	R. 43, 226r.

90.	R. 44, 14r.

91. R. 43, 215v.
92. Bo. 1545 reveals that the *Studium*'s furnishing were already prepared in September and had been ordered from the carpenter Niccolò, nicknamed *il Ciomba*: in September, 'al Ciomba falegname scudi cinque de iulii diece per il scudo sonno a bon conto de' suoi legnami et manifattura tanto delle cathedre per li novi lectori quanto per li banchi per li studenti et ancora a bon conto delle porte et chiustrini delle presoni per causa dello Studio del solito locho mutate'; in December, 'per una porta de legname fatta al novo Studio scudi quattro, per una tavola per li scolari et bidello iulii 25, per una porta nova fatta alla sala dello Studio scudi dui, per due belle cathedre per li lectori scudi diece'.
93. R. 43, 218r.
94. In fifteenth- and sixteenth-century Modena too, medics were usually responsible for lectures in law and philosophy. On this subject, see Emilio Vicini, 'Le letture pubbliche in Modena nei secoli XV–XVII', *Rassegna per la storia della Università di Modena e della cultura superiore modenese*, 5 (1935), 47–170.
95. This custom was ubiquitous. Similarly, lectures on the third book of Avicenna were reserved for recent graduates in medicine and lectures on introductory texts in logic and moral philosophy were reserved for recent philosophy graduates.
96. R. 44, 53r.
97. R. 43, 230r.
98. On the potential ideological value of the lecture celebrating beginning of the academic year, see Carla Frova, 'Il maestro universitario nel Medioevo: forme di autorappresentazione', in Brizzi and Verger (eds), *Università dell'Europa*, 137–55; for examples from fifteenth-century Rome, see Carla Frova and Rita Nigri, 'Un'orazione universitaria di Paolo Veneto', *Annali di Storia delle Università italiane*, 2 (1998), 191–7; and Anna Esposito, 'Un'inedita orazione quattrocentesca per l'inaugurazione dell'anno accademico dello *Studium Urbis*', Giulia Barone, Lidia Capo, and Stefano Gasparri (eds), *Studi sul Medioevo per Girolamo Arnaldi* (Rome, 2001), 205–33. Frova observes of university oratory: 'We find orations declaimed at the Universities for the most diverse official occasions: candidates' presentation at their final examination, promotion to academic ranks, appointment of the chancellor, *principia* of the academic year or of *lecturae*, feast days of patron saints. [...] The orations declaimed for the beginning of the academic year were surely the most extensive, and their main theme was the praise of the disciplines; the *principia* of the courses are primarily pedagogical in focus; while te declamations in honour of the patron saints represent a separate genre. [...] As early as the 1960's, Celestino Piana made extensive use of some important compilations containing examples of university oratory to discover information about teachers and students [...] later on, various scholars drew on this type of source, considering it not only as repository of information for the extension

of prosopographical data, but also as a witness to the culture, mentality, values, and aspirations of the university population' (196). With regard to the Viterban inaugural oration, in R. 43, 230r, we read: 'oratio Studii per discretum adulescentem *** domini Innocentii Ugonii'; in Bo. 1545, in December 1546, it is specified that one *scudo* was paid to 'erudito Giovanni Francisco di messer Innocentio per haver recitato la oratione dello Studio in Santo Lorenzo'. In Bo. 1545, it is noted that a payment was made in September 1547, probably for the beginning of the first academic year following foundation, to 'magistro Cesare Busso della comunità nostro advocato et in questi giorni passati ad una con magistro Iacomo Sacchi et Antonio Gentile in Roma per occurrentia della comunità nostra ambasciador, [of] iulii cinque per la scrittura della oratione fatta scrivere in Roma per recitare in principio di Studio'. The orator of 1547 was the 'letterato et erudito giovane Cesare di Peroni', to whom one *scudo* was paid in November 'secondo il solito dell'anno passato' (Bo. 1545); on this occasion the oration took place 'in S. Agnilo'.

99. R. 43, 230v.
100. Ibid.
101. R. 43, 232v.
102. Ibid.
103. R. 43, 237r.
104. Payment was in three instalments and not *de bimestre in bimestre* as announced in the papal brief. This was in fact that normal schedule, conventional for other civiv officers: the three instalments were usually paid on 1 November, on 1 March, and on 1 August. In 1566, it was specified that the instalments would be paid on Christmas Eve, on the feastday of *Carnis privii* (the last Sunday before Lent) and at Easter.
105. Bo. 1545.
106. R. 45, 41r.
107. Bo. 1548.
108. R. 50, 25r.
109. R. 52, 26r.
110. R. 57, 98v.
111. R. 57, 142v.
112. R. 58, 105r: '20 octobris. Magnificus dominus Ascanius Salimbenius Institutionum lector dicta die pro principio novi Studii disertissimam et eloquentissimam orationem habuit in palatio magnificorum dominorum Priorum etc. 21 eiusdem. Magister Iohannes Turcus lector logice etiam pro principio Studii orationem disertissimam habuit'.
113. R. 58, 120r.
114. The *doctor*'s activity was not therefore restricted to the public school, but we cannot be certain that this implied a private revenue apart from the salary guranteed by the commune. The possibility that lecturers would teach outside the places designated for public instruction had already been raised in 1567 (R. 57, 203v) when, in Council, Giovanni Turco himself suggested

that it should be permitted 'che li lettori leggerno in casa a tempo delle vacantie et li lettori siano affabili et domestici'.
115. R. 158, 194r.
116. R. 59, 30r.
117. R. 59, 37r.
118. R. 57, 14v.
119. That is the printer mentioned above.
120. R. 65, 227v.
121. *I.*: *Institutiones*; *L.*: Logic; *P.*: Philosophy; *D.*: Dialectic; *C.*: Beadle.
122. Bo. 1575, April 1575.
123. On 3 November 1575, 'de sero et hora 22 [...] in aula palatii [his first lecture was] de contractis, venditionibus et obligationibus' (*Inst.*, Lib. III, Tit. XIII, 'De obligatione'; Tit. XXIII, 'De emptione et venditione').
124. Bo. 1575, December 1575, April 1576, June 1576; R. 61, 13v.
125. 6 November 1576, an oration 'de laudibus philosophiae et logicae facultatis'.
126. Bo. 1575, January, April, and June 1577; R. 61, 13v.
127. 4 November 1577, first lecture about 'titulum de usucapionibus et de aquirendo possessione' (*Inst.*, Lib. II, Tit. VI, 'De usucapionibus et largi temporis possessionibus').
128. Bo. 1575. January and March 1578; Bo. 1578, June 1578; R. 61, 312v.
129. Bo. 1578, March and April 1579.
130. Bo. 1578, December 1579; January, February, and July 1580.
131. 3 November 1582, 'de sero [his first lecture] in quam de anno proxime venturo interpretare velle proposuit et affirmavit et de testamentis et desuper se multum extendit'.
132. 3 November 1582, 'de mane [an oration] de nomine et laudibus philosophiae in qua summopere optimum ordinem a magnifica communitate introductum, ut duodecim iuvenes bonarum studiis artium incumbentes aere publico in alienis regionibus in quibus Gymnasii florent subvenire etiam commendant'.
133. R. 64, 165r.
134. He gave an oration on 7 November 1583, 'de sero in hoc venturo anno se et de donationibus interpretaturum fore promisit'. (*Inst.*, Lib. II, Tit. VII, 'De donationibus').
135. R. 64, 239v.
136. R. 65, 65v.
137. 4 November 1585, 'de mane titulum de his qui alienari possunt se lecturum et explicaturum promisit' (*Inst.*, Lib. II, Tit. VIII, 'Quibus alienare licet vel non').
138. R. 65, 149r.
139. R. 65, 232r.
140. Bo. 1590, June 1590.
141. Bo. 1590, January and March 1592; R. 68, 148r.

142. Instances of this ceremony are recorded in the sixteenth-century *Libri delle Riforme*: 1562 (R. 55, 173r), Aristofilo Florenzolo; 1563 (R. 56, 84v) Giovanni Battista Fustino and (176r) Alessandro di Giovanni di maestro Galieno Almadiani; 1568 (R. 57, 300r) Fausto Alosio; 1569 (R. 58, 67r), Giovanni Battista Nino; 1571 (R. 59, 37r), Paride Turellio; 1574 (R. 60, 45r), Pietro Pollione; 1577 (R. 61, 228r), Vincenzo Franceschino, and in May 1577 Bo. 1575 registers: 'a messer Vincenzo Franceschini dottore di leggi scudi diciotto quali segli danno per la sovvenzione dello studio secondo la forma di nostri statuti e secondo il solito'; 1577 (R. 62, 288r; Bo. 1575, August 1577) Annibale Regio; 1578 (R. 62, 145v; Bo. 1578, September 1578), Domenico Ferro; 1579 (R. 62, 203v), Giulio Durante; and 1579 (R. 62, 254r; Bo. 1578, August 1579), Alessandro Iacomucio; 1585 (R. 65, 163v), Santoro Paulonio; 1586 (R. 65, 143v), Orazio Bussi and (R. 65, 178v) Ascanio Delicato; 1587 (R. 66, 19r), Coloniso Sannello; 1588 (R. 66, 140r), Roscio Malagriccia; 1589 (R. 66, 146v), Agostino Ciosa; 1593 (R. 70, 174r), Lepido Bussi.
143. The ceremony is clearly modelled on the *conventus* or *publica*.
144. To be more precise 'ab conventu Sancte Marie supra Quercum' (R. 58, 67r; R. 60, 45r) and 'a conventu Beatae Mariae Paradisi' (R. 57, 300r; R. 59, 37r). This fact seems not to indicate that the graduates in question were in holy orders. One might speculate that the civil ceremony was in some cases preceded by private worship.
145. In 1563 (R. 56, 84v), Giovan Battista Fustino delivered is oration *de legibus*. In the same year (R. 56, 176r), Alessandro Almadiani gave an oration 'continens in se quantum sit utile ius civile et leges et quantum precedat aliis in medicina doctoribus'. The oration delivered by Annibale Regio in 1577 (R. 62, 228v), was 'de laudibus iuris civilis scientie'. In 1582 (R. 66, 19r), Coloniso Sannello pronounced an oration 'super laudibus predicte magnificae communitatis et presertim istituto alendi scolares in Studiis publicis'; after which he gave a public defence of 'conclusiones in logica, phisica et universa philosophia et medicinis'.
146. Miglio, *Cultura umanistica*, 17.

Scholarly Reputations and Institutional Prestige: The Fashioning of the Public Image of the University of Helmstedt, 1576–1680

Richard Kirwan

This article examines the manner in which the public profiles of universities were fashioned in the Holy Roman Empire in the sixteenth and seventeenth centuries. It argues that in this period of growing competition between universities the need to influence perceptions of institutional prestige became increasingly important. Taking the University of Helmstedt as a case study, it finds that a variety of representational strategies were deployed to cultivate the public image of a university. Chief among these was the endeavour to fashion the reputations of a university's scholars; an enterprise which lent specificity to representations of institutional fame. This particular aspect of institutional image construction provides the main focus of analysis.

The number of universities operating in the Holy Roman Empire increased significantly over the course of the sixteenth and seventeenth centuries.[1] New universities did not emerge organically from the gathering of scholars but were founded by princes or city governments to serve the interests of the host polity and its rulers. As such they are commonly described as 'territorial' universities. One natural effect of the growth in the number of universities was the heightening of competition between institutions for students, teachers, and patronage. Within this climate, perceptions of the relative merits of a university were crucial to its welfare. As a consequence, professors became ever more deliberate in their attempts to cultivate the good name and reputation of their university. This was especially the case at newly established institutions which suffered from an inevitable deficit of prestige. In such cases professors were especially enthusiastic in their efforts to tend to the public image of the institution and proved particularly adept at utilizing novel instruments of representation to fashion and publicize the image of their university.

When cultivating a university's reputation professors sought to convey merit according to a wide range of criteria, all of which aimed to feed the expectations of potential clients. Representations of institutional character thus described, among other attributes, the corporate identity of a university, its relations with ruling authorities, its political and social functions, the nature of pedagogy offered, the renown of its professors, and its environmental and architectural character.

Opportunities to promote the image of a university tended to be bound by occasion. Larger scale events such as inauguration or jubilee festivals permitted a high degree of representational activity. Such events were also the least frequently occurring. More common occasions for publicizing a university were presented by smaller scale events in the academic ritual cycle such as commencement ceremonies or social events like professorial marriages and funerals. As a consequence, much of the fashioning of the image of a university was enacted via the celebration of its scholars both individually and collectively.

The reputations of universities had always been built, at least in part, upon the profiles of their more famous scholars. The corporate celebration of exemplary scholars occupied a central place in projections of institutional prestige. Over the course of the sixteenth century, as competition between institutions became more intense, celebrations of the individual began to extend with greater frequency to the lesser men of a university, offering a broader characterization of the academic cohort and thus providing a more complete indication of institutional worth.

Academic self-fashioning in the early modern period

The notion that university academics recognized themselves as a distinct social category in the early modern period is one that has received a cautious response from historians. This is in part a consequence of a general lacuna in existing scholarship on questions of academic social identity. In recent years, however, scholars investigating various facets of academic culture have sought to fill this gap.[2]

The constituency and social character of academic groups are often difficult to define.[3] Medieval and early modern universities played host to teachers, students, and servants of various types. Within each category there existed further subsets and distinctions, which varied according to local situation.[4] Faculties, each with a distinct functional identity, for example, separated groups of professors and students. The identification of coherent groups is also made difficult by the fact that scholars generally held allegiances external to the university. At municipal universities such as Altdorf, for example, scholarly and urban elites were highly integrated.[5] In Catholic universities scholars often belonged to clerical orders, which inevitably led to a diffusion of allegiance.[6] It was also common for professors to hold non-academic posts in the church, city or state. Given this diversity of associations, it is, therefore, unsafe to assume that scholars tended to categorize themselves as university men in the first instance.

In spite of these complexities, it is evident from the self-characterizations of scholars that they often perceived themselves as belonging to an academic social category, however nebulous that association might have been. In the quest for precision there is a risk of paying greater heed to the exact definition of boundaries of social distinction than was exhibited by the subjects of our analysis. This is not to ignore the fact that concerns for social categorization and symbolic differentiation were often central to social negotiation within and outside of the university in the early modern period.[7]

Early modern academic self-characterizations combined traditional symbolic and ceremonial practices with newer humanistic and ultimately baroque forms of representation. The more traditional practices, which often had their origins in the medieval period, remained fundamental as vehicles of social expression. Such mechanisms were deployed in society generally to delineate social purpose and inscribe agency. In academic contexts these included, for example, the various ceremonies and ritual habits that regulated hierarchies, the pedagogical process, and academic social life in general. Similarly, sumptuary signifiers; articles of academic power such as maces, seals, and keys; and monumental and architectural forms belong to this category. In the main, such instruments depicted generic characteristics and were not centred on the traits of individuals. They conveyed conformity to established models of what a university or scholar should be.

While academics were clearly engaged in the business of constructing self and corporate image in the medieval period, their preoccupation with such matters intensified over the course of the sixteenth and seventeenth centuries. This is evidenced by the proliferation of new

forms of representation which served to augment the effects of traditional symbolic and ceremonial devices. Importantly, there was considerable exploitation of print, which permitted a great deal of specificity in
the representation of character. Deployed in conjunction with more
traditional forms, these instruments allowed for the presentation of a
more nuanced image of a particular university and its scholarly society.
The surge in self-fashioning activity suggests that there was a growing need to define academic social character in this period. The
increased concern for self-representation corresponds with and was in
part a consequence of a general transformation of the role of scholars
which saw them act increasingly as bureaucratic functionaries of the
territorial state.[8] This was a process which led to some diminishment of
the medieval ideal of the mobile scholar operating in a supra-territorial
sphere.

The public life of the scholar

Academic legal and social identity was, in the first instance, ascribed to
the individual through a series of rituals that marked transitions in status.
Such rites of passage corresponded to career progression and included
matriculation, deposition, commencement, and appointment ceremonies. These ceremonies of transition also served to describe and realign
the hierarchical structure of the university.

Deposition rituals, for example, were fundamental to the formation of
scholarly character.[9] Violent in their application, they facilitated incorporation into student society by forcing the passenger to abandon his
previous social demeanour (or the status of *beanus*) and to assume
characteristics befitting a scholar.[10] Once the newcomer was admitted
to student society, scholarly character was ascribed through various
means, including participation in pedagogical practices, university ceremonial, and the communal life of the university and college. In addition, students were often distinguished by legal means, being subject to
the jurisdiction of the university corporation in certain matters.

Examination and commencement ceremonies, rites of passage
signalling the maturation of a scholar, brought about the alteration of
academic identity.[11] In addition to their obvious performative effects,
commencement ceremonies had many representational functions. They

described, for example, the characteristics of different academic ranks. The pedagogical practices of the university were also portrayed during such rituals via the staged examination of candidates. In addition, academic identity could be derived from social interactions between scholars both formal and casual. From the sharing of meals and living spaces to the celebration of academic marriages or the commemoration of deceased scholars, such interactions served to promote a sense of communal belonging among scholars.

Importantly, the public profile of the scholar was also fashioned in an array of representational forms including, for example, celebratory or commemorative literary devices, portraits, sculpture, and monuments.[12] Occasional literary forms, often highly classicized, emerged from humanistic culture. Similarly, they followed the cultural innovations of the court where humanist poets were often engaged to celebrate princes in occasional works. Occasional pamphlets became increasingly popular in the celebration and commemoration of academic life and death from the mid-sixteenth century and by the seventeenth their use was relatively habitual. It should be noted that the use of occasional publications outside of the princely court was not exclusively academic. Celebrations of marriage and funeral pamphlets, for example, were popular among those social elites who could afford their production. Indeed, academic poets, especially laureates, were frequently sought after to compose or contribute to such works.

Occasional publications were produced to mark key events in the academic career of the scholar. These works, for example, were printed to celebrate ritual transitions such as commencement or the installation of a rector. Other events outside of this institutional matrix also prompted such activity. Academic marriage, for example, was often celebrated through the publication of wedding songs. Exceptional achievements such as the naming of a scholar as poet laureate could be marked in this fashion. The death of members of a scholar's family frequently occasioned the printing of commemorative orations, sermons, and poems. A scholar's own death, in particular, could prompt the publication of commemorative works. Portraits were also deployed in the characterization of scholars, often printed alongside commemorative pieces or in editions of scholarly writings.

In addition, more substantial pamphlets were produced to celebrate a university's 'greatest' scholars in collective fashion. These works sometimes reutilized text and portraits from older celebratory and commemorative pieces to build a portfolio of famous professors, providing accounts of their lives and deeds, all in the service of the *fama* of the university. Examples of this type of publication include the *Annales Ingolstadiensis Academiae* (1580), *Imagines Professorum Tubingensium* (1596), *Effigies et Vitae Professorum Academiae Groningae et Omlandiae* (1654), and the *MONUMENTA JULIA Memorias Professorum Helmstadiensium* (1680).*

The sponsorship of individual reputations in occasional publications was not universal. While the degree to which a reputation could be supported in such media depended on the extent to which a scholar's career had progressed, it was not automatic that the reputations of the most senior scholars of a university were also the most endorsed. Not each and every scholar could gain (or be seen to gain) admission to a university's 'pantheon' since the legitimacy of such representation was based on its selectivity. In this way, graded distinctions in the sponsorship of reputations suggested a certain order and hierarchy of esteem.

The University of Helmstedt

The University of Helmstedt was founded by Duke Julius of Braunschweig-Wolfenbüttel in 1576. Its foundation was part a general programme of reform in the Duchy which commenced upon Julius' accession in 1568 and was primarily focused on the implementation of a Lutheran reformation.[13] Due to the fact that the university was founded without tradition as an imposition of ducal policy it suffered from a reputational deficit in its early years. Efforts to compensate for this situation were, as a result, considerable, both at the time of foundation and in the years that followed.

Helmstedt's inauguration provided a vital platform upon which favourable projections of the university could be staged. Inauguration ceremonies were ripe for the demonstration of a new university's merits and were typically marked by major festivities, although this depended on the circumstances of a university's foundation and the founder's willingness to exploit the opportunity.[14] Inauguration festivals allowed

---

* On the production of biography-based University histories see Richard Kirwan, 'The paper monument: University histories and the fashioning of institutional prestige in early modern Germany' in Anthony McElligott et al. (eds.), Power in history from the medieval to the post-modern world (Dublin, 2011), 83–108.

a prince to declare the merits of his reign by identifying his founding of the university as a monumental commitment to the welfare of his territory and a sign of his extraordinary stature among princes. Inauguration ceremonies had key performative functions necessary for the institution of the university as a legal entity, the appointment of university officers, and the introduction of the professors as a social body to the host city and territory. At Helmstedt the inauguration festival was an event of particular significance. A three-day festival comprising numerous ceremonies, processions, and entertainments, it facilitated the university's constitution and demonstrated its academic and ultimately its social functions. It was attended by academic, ecclesiastical, civic, and political dignitaries drawn mainly from the Duchy and the surrounding territories.[15] In order to capitalize on the representational potential of the inauguration, a festival book was compiled and printed in 1579 with the agreement of the Duke.[16] This text relates the history of the foundation, describes the inauguration festival, and reproduces ceremonial orations and celebratory poetry. The final section of the pamphlet contains a catalogue of all notables present during the festival, including princes, counts, lords, prelates, and nobles.[17] In an effort to demonstrate the academic strengths of the university a list of its professors is also provided. In a telling remark revealing the urgency of the need to convey the academic merits of the university the reader is assured that this list of professors is soon to be augmented, that '[p]lures sunt in expectatione'.[18]

Following the institution's inauguration, the public image of the university continued to be cultivated with enthusiasm. The level of publicity and interest generated by the opening festival could only be reproduced infrequently, however. The opening of grand new university buildings in 1612, for example, provided such an opportunity.[19] Similarly, the university's centenary afforded a commodious stage upon which to project institutional prestige. Both events were marked by festive celebration and occasioned considerable output of celebratory publications, in each case including festival books.[20] The highly ornamental university architecture also had important representational functions describing the stature and purpose of the institution.[21] The building of the university's reputation, however, was not limited to the opportunities presented by these major events. The merits of the institution were communicated in a more persistent if less dramatic way through the ceremonial practices of the academy and the celebration of the life and achievements of individual scholars. These more common and habitual representational practices are the main focus of this article.

The celebration of commencement in print

As a key moment in a scholar's professional and social development, commencement presented a natural opportunity for the publication of celebratory pamphlets. However, at Helmstedt the celebration of commencement in print was relatively infrequent. For the period between 1576 and 1626, for example, just fifty-three pamphlets celebrating commencement are extant. During the same period 667 degrees were awarded.[22] This disparity suggests that only those scholars most richly endowed with financial or social capital were in a position to engineer the publication of pamphlets to mark their achievement. It also suggests an endeavour to differentiate between scholars beyond the award of degrees. Investment in the reputations of scholars at this level, therefore, was far from uniform.

A level of regularity did exist in the content of these occasional texts. In general it can be observed that individuals were praised in a conventional and patterned manner. This ultimately had the effect of identifying ideal scholarly characteristics. More specific characterisations of individuals tended to occur in celebrations of established scholars or in commemorative works. Thus, with respect to junior scholars, it was more the act and artefact of praise which served to advertise distinction.

Printed celebrations of commencement took various forms. On occasion they were dedicated to all candidates, usually taking the form of a single sheet listing names and origins, with a short celebratory verse and generous use of printer's ornaments. Another format was a pamphlet offering a compilation of verses dedicated variously to the different candidates. Candidates promoted to the upper academic grades were often celebrated in publications dedicated exclusively to them. Indeed numerous pamphlets could be produced in praise of a single scholar. Celebratory pamphlets typically contained verses from a number of different authors. It should also be noted that commencements often provided an impetus for the publication of academic orations, dissertations, and other texts relating to the examination process. Such materials exhibited important representational functions.

For the most part, celebratory texts concentrate on the description of scholarly progress, mobilizing narratives of effort and reward, as well as pointing to the importance of innate ability. This results in the identification and idealization of patterns of behaviour and achievement typical of successful scholars, i.e. those achieving academic grades. Observations on the taxing nature of scholarly effort are common. In a text published in praise of Samuel Satler in 1603, for example, Johannes Arendes compares scholarly effort to the labour of the farmer.[23] The mundanity of such comparison is common. Andreas Creicius, for example, draws similar analogies between the work of artisans and scholarly endeavour by suggesting that the latter is akin to a shoemaker's exertions and infused with a similar workmanlike commitment.[24] Descriptions of the nature of studies are not universally pedestrian, however. Creicius, for example, goes on to compare academic study to a perilous sea voyage, highlighting the difficult but ultimately profitable nature of the endeavour.[25] The poet's preoccupation with arduous transit resurfaces when suggesting that the scholarly efforts of his subject, Johannes Wegener, had brought him to the Parnassian summit, a standard characterisation of academic achievement.[26] Such rhetorical measures served to portray diligence as a normative attribute of the successful scholar.

In all instances the reader is made aware of the magnificence of the reward for academic effort. Elaborate references to commencement ceremonies are frequent.[27] Allusions to the symbols of academic dignity obtained during such ceremonies are especially common. This has the effect of lauding both prize and recipient. Anthonius Herringius, for example, writing in praise of Joannes Wegener in 1581, draws attention to the rhetorical and real symbols of academic rank, i.e. the laurel crown and the scarlet *pileum*.[28] Descriptions of the receipt of the symbols of academic dignity are often located towards the end of a celebratory poem, in this way mimicking the ceremonial action. References to these symbols are designed not to isolate the candidate for special praise but to advertise his incorporation into the upper tiers of the academic hierarchy.

The provision of biographical information is generally quite limited in the celebrations of commencement. On occasion passing references to a scholar's peregrinations, former teachers, and colleagues can be observed. In certain cases, however, where the scholar's background or career was unusual, such information is furnished more readily. This is the case in texts celebrating the commencement of 'foreign' scholars. The biography of Scottish scholar Duncan Liddel, for example, is described in detail in a pamphlet celebrating his commencement in 1596.[29] In his contribution to the pamphlet Johannes Caselius describes Liddel's *peregrinatio academica* with special reference to his time spent at Rostock, a former institutional home of the author. Caselius also takes care to describe Liddel's Scottish origins.[30] A similar case is that of another Scot, Duncan Burnet, who was awarded a doctoral degree in 1608.[31] In a text celebrating this event, Johannes Caselius retraces Burnet's academic travels, describes his studies at Helmstedt, and mentions his prospective appointment as a physician at Norwich. In his celebration of Burnet Johannes Cellarius points out that the Scot chose Helmstedt as the place to take his degree over many other universities.[32] In this way the university's ability to attract scholars from distant lands is celebrated. It was not only shown to be an important stop on an academic tour but also to be the most critical one. The unusual provision of biography in both cases thus advertises the particular merits of the university, serving to emphasize its relative fame in inter-institutional and trans-territorial prestige economies.

References to the potential future fame of promoted scholars are prolific in celebratory texts, where it is often suggested that recognition comes with newly acquired academic rank. Adam Lucht's remarks on Duncan Liddel's emerging reputation are typical. Lucht suggests that the acquisition of doctoral status will enhance his good name.[33] Theodor Berckelman displays a similar interest in the future fame of Heinrich Boethius in his celebratory text of 1616. Berckelman's remarks on the matter also refer to the responsibilities that come with such recognition. He insists that, as a doctor of law, Boethius must protect the interests of innocent clients and repel public injury.[34] References of this nature could on occasion be more exuberant. Cellarius' praise of Duncan Burnet's renown, for example, is enthusiastic. Cellarius describes Burnet as a light of his native *patria*, of *Germania*, and of the university.[35] Typically, such energetic praise of newly graduated scholars was avoided, having the potential to disrupt hierarchies of merit within the university. At the time of his commencement, Burnet was exiting academic society at Helmstedt, having secured a medical position in Norwich. Thus Cellarius' vigorous praise did not threaten the hierarchical balance of status and reputation within the university.

The content of celebrations of commencement reveals a degree of uniformity in the praise of individual scholars. The individual is shown to exhibit strength of character which has allowed him to obtain academic dignity. These characteristics are found to be normative rather than exceptional. Individual achievement is shown to reflect that of the university's scholars in general. Thus its celebration serves to represent the merits of the academic group as a whole. Celebrations of commencement acted as a first step in the cultivation of individual scholarly reputations; a process which continued over the course of a career and lifetime.

Marriage pamphlets and the representation
of professorial community

Of the various occasional media deployed in the celebration of the individual scholar one form, the wedding pamphlet, proved especially suited to the fashioning of academic community. At Helmstedt marriage was one of the primary tools through which the cogency of academic society was secured. It was employed strategically to promote bonds between professors and their families, thus assisting in the construction of community, ultimately leading to the development of a family university; a type of institution in which strong professorial dynasties dominated through the generations.[36] Helmstedt's professors did not rule out marital alliance with other social groups. Networking of this type facilitated the accumulation of power within the territory and beyond. The enthusiasm for the celebration of academic marriage in publication corresponded to the levels of commitment to the enterprise itself. For example, 142 pamphlets celebrating academic marriage are extant from the period 1576 to 1626. Given the ephemeral nature of these pamphlets it can be assumed that survival rate does not reflect the full scale of production.

As a response to the activity which was most central to academic social enterprise, published *epithalamia* and other celebrations of marriage served as vehicles for idealized representations of the group and preferred patterns of social behaviour.

A genre of classical origin, the *epithalamium* enjoyed popularity in the early modern period. During the Middle Ages it developed into a devotional form.[37] Humanistic studies drew the genre back to its original purpose by reviving its use as a means of celebrating 'earthly' marriage. Analysis of the listings of the *Verzeichnis der im deutschen Sprachbereich erschienenen Drucke des 16. Jahrhunderts* (*VD 16*) reveals a significant increase in the publication of *epithalamia* from the late 1560s.[38] It also demonstrates that the form was exploited by groups attempting social escalation in this period such as merchants or bureaucrats. Among the reasons for the *genre*'s revival was its perceived utility as a means of a presenting a positive image of those it celebrated. Writing on the *epithalamium*, Julius Caesar Scaliger, for example, emphasized its representational potential.[39] Advising on which classical references a poet should use, how he should use them, and to what effect, Scaliger instructs that '[y]ou must choose what is especially splendid, seeking farther afield if what is close at hand seems less noble; all else must be either veiled or wrapped in silence'.[40] The purpose of the *epithalamium*, therefore, was not to present a plain description of the parties involved but to fashion a favourable if somewhat fabricated image of them.

The diverse formal possibilities of marriage pamphlets made them especially suited to the representation of community. The formal arrangement of Heinrich Meibom's *Cento Vergilianus* of 1579, for example, conveys the extent of communal involvement in the marriage it celebrates. The pamphlet was occasioned by the marriage of Johannes Olearius, Professor of Hebrew, and Anna Heshus, daughter of Helmstedt Professor of Theology, Tilemann Heshus.[41] The work takes the form of a *Chorus Musarum*, presenting a series of verses attributed to Apollo and the Muses. Each verse is dedicated to a particular individual, set of people, or theme.[42] Verses are dedicated to the bride and groom, both separately and as one, to the father of the bride, and ultimately to the wedding guests. Thus, in its formal structure, the work mirrors the gathering of a community of revellers at the wedding festivities. Indeed, the dedications suggest that Meibom's *Cento* was in fact recited at some point in the company of those listed. The formal mechanism is effective in drawing the reader's attention to the communal nature of the celebrated event, demonstrating the existence of a coherent academic community. The feigned interaction between the Muses and the academic gathering, made possible by the formal conventions of the *Chorus Musarum*, also espouses a level of cultural sophistication, advertising the social distinction of the professorial group to the reader.

An extremely popular format of celebration was a work containing poems from different authors, *scripta ab amicis*. Again this formal mechanism has the effect of simulating a communal celebration of marriage and thus communicating the cogency of the group to the reader. The greater the number of contributing poets involved, the more convincing the representation of the group's communal nature. Similarly, the number of contributions indicated the degree to which the marriage was supported by the community. Academic colleagues, students, and sometimes non-academic associates contributed to these publications.

The response to the marriage in 1585 of Helmstedt Professor Heinrich Meibom and Sophie Bökel, daughter of the court surgeon of Duke Heinrich, and niece of Professor of Medicine Johann Bökel, provides an example of the use of this format. Two pamphlets published in celebration of this marriage survive. The *GRATVLATORIA aliquot Carmina* contains six poems, each by separate authors, most of whom had an academic background.[43] A second publication, the *EPITHALA-MIA IN NVPTIAS...M. HENRICI MEIBOMII...Et LECTISSIMAE VIRGINIS SOPHIAE BOKELIAE* comprises seven poems, again from separate authors including Helmstedt's Vice-Rector, Basilius Satler, Professor of Medicine Johannes Bökel, a second Professor of Medicine, Hermann Neuwalt, Professor of Hebrew Henricus Boëthius, and Master Martin Chemnitz.[44]

The extensive and varied authorship of poems in these pamphlets reveals the cohesive nature of academic society at Helmstedt. Pamphlets *scripta ab amicis* thus allowed for a precise representation of the social texture of academic society. The format facilitated the espousal of communal unity and the demonstration of the group's advanced social status.

Like the effect of form and presentation, the content of the wedding songs served to characterize academic society in terms which advertised social sophistication and worth. In addition, the wedding songs helped to promote marriage as a preferred pattern of social behaviour.

As is common in academic occasional forms, a classicized rhetoric predominates. Although conventional by the mid-sixteenth century, the representation of academic social action in this manner set the community apart in a local context, reinforcing claims to superiority.[45] In this setting a neo-classical rhetoric constituted a 'language' of social celebration which was relatively unique to the scholarly group and its associates. The extraordinary nature of this celebratory 'language' both enhanced internal communal unity and advertised the users' cultural distinction and agency to the outside observer, operating as a boundary expressing symbol.[46]

A core function of the Helmstedt wedding songs is the advancement of the social ideology of the family university. This is achieved through the promotion of attitudes to encourage academic marriage and the development of strong professorial family networks.

In many of the poems considerable effort is made to undermine the tradition of scholarly celibacy and to advance a newer protestant culture of academic marriage.[47] The contrast between these two competing modes of behaviour is evident in poems published to mark the marriage of Jeremias Reichelm and Elisabeth Borcholt in 1590.[48] In his poem, Conrad Memmius characterizes the groom as a scholar eager to avoid marriage.[49] This reticence is associated with Reichelm's dedication to his studies. His encounter with the daughter of Helmstedt's Professor of Law, however, is shown to have motivated a change in perspective, the ultimate outcome of which was their marriage. This account outlines an appropriate behavioural pattern for a scholar, where marriage follows the completion of studies in the process of his personal maturation.

Throughout the Helmstedt *epithalamia*, the love experienced by professors is characterized as morally pure. Nicolaus Volcerus' poem celebrating the marriage of Friedrich Dasypodius and Elisabeth Schösgen, for example, is dedicated entirely to this theme.[50] Voclerus contrasts corrupt and morally correct forms of love.[51] Inevitably, the chaste type is characterized as that expressed in marriage, which the poet represents as divinely sanctioned. The subtext of this argument is that where professors do not marry they are at risk of operating in a deviant amorous mode. Thus marriage is portrayed as being vital to the moral health of the professoriate.

In addition to the encouragement of conjugality, academic marriage is promoted through commentary on its social and communal merits. There is a distinct focus on the importance of choosing a bride appropriately on the basis of her social background. Correspondingly, the poems often dwell on questions of lineage. The benefits of building alliances between academic families are also remarked upon, as is the importance of perpetuating professorial dynasties by means of procreation.

The preoccupation with lineage has both a celebratory and advisory function. In first instance, the individual social prestige of bride and groom, and of the families which they represented, is advertised. This serves to emphasize the importance and potential benefits of an apt marital choice. Barvvardus Rhesenius' celebration of the marriage of Johann Siegfried, Professor of Medicine, and Anna Bökel, daughter of Professor Johann Bökel, provides an example of this tendency.[52] The suitability of the bride is attested to by drawing attention to the prestige of her family. In contrast, the groom's suitability is advertised not by reference to his family name, but to his merits as a scholar and his professorial rank. Rhesenius' characterisations of bride and groom reflect recurring patterns in the Helmstedt *epithalamia*.

Having established the merits of each party, it was typical for a poet to anticipate certain favourable outcomes from the union. The merging of great academic families was a cause for much joy. Naturalistic metaphors are frequently deployed to demonstrate the new social strength arising from such marriage. This serves to emphasize the individual merits of each line and dynastic strength achieved as a result of the marriage. Representations of the benefits of dynastic union could also be enacted in non-textual devices. Illustrations included in pamphlets celebrating the Meibom-Bökel marriage of 1585 provide an instructive example of this tendency.[53] An illustration of the respective familial arms of bride and groom is printed in each pamphlet.[54] The arms are depicted facing one another on an equal basis, each one inclined towards and supported by the other. This depiction suggests an equality, mutual dependency, and combined strength. The illustration also reflects the 'dynastic' ambitions and noble pretensions of these professorial families. Indeed both the Meibom and Bökel families were to remain important at Helmstedt for generations.

Thus clear representational strategies are evident in the content of celebrations of marriage at Helmstedt. In the first instance, the married state is promoted as being important to the moral welfare of the individual. Professorial marriage is also promoted in order to facilitate the emergence of an academic community supported by strong professorial dynasties. A persistent concern with lineage and the commentary on the appropriateness of the marriages celebrated serve to reinforce the ideology of the family university. Representations of marriage also facilitated the characterization of the academic society. This served to encourage scholars to identify with one another in recognition of their common culture and to project a favourable image of the community to outside observers.

Within the structure of a scholar's social development at Helmstedt, marriage often played a significant role. It provided an opportunity for further integration into professorial society. Indeed the career of a scholar could be advanced through an appropriately chosen union to an established professor's daughter. The celebration of a scholar's marriage in print constituted a further instance of reputational sponsorship on the part of his colleagues. As artefacts and in terms of their content, these publications served to identify the scholar's continuing advancement and integration into the professorial group. They also helped to characterize the academic group. The mechanisms of form, for example, permitted poets to convey the cogency and exclusivity of academic society to the reader. Similarly, professorial social sophistication could be espoused in the classicism of the poetry's content. The Helmstedt wedding songs also facilitated the expression and promotion of the social logic behind academic marriage strategies. Thus the action of celebrating the individual scholar on the occasion of marriage served to promote his public profile, to encourage community-building enterprises, and to fashion an empowering image of academic society.

The commemoration of scholars in print

Far from bringing an end to the communal and institutional sponsorship of a scholar's reputation, his death often resulted in a flourish of representational activity. University professors were commemorated in printed orations, funeral sermons, poetry, and portraits. Monuments and headstones were also utilized to commemorate deceased scholars.[55] Commemorative texts provided considerable detail of a scholar's life and achievements and registered a level of enthusiasm in the praise of his individual merits which was relatively unknown in celebratory publications produced during his lifetime. The death of a professor, of course, marked the end of his academic career and movements. Consequently, in death his public profile became perennially wedded to that of the institution. Thus there was particular advantage for the university in celebrating and promoting the fame of deceased scholars.

Academic funerary publications typically comprised conventional commemorative forms such *programmata,* sermons, orations, and poems.[56] *Programmata*, sermons, and orations were particularly suited to the expression of corporate grief. Commemorative poetry allowed for more individualized expressions of grief. However, commemorative poems were often printed alongside one another and, as a result, conveyed a communal expression of loss. At Helmstedt the publication of pamphlets commemorating professors was frequent in the late sixteenth and seventeenth centuries. From the years between 1576 and 1626, for example, thirty-three pamphlets commemorating twenty-five professors are extant. This mirrors trends at other territorial universities. Deceased professors were often commemorated in multiple publications, each of which could contain a number of separate contributions.

The response to the death of Johannes Caselius exhibits patterns common throughout commemorative texts published in Helmstedt. A prominent humanist, Caselius was one of Helmstedt's most renowned professors. Even without its cultivation by colleagues, his reputation enhanced the prestige of the university. His death in 1613 was at once a blow to the institution and an opportunity. Thus in their printed response to his demise, his former colleagues sought to preserve the memory of his greatness, and to record the exceptional nature of his life, achievements, and talents. His association with Helmstedt was inevitably brought to the attention of the reader. In this respect, he was repeatedly cast as an exemplar of Helmstedt's professoriate; a prominent strategy in commemorative texts. Caselius' death occasioned a series of commemorative publications. The representational contents of a selection of these pamphlets will now be considered by way of illustration.

DE VITA, OBITV ATQVE OBITER HAC OCCASIONE DE ORIGINE V. CL. IOANNIS CASELLI, a *programma academicum*, constitutes a corporate statement of commemoration.[57] This text registers the grief of the academic community; remarks upon Caselius' standing and reputation; describes his family background and origins; gives an account of his education and academic travels; comments upon his early career; describes the circumstances of his move to Helmstedt; and provides details of his demise and death. As such it conforms fully to generic convention.

The pamphlet commences with salutations to the academic audience and proceeds to comment upon the severity of the grief now felt by this group.[58] It also remarks upon the greatness of Caselius, reminding the reader of the extent of his fame in elevated circles, and suggests that he will continue to be renowned among future generations of scholars.[59] The text then proceeds to describe Caselius' family background in detail stretching into the distant past.[60] The quality of his lineage is attested to with remarks upon his family's associations with emperors and other men of stature. The erudition of Caselius' father is a particular focus of attention.[61] Such commentary is ripe with suggestions of inherited brilliance, a common trend in the characterization of scholars. Commentary on Caselius' mother, Catherine Calobrad, is focused almost exclusively on the quality of her lineage.[62] As is conventional in such texts, the deceased's place and date of birth are noted.[63] This is followed by an account of Caselius' early education. Considerable detail of

Caselius' university education is then provided. In this respect, the text describes the various universities he attended and his most prominent teachers and associates.[64] The text draws particular attention to Caselius' time in Italy.[65] Moving from his education to his early career, the manner in which Caselius came to be employed at Rostock is then related.[66] Caselius' biography continues with the account of his marriage to Gertrud Mylius, daughter of the well-placed Andreas Mylius, a councillor of the Mecklenburg Duke.[67] The circumstances of Caselius' move to Helmstedt are then described.[68] In keeping with convention, the *programma* concludes with an account of Caselius' illness and death.[69]

The *ORATIVNCLVLA in funere Clarissimi longequé praestantissimi viri, IOANNIS CASELII* comprises three separate contributions.[70] Most prominent is an oration in honour of the deceased by Christoph Heidmann. This is accompanied by two short verses, the first by Ducal councillor Tobias Pauremeister von Kochstet and a second by Heinrich Meibom. Heidmann's oration begins with a reference to the sorrow felt by his academic audience.[71] Heidmann remarks that the professors have lost the friendship of a colleague, the young students an incomparable teacher, and the university one of its greatest scholars.[72] He reminds the audience that Caselius' death will be mourned far beyond Helmstedt, having dealt a great blow to Saxony and Germany.[73] Caselius' future reputation is a predominant concern of Heidmann. He is certain that the fame of Caselius will live in the minds of good men who serve as custodians of his reputation.[74] The commemorative activities of the academic community are self-consciously regarded as having an important role in the propagation of the good name of the deceased.

The death of a scholar represented an opportunity for the consolidation of his reputation by his academic peers. Unlike those enterprises which sought to promote a scholar's public profile mid-career, the celebration of a deceased professor could be conducted with less regard to the sensitivity of colleagues. As a result praise could be offered more freely. Nonetheless, strong patterns and a tendency towards uniformity are evident in commemorative texts. Here one can note the idealisation of general scholarly character according to key biographical patterns. Thus commemorative texts focus their attentions on the description of the deceased's origins, lineage, early promise, education, scholarly networks, academic career, erudition, teaching abilities, marriage, and progeny. The repetition of biographical patterns led to the emergence of an image of the archetypal Helmstedt scholar. In this way ownership of a defunct scholar's reputation was assumed by the publicizing institution. The branding of scholars as exemplars of institutional professorial excellence inevitably favoured the projection of the university's public image. Indeed it effectively led to the gradual construction of a 'pantheon' of institutional greats. By such means, the representational benefits of individual scholarly reputation accrued to the university.

The *Monumenta Julia* and the perpetuation of scholarly reputations

Celebratory and commemorative publications, bound as they were to occasion, provided a platform for further representational activity. When published, these texts added to a *corpus* of representation which served to promote a scholar's public profile. Taken as a whole this body of material intimated the extent to which the reputation of a scholar was supported by colleagues and community. This body of celebratory material often fed into and informed other representational texts. Printed portraits were reused, lines of poetry quoted, and biographical detail borrowed and reprinted. Such materials served as an important resource for publications which sought to recall the glories of the institution or provide a history of its development through the celebration of its greatest professors.

Gebhard Theodor Meier's *MONUMENTA JULIA Memorias Professorum Helmstadiensium, qui diem suum obierunt* (1680), a biographical dictionary of deceased professors of Law and Theology, relied heavily on this existing corpus of representational material. This was one of a number of lengthy publications occasioned by the university's jubilee in 1676.[75] Its purpose was to present the university's history through an account of lives and deeds of its former professors. An additional function was to rejuvenate those earlier representations of the defunct scholars and to maintain their fame. The *Monumenta Julia* demonstrates the store put in prefabricated representations of scholars and the longevity of their representational value. The trajectory of reputation fashioning it seems could continue long after a scholar's demise.

Like the celebratory and commemorative texts upon which it drew, the *Monumenta Julia* conformed to convention in its relation of scholarly biography.

Thus, in the *Monumenta Julia,* biographies commence with the description of a scholar's family background and origins. Parents are shown to have been pious and their eagerness to educate their sons significant.[76] If it is possible to advertise the high social rank of the family, Meier does not hesitate to do so. By the same token, in situations where a scholar was of more humble origins, the author celebrates the overcoming of adversity and resilience of the academic character.[77] Descriptions of a scholar's early education usually follow such commentary with mention of schools attended and notable teachers. Meier's biographies generally progress to an account of a scholar's experiences as a university student. This usually incorporates favourable remarks on the diligence and abilities of the student. In the event that the commemorated individual had spent his student days at Helmstedt, Meier frequently provides an account of his movement up the academic ranks. Similarly, a scholar's early associations and student networks at Helmstedt are described with particular care.[78] As is common in funeral pamphlets, the academic travels of the deceased professor are described in detail. Such description serves to identify the importance of Helmstedt as a university of international significance, its merits being sufficient to attract wandering scholars and to encourage professors to remain.

Meier's accounts of mature academic careers at Helmstedt also reveal strong patterns. Typically, they begin by providing details of the manner of appointment. Where permissible, the role of the Ducal patron in attracting the scholar to Helmstedt is remarked upon. Indeed, accounts of the appointment of the university's earliest professors facilitate the description of its early history. Inevitably, further advancements in rank and position are noted.

The academic merits of Meier's celebrated subjects are also advertised through the description of scholarly output. Eberhard Speckhan's scholarly merits, for example, are measured by the extent of his writings.[79] Commentary on the quality of a professor's teaching is also employed in the identification of individual accomplishment. Heinrich Boethius' merits as a teacher, for example, are praised highly.[80] Meier also often remarks upon the esteem in which a professor was held within and outside of the university. The social lives of professors also prove worthy of comment. In particular the scholar's marriage and family life are remarked upon. The careers and marriages of a professor's children are also noted.

The relative lengths of the biographical accounts provided by Meier vary considerably. This suggests a hierarchy of merit to the reader. Even in such historically reflexive works, some reputations are supported more than others, thus mimicking the action and effects of the structure of the reputational corpus as a whole. The *Monumenta Julia*, therefore, stands in a firm relationship with this existing body of occasional publications. It refers constantly to these earlier works and frequently quotes passages from this body of celebratory poetry and prose. Relying on these earlier works for its content, it mirrors the relative size of the original celebratory efforts in the allocation of space within the volume. Thus Meier's work brings truth to the assertion common in many eulogistic texts that their act of commemoration would ensure the longevity of the subject's fame. The rejuvenation of the reputations of deceased professors ultimately serves to demonstrate the merits of the university on the occasion of its jubilee. Indeed the fashioning of institutional reputation was the central function of the *Monumenta Julia*.

Conclusion

The cultivation of scholarly reputations was a central component in the fashioning of the public image of an early modern university. Generic representations of scholarly identity, usually enacted in ceremonial and symbolic devices, served to demonstrate a university's conformity to established traditions. However, the pressures of competition arising from the growth in the number of universities in the Empire in the sixteenth and seventeenth centuries necessitated an approach which would also publicize the specific merits of a particular institution and its scholarly cohort. This was achieved primarily through the fashioning of scholarly character, both individual and communal, in an array of occasional literature.

The public profile of a scholar took shape at key intervals during his professional and social life. In particular scholarly identity was ascribed during ceremonies of transition which in turn provided a platform for the fashioning of reputations in print. The social enterprises of a scholar also provided impetus for the publication of texts in which his public image could be developed. Similarly, the commemoration of deceased scholars allowed considerable scope for the elaboration of character.

The more a scholar advanced within a given academic society, the greater the opportunity for the sponsorship of his reputation in representational media. The support of reputations in this manner was selective, however. This differentiated distribution of praise ensured that representations of institutional prestige remained convincing and ultimately allowed for the fashioning of a pantheon of a university's greatest scholars. The memory of esteemed scholars continued to be cultivated long after they were deceased in commemorative works which drew heavily upon extant bodies of occasional publications.

The cultivation of scholarly reputations was central in the representational enterprises of universities within the Empire in the sixteenth and seventeenth centuries. The celebration of the lives and achievements of individual scholars ultimately facilitated the enactment of representations of institutional distinction. The cumulative fashioning of an individual scholar's public profile allowed for the construction of traditions of excellence specific to an institution. Such specificity was of great importance in allowing universities to compete effectively within those prestige economies vital to their welfare.

School of History
University of St Andrews

REFERENCES

1. For patterns of university foundation in the early modern period see, for example, Willem Frijhoff, 'Patterns' in *A history of the university in Europe, ii: Universities in the Early Modern Period*, ed. Hilde de Ridder-Symoens (Cambridge, 1992), 43–110, esp. 70–110.
2. Examples of recent scholarship in this general area include William Clark, *Academic charisma and the origins of the research university* (Chicago, 2006); Marian Füssel, *Gelehrtenkultur als symbolische Praxis. Rang, Ritual und Konflikt an der Universität der Frühen Neuzeit* (Darmstadt, 2006); Andrea von Hülsen-Esch, *Gelehrte im Bild. Repräsentation, Darstellung und Wahrnehmung einer sozialen Gruppe im Mittelalter* (Göttingen, 2006); Richard Kirwan, *Empowerment and representation at the university in early modern Germany: Helmstedt and Würzburg, 1576–1634* (Wiesbaden, 2009); Stefanie Knöll, *Creating academic communities. Funeral monuments to professors at Oxford, Leiden and Tübingen 1580–1700* (Haren, 2003); Rainer Christoph Schwinges, *Studenten und Gelehrte. Studien zur Sozial- und Kulturgeschichte deutscher Universitäten im Mittelalter = Students and Scholars. A social and cultural history of German medieval universities* (Leiden, 2008).
3. The difficulties of defining the professoriate are discussed, for example, in Stefanie A. Knöll, 'Collective identity: funeral monuments to academics in

Northern Europe', *History of Universities*, 28/1 (2003); Peter A. Vander-meersch, 'Teachers' in Ridder-Symoens (ed), *History of the university in Europe*, ii. 210–55.

4. See, for example, Schwinges, *Studenten und Gelehrte*, 237–337, 440–53.
5. On the relationship between cities and universities see, for example, Thomas Bender (ed.), *The university and the city. From medieval origins to the present* (New York, 1988) and Erich Maschke und Jürgen Sydow (eds), *Stadt und Universität im Mittelalter und in der früheren Neuzeit* (Sigmaringen, 1977).
6. Jesuits, in particular, were often in this position. See Karl Hengst, *Jesuiten an Universitäten und Jesuitenuniversitäten. Zur Geschichte der Universitäten in der Oberdeutschen und Rheinischen Provinz der Gesellschaft Jesu im Zeitalter der konfessionellen Auseinandersetzung* (Paderborn, 1981).
7. On the nature of such preoccupations see, for example, Füssel, *Gelehrtenkultur als symbolische Praxis* and Thomas Weller, *Theatrum Praecedentiae. Zeremonieller Rang und gesellschaftliche Ordnung in der frühneuzeitlichen Stadt, Leipzig 1500–1800* (Darmstadt, 2006). Anthony Cohen's observations on the symbolic constitution of communities are instructive when confronting these problems. He maintains that the boundary encapsulates the identity of the community. At the same time, however, he suggests that such boundaries are not objective constructs. They exist, rather, in the 'minds of their beholders' and thus can be perceived in different terms by different elements within the same community. See Anthony P. Cohen, *The symbolic construction of community* (London, 1985), 12.
8. On the relationship between the university and the territorial state see, for example, Peter Baumgart, 'Universitätsautonomie und landesherrliche Gewalt im späten 16. Jahrhundert', *Zeitschrift für Historische Forschung*, 1 (1974), 25–53; Notker Hammerstein, 'Relations with authority' in Ridder-Symoens (ed.), *History of the university in Europe*, ii. 114–54; Frank Rexroth, *Deutsche Universitätsstiftungen von Prag bis Köln. Die Intentionen des Stifters und die Wege und Chancen ihrer Verwirklichung im Spätmittelalterlichen deutschen Territorialstaat* (Cologne, 1992); Rudolph Stichweh, *Der frühmoderne Staat und die europäische Universität. Zur Interaktion von Politik und Erziehungssystem im Prozess ihrer Ausdifferenzierung (16.-18. Jahrhundert)* (Frankfurt, 1991).
9. For descriptions of deposition rituals see Andreas Meinhardi, *The Dialogus of Andreas Meinhardi. A utopian description of Wittenberg and its university, 1508*, trans. Edgar Carl Reinke (Ann Arbor, 1976), 274–89; *Orationes Duae; De Ritu & Modo Depositionis Beanorum* (Strasburg, 1680); *The Manuale Scholarium. An original account of life in the mediaeval university*, trans. Robert Francis Seybolt (Cambridge, 1921), 24–33.
10. For analysis of deposition rituals see Jonathan Davies, *Culture and power. Tuscany and its universities 1537–1609* (Leiden, 2009), 143–5; Marian Füssel, 'Riten der Gewalt. Zur Geschichte der akademischen Deposition und des Pennalismus in der frühen Neuzeit', *Zeitschrift für historische*

Forschung, 32 (2005), 605–48; Ruth Mazo Karras, *From boys to men.
Formations of masculinity in late medieval Europe* (Philadelphia, 2003),
67–108; Helga Robinson-Hammerstein and Richard Kirwan, 'University
ritual and the construction of the Scholar' in Per Anderson et al. (eds.), Liber
Amicorum Ditler Tamm: law, history and culture (copenhagen, 2011), 201–
214. Rainer Christoph Schwinges, 'Mit Mückensenf und Hellschepoff: Fest
und Freizeit in der Universität des Mittelalters (14.-16. Jahrhundert)', *Jahrbuch für Universitätsgeschichte* 6 (2003).

11. Commencement ceremonies and their effects have been the focus of considerable historiographical attention in recent years. See, for example, Kirwan,
Empowerment and representation, 87–97; Rainer A. Müller (ed.), *Promotionen und Promotionswesen an deutschen Hochschulen der Frühmoderne*
(Cologne, 2001); Rainer Christoph Schwinges (ed.), *Examen, Titel, Promotionen. Akademisches und staatliches Qualifikationswesen vom 13. bis zum
21. Jahrhundert* (Basel, 2007). Commencement ceremonies reveal progression between phases of 'separation', 'liminality' and 'aggregation', and as
such conform to the general template for rites of passage as set out by Arnold
van Gennep and Victor Turner. Arnold van Gennep, *The rites of passage*,
trans. Monika B. Vizedom and Gabrielle L. Caffee (Chicago, 1960); Victor
Turner, *The ritual process. Structure and anti-structure* (London, 1969).

12. See Kirwan, *Empowerment and representation*, 85–142.

13. On the early history of Helmstedt see, for example, Peter Baumgart, 'Die
Gründung der Universität Helmstedt' in Peter Baumgart and Notker Hammerstein (eds). *Beiträge zu Problemen deutscher Universitätsgründungen
der frühen Neuzeit* (Nendeln, 1978), 217–41; Franz Haeberlin, *Geschichte
der ehemahligen Hochschule Julia Carolina zu Helmstedt* (Helmstedt,
1876); Hermann Hofmeister, *Die Gründung der Universität Helmstedt*
(Marburg, 1904).

14. See Füssel, *Gelehrtenkultur als symbolische Praxis*, 136–49; Kirwan,
Empowerment and representation, 31–83; Jan Könighaus, *Die Inauguration
der Christian-Albrechts-Universität zu Kiel 1665. Symbolgehalt und re-
chtliche Bedeutung des Universitätszeremoniells* (Frankfurt, 2002); Frank
Rexroth, 'Ritual and the creation of social knowledge. The opening celebrations of medieval German universities' in *Universities and schooling in
medieval society*, ed. William J. Courtenay and Jürgen Miethke (Leiden,
2000).

15. Descriptions of these festivities are provided in two contemporaneous
sources: an account by Francis Algerman, reproduced in *Feier des Gedächt-
nisses der vormahligen Hochschule Julia Carolina zu Helmstedt*, ed. F.R. von
Strombeck (Helmstedt, 1822), 165–246 and the *HISTORICA NARRATIO DE
INTRODVCTIONE VNIVERSITATIS IVLIAE . . .* (Helmstedt, 1579).

16. The resulting publication being the *HISTORICA NARRATIO*. An extensive
correspondence between various parties, ducal and academic, concerning
the publication of this work is evident from 1576 to the date of publication.
See Niedersächsische Staatsarchiv, Hannover, Cal. Br. 21 Nr. 3756.

17. *HISTORICA NARRATIO*, [284–289]. Note on pagination: Square brackets are used where page numbers have not been printed. Pages are counted from the first page upon which text is printed following the frontispiece.
18. Ibid., [290].
19. Accounts of the festival are provided in Andreas Cludius, *ΠΑΝΗΓΥ ΡΙΣΜΟΣ Siue INAVGVRATIO Splendidissimi noui Musarum Theatri, in illustri Academia Iulia Helmstadij* (Helmstedt, 1613) and in the first oration of Christopher Heidmann, *ORATIONES DVAE. Quarum altera De IVLEO NOVO...* (Helmstedt, 1613).
20. The centenary festival was celebrated in the *HISTORIA FESTI SECV-LARIS...* (Helmstedt, 1678). The opening of the university buildings occasioned the publications listed in note 19 above.
21. For analysis of the representational functions of these buildings see Kirwan, *Empowerment and representation*, 176–82.
22. These statistics are extracted from Friedrich Welcken, 'Helmstedter Promoviertenliste', *Mitteilungen der Zentralstelle für Deutsche Personen- und Familiengeschichte*, 15 (1917), 51–79 and Paul Zimmermann (ed.), *Album Academiae Juliae. Abteilung 1: Studenten, Professoren etc. der Universität Helmstedt von 1574–1636; voran geht ein Verzeichnis der Schüler und Lehrer des Pädagogium Illustre in Gandersheim, 1572–74 (Album Academiae Helmstadiensis, Vol. I,* Hannover, 1926).
23. *VIRTVTE SIMVL ET Eruditione ornatissimo viro-iuueni SAMVELII SATLERO De summo in Philosophia gradu Gratulantur Amici* (Helmstedt, 1603), [4].
24. *CARMINA GRATVLATORIA IN HONOREM DOCTISSIMI...IVVENIS D. IOHANNIS VVEGENERI...* (Helmstedt, 1581), [2–3]: 'Quem iam petis VVEGNERE docte & obtines,/Hoc es gradu dignissimus:/Hunc es tuo meritus labore plurimo,/Noctes diesque literis/Dum semper incubuisti honestis sedulus,/Easque didicisti impiger. [...] Et sic labori impendit omnem industri?,/Graui quidem ast ignobili:/Fragilia sartor vestimenta consuit,/ Sutor terendos calceos:...'.
25. Ibid., [1–8].
26. Ibid., [4]: 'Nempe ardui superare Parnassi iuga,/Superanda raris, culminis,/ Semper laborasti pio conamine'.
27. For example in Meibom, *CARMEN GRATVLATORIVM...ad...HENRICVM BOETHIVM...LAVRENTIVM SCHEVRLE...HENRICVM PAPAEBV-GERVM...IOHANNEM PANDOCHEVM...CASPARVM PFAFRADIVM... GOTFRIDVM SLVTERVM...: Quibus XXX. die Maij Anno M.D.IIC. summa in Theologiâ dignitas ab amplissimo Collegio Theologorum academiae Iuliae solenni ritu attributa est...* (Helmstedt, 1598) [1]: 'Vos ego, vos sancti manes, & principis vmbra/Guelfiadae, cui post Iouam nos nostraque cuncti/ Debemus, vos Elysio de colle vocarem/Spectatum has pompas atque haec solemnia sacra'.
28. *CARMINA GRATVLATORIA IN HONOREM...D. IOHANNIS VVEGEN-ERI*, [10]: 'Non ignara tui Pallas VVegenere laboris/Iam tua Daphnëis

exornat tempora lauris,/Purpureamque ferens tibi IVLIA diua tiaram,/ Ampla Magisterij designat nomina docti'.

29. *VIRO Clarissimo & excellentissimo dn. DVNCANO LIDDELIO SCOTO ... gratulantur COLLEGAE ET FAMILIARES*, (Helmstedt, 1596).

30. For example, Ibid., [2]: 'Hinc Dunae geminum, gente satum & te Caledonia,/Te Brucaeus amabat, coluit Duditius, Braha/Demiratur acumen genij Scotigenae inclytus'.

31. Johannes Caselius, *GRATVLATIO AD CL. V. DVNCANVM BVRNETVM, Abredoniensem, Scotum, ...* (Helmstedt, 1608).

32. 'Joannes Cellarius, *Cl. & excellentiss. Viro, DVNCANO BVRNET SCOTO, Medico publ. Noruici in Anglia, insignia Doctoralia iam capessenti* (Helmstedt, 1608), [2]: 'Fortè nefas fuerit, stipato hîc artibus, illic/Aut alibi Artificis symbola docta capi./IVLIA pergratum lustro sibi fouit alumnum/ Te, patriaeque Patris fouit & auxit ope'.

33. *VIRO Clarissimo & excellentissimo dn. DVNCANO LIDDELIO*, [10]: 'At quae nunc tibi surgit ampla fama/Et nomen, potiora credo habebit/Cui finita cupido honoris escit.'

34. *V. Cl.mo HENRICO BOETHIO, HENRICI THEOLOGI FILIO, De gradu DOCTORIS INV.I ...* (Helmstedt, 1616), [2]: '.../Quos vt porrò etiam famâ & virtutibus auctes,/Praesidioque tuo innocuos tutere clientes,/Consilioque iuues, & publica damna repellas;/Te tranquillet honos, foueat sors laeta labores,/Sit tibi vita, & opes, animusque in tristibus aequus,/Numinis atque timor, quod cuncta haec donat & aufert'.

35. Joannes Cellarius, *Cl. & excellentiss. Viro, DVNCANO BVRNET SCOTO ...*, [3].

36. See Matthias Asche, 'Über den Nutzen von Landesuniversitäten in der Frühen Neuzeit - Leistung und Grenzen der protestantische "Familienuniversität" ' in Peter Herde and Anton Schindling (eds), *Universität Würzburg und Wissenschaft in der Neuzeit. Beiträge zur Bildungsgeschichte gewidmet Peter Baumgart anläßlich seines 65. Geburtstages* (Würzburg, 1998), 133–50.

37. Virginia Tufte, *The poetry of marriage. The epithalamium in Europe and its development in England* (Los Angeles, 1970), 9–85.

38. See Kirwan, *Empowerment and representation*, 151–2.

39. Julius Caesar Scaliger (1484–1558), *Poetices libri septem* (Lyon, 1561). Reproduced in English translation as 'On the epithalamium', trans. Jackson Bryce, in Heather Dubrow, *A happier Eden. The politics of marriage in the Stuart epithalamium* (Ithaca, 1990), 273–96.

40. From Scaliger in ibid., 273.

41. *CENTO VERGILIANVS IN HONOREM NVPTIARVM REVERENDI ET CLARISSIMI VIRI D. IOHANNIS OLEARII VVESALIENSIS ... & castissimae virginis ANNAE HESHVSIAE ...* (Helmstedt, 1579). This is one of five pamphlets published in celebration of their marriage.

42. The verses are dedicated as follows: APOLLO; CALLIOPE, *Invocatio Divini auxilij*; CLIO, *Gratulatio ad Sponsum*; THALIA, *Gratulatio ad Sponsam*;

EVTERPE, *Ad D. Heshusium*; ERATO, *Psalmus 128*; POLYMNIA, *Nocumenta Veneris inconcessae*; MELPOMENE, *Dehortatio à Libidine*; TERPSICHORE, *Ad Sponsum & Sponsam*; and finally VRANIE, *Ad Convivas*.

43. *GRATVLATORIA aliquot Carmina. HONORI NVPTIARVM CLARISSIMI VIRI...Dn: M. Henrici Meibomij...& lectissimæ virginis SOPHIAE BOKELIAE...* (Helmstedt, 1585).
44. *EPITHALAMIA IN NVPTIAS...M. HENRICI MEIBOMII...Et LECTISSIMAE VIRGINIS SOPHIAE BOKELIAE...* (Helmstedt, 1585). Martin Chemnitz was the son and namesake of the prominent Lutheran theologian and Superintendant of Braunschweig.
45. On humanistic character of scholarly social culture see, for example, Christine Treml, *Humanistiche Gemeinschaftsbildung. Sozio-kulturelle Untersuchung zur Entstehung eines neuen Gelehrtenstandes in der frühen Neuzeit* (Hildesheim, 1989) and Erich Trunz, 'Der deutsche Späthumanismus um 1600 als Standeskultur', *Zeitschrift für Geschichte der Erziehung und des Unterrichts*, 21 (1931), 17–53.
46. For further analysis of the effects of such characterization see Kirwan, *Empowerment and representation*, 160–5.
47. For further discussion of the emergence of this culture see Gadi Algazi, 'Scholars in Households: Refiguring the Learned Habitus, 1480–1550', *Science in Context*, 16/1 (2003), 9–42.
48. *Nuptijs IEREMIAE RICHELMII & ELISABETHAE BORCHOLDIAE. Carmen Conradi Memmij. Aliud Friderici Corfinij* (Helmstedt, 1590) and *Nuptijs IEREMIAE RICHELMII & ELISABETHAE BORCHOLDIAE. Carmen Ioannis Caselij. Aliud Alberti Clampii* (Helmstedt, 1590).
49. 'Memmius & Corfinius, *Nuptijs Ieremiae Richelmii*, [1–2]: 'Et quis adhuc stulte speret spicula amoris /Effugere? aut latere inuasus discedere tecto?/O flos & Reichelmiadorum gentis ocelle./Cum tu necquidquam assiduo multoqué labore /Euitare studens casses retia amoris,/Munieris pectus doctrina, & rebus honestis./Ergo age virgo ades, & quae incendia prima dedisti,/ Prima quoque efflictim ardenti succurre marito,/Ne tua quando olim torrebit flammeus ardor/Pectora, nec quidquam cupida tu? mente requiras,/Quem nunc, cum potis es, miserum seruare recuses'.
50. *NVPTIIS CLARISSIMI AC DOCTISSIMO VIRI DN. FRIDERICI DASYPODII...Et ELISABETHAE, Reuerendi viri CASPARI SCHOSGEN...filiae* (Helmstedt, 1591). Dasypodius was an extraordinary professor of law and Elisabeth was the daughter of Kaspar Schösgen, Abbot of Marienthal.
51. Ibid., [2–3]: 'CYPRIS amat fraudes, furta, dolosque vafros/Est VENVS orta Salo, quae turpes nutrit amores,/Multaque offendunt NVMINA SANCTA facit. [...] Altera sed VENVS est coelo sata, CASTA, PVDICA,/Coniugiuj praeses religiosa sacri'.
52. Ibid., [6–9].
53. *GRATVLATORIA aliquot Carmina* (Helmstedt, 1585) and *EPITHALAMIA IN NVPTIAS CLARISSIMI ET ORNATISSIMI VIRI DN. M. HERICI MEIBOMII* (Helmstedt, 1585).

54. The image can be viewed at http://diglib.hab.de/drucke/129-helmst-dr-7/start.htm [Persistent URL].
55. On the social uses of funeral monuments at early modern protestant universities see Knöll, 'Collective identity' and Knöll, *Creating academic communities*. Professorial funeral monuments were popular at Helmstedt during this period. Such monuments remain visible in the St. Stephani Kirche in Helmstedt.
56. For a treatment of academic funeral sermons and orations see Horst Schmidt-Grave, *Leichenreden und Leichenpredigten Tübinger Professoren (1550–1750). Untersuchungen zur biographischen Geschichtsschreibung in der frühen Neuzeit* (Tübingen, 1974). There is growing historiography on the functions of the funeral sermon in early modern Germany. See, for example, Cornelia Niekus Moore, *Patterned lives. The Lutheran funeral biography in early modern Germany* (Wiesbaden, 2006).
57. *DE VITA, OBITV ATQVE OBITER HAC OCCASIONE DE ORIGINE V. CL. IOANNIS CASELLI, Programma publicum & breuis narratio* (Helmstedt, 1613).
58. Ibid., [1–2].
59. Ibid., [4].
60. Ibid., [5].
61. Ibid., [7]: 'In his Matthias est natu quintus, IOANNIS CASELLI pater, homo boni ingenij, optimè eruditus, integri placidique animi'.
62. Ibid., [8]: 'Huius maximus natu filius fuit IOANNES CASELIVS, natus hoc, quem dixi, patre, matre autem, CATHARINA CALOBRADEA, femina primariae familiae, quae, cum nonaginta quinque annorum esset, & multas calamitates difficillimis temporibus cum marito pertulisset, mortua est Arxlebij, qui vicinus nobis locus est, apud filium natu minimum DANIELEM. Euis verò Calebradeorum familiae, praeter paucos propinquos, inter quos Seligeri, & Transfeldij, atque praeter hos etiam adfines, inter quos Rhumanni, vestigia vix vlla sunt'.
63. Ibid., [8–9].
64. Ibid., [9–12].
65. Ibid., [12].
66. Ibid., [12].
67. Ibid., [13].
68. Ibid., [13–14].
69. Ibid., [15].
70. *ORATIVNCLVLA in funere Clarissimi longequé praestantissimi viri, IOANNIS CASELII, dicta Ad Illust. Academiam IVLIAM altero die post exequias à CHRISTOPHORO HEIDMANO* (Helmstedt, 1613).
71. Ibid., [3].
72. Ibid., [7].
73. Ibid., [3].
74. Ibid., [17]: 'Quare quotquot dicendi facultate & scribendi polletis, auditores, agite, ingenij neruos intendite, & magni CASELII nomen, quod

sese longè iam lateque, sua ipsius opera, suis meritis diffudit, praedicatione vestra, pio vestro studio, vlteriùs etiam, quod in vobis est, propagate, & ad posteritatis memoriam transmittite. Hoc pacto non tantum ipsi debitum officium praestiteritis, sed vobis etiam claritatis, & famae bonae permultum comparaueritis'.

75. The most significant jubilee publication was the *HISTORIA FESTI SECVLARIS*... (Helmstedt, 1678).

76. For example, in the case of Johann Jageman: *MONUMENTA JULIA*, 84: 'Est in agro Eichsfeldia [con]ditionis hodie Moguntinae Hilgenstadium, oppidum non inelegans. In eo natus erat Jagemannus, anno 1552. sub finem mensis Novembris & quidem die vigesimo septimo, ut nonnulli autumant. Ejus Parens, Vir honestus & reformatae relligioni addictus, eum ad pietatem rectè colendam eduxit'.

77. This is the case in his decription of Heinrich Boethius' ascent from humble social origins: 17: 'Erat hic vir optimus, natus in pago quondam agri Lynaeburgensis, Steinbeca, non procula Supplinburgo, anno 1551, parentibus honestis, etsi, ut fere solent istius loci homines, fortuna uterentur angustiore. Quae tamen res eos non deterruit, quo minus filium ad pietatem in bonis literis educari curarent.' Also Ibid., 17: 'Quarum rudimenta, puer etiam tum, didicit in ludo literario Helmstadiensi, quod is locus à patrio solo vix quatuor abesset passuum millibus,...'.

78. For example, in his account of the student career of Johannes von Fucht: Ibid., 27: 'Itaque fundamentis probè jactis in hanc Juliam adolescens venit, eamque operam optimis artibus navavit, usus institutione & convictu praestantium virorum, ut anno 1590. Philosophiae gradu decoraretur à Clmo. Henrico Meibomio Poëta & Historico, cum inter reliquos etiam renunciarentur Henricus Schaperus Mathematum postea hic Professor, Georgius Buscherus Gottingensis ac dein Hannoveranae Scholae Rector: & Samuel Scharlachius Medicinae dein Doctor & in Academia ad Oderam Professor'.

79. Ibid., 98–9.

80. Ibid., 19: 'Docendo & disputando officium suum fecit gnaviter. Magistratum Academicum quinquies gessit. Henricum Julium Strubium, Joannem à Fucht, Theodorum Berckelmann & Georgium Calixtum, Anno 1616. Theologiae Doctoris renunciavit'.

The Conflict of the Faculties: Hierarchies, Values and Social Practices in Early Modern German Universities*

Marian Füssel

Conflict of the Faculties has been a byword for academic culture at least since the publication of Immanuel Kant's work of that name in Königsberg in 1798. On closer inspection, however, it seems that the hierarchy of the four faculties of theology, law, medicine, and philosophy has been wrongly thought to be relatively static and the history of the numerous upgradings, downgradings, and re-evaluations within the hierarchy, has not yet been written. From the medieval roots of the university until the end of the so-called pre-classical period, academic cultures were marked by the omnipresence of the classical four-faculty scheme, a hierarchy which, however, never went unchallenged.[1] The slow emancipation of the faculty of arts from philosophy, the gradual professionalization of medicine, the rise of jurisprudence as leading academic discipline in early-modern statebuilding, and, lastly, theology's gradual loss of authority form the background for a host of tightly interwoven conflicts. But how were tensions concerning these developments experienced in everyday academic life? How was the traditional hierarchy of the faculties defended, or challenged? How were the conflicts between the faculties settled? As yet, we know surprisingly little about the actual conduct of these disputes, which are as old as the faculties themselves. This article, therefore, will not offer a traditional history of thought and ideas, examining contemporaries' discussions of the shifts in values in academic culture. It will instead reveal the actual social practice in circumstances where even the fist could occasionally replace the pen as a tool for settling conflicts.[2] Rank and hierarchy dominated academics' perception of the scholarly community and their sense of position in every situation from the ordering of the written text to the order of a funeral procession. The validity of an intellectual argument could not be separated from the social status of its proponent. This situation was to be modified by the emergence, primarily in the German territories of the late eighteenth century, of the modern research university as a new socio-epistemic regime.[3]

On the basis of selected examples from the seventeenth and eighteenth centuries, this article will demonstrate how individuals utilized a variety of media and strategies in disputes over the value of their professions. From controversies over ceremonial rank and order to the satire and polemics in enlightened journals, it can be shown that controversies over the re-evaluation of the professions were based on social as well as epistemological claims. Social rules governing interpersonal relations in academic societies were similar to those in force elsewhere. Honour for example was a guiding principle for the academic as well as for the nobleman or the soldier. However, academic hierarchies did not simply mirror broader social hierarchies. Nor did the academy offer an alternative, egalitarian culture governed by ideas divorced from social conventions. Their hierarchies were shaped by internal and external forces, and it is on this basis that one may propose a new and less linear historical account of the changing fortunes of academic disciplines.

1. Order of Values as Order of Precedence – the Faculties in the *Theatrum Praecedentiae*

The order of faculties was expressed through various metaphors, and also through scholarly practices, institutional mechanisms, and juridical discourses. This order produced a specific culture of precedence integrated in the common cultural representations of the early modern ordered society and its ubiquitous claims of rank.

Contemporary scholars tried repeatedly to illustrate the hierarchical order of the four faculties by means of analogies – not always felicitous. For some medieval professors the faculties represented the 'four rivers of paradise'. In 1682 Ernst Gockel related them to the four elements (fire, air, water, and earth) or the four forms of being ('esse' for theology, 'vivere' for jurisprudence, 'sentire' for medicine, 'intelligere' for philosophy).[4] In the Middle Ages Bonaventure had already compared the *artes* with the fundament, law and medicine with the walls, and theology with the roof and apex of a building.[5] These illustrations seem to demonstrate simple and persistent conventions for ordering the faculties in medieval and early modern academic culture.

On closer inspection, however, one sees that the hierarchy of the faculties was arranged according to various distinctions. First of all there was the separation between philosophy and the three higher faculties, then between medicine and jurisprudence, and between jurisprudence and theology. These distinctions persisted despite the special characteristic of the pre-modern ordering of the faculties known as 'moving up'.[6] It was in no way unusual for an academic starting in the faculty of arts to be promoted up through the hierarchy of the chairs into the faculties of theology or law. The rise of the 'mono-disciplinal career' came only in the eighteenth century.[7] A philosopher like Kant remained a philosopher and entertained no ambitions of moving up into the higher faculties by acquiring a new specialism. With respect to the conflict of the faculties, this fact indicates the degree to which differences and areas of conflict were institutionalized; they could be detached from the personalities of the individual scholars in question. The faculty had a quasi super-personal institutional identity which could be newly assumed by an individual who succeeded in 'moving up'.

The concept of 'rank/status' is now used more metaphorically than in the past; particularly in scientific or academic work, it is applied in a way that disconnects it from the social reality. This modern usage must be avoided if we are to understand how claims concerning the professions' value, precedence, and position in the academic hierarchy were communicated in practice. The hierarchical structure of the faculties was vividly expressed at the numerous ceremonial occasions where members of the corporation moved to the choreography of a rigidly observed order of precedence.[7] At all academic *actibus publicis* or public acts at which the university appeared as a corporation, the members sat, stood, and walked according to the classical hierarchy of the faculties. Moreover, the office of rector rotated at the early modern university, passing through the hierarchy of the faculties.[8] Scholars' names were listed according to their place in the same hierarchy. This practice originated with the medieval *rotuli*, the annual submission to the papacy of candidates for benefices. The same order was observed in other official documents such as library catalogues, *Leichencarmina* (funeral songs) and course catalogues.[9] The differentiation of the faculties was made visible too in the different colours of the gowns. In Erlangen, for example, the theologians wore black caps and gowns, the jurists scarlet, the physicians green, and the philosophers dark blue.[10] Finally, in addition to symbolic differentiations in clothing and ceremony, different salary brackets reflected the hierarchy of the faculties (already demonstrated by the medieval *rotuli*).[11] The gap between salaries paid to theologians and to members of the faculty of arts could be considerable.

Most research on changes in the academic hierarchy originating from the field of history of ideas accords the concept of 'rank/status' its contemporary significance of reputation or prestige without considering the legal, economic or ceremonial implications for everyday life. Rainer Christoph Schwinges determined for the medieval university that the orders of rank 'granted the theologians the highest rank as well as precedence in assemblies and processions, but this traditional standing was more of a symbolic nature [*sic!*] and could not be translated into real social prestige. Jurists ranked first almost everywhere and – even more importantly – also got their position accepted almost everywhere'.[12] Such a position suggests that the 'merely symbolic' was ultimately of lesser significance. In his *Praise of Folly* Erasmus of Rotterdam noted, 'Among these I suppose the lawyers will shuffle in for precedence, and they of all men have the greatest conceit of their own abilities'.[13] This observation demonstrates that for Erasmus, jurists' success in acquiring recognition and respect were not concomitant with an actual ceremonial position of rank. At the Sorbonne in Paris the status-conscious jurists were already attacked by the theologians in the late Middle Ages as 'idiots politiques' because of their function as political advisors.[14]

With regard to the situation during the seventeenth and eighteenth centuries, the research also refers again and again to the precedence of jurisprudence, which had replaced theology as the leading academic discipline at the enlightened reformed universities of Halle and Göttingen. Notker Hammerstein states: 'The law faculty became the most distinguished and in reality [!] the first in importance'.[15] In his history, *Verfassung und Verwaltung deutscher Universitäten*, Christoph Meiners wrote in 1802: 'In our fatherland Hanover, jurisprudence indisputably claims first place among the various scholarly subjects, pharmacology/medicine second, theology third, and philosophy fourth'.[16] A similar assessment can already be found in earlier self-descriptions, for example in Samuel Stryk's dictum that *corpus juris* is 'considered the main course of a meal; the other scholarly disciplines, however, [are regarded] merely as collations and *hors d'oeuvres*'.[17] Nevertheless, the traditional order of precedence still persisted in Halle. Christian

Thomasius even called the division into the four classic faculties a 'papal invention' to gain control over others.[18]

Moreover, the early modern era was familiar with its own legal discipline, the so-called *jus praecedentiae*, in which the attempt was made to bring the social order of the estates [*Ständegesellschaft*] into a fixed, linear order of precedence.[19] Within this pre-modern 'science of subtle distinctions', the hierarchy of the faculties became an object of scholarly attempts at systematization time and again. Poly-historical scholarship was at pains to collect and order all relevant precedents. From the Middle Ages on, the justification of hierarchy was accomplished mainly with reference to the subject matter studied within each faculty.[20] But the value attached to this subject matter fluctuated, so that the conflict of the faculties was always a dispute about the esteem in which they were held. The eighteenth century in particular witnessed numerous attempts to re-evaluate the traditional hierarchy, as will be demonstrated. The academic order of precedence was an integral part of most of the texts of the law of precedence in which the privileges and criteria of individual ranks were discussed. In the middle of the eighteenth century, Johann Theodor Hellbach, one of the most important authors of this discourse, distinguishes between 'dignitates certae' and 'dignitates vagae' in his *Meditationes de Iure proedriae*. He counts among the certain ranks or standings the sequence of the faculties, which consists, in descending order, of theology, jurisprudence, medicine, and philosophy.[21] Yet, upon closer inspection, the order of precedence of the faculties was even then the subject of frequent controversy.[22]

The strongly Aristotelian argumentation of the French jurist Barthélemy de Chasseneux (1480–1541), who made the assessment of a subject's place in the hierarchy dependent on its subject matter, provided one of the fundamental points of reference for legitimizing the hierarchy of subjects.[23] With his *Catalogus Gloriae Mundi*, which appeared for the first time in 1529, Chasseneux produced the first major compendium of the law of precedence which was later cited time and again as an authority.[24] The tenth chapter of the *Catalogus* is dedicated to the rank of the academic disciplines.[25] Theology stands at the top of the hierarchy of subjects; its precedence over all the other subjects is based on the special dignity of its subject matter. It has in God himself the highest object (*nobiliores materia*), incontrovertible truths (*certiores veritates*), the most dignified material (*dignitissima materia*), and the most noble and most stable goals (*potioris/nobilioris/stabilioris finis*).[26] Moreover, it is particularly useful (*utilitas*) and has outstanding teachers (*excellentiores doctores*) as well as excellent students (*discipulatus perfectio*).[27] Canon law and civil law are the subjects valued mostly highly after theology.[28] The argument for the precedence of jurisprudence over medicine occupies a large part of Chasseneux's discussion. The question is thus posed as to whether medicine should not rank higher than law since it is concerned with the substance, but law only with the accidents. Concerning this question, however, Chasseneux ultimately reaches a clear decision in favour of the jurists.[29] Finally, the rank of the faculty of arts is taken up, with Chasseneux first explaining once again why physicians have priority over members of the arts faculty. Within the arts, the rank, in descending order, is organized as follows: poetics, history, grammar, dialectics, mathematics and arithmetic, geometry, music, and finally astronomy or astrology.[30]

The Hanoverian jurist Jacob Andreas Crusius (1636–80) also dedicates several chapters of his voluminous *Tractatus politico-juridico-historicus de praeeminentia, sessione, praecedentia, et universo jure proedrias magnatum in Europa* to the precedence of academics.[31] They are treated in the last seven chapters of the work and thus form the final stage of the part of society 'capable of precedence' which consists of, above all, the religious and the secular nobility. In many points Crusius explicitly follows the arguments already presented by Chasseneux. For Crusius, the rank of a discipline is also proportionate to the dignity of its subject matter. Accordingly, the highest rank is awarded to theology.[32] That four of six chapters are dedicated exclusively to jurists can be explained by the differentiation and new developments within this faculty, and by the fact that here the really tricky question concerning rank is not articulated within one of the orders, but between different orders.[33] Hence the jurists asserted the ennobling character of their doctorate with singular vehemence, making a claim for recognition and respect well beyond the narrow academic context.[34]

We have three major reasons for the vehemence with which early modern academics engaged in quarrels about precedence in the order of the faculties: first, rank meant honour and claims for precedence always put personal honour as well as the corporate honour of the institution to the test; second, honour and rank were juridical categories that could be regulated by law and therefore meant more than mere courtesy; third, the law faculty accordingly played a central role in allocating and contesting the ranks.

Political Body vs. Individual Body:
Jurists contra Physicians

As we have already seen, discussion of the rank of the law faculties was the most complex. In particular, the precedence dispute between the juristic and the medical faculties was part of a long-running conflict.[35] In 1641 a real feud broke out between the physicians and the jurists at the University of Leipzig, lasting almost twenty years.[36] The starting point was the question of whether jurists with a doctorate who were not members of the faculty nonetheless had precedence over the professors of medicine. A settlement that was reached soon thereafter, granting the medical professor their privilege, provoking instant dissent and protest from the medical doctors. Violent brawls occurred during the university's religious services and ceremonial processions. Both parties addressed numerous petitions to their sovereign, the Prince Elector of Saxony, revolving essentially around the question of whether faculty membership or individual office was the decisive factor. In 1643 the conflict escalated once again when two medical doctors were offered chairs; one of them had started the dispute two years earlier. Both eventually resigned their professorships and bombarded the university with insults. One of them – this was, after all, the last phase of the Thirty Years' War – even defected to the Swedish army. It seems that the conflict gradually petered out; at least no further correspondence has survived. But in 1662 the dispute was repeated with new adversaries, the same points being argued. Again, however, the physicians did not succeed in pushing through their demands, and on the 19th of September 1662 Prince Elector Johann Georg II ruled that 'the doctors of law, without exception, have, as a general rule, priority over physicians who may or may not be professors and assessors in the faculty of medicine.'[37]

At the University of Vienna too, seventeenth-century ceremonial interaction was an occasion for representatives of the faculties to articulate academic-discursive claims to precedence. Such quarrels between jurists and medical professors arose frequently there, and were on occasion raised in the course of public speeches during doctoral celebrations.[38] Thus Sigismund Geissler discussed the question of precedence with regard to medicine and jurisprudence at the conferral of a doctorate in medicine in 1624, just as Paul de Sorbait did in 1667.[39]

This long-running conflict had already featured in polemic, in Hein-rich Cornelius Agrippa von Nettesheim's work *De incertitudine et vanitate scientiarum*, first published in 1530. According to Agrippa, the medical professors argue as follows:

There are three kinds of goods with a particular order of priority, namely spiritual, physical, and worldly. The theologian takes care of the first, the physician the second, and the jurist the third. For this reason the physicians deserve the middle position, thus the one ahead of the jurists, since health and the strength of life take priority over happiness and wealth. But a judge put an end to these precedence conflicts of the two parties during a court hearing by asking the intelligent question with respect to what the order of priority would be according to origins and the legal system if a convicted person were led to the execution, whether the robber or the executioner would lead the way. Respond-ing to the answer that the executioner follows the robber he decided: The jurists should take precedence over the physicians. With this response he wanted to express that the jurists rob the people and the physicians thoughtlessly kill them.[40]

This story was still being circulated in similar form over two hundred years later, propagated by the Enlightenment philosopher Friedrich Nicolai of Berlin among others. Nicolai's *Vade Mecum für lustige Leute* describes a conflict of precedence between a physician and a jurist during a funeral procession in which the jurist finally prevails. 'One of the rest of the company said, "That is also only just" since recently when the authorities had sentenced wrongdoers to death, the one who had taken the money went first and the one who was in the habit of taking life followed'.[41] This anecdote shows how traditional elements of satire concerning professions and estates could be linked to academic discus-sion about the value to be placed on subjects in the different contexts of their functions. In his *Gesichte Philanders von Sittewald* (1642) Johann Michael Moscherosch also treats the precedence dispute between phy-sicians and jurists.[42] Here the jurists argue that the law existed before the fall of man, and for this reason priority is due to them. To support their precedence the physicians assert 'that the body is more than clothes and temporal goods'.[43] Most of the authors gave medicine a lower status than jurisprudence because it only deals with the body and not with the mind. This 'logo-centric' argument can be found in most attempts to legitimize the hierarchy of subjects. An anonymous author thus argues in the *Dresdner Gelehrte Anzeigen* of 1753 that 'jurisprudence undoubt-edly has a greater influence in human life and society than medicine' because it 'promotes the well-being of entire nations', whereas medicine only saves 'individual people through the skill of medical scholars'.[44]

Moreover, many people regarded the medical profession as a craft rather than a science. This was detrimental to the reputation of university medicine even though it was studied from books alone in many places until the eighteenth century.[45] In 1720, however, Heinrich Caspar Abelius insisted in his *Medizinischer Gewissens-Spiegel* that 'a doctor of medicine should precede the doctor of law', for, on the one hand, the *medici* enjoy a good reputation with kings and princes owing to their learning and, on the other hand, a great ruler, 'without advice on physical matters and health' walks on 'only one foot/and does not embody his magnificence'.[46] In 1750 Heinrich Johannes Schoenau, doctor of philosophy and medicine, devoted an extensive treatise to the question of precedence between physicians and jurists, refuting explicitly the precedence of jurists over physicians as supported by Chasseneux's '*argumentis ridiculis*'.[47] Among his counterarguments, he denies that physicians enter into service for money while jurists receive a fee as an honorarium; that physicians, unlike jurists, admit Jews to the doctorate since they have not attained it *de jure;* and that physicians are essentially worth no more than midwives. Here it is perfectly clear how one could attempt to discredit physicians and denigrate their rank and dignity by linking them with social groups at the bottom of the system of estates like Jews and midwives. Schoenau tried to respond to this strategy by pointing repeatedly to the physicians' status as rulers' personal medics.[48] In the article 'Facultät' in his *Philosophisches Lexicon,* the theologian Johann Georg Walch of Jena supports a similar alteration in the classical hierarchy of the faculties, granting the physicians precedence over the jurists with the following argument: The faculties

justly have the following rank among themselves. At the top is theology since it shows the way to eternal bliss, although one should not assume scholastic theology here, but the true theology whose merit in itself cannot be considered doubtful despite even the prestige accorded to the subject by the papacy. Medicine follows hereupon which looks after the health of the body and since the well-being of the body is properly the most noble among the temporal goods, it should thus follow immediately after theology and then jurisprudence ends it all. This is the natural order.[49]

Although the differentiation of the ranks is legally binding and usually regulated by statutes and other magisterial ordinances, differentiation in the area of academics' lifestyles is less fixed since what Bourdieu called the scholarly '*habitus*' also served as a medium of differentiation.[50] Here, however, one must distinguish between characterics attributed by contemporary observers, often stereotyped, and actual lifestyles. The drastic characterization of Leipzig academics by Georg Friedrich Rebmann in his *Kreuzzüge durch Deutschland,* written at the close of the eighteenth century, demonstrates how differently the *habitus* of representatives of different faculties could be perceived. His criticism of theologians is the most severe: 'They are poor, unknowledgeable, grovelling, contemptible, proud, and dirty. The latter ensures that one can find them among all the others and detect their studies from the odour they spread around themselves'.[51] Having completed the description of the theologian with great attention to detail, Rebmann continues in accordance with the hierarchy to the law faculty, where gallantry rather than pedantry dominates.[52] The members of the medical faculty would be a credit to the university, but can hardly be mentioned because of their small number. He deals last with the 'fine-arts scholars' as representatives of the philosophical faculty. They are described as small and sickly people who, 'more or less gallantly', try for a 'genius-like appearance'.[53] Even though the polemical exaggeration of Rebmann's comments can hardly be surpassed, they still provide an insight into the different lifestyles of the highly distinctive representatives of the various subjects.[54]

The quarrel between jurisprudence and medicine reveals, underlying the discussion of principles, a social distinction between a faculty with pretensions to noble status and one slowly distancing itself from the association of a craft.

'Barren Jurisprudence' vs. 'World Wisdom': A Precedent from 1713

Jurists' disagreements over rank were not confined to the faculties which could be described as their neighbours in the conventional academic hierarchy. A 1713 precedence dispute between a lawyer and a master of philosophy demonstrates that the actual conduct of a conflict within the framework of hierarchized interaction incorporated use of the arguments expressed in the relevant treatises cited above.[55] The case was included in a legal collection of consultations and petitions by Hellbach, who has already been mentioned, and shows how the conflict of the faculties could make itself felt in ceremonial practice.

A master of philosophy complained to the local consistory about the precedence assumed by an official public lawyer in church, during a baptism. His petition and the lawyer's response illustrate the different claims made for the subjects which the disputants represent. Moreover, the fact that the conflict took place outside the narrower confines of a university reveals the important social role which the hierarchy of the faculties played beyond the academic field to justify social orders of precedence.

With several 'irrefutable syllogisms and conclusions of reason, *ex omnibus disciplinis Philosophiae tam theoreticae, quam practicae* as well as *ex Theologia morali, nec non principiis Juris naturae et Gentium*', the philosopher strives to maintain and demonstrate that the philosopher, not the lawyer, deserves the 'higher position'. Here he expresses the fear that his opponent might possibly not be in a position to understand his argument since he might not have got so far in his studies as to understand them with his '*sensu communi*' or 'to discern' them with his '*Judicio*'. He thus decides to defeat his opponent through his own principles (*propriis principiis*) and to make it clear to him how, in his arrogance, he has contravened central '*Praecepta Juris*'. Hence he begins to justify the precedence of philosophy according to content, for what would 'barren jurisprudence' be, he asks, if it did not have philosophy? The legal profession would be a 'mere pettifoggery' without philosophy, and thus philosophy could manage without jurisprudence, but the latter could not get along without philosophy. Whereas jurisprudence is tied to a particular place, philosophy extends over the entire church and the entire community, indeed it produces the best kings worldwide since these, as is generally known, are the philosophical kings. The precedence of the philosopher is thus settled. By virtue of his philosophy he is also able to communicate 'to the scholarly world the most infallible judgements of theological, legal, medical, philosophical, historical, oratorical, poetical, mathematical, mechanical, economical and, in one word, of all books in all sorts of languages and to write the most splendid journals ... '. Mockingly he adds, the lawyer will have to 'leave this as it is'.

The lawyer, of course, could not accept this attack and wrote a detailed response. Although he is quite prepared to leave 'Mr. Complaint-Maker' his 'cap of honour,' he does not risk the reproach of 'untimely faint-heartedness', by appearing to forgive his colleague rather than repudiate his '*praetensiones*'. He does not want to demonstrate his erudition at length or boast with 'great world- wisdom', but he has indeed studied '*humanioribus*' and '*Philosophia*' to the degree necessary for his profession. Resisting his opponent with his own weapons, he proceeds with further flights of philosophical fancy. His '*sensus communis*' [can] comprehend and his understanding [can] judge this much, that with all the syllogisms as well as abstractions from '*qualitatibus occultis*' or all the Aristotelean virtues, the fantasy of his opponent attempts in vain to justify philosophers' precedence. After further ironic responses, the lawyer expounds three principles. He cannot see his profession trampled on; the arrogant philosopher must be curbed; and the 'lower position' must be accorded to him who deserves it by virtue of his origins. Jurists enjoy imperially documented privileges and they, finally, are 'exactly those *philosophi, qui veram, non simulatam, Philosophiam profitenter* and through whom the world is ruled'.

We do not know how the dispute of the two anonymous parties involved in the conflict was finally decided. For our purposes, however, it is more important to note the form of the argumentation, which used precise accusations to discredit opponents and deny their scholarly ability, while seeking to assert superiority by meeting contemporaries' expectations as to eloquence. Thus, after responding to the philosopher's claims to recognition and respect, the lawyer notes with reference to Crusius, that the latter, 'with great circumspection, dedicated the last and final *Caput tractationis* to the *Magister Philosophiae* so that they might not get lost *extra suam sphaeram* and overdo it.'[56] But this clearly seems unseemly to representatives of '*Philosophiae peripateticae*'. The way in which legal justification of social privilege is combined with academic claims for validation and respect clearly shows that prestige derived from academic hierarchies is linked to prestige in social hierarchies outside the university. Thus the hierarchy of the faculties not only constituted the organizational principle according to which precedence was regulated within the pre-modern university corporation, but also implied claims for validation and respect of a considerably more general sort which could be applied to other social contexts.

The Servant's Long Journey: the repositioning of philosophy in the eighteenth century

The historic difference between the philosophical faculty or faculty of arts and the three superior faculties is apparent from the fact that, for a long time, a master's degree was the highest it could award. This could produce conflict as masters of the faculty of arts were nonetheless apt to claim equal status with the doctors of the higher faculties.[57] The doctor of philosophy only arrived at German universities in 1771, authorized by the Prussian minister Zedlitz. Since this doctorate was a double degree, as it were, candidates incurred a double charge, with the new doctoral fee added to the existing cost of the master's degree.[58] The difference between the philosophy faculty and the three higher faculties also found its symbolic expression in the contemporary forms of address. 'If the patron is a professor of theology, law or medicine, then one gives him the title: Your Magnificence. If he is a professor of philosophy, then it is: Highly esteemed Professor, or: My Patron, or also perhaps: your Excellence'.[59] In many instances only members of the three higher faculties had the right to a seat in the sessions of the academic senate. The philosophers had to stand. In Helmstedt, for example, the philosophical faculty, by fighting hard, first obtained the right to chairs in the middle of the eighteenth century. The Helmstedt philosophers asked their sovereign in June of 1746 to put an end to this form of 'distinction' from the higher faculties so that they 'might be respected as *docentes*'.[60] After all, they had the right to call themselves '*Doctores philosophiae*' and would take on the task of lecturing with no less diligence and effect than other *graduati*', so that they should not be placed after those of the other faculties with doctorates. Although the sovereign took the view as a matter of principle that 'the *dignitas* of a *magistri* follows the *dignitati doctorali*, he permitted the philosophers to take seats in '*consistorio publico*' in order to 'encourag[e] their diligence'.[61] On this occasion the dispute about seating is less a question of comfort than a fundamental practice of symbolic differentiation within the early modern society of estates. The philosophical faculty's fight for equal rights and recognition within the relevant forms of institutional micro-politics was to continue through the entire century.

During the eighteenth century the philosophy gradually changed from propaedeutics into a leading science.[62] The philosophy of Christian Wolff supplied the theory underlying a fundamental re-evaluation of the relationship of the three higher faculties to philosophy or 'world wisdom'.[63] The self-awareness acquired from the new methodical status of philosophy becomes apparent when Wolff acknowledges that 'world wisdom is the servant of the higher faculties inasmuch as a woman would have to grope in the dark and would fall repeatedly if the servant did not light the way for her.'[64]

Starting out from a characterization of the four faculties, the Saxon Privy Counsellor and Counsellor of Justice, Adam Friedrich Glafey (1692–1753), undertakes a reform of the classical hierarchy of the faculties in his *Recht der Vernunft* (1746). His account demonstrates how philosophers' understanding and assessment of their faculty developed under the influence of natural law.[65]

The theologian leads people to eternal bliss, the jurist, however, teaches how the same people are to manage their behaviour when they want to be able to live together contractually in a state. The physician attempts to maintain the body and, where it deteriorates into sickness, to return it to its former health. The philosopher, however, prepares the ground by means of which one must achieve all this, but first and foremost this same philosopher teaches how one should live properly, remedy the flaws that appear, and stand in good stead.[66]

From this Glafey concludes: 'Reason thus creates the order among the faculties, [namely] that the doctor of theology leads the way, the doctor of philosophy or master immediately follows him and has the doctor of law behind him, but that the doctor of medicine brings up the rear of the procession'.[67] Here Glafey emphasizes over and again the quality of utility. Thus discrete academic subjects (metaphysics, poetry, language) are treated as follows: poetry is above all for 'souls who love the skins more than the core'. The poets are therefore 'placed far behind/[a] lecturer or scribe/who teaches such things/that can be of use in ordinary life'.[68] Language is understood as a pure means to an end, that is, for the communication of content; the language teachers, therefore, cannot claim any priority.[69] The mastery of languages is seen as useful, but not worthy of public recognition. This is, in point of fact, a significant change in comparison to the status-consciousness of humanist secretaries and lawyers who justified their rank above all with reference to their mastery of letters and the art of writing.[70]

With the anthropological turn of the eighteenth century, some scholars, such as Giessen professor of rhetoric Christian Heinrich Schmid
(1746–1800), re-evaluated the traditional hierarchy as constructed by
subject matter so as to elevate the science of the human above all.[71] In
Schmid's opinion, 'popular prejudices, which are over and done with,
and bourgeois orders of rank' should no longer determine the hierarchy
of subjects.[72] Thus the traditional precedence of theology is fundamentally challenged as well: 'All the other colours have to give way to the
black frock, but the merit of theology does not lie in the colour'.[73] 'The
ranking of the so-called four faculties' is, in his opinion, 'so arbitrary
and arose in such dark times that, at most, it only proves according to
which gradation one saw the necessity of public instruction'.[74] Finally,
in order to '[spread] the cosmopolitan way of thinking' he advocates
letting all sciences or academic disciplines stand side by side with equal
rights.[75] Although Schmid's position had no direct influence on the
organization of the disciplines, it is nevertheless typical of the effort to
establish new, 'anthropologically'-oriented classifications and, simultaneously, to criticize the 'pride' individual 'classes of scholars' took 'in
their handicraft' at the expense of brotherly collaboration.

At the end of the eighteenth century, Immanuel Kant undertook what
is probably the best-known re-evaluation of the relationship of the
philosophical faculty to the three higher faculties in *The Conflict of the
Faculties* (1798).[76] Kant starts from the premise that the order of the
faculties is not based on chance, but on reason: 'a priori . . . [on] a
principle of division which seems otherwise to be of empirical origin'.
According to reason, then, 'the incentives' of the government to carry
out such a division are the following: 'first comes the *eternal* well-being
of each [person], then his *civil* well-being as a member of society, and
finally his *physical* well-being (a long life and health)'.[77] But the
decisive twist in Kant's justification lies in the connection of all these
aims to the goals of the government, as he goes on to say:

By public teachings about the *first* of these, the government can exercise very
great influence to uncover the inmost thoughts and guide the most secret inten-
tions of its subjects. By teachings regarding the *second*, it helps to keep their
external conduct under the reins of public laws, and by its teachings regarding
the *third*, to make sure that it will have a strong and numerous people to serve its
purposes.

Thus this 'customarily assigned' hierarchy of theology, law and medicine is initially confirmed by 'reason'. If, however, it were a matter of

'natural instinct', then 'men consider the physician most important, . . . [a]nd only last (almost at the point of death) do they send for the clergyman, though it is their salvation that is in question'.[78] The three higher faculties, however, draw their legitimation solely from authoritative writings which speak through them:

So the biblical theologian (as a member of a higher faculty) draws his teachings not from reason but from the *Bible*; the professor of law gets his, not from natural law, but from the *law of the land*; and the professor of medicine does not draw his *method of therapy as practised on the public* from the physiology of the human body but from *medical regulations.*[79]

The power of the higher faculties is therefore less based on a rational grasp of the respective subject matters than on the power they receive by virtue of the authority of the government in the perception of the people, for the people, who 'want to be *duped*', think they have enough reason and can do without the abilities of the philosopher. The higher faculties, however, exert nothing short of a magical pull on the people by means of what they promise.[80] The philosophical faculty acquires its freedom precisely from not being oriented toward the higher faculties' 'magical' effect on the public, but only by serving the pursuit of 'truth'. The independence of the true science of philosophy claimed here refers at the same time to the differentiation of the social systems of scientific study and politics and thus goes far beyond a pure re-evaluation of the hierarchy of subjects.[81] Nevertheless, Kant did not lose hope that 'it could well happen that the last would some day be first (the lower faculty would be the higher) – not, indeed, in authority, but in counseling the authority (the government).'[82] Using the formulation of Rudolf Stichweh, one could say that the traditional hierarchy of the faculties, as a classification of the scholarly disciplines according to rank, was '*theoretically* discredited in the eighteenth century, but *institutionally* fixed and, as a result, of abiding effectiveness'.[83]

Changes in the Organisation of Scholarly Studies

In the area of the ceremonial representation of the faculties, however, corresponding processes of change took place only slowly. It should not be forgotten that the hierarchy of the faculties was also a material hierarchy, a fact that was expressed in the different salary levels. In this connection the Swiss mathematician Jacob Bernoulli, for example, had already delivered an emphatic criticism of the hierarchy of the faculties in a memorial and remonstrance presented to the University of Basel in 1691.[84]

In his *Philosophisches Lexikon*, almost one hundred years later, Johann Georg Walch also advocated abolishing 'the priority and rank of the teachers according to the faculties' and argued for giving 'everyone the same salary all the time,' whereby 'a lot of trouble that is otherwise fosterd by ambition or avarice would be prevented'.[85]

In Berlin's Wednesday Society, which was centred around Friedrich Nicolai, the abolition of the order of the faculties was also avidly discussed within the framework of general considerations concerning reform.[86] Wilhelm Abraham Teller, for example, demanded the following: 'The monastic division into faculties, in which philosophy as the servant walks at the back, should cease to apply.... The division into four faculties stems of course from the times when one still wandered in the twilight, and so it has many defects and flaws'.[87] In order to counter this 'scholastic' hierarchizing Teller therefore advocates the establishment of a rigorous principle of seniority: 'Would it not be enough if one left it as such and only made the arrangement that persons of all four faculties, among themselves, follow each other at celebrations and in social settings according to their term of office and not according to the order of these faculties?'[88] Subject to the condition that corresponding modifications be made, most of the members of the Wednesday Society nevertheless argued in principle for the retention of the faculties.[89]

The reordering of books listed in auction catalogues by the Leipzig publisher Philipp Erasmus Reich, who arranged the *Catalogus Universalis* in 1759 not according to the traditional hierarchy of the faculties but in alphabetical order, can also serve as an indication of the gradual process of change.[90] The University of Göttingen had two course catalogues which show this process of change particularly clearly. One was published in a Göttingen journal in 1748; the introduction states that, 'without considering rank, one favoured an order in which all those lectures that belong to the same faculty can always be found together.'[91] Although the hierarchy of the faculties is still preserved, a change already seems to be imminent, with ordering by rank of scholars within the faculties suspended.[92] The shift can be seen most clearly in 1755–6 when the ordering of professors within the faculties is replaced by a division by topics and groups of subjects.[93] In his 1789 report to

Friedrich Wilhelm concerning the two course catalogues, Gedicke writes that in Göttingen there are '1) a Latin catalogue where the professors announce their lectures one behind the other according to seniority... [and] 2) a German catalogue according to a methodical, systematic order'.[94] On a macro-structural level the structural change in the organization of scholarship and classification which began in the eighteenth century has been described as a switch from the stratificational differentiation of a hierarchy of the faculties to a functional differentiation of subjects.[95] Here the 'old' stratificational system and the 'new' functionally differentiated system exist side by side, as it were, the use of different languages for each catalogue further emphasizing the distinction.[96] Along with Rudolf Stichweh, however, one can assume 'that for students and university scholars for the greater part of the eighteenth century the formation of expectations [was] still determined by a hierarchically oriented perception of university reality.'[97]

Between the second half of the eighteenth century and the beginning of the nineteenth, seniority gradually prevailed over the traditional hierarchy of the faculties as the criterion for rank.[98] In a decree of the Württemberg Ministry of the Interior dated 28 January 1818 it was ordained 'that the personal ranks of the professors, irrespective of the faculties, are determined solely according to the time of their appointment to full or as the case may be to associate professorships, though the associate professors should always go after the full professors.'[99] The classical hierarchy of the faculties seemed increasingly odd to early nineteenth-century scholars. Schleiermacher, for instance, writes: 'It has been observed frequently and at length that our four faculties, the theological, juridical, medical, and philosophical, and still in this order as well, give the universities a very grotesque appearance'.[100] Others endeavoured more or less successfully to conjure unity from the distinction. For example, in a vice-rector's speech in 1859 Franz Delitzsch declared with respect to the colours of the faculty robes: 'We wear the four colours on white since, if all colours are children of white light, then all the faculties are children of one truth and each serves in its own way the God of truth, the father of lights. . . . Let them all be like the colours of the rainbow which do not stand apart from one another in a hostile way, but signify peace together!'[101] This marks the growing discomfort with the display of strict hierarchies, which now seemed odd to many observers. What really undermined the centuries-old rankings, however, was a formal transformation in the practice of ordering and constructing hierarchies, not a simple attempt to re-evaluate positions within the existing hierarchies.

Conclusions

The various sources examined illustrate conflicts over faculty hierarchies which did not, for the most part, lead to actual institutional revisions of the classical hierarchy of the faculties, but still offer a vivid insight into the changing assessments of the categories attached to individual academic subjects. Thus jurists and physicians, for example, frequently argued about the question of whether priority should be attached to the individual or to the collective body of the community. The philosophers had first to struggle to be recognized by the three higher faculties as a real, independent discipline offering more than a propaedeutical role. At the same time, the rise of philosophy indicated its new function in the generation of values. Simply put, philosophers' self-presentation as new, secular 'experts in value' incorporated simultaneous symbolic enhancement of their own position. So if we discard the Aristotelian notion that the subject corresponding to a certain discipline determines its rank and instead take into account the cultural impact the ordered society had on these distinctions, the dynamics of the numerous scholarly debates on the contest of the faculties appear in a new light. This is not to advocate a simple deterministic view of these conflicts, but to recognise the complex reciprocal negotiations of values and hierarchies both social and epistemic.

Finally, the switch to formal criteria of order, which began during the course of the 'saddle period' [*Sattelzeit*] around 1800, relocated the communication of social valorization, giving the epistemological value-dispute its autonomy, as it were. One could continue to argue about the evaluation of the individual faculties, beginning with the esteem for their subject matter, but without linking this debate with juristically legitimized social claims for validation and respect. In the pre-modern culture of knowledge, values in the sense of principles like God, political-social order, physical health or reason could not be separated from values in terms of symbolic and material goods like honour, rank, and salary bracket. The structural disconnection of the two value-dimensions achieved during the differentiation of science or scholarship as an autonomous social system first made it possible to work out conflicts about values, at least in principle, without recourse to a prior hierarchical order. Changes in the autonomy of the intellectual field during the emergence of the research university certainly did not mean an end to academic distinction. But some of the fundamental structures of pre-modern systems of inequality were transformed. Rank was no longer a juridical category which could be claimed at court and the order of precedence lost the earlier overwhelming importance which had formerly been expressed through all forms of communication.[102] There was no longer any cultural necessity for a definite spatialized hierarchical distinction between superior and inferior and covering every possible eventuality.

Nevertheless, one should not proceed on the assumption that, as a result, the significance of symbolic orders and of conflicts about resources has become fundamentally less important in the academic area. Precisely from today's perspective, it seems that Kant's appeal has not gained final acceptance, since representatives of the classical three higher faculties still claim precedence in current surveys and so-called occupational-prestige rankings. When answering the question about which professional groups they believe to be most honest, today's Germans put doctors in the first place, followed by clergy and judges and, somewhat further down the scale, scholars and university professors as such.[103] Certainly, we should not over-estimate the usefulness of such surveys, but they do suggest that the persistence of the long tradition of both epistemic and social valorization still lends the three higher faculties a special charisma even in a differentiated, post-metaphysical society.

Georg-August-Universität Göttingen
Seminar für Mittlere und Neuere Geschichte
Platz der Göttinger Sieben 5
37073 Göttingen
Germany

REFERENCES

* Earlier drafts of this paper were presented at the Eleventh International Congress of the International Society for Eighteenth-Century Studies, August 3–10, 2003, Los Angeles; Conference of the International Max Planck Research School for the History and Transformation of Cultural and Political Values in Medieval and Modern Europe, September 23/24, 2004 at the Max-

Planck Institute in Göttingen; and 'Breaching the Ivory Tower' – Universities in Context (16th-18th Cent.) 12–13 December 2007 at the European University Institute, Florence. I would like to thank all the participants for their helpful comments. An earlier, German version of this essay appeared as Marian Füssel, 'Der Streit der Fakultäten. Zur sozialen Praxis des Wertewandels in der frühmodernen Gelehrtenkultur', Marie Louisa Allemeyer, Katharina Behrens, and Katharina Ulrike Mersch (eds), *Eule oder Nachtigall? Tendenzen und Perspektiven kulturwissenschaftlicher Werteforschung* (Göttingen, 2007), 104–133.

1. Marian Füssel, *Gelehrtenkultur als symbolische Praxis. Rang, Ritual und Konflikt an der Universität der frühen Neuzeit* (Darmstadt, 2006). In the Holy Roman Empire exceptions from the four faculty system only occurred at purely Jesuit universities: see Karl Hengst, *Jesuiten an Universitäten und Jesuitenuniversitäten. Zur Geschichte der Universitäten in der Oberdeutschen und Rheinischen Provinz der Gesellschaft Jesu im Zeitalter der konfessionellen Auseinandersetzung* (Paderborn, 1981).

2. Interpretations mainly oriented to the history of ideas are Notker Hammerstein, 'Der Wandel der Wissenschafts-Hierarchie und das bürgerliche Selbstbewußtsein. Anmerkungen zur aufgeklärten Universitäts-Landschaft', in Wilfried Barner (ed), *Tradition, Norm, Innovation. Soziales und literarisches Traditionsverhalten in der Frühzeit der deutschen Aufklärung* (Munich, 1989), 277–91; Notker Hammerstein, 'Vom Rang der Wissenschaften. Zum Aufstieg der philosophischen Fakultät', in Armin Kohnle and Frank Engehausen (eds), *Zwischen Wissenschaft und Politik. Studien zur deutschen Universitätsgeschichte* (Stuttgart, 2001), 86–96; Martin Kintzinger, 'Die Artisten im Streit der Fakultäten. Vom Nutzen der Wissenschaft zwischen Mittelalter und Moderne', *Jahrbuch für Universitätsgeschichte* 4 (2001), 177–94; Günter Gawlick, 'Ein Hallischer Beitrag zum Streit der Fakultäten: Georg Friedrich Meiers „Betrachtungen über das Verhältnis der Weltweisheit zur Gottesgelahrtheit (1759)" ', in Robert Theis and Claude Weber (eds), *Von Christian Wolff bis Louis Lavelle. Geschichte der Philosophie und Metaphysik. Festschrift für Jean Ecole zum 75. Geburtstag* (Hildesheim, Zurich und New York, 1995), 71–84; Hanspeter Marti, 'Plädoyer für Unbekannt. Bemerkungen zum Streit der vier Fakultäten im vorkantschen Gelehrtenschrifttum', in: Heinrich P. Delfosse and Hamid Reza Yousefi (eds), *'Wer ist weise? der gute Lehr von jedem annimmt'. Festschrift für Michael Albrecht zu seinem 65. Geburtstag* (Nordhausen, 2005), 173–84.

3. William Clark, *Academic Charisma and the Origins of the Research University* (Chicago and London, 2006); Charles E. McClelland, *State, Society and University in Germany 1700–1914* (Cambridge and London, 1980).

4. Ernst Gockel, *Deliciae academicae in quibus natura et pleraeque civitates universitatum [...] exponuntur* (Augsburg, 1682), par. xxx, 50–1. Johann Schwimmer's analogy with the planets in 1672 does not seem immediately obvious either in view of the hierarchization of the faculties: he compares theology to Jupiter, jurisprudence to the moon, and philosophy to

Mars. Johann Schwimmer, *Tractatus politicus de academicis omnium fa-cultatem professoribus academia et studiosus* (Jena, 1672), thes. vii & lxi; see further the reference to Gockel and Schwimmer in Clark, *Academic Charisma*, 517n.

5. Aleksander Gieysztor, 'Management and Resources', in: Hilde de Ridder-Symoens (ed.), *A history of the university in Europe: Vol. I, Universities in the Middle Ages* Cambridge 1992, 1993), 108–43, here 111–12.

6. Füssel, *Gelehrtenkultur*, 100–1; Clark, *Academic Charisma*, 42–3.

7. Concerning this point Zedler's encyclopaedia states: Owing to 'rank and precedence at universities as well as outside them this order is observed as a rule: that the doctors of theology precede all the others, being followed by the jurists and after them by the physicians; although every faculty pays attention to the seniority of the doctor and thus establishes precedence, this is not manifested across the faculties so that a young doctor of jurisprudence does not follow an older medical doctor unless some external source con-tains a relevant regulation to the contrary or a doctor of medicine also holds some office which bestows on him a particular rank and a position of honour, in which case a medical doctor may even precede a jurist and this person a theologian, however not as a doctor, but in consideration of his office; one should also observe the custom of the place,' Johann Heinrich Zedler, *Großes Universal-Lexicon aller Wissenschafften und Künste, welche bißhero durch menschlichen Verstand und Witz erfunden und ver-bessert worden* (68 vols, Halle and Leipzig, 1731–54).

8. Cf. Marian Füssel, 'Zeremoniell und Verfahren. Zur Wahl und Einsetzung des Rektors an der frühneuzeitlichen Universität', in Daniela Siebe (ed.), *'Orte der Gelahrtheit': Personen, Prozesse und Reformen an protestan-tischen Universitäten des Alten Reiches* (Stuttgart, 2008), 119–42.

9. On *rotuli* see Donald E. R. Watt, 'University Clerks and Rolls of Petitions for Benefices', *Speculum* 34/1 (1959), 213–29. For hierarchies in written orders see William Clark, 'Parades académiques: Contribution à l'écono-mique politique des livrets universitaires', in *Actes de la recherche en sciences sociales* 135 (2000) 6–24; Clark, *Academic Charisma*, 33–67; Peter Burke, *A social history of knowledge. From Gutenberg to Diderot* (Cambridge, 2000), 91ff.

10. Franz Delitzsch, *Die akademische Amtstracht und ihre Farben. Rede zum Antritt des Prorectorats der Königl.-Bayerischen Friedrich-Alexander-Uni-versität Erlangen* (Erlangen, 1859). Concerning the history of gowns and for additional literature see Marian Füssel, 'Talar und Doktorhut. Die akademische Kleiderordnung als Medium sozialer Distinktion', in Bar-bara Krug-Richter and Ruth-E. Mohrmann (eds), *Frühneuzeitliche Uni-versitätskulturen. Kulturhistorische Perspektiven auf die Hochschulen in Europa* (Cologne, Weimar, and Vienna, 2009), 245–71.

11. Concerning salary relationships see Füssel, *Gelehrtenkultur* and citations, 98–100; for the fact that little changed in the eighteenth century with respect

to the traditional hierarchy see for example the table in Hans Haering, *Die Spätzeit der Hohen Schule zu Herborn (1742–1817). Zwischen Orthodoxie und Aufklärung* (Frankfurt, 1994), 327.

12. This part was added in the german edition of the volumes see Rainer Christoph Schwinges, 'Der Student in der Universität' in Walter Rüegg (ed), Mittelalter. Geschichte der Universität in Europa, Vol. I (Munich, 1993), 181–223, here 197, for the shorter version in English see Rainer Christoph Schwinges, 'Student Education, Student Life', in Ridder-Symoens, Universities, 195–243. Bettina Bubach criticizes Schwinges's interpretation of the predominance of jurists in the case of rectoral elections, using the example of Freiburg: *Richten, Strafen und Vertragen. Rechtspflege der Universität Freiburg im 16. Jahrhundert* (Berlin, 2005), 114–5.

13. Erasmus of Rotterdam, *In Praise of Folly*, ed. Horace Bridges, trans. White Kennett, (Whitefish MT, 2004), 121.

14. Jacques Krynen, 'Les légistes 'idiots politiques'. Sur l'hostilité des théologiens à l'égard des juristes en France au temps de Charles V', in *Théologie et droit dans la science politique de l'État moderne* (Rome, 1991), 171–98.

15. Notker Hammerstein, 'Die deutschen Universitäten im Zeitalter der Aufklärung', *Zeitschrift für Historische Forschung* 10 (1983) 73–89, here 76.

16. Christoph Meiners, *Über die Verfassung und Verwaltung deutscher Universitäten* (2 vols, Göttingen, 1801–2), ii. 58.

17. Johann Christian Förster, *Übersicht der Geschichte der Universität Halle in ihrem ersten Jahrhunderte* (Halle, 1794), new edition revised and provided with an appendix by Regina Meyer and Günter Schenk (Halle, 1998), 44. Characteristic for the perception of the classical hierarchy in the mid-eighteenth century is the following anecdote about Frederick the Great: 'As he visited Halle in 1754 and all the professors of the university appeared in their hierarchical order at the house in which he stayed, he expressed his displeasure with the parade because the theologians, or in his words the shavelings, were ranked in first place', Anton Friedrich Büsching, *Character Friedrichs des zweyten. Königs von Preussen* (Karlsruhe, 1789), 131.

18. See 'Facultät', Johann Georg Walch, *Philosophisches Lexikon,* (2 parts, Leipzig 1775; rprn Hildesheim 1968), col. 1208.

19. Barbara Stollberg-Rilinger, 'Die Wissenschaft der feinen Unterschiede. Das Praezedenzrecht und die europäischen Monarchien vom 16. bis zum 18. Jahrhundert', *Majestas* 10 (2002), 125–50; concerning the scholars see Füssel, *Gelehrtenkultur*, 73–93.

20. William Clark's conclusion that 'the order of precedence of the four faculties formed a moral or juridical order, that is, a canonical order, not an epistemic one' (Clark, *Academic Charisma*, 47) must, in my opinion, be modified to the effect that the order of the four faculties was also an epistemic order, but not one independent of the social mechanisms of validation or recognition. Academic and social validation simply cannot be separated here.

21. 'Inter certas referrimus ordinem Facultatum,' Johann Theodor Hellbach, *Meditationes iuris proedriae moderni oder Abhandlungen von den heutigen Rechten des Ranges, Vorzugs und Vorsitzes* (Leipzig, 1742), 27.
22. Concerning the contemporary debate see Johann David Dietrich (praes.) and M. Johannes Andreas Siepius (resp.), *De Non Adaequata Eruditionis In Quatuor Facultates Divisione* (Wittenberg, 1730).
23. Thus Jacob Gothofredus was content with the remark: 'Non in umbraticas quaestiones excurremus, utrum Doctor Iuris Civilis praeferendus sit Doctori Iuris Canonici: an Iurisconsultus, Medico: Miles Nobili, Doctor, Militi: In quibus omnibus Chassanaeus prolixe versatur' (Jacobus Gothofredus, *Diatriba de iure praecedentiae repetitiae praelectionis* (Geneva, 1664), 17). In his influential compendium Johann Christian Itter also refers to Chasseneux extensively in the tenth chapter, which is dedicated to precedence: Johann Christian Itter, *De honoribus sive gradibus academicis liber. Editio nova* (Frankfurt, 1698), 367–422.
24. Bartholomaeus Cassaneus [Barthélémy de Chasseneux], *Catalogus Gloriae Mundi* (Lyon, 1529). Numerous new editions followed, among others in 1546, 1569, 1571, 1576, 1579, 1586, 1603, 1612, 1617, 1649, 1657, 1690, 1692. With respect to Chasseneux cf. Christian Dugas de la Boissonny, *Barthélémy de Chasseneuz (1480–1541)*, thesis (Dijon, 1977).
25. Chasseneux, *Catalogus*, chapter 10, 1–52 (The text is not paginated; this would be c. 448–510).
26. Ibid., ch. 10, 10–12.
27. Ibid., ch. 10, 15–16.
28. Ibid., ch. 10, 17.
29. 'Universalis ergo et generalis erit conclusio in qua non est dubium quo ad ecclesiam et quo ad temporalitatem in curia romana et in gallia doctores in iure canonico et civili vel in altero tam preferuntur doctoribus in medicina' (Chasseneux, *Catalogus*, ch. 10, 25).
30. Ibid., ch. 10, 45–52.
31. Jacobus Andreas Crusius, *Tractatus politico-juridico-historicus de praeeminentia, sessione, praecedentia, et universo jure proedrias magnatum in Europa, [...] Libris 4 absolutus [...]* (Bremen, 1665), especially chapters 29–35.
32. 'Theologia dignior est aliis scientiis ratione certioris veritatis' (Crusius, *Tractatus politico-juridico-historicus*, 843); concerning theological faculty, 843–6.
33. The subject matter of the first two chapters dedicated to jurists is precedence between the military and jurists and between the nobility and jurists, ch. XXXI, 'De praeeminentia Togatae & armatae militae, & an Doctores Juris praeferendi viris in militari dignitatae constitutis?' and ch. XXXII, 'De ordine sessionis Iu[ris]c[onsul]torum, quod nobiles, & utrum hi illis praeferendi?', 886–901. The third chapter is dedicated to precedence within the faculty of law, ch. XXXIII: 'De ordine sessionis & Praecedentiae inter ipsos Juris doctoris', 901–18. And, finally, in the fourth chapter the rank of jurists

and physicians is treated, ch. XXXIV, 'Vtra artium, Medicinae, an juris Civilis praestet, & an Doctores Juris indistincte Doctoribus Medicinae in sessione praefereudi?,' 918–44.

34. Concerning the social claims of the jurists to recognition cf. also Hermann Lange, 'Vom Adel des doctor', in Klaus Luig and Detlef Liebs (eds), *Das Profil des Juristen in der europäischen Tradition. Symposion aus Anlaß des 70. Geburtstages von Franz Wieacker* (Edelsbach, 1980), 279–294; Ingrid Baumgärtner, '„De privilegiis doctorum". Über Gelehrtenstand und Doktorwürde im späten Mittelalter', *Historisches Jahrbuch* 106 (1986), 298–332; Karl Heinz Burmeister, *Das Studium der Rechte im Zeitalter des Humanismus im deutschen Rechtsbereich* (Wiesbaden, 1974), 13–17.

35. See Coluccio Salutati, *Vom Vorrang der Jurisprudenz oder der Medizin. De nobilitate legum et medicinae*, translated with commentary by Peter Michael Schenkel (Munich, 1990); Fridericus Gerdesius (praes.) and Bernhardus Friese (resp.), *Discursus Inauguralis De Jure Precedentiae* (Greifswald, 1674), ch. VI, part 3; cf. also the information in Johann Christian Hellbach, *Handbuch des Rangrechts in welchem die Literatur und Theorie, nebst einem Promtuar über die praktischen Grundsätze derselben, ingleichen die neuesten vorzüglichen Rangordnungen im Anhange enthalten sind* (Ansbach, 1804), 131; Lynn Thorndike, 'The debate for precedence between medicine and law: Further examples from the 14th to the 17th century', *Romanic Review* 27 (1936) 185–90; idem, *Science and Thought in the Fifteenth Century: Studies in the History of Medicine and Surgery, Natural and Mathematical Science, Philosophy, and Politics* (New York, 1967), 24–58, 261–4.

36. This conflict found its way into Hellbach's collection of consultations: Hellbach, *Meditationes, Enunciatum* XXVI, 71–2; see further the dispute between a doctor of jurisprudence and a physician, ibid., 54ff.; the same case is also reported in Itter, *De Honoribus*, 385–6; cf. additional, similarly structured cases in Hellbach, *Meditationes*, 149–154. See Füssel, *Gelehrtenkultur*, 219–22; Thomas Weller, *Theatrum Praecedentiae. Zeremonieller Rang und gesellschaftliche Ordnung in der frühneuzeitlichen Stadt: Leipzig 1500–1800* (Darmstadt, 2006), 272–89.

37. Weller, *Theatrum Praecedentiae*, 289.

38. Leopold Senfelder, ed., *Acta Facultatis medicae Universitatis Vindobonensis*, v: *1605–1676* (Vienna, 1910), p. xxxvi.

39. 'Deinde ergomet authoritate apostolica et caesarea, praehabita prius oratione ad promotionem accomodata de praestantia et primatu medicinae, adque praecedentia contra juristas, nimirum utra facultas sit praeferenda alteri, juridicane medicae, an medica juridicae?', ibid., 178.

40. Heinrich Cornelius Agrippa von Nettesheim, *De incertitudine et vanitate scientiarum et artium/Über die Fragwürdigkeit, ja Nichtigkeit der Wissenschaften, Künste und Gewerbe*, with an epilogue ed. Siegfried Wollgast, translated and annotated by Gerhard Güpner (Berlin, 1993), ch. 82, 200–1. On the propagation of this anecdote in the satirical literature of the

seventeenth and eighteenth centuries see Elfriede Moser-Rath, *'Lustige Gesellschaft'. Schwank und Witz des 17. und 18. Jahrhunderts in kultur- und sozialgeschichtlichem Kontext* (Stuttgart, 1984), 192, note 12. It can also be found in Johann Burckhard Mencke, *Herrn Jo. Burckhardt Menckens Zwey Reden von der Charlatanerie der oder Marktschreyerey der Gelehrten, nebst verschiedener Autoren Anmerckungen. Mit Genehmhaltung des Hn. Verfassers nach der letzten vollständigsten Auflage übersetzt* (Leipzig 1716, rprn Munich 1981), 265–6.

41. Friedrich Nicolai, *Vademecum für Lustige Leute* (10 vols, n.p. 1764–92), i. 143; printed in Siegfried Armin Neumann (ed.), *Den Spott zum Schaden. Prosaschwänke aus fünf Jahrhunderten* (Munich, 1977), 343.
42. Johann Michael Moscherosch, *Visiones de Don Quevedo. Wunderliche und Warhafftige Gesichte Philanders von Sittewald* (Strasbourg, 1642), 288ff.
43. Ibid.
44. 'Th***' [Anonymous], 'Ob ein Doctor Medicinae den Rang mit Recht nach den Doctoribus Juris habe?', in *Dreßdnische Gelehrte Anzeigen* 4 (1753) art. 80, cols 451–6, here cols 453–4. With an appeal to Aristotle the author also argues here for the precedence of jurisprudence over medicine because 'the former, with respect to the criticism of its activities, has the soul, but the latter the human body' (ibid., col 453).
45. Concerning the professionalization of physicians in the eighteenth century see Thomas H. Broman, *The transformation of German academic medicine: 1750–1820* (Cambridge, 1996).
46. Heinrich Caspar Abelius, *Lang-gewünschter medizinischer Gewissens-Spiegel* (Frankfurt am Main, 1720), 9–10. Here Abel refers to authors of the *Ius praecedentiae* such as Horn or Zwantzig, claiming not to undestand why jurists should be given precedence. In the same context he alludes to Agrippa von Nettesheim's analogy, quoting: 'Quod fur praecedat, Carnifex sequatur' (ibid.).
47. Heinrich Johannes Schoenau, *De Justa Themidis sententia, medicinae doctoribus, prae causidicis sive advocatis competere praerogativam dignitatis: adeoque jus praecedentiae rationibus decidendi ad summam medicae facultati dignitatem et gloriam demonstrata* (Frankfurt am Main, 1750), see the chapter 'Nugatoria Chassanei argumenta, quibus medicorum dignitatem imminuere adnititur, exploduntur ac refutantur', 63–9.
48. On the relationship between 'consultative functions' of physicians and claims to precedence see also Rudolf Stichweh, *Der frühmoderne Staat und die europäische Universität. Zur Interaktion von Politik und Erziehungssystem im Prozeß ihrer Ausdifferenzierung, 16.- 18. Jahrhundert* (Frankfurt am Main, 1991), 371.
49. 'Facultät', in Walch, *Philosophisches Lexikon* (2 parts, Leipzig 1775; rprn Hildesheim 1968), cols. 1207–9, here 1209.
50. Cf. Marian Füssel, 'Akademische Lebenswelt und gelehrter Habitus. Zur Alltagsgeschichte des deutschen Professors im 17. und 18. Jahrhundert', *Jahrbuch für Universitätsgeschichte* 10 (2007), 35–51.

51. Georg Friedrich Rebmann, *Kreuzzüge durch einen Teil Deutschlands (1795)*, (Leipzig, 1990), 83.
52. 'The small pack of jurists is more scholarly than the throng of theologians. A respectable tone prevails among them, their *mores* are finer, and, on the whole, their clothing is a step above the average. That blind devotedness [of theologians] to their studies and their teachers is not found among them, they do justice to each person, and they do not try to gain the advantage by forceful means since they have it anyway. They seldom tote satchels, carry no inkwells, have at most two books with them, sit in the collegium on chairs which they pay for, thus do not make the streets unsafe, do not so inanely write things down, and one can approach their lecture halls without a bottle of smelling salts': ibid, 85.
53. Ibid., 85–6.
54. One still sees attempts to link the different styles of the faculties to their clothing; e.g. Florentine Fritzen, 'Die Uniformen der Uni', in *Frankfurter Allgemeine Sonntagszeitung*, no 2, 14 January 2007, 49 and Stefanie Stegmann, *'got the look!' – Wissenschaft und ihr Outfit. Eine kulturwissenschaftliche Studie über Effekte von Habitus, Fachkultur und Geschlecht* (Munster, 2005).
55. The corresponding petitions are described anonymously in Hellbach, *Meditationes*, 194–8, originally in: Johann Friedrich Hertel, *Institvtionum Imperialivm Praxis Forensis oder Practicalischer Handgriff der Keyserl. Rechts-Lehre* (Jena, 1717), par. 3, n. 8, 63ff; see also Barbara Stollberg-Rilinger, 'Rang vor Gericht. Zur Verrechtlichung sozialer Rangkonflikte in der frühen Neuzeit', *Zeitschrift für Historische Forschung* 28 (2001) 385–418, here 385–87.
56. Ibid., 198.
57. With respect to Ingolstadt see Arno Seifert, *Statuten- und Verfassungsgeschichte der Universität Ingolstadt (1472–1586) (Ludovica Maximilanea 1)* (Berlin, 1971), 164ff; see also chapter XXXV in Crusius, *De praecedentia, dignitate, & praerogativis Magistrorum, Baccalaureorum & c. cum poeris totius Epilogo*, 944–56, as well as, in general, William Clark, 'On the Ironic Specimen of the Doctor of Philosophy', *Science in Context* 5 (1992), 97–137.
58. Conrad Bornhak, *Geschichte der preussischen Universitätsverwaltung bis 1810* (Berlin, 1900), 90; Clark, 'Doctor of Philosophy', 110–1.
59. August Bohse, *Der getreue Hoffmeister adelicher und bürgerlicher Jugend oder auffrichtige Anleitung, wie so wohl ein junger von Adel als anderer der von guter Extraction, soll rechtschaffen aufferzogen werden [. . .] an das Licht gegeben von Talandern [i.e. August Bohse]* (Leipzig, 1706), 122.
60. See the petition of the members of the faculty of arts to the sovereign, dated 30 June 1746: Niedersächsisches Staatsarchiv Wolfenbüttel, 37 Alt/326; see also Füssel, *Gelehrtenkultur*, 235–37.
61. Ibid., official reply to the university from 6 July 1746.

62. Hans Erich Bödeker, 'Von der 'Magd der Theologie' zur 'Leitwissenschaft'. Vorüberlegungen zu einer Geschichte der Philosophie des 18. Jahrhunderts', *Das achtzehnte Jahrhundert* 14 (1990), 19–57, here 31ff.

63. Christian Wolff, 'Ausführliche Nachricht von seinen eigenen Schrifften, die er in deutscher Sprache von den verschiedenen Theilen der Welt-Weißheit herausgegeben' (Frankfurt am Main, 1733), reprinted in *Gesammelte Werke*, (Hildesheim and New York, 1962-), I.ix. 532ff., pars 193ff.; Regina Meyer, 'Das Licht der Philosophie. Reformgedanken zur Fakultätenhierarchie im 18. Jahrhundert von Christian Wolff bis Immanuel Kant', in Notker Hammerstein (ed.), *Universitäten und Aufklärung* (Göttingen, 1995), 97–124.

64. Wolff, 'Ausführliche Nachricht,' 536.

65. Adam Friedrich Glafey, *Recht der Vernunfft, worinnen die Lehren dieser Wissenschafft auf feste Gruende gesetzt und nach selbigen, die in Welt-Haendeln [...] vorgefallenen Streitigkeiten eroertert werden* (Frankfurt and Leipzig, 1746), 519–34 (pars 69–108). Glafey also comments on the precedence of a doctor over a princely councillor and nobleman in his *Kern der deutschen Reichs-Geschichte* (Leipzig, 1722) and in his *Anleitung zu einer weltüblichen deutschen Schreib-Arth* (Frankfurt am Main, 1730), 531.

66. Glafey, *Recht der Vernunfft*, 525–6 (par. 83).

67. Ibid., 528–9 (par. 91). Among the academics, the full professors were distinguished from the doctors and masters. The 'academic lecturer' always went ahead of the ordinary teacher: ibid., 522 (par. 75).

68. Ibid., 523 (par. 79).

69. Ibid., 524 (par. 81).

70. Jacob Burckhardt, *Die Kultur der Renaissance in Italien* (Stuttgart, 1988), 164–5.

71. Christian Heinrich Schmid, 'Über die Klassifikation und Rangordnung der Wissenschaften', in *Gothaisches Magazin der Künste und Wissenschaften* (1779), ii. 231–51; concerning this see Ulrich Dierse, *Enzyklopädie: zur Geschichte eines philosophischen und wissenschaftstheoretischen Begriffs* (Bonn, 1977), 46ff. Schmid ranks the academic disciplines as follows: 1. knowledge of the human body (a. externally = physiology, b. internally = theoretical medicine), 2. knowledge of the human spirit (philosophy, psychology, and aesthetics), 3. culture of the body (gymnastics, practical medicine), 4. culture of the spirit (practical logic, language studies, philology, morals as the doctrine of our duties towards ourselves, liberal arts and sciences), 5. knowledge and culture of society (laws of reason, morals as the doctrine of our duties towards others, political sciences, jurisprudence, history of humanity, world history), 6. insentient and lifeless material world (physics, mathematics), 7. theology, 8. ontology (= 'ultimate academic discipline', the study of general terms), ibid., 237–48.

72. Schmid, 'Klassifikation', 249.

73. Ibid.

74. Ibid.

75. Ibid., 251.
76. Rudolf Stichweh, *Zur Entstehung des modernen Systems wissenschaftlicher Disziplinen in Deutschland 1740–1890* (Frankfurt am Main, 1984), 31ff. On Kant's work in the historical context of the university, see Steffen Dietzsch, *Immanuel Kant. Eine Biographie* (Leipzig, 2003), 253–60; Riccardo Pozzo, 'Kant's *Streit der Fakultäten* and Conditions in Königsberg', *History of Universities* 16 (2000) 96–128; Reinhard Brandt, *Universität zwischen Selbst- und Fremdbestimmung. Kants 'Streit der Fakultäten'*, with an appendix on Heidegger's 'Rektoratsrede', (Berlin, 2003).
77. Immanuel Kant, *Der Streit der Fakultäten*, in *Werke*, (12 vols, Frankfurt am Main, 1968), xi. 12, 13, 283; English edition, *The Conflict of the Faculties*, trans. with introduction by Mary J. Gregor (Lincoln NE, 1992), 31.
78. Kant, *Streit der Fakultäten*, A 12, 13, 283f.; *Conflict of the Faculties*, 31 and 33.
79. Kant, *Streit der Fakultäten*, A 16, 285; *Conflict of the Faculties*, 35.
80. 'But now the people are approaching these scholars as if they were soothsayers and magicians, with knowledge of supernatural things; for if an ignorant man expects something from a scholar, he readily forms exaggerated notions of him. So we can naturally expect that if someone has the effrontery to give himself out as such a miracle-worker, the people will flock to him and contemptuously desert the philosophy faculty. But the businessmen of the three higher faculties will always be such miracle-workers, unless the philosophy faculty is allowed to counteract them publicly – not in order to overthrow their teachings but only to deny the magic power that the public superstitiously attributes to these teachings and the rites connected with them – as if, by passively surrendering themselves to such skillful guides, the people would be excused from any activity of their own and led, in ease and comfort, to achieve the ends they desire'. Kant, *Streit der Fakultäten*, A 32, 33, 294; *Conflict of the Faculties*, 49, 51.
81. Stichweh, *Entstehung*, 35–6. The establishment of one's own code or of a 'symbolically generalized communications-medium' can be regarded as a characteristic of differentiation, and in the case of the scholarly scientific system as a characteristic of the defining difference between true and false. See also Niklas Luhmann, *Die Wissenschaft der Gesellschaft* (Frankfurt am Main, 1994).
82. Kant, *Streit der Fakultäten*, A 43, 44, 300; *Conflict of the Faculties*, 59.
83. Stichweh, *Entstehung*, 31.
84. Bernoulli asked '[w]hether variation in salaries and differentiation in seating by rank and faculty have not been major causes of the lack of seriousness that has prevailed until now, since self-interest and ambition have been so great that even those who could call their professions praiseworthy were dissatisfied, always aspiring to richer and higher professions for which they were not so well qualified; another person furthermore, not yet a professor, could not wait until a position became vacant which was appropriate for him, but in the meantime took another for which he was not suitable at all

for the sole purpose of gaining access to others much more easily. Would it not therefore be quite useful where such conditions now exist to abolish completely the inequality in salaries and to range professors in future according to their seniority, irrespective of the ranks and faculties, as is common at all well-organized universities', cited in Andreas Staehelin, *Geschichte der Universität Basel 1632–1818* (Basel, 1957), 436.

85. Art. 'Facultät', in Walch, *Philosophisches Lexikon* i. cols. 1207–9, here 1209.
86. A. Stölzel, 'Die Berliner Mittwochsgesellschaft über Aufhebung oder Reform der Universitäten (1795)', in *Forschungen zur Brandenburgischen und Preußischen Geschichte* 2 (1889), 201–22.
87. Ibid., 206.
88. Ibid., 207.
89. See e.g. B. Nicolai, ibid., 210 or Selle, ibid., 220.
90. Mark Lehmstedt (ed.), *Philipp Erasmus Reich (1717–1787). Verleger der Aufklärung und Reformer des deutschen Buchhandels* (Leipzig, 1989), 71.
91. *Göttingische Zeitungen von gelehrten Sachen* 31 (1748), 241–8, here 241. Concerning the following see Clark, *Academic Charisma*, 33–67. On the lecture catalogues see also Horst Walter Blanke, 'Bibliographie der in periodischer Literatur abgedruckten Vorlesungsverzeichnisse deutschsprachiger Universitäten 1700–1899', *Berichte zur Wissenschaftsgeschichte* 6 (1983), 205–27, 10 (1987), 17–43. Our knowledge about the emergence of the lecture catalogue has very recently been revolutionized by the work of Ulrich Rasche, 'Seit wann und warum gibt es Vorlesungsverzeichnisse an den deutschen Universitäten?', *Zeitschrift für Historische Forschung* 36 (2009), 445–78.
92. In 1770 Johann David Michaelis asked, '[w]ould it not be more seemly if the full professors were simply ranked according to seniority, as is done in other colleges, so that the older professor of medicine or philosophy would go ahead of the younger professor of theology, if he had no further title, and would also take a seat above him in assemblies?' (Johann David Michaelis, *Räsonnement über die protestantischen Universitäten in Deutschland* (Frankfurt and Leipzig, 1768–76, rprn Aalen 1973), ii. 405.
93. *Göttingische Zeitungen von gelehrten Sachen*, 117 (1755) 1085–98.
94. Richard Fester (ed.), 'Der Universitäts-Bereiser' Friedrich Gedike und sein Bericht an Friedrich Wilhelm II.', in *Archiv für Kulturgeschichte*, supplementary issue 1 (1905), 26; regarding Gedike's report see also Elena Barnert, 'Headhunter Seiner Majestät. Der "Universitäts-Bereiser" Friedrich Gedike evaluiert Deutschlands Professoren für Preußens Universitäten', *Rechtsgeschichte* 4 (2004), 256–63.
95. The 'hierarchy is replaced by a juxtaposition of functional systems with increasing heterogeneity': Stichweh, *Entstehung*, especially 31–9, here 35.
96. The first German-language course catalogue was apparently published in Halle in 1729: Clark, *Academic Charisma*, 61.

97. Stichweh, *Entstehung*, 32–3.
98. Gedike thus reports from Mainz in 1789: 'By the way, the professors are not ranked according to their faculties, but according to seniority irrespective of the faculty' (Fester, 'Gedikes Bericht,' 46); see also Andreas Staehelin, 'Der Rang der Fakultäten in der Geschichte der Universität Basel', *Universität Basel 1469–1960 Sonderheft der Schweizerischen Hochschulzeitung* 33 (1960), 72–6.
99. 'Erlaß des Ministeriums des Inneren an den akad. Senat, betr. den Rang der Fakultäten und Professoren untereinander vom 28. Januar 1818', in August Ludwig Reyscher (ed.), *Universitätsgesetze*, revised by Theodor Eisenlohr (*Vollständige, historisch und kritisch bearbeitete Sammlung der Württembergischen Gesetze, Vol XI:3*, Tübingen, 1843), no.13, 610–11. But of course there are still occasions at which the university and senate appear according faculty, and here the traditional order is still observed, now complemented by the Catholic theological faculty in second place and the political-economic faculty in sixth place.
100. Friedrich Daniel Ernst Schleiermacher, 'Gelegentliche Gedanken über Universitäten im deutschen Sinn [1808]', in Ernst Müller (ed.), *Gelegentliche Gedanken über Universitäten von Engel, Erhard, Wolf, Fichte, Schleiermacher, Savigny, v. Humboldt, Hegel* (Leipzig, 1990), 159–236, here 198.
101. Delitzsch, *Amtstracht*, 10.
102. The latter resulting from a general shift away from relational inequalities towards distributive regimes of inequality: Füssel, *Gelehrtenkultur*, 24–5.
103. See Elisabeth Noelle and Thomas Petersen, 'Das Ende von Humboldts Universität', in *Frankfurter Allgemeine Zeitung*, 15 November 2006, no. 266, 5.

The Netherlands, William Carstares, and the Reform of Edinburgh University, 1690–1715[1]

Esther Mijers

Aims & Objectives

The University of Edinburgh was one of the great institutions of the eighteenth century. Many of its professors were luminaries of the European Enlightenment, and throughout the period the University attracted students from around the globe. Yet its history and development are perhaps less well known than they ought to be. Both the development of the Scottish Enlightenment and the emergence of Edinburgh have deep roots in the seventeenth century. The earlier history of Scotland's universities is currently receiving renewed interest.[2] This article aims to make a contribution to this historiographical development. It addresses the different attempts to reform the Scottish universities, in particular the University of Edinburgh, in the late seventeenth and early eighteenth centuries. First it considers the reforms of the 1690s as a Presbyterian backlash, following on from the Revolution of 1688/9, opposing the more lenient academic climate of the 1680s and aiming to bolster the re-established Presbyterian Church. Second, it traces the roots of the reform of 1708 by the Principal William Carstares and investigates to what extent his reforms originated his Dutch connections, the time he spent in the Netherlands, and the example of its universities. The four main Dutch universities - Leiden, Groningen, Franeker and Utrecht - were civic institutions, founded after the Reformation, designed to train magistrates rather than being tied to the church. The University of Leiden especially was a national university, which not only attracted pupils from all Dutch provinces but also acted as the country's national academy. William Carstares sought to emulate the example of the Dutch universities, and of Leiden in particular, in Scotland.

William Carstares's initiatives were firmly rooted in the seventeenth century tradition of educational change. Moreover, these reforms were part and parcel of Carstares's personal agenda, to which his own time abroad, as a student at the Dutch universities of Utrecht and Leiden, his dual role in Scottish politics and the Scottish Kirk, and his own religious beliefs and personal interests all contributed in varying degrees. Given his experience it is not surprising that he turned to the continent for inspiration, as others had done before him. Their innovation was the successful transformation of Edinburgh from a protestant 'seminary' into a civic university.[3] Once realised, their reforms had more in common with a number of Episcopalian initiatives of the 1680s than with the hardline Presbyterianism of the 1690s.

While others - John Cairns, Roger Emerson, Christine Sheperd (King), and M.A. Stewart - have considered this period, much archival material has remained under-used and further synthesis is needed.[4] For this account, the Visitation Papers in the National Archives of Scotland (NAS), the *State-Papers and Letters Addressed to William Carstares* edited by his first biographer, Joseph McCormick,[5] the Carstares Papers in the University of Edinburgh Library (EUL), and the Stirling Papers in the University of Glasgow Library (GUL) have all been consulted, as has some of the Dutch correspondence between William Carstares and Willem Bentinck, the future Earl of Portland and the politician who would 'manage' Scotland on behalf of William III throughout most of the 1690s. The picture that emerges is one of longstanding Scottish religious and political concern with educational reform, which owed as much to domestic initiatives as it did to Dutch influences. Paradoxically enough the Scottish-Dutch moment of 1688/9 provided somewhat of a break in an otherwise continuous development, which found its culmination in Carstares's 'Dutch' reforms. Although we lack a complete picture of his activities in the Netherlands, it is possible to give a fairly comprehensive account of the reforms of Edinburgh University on the eve of the Scottish Enlightenment.

Before Carstares

Throughout the seventeenth century, the Dutch Provinces provided a model for economic prosperity and emulation for much of Protestant

Europe, and for Scotland in particular. The two countries were closely tied in terms of trade, religion, and intellectual outlook.[6] Already host to a substantial Scottish community before 1660, the country became a haven for Scottish, Presbyterian exiles after the Restoration of the Stuart monarchy.[7] In the wake of the Revolution of 1688/9, a substantial number of these Scots returned from their Dutch exile. They brought back with them a range of experiences, many of which were educational. A number of these exiles involved themselves with the issue of the schools and universities in Scotland, which had suffered from a lack of Presbyterian scholars, textbooks, and 'zeal', throughout the Restoration period but especially during the 1680s. It is tempting to see in the educational purges and reforms that subsequently took place the beginning of a new enlightened era for the Scottish universities, preceding the famous university reforms of the first quarter of the eighteenth century, which concerned both curriculum and spirit. The truth is rather more complicated. For a full appreciation of what happened in the 1690s, we need to look both backwards, to the 1680s, and forwards, to the personal involvement of perhaps the most famous of all Scottish students and exiles in the Netherlands, the Reverend William Carstares (1649–1715), King William of Orange's chief advisor on Scottish ecclesiastical affairs and the Principal of Edinburgh University from 1703 until his death in 1715.

Education was a longstanding concern in Scotland and the perceived necessity for university reform can be traced back to the Reformation. The importance of a basic education for everyone had been stressed by John Knox, as it was by continental reformers. Public authorities and the church were to co-operate to achieve this. Educational renewal was first proposed by Andrew Melville (1545–1622), Knox's successor and Principal of Glasgow University from 1574 to 1580. Melville turned to Geneva for inspiration and introduced Ramism to Scotland, as well as specialist teaching. In Edinburgh, Melvillean reforms were introduced by the University's first Principal, Robert Rollock, although a complete transformation was never achieved.[8] Educational matters were relevant not only to teaching but also to religion and politics. On the foundation of the Tounis College, the future University, in Edinburgh in 1582, the Scottish Parliament had sanctioned statutes and laws for the institution, as had the Town Council and the new kirk.[9]

Despite Melville's reforms, the teaching method of regenting, where a year or class was taken through the arts curriculum by a single tutor, rather than by separate, specialist professors, was never abolished. This as well as the practice of dictating lessons continued to worry Scotland's educators.[10] Throughout the seventeenth century, educational renewal was addressed by a number of Visitation Commissions, which were as much concerned with religious and political conformity as with teaching.[11] The educational interests of the new Williamite Presbyterian establishment as well as those of Carstares must be viewed in this context.

The state of the universities at the time of the Revolution of 1688, contrary to the conventional historiography or even the contemporary Presbyterian opinion, was far from desperate.[12] Although Charles II's persecution of the clergy had stretched as far as the universities, forcing Presbyterian Scottish ministers, students, and scholars into exile, the resulting political and religious conformity had never really put a strain on the universities' 'intellectual vitality'.[13] The regents' basic philosophy teaching incorporated new ideas from the continent, and logic, the sciences, mathematics, and some medical teaching all underwent renewal. During the second half of the seventeenth century, the new science and its methods found their way into the Scottish universities' curriculum. The first references to Cartesian physics date to the 1650s and appear in graduation theses; Newtonianism began to make its appearance some thirty years later.[14] In mathematics, the new science was introduced by James Gregory (1668–74) at St Andrews, where he was the first Regius Professor of Mathematics. He was the first to use the works of Kepler, Galileo, and Descartes for his teaching. His brother David Gregory (1661–1708) taught at Edinburgh before moving to Oxford. He was one of the first to lecture on Newton at Edinburgh, and was succeeded there by his nephew James Gregory (1666–1742), who had taught earlier at St Andrews. Glasgow and Aberdeen soon followed the examples of Edinburgh and St Andrews.[15] By the late 1680s, the Scottish universities' science curriculum had, to an extent, been modernized. In law, a renewal had taken place *extra muros*.[16] In the early 1680s two legal texts of crucial importance to the future discipline of Scots Law appeared, Stair's *Institutions* and Mackenzie of Rosehaugh's work of the same name, and there were extra-mural lecturers in civil law teaching in Edinburgh.[17]

William Carstares was not the first to establish professorships at Edinburgh. Divinity had always had its own chair. In 1642, a Professor of Hebrew was appointed to teach alongside the four existing regents. In 1674, James Gregory was appointed Professor of Mathematics. In the 1680s, Scottish academic life flourished under the Duke of York, the future King James VII and II, and a largely Episcopalian intellectual establishment. He gave patronage to the establishment of three medical chairs, and tried to found chairs in law and history. In Glasgow as well there had been attempts to establish a specialised teaching system, in 1681 and 1695.[18] Royal patronage made other contributions to Scottish learning. The Royal College of Physicians, the Physic Garden, and the Advocates' Library were founded with the Duke of York's support in response to initiatives by Scotland's Episcopalian intellectual community.[19] The immediate result for Edinburgh University was the appointment in 1685 of three Professors of Physic (Medicine), the Dutch-educated *virtuosi* physicians Sir Robert Sibbald of Kipps, Archibald Pitcairne and James Halkett, none of whom taught so far as is known.

The intellectual connections with the United Provinces, from which Carstares was to draw much of his thought, were already in place in the 1680s. The contributions of the Royalist, Episcopalian intellectual establishment of the 1680s to the curriculum, and its members' use of Dutch textbooks, paved the way towards what has been called the 'Dutch phase' of the Scottish universities.[20] Moral and natural philosophy, logic, metaphysics, law, medicine, and divinity were all taught from compendia produced in the Netherlands, by Grotius, De Vries, and the German Pufendorf. These were supplemented with the works of the Cambridge Platonists, astronomers like Kepler, Brahe, and Galileo and English and 'Dutch' philosophers. References were certainly made to the works of Descartes, as well as to Spinoza and Hobbes, who were refuted. Locke was probably taught as well. Recent experimental work by continental scientists and the members of the Royal Society in London and the Académie des Sciences in Paris was also discussed in virtuoso circles.[21] Paradoxically enough, the Dutch teachings in moral and natural philosophy were to come under attack from the 1690–5 Visitation Commission, which was partly made up of men who had been in exile in the Netherlands during the 1680s.

The 1690–5 Visitation - 1702

The concerns to renew Scottish higher education survived the Revolution of 1688/9, and as part of the Kirk's victory over episcopacy and comprehension, took on a new urgency. Religious & political conformity were once again at stake. Following on from the Revolution and in accordance with the impending Presbyterian settlement, a *Commission for Visiting Universities Colledges & Schools* was appointed on 4 July 1690.[22] Its members were 'the Duke of Hamilton, the Earl of Argyle, Earl of Crawford, &c' plus 'sixty others, consisting of noblemen and gentlemen,' who were appointed as 'visitors.'[23]Although such initiatives were not new- after every change of power a number of more or less drastic measures against the universities tended to take place- the Visitation of 1690–5 was both severe and ambitious.[24] By the end of July, the Commission had created a number of committees to sit at the different universities, with an ever-changing membership.[25] The core of the Edinburgh committee was Gilbert Rule (*c.*1629–1701), the strict Presbyterian principal of Edinburgh University who replaced his outed predecessor Alexander Monro (d. 1698), the Duke of Hamilton (1635–94), the Earl of Crawford (1644–98), the Duke of Argyll (d. 1703), Sir James Dalrymple, Viscount Stair (1619–95) and Sir Patrick Hume of Polwarth, the first Earl of Marchmont (1641–1724). The latter three had all been in exile in the Netherlands in the 1680s and returned with William of Orange; Gilbert Rule had been imprisoned for his religious convictions.

    Subdivided into several committees and driven by political conviction as well as Presbyterian zeal, the Commissioners set out:

to meitt and visite the separate colledges and schools [...] and to report [...] what persons they find to be erroneous scandalous negligent insufficient or disaffected to ther Majesties government and who shall not subscryve the said confessione of faith and swear and subscryve the said oath of alledgeance and submitt to the government of the church now settled by law [...] and for ordering the saids universities colledges and schools ther profesions and maner of teaching them and all els relaiting therto according to the foundations therof and consistant with the present establisht government of church and state [...] [26]

Piety and discipline were deemed crucial for the proper education of Scotland's youth, especially her future clergy. To the Commission, Episcopalianism, Arminianism, and Socinianism were all cause for concern. Every member of the university, including the librarians and the hall masters, was called before a university committee and questioned extensively about their religious beliefs and morals, as well as about the discipline within the university, students' church attendance, and observation of the Sabbath.[27] The Principal and the Professors of

Divinity were also questioned on the 'books that are taught for sacred lessons', which concerned all the students. The *Whole Duty of Man* and Grotius, *De Veritate Religionis Christianae*, were among the recommended texts.[28] Moreover, the committees demanded that every university member sign the Westminister Confession of Faith, take the oath of allegiance to the Crown, subscribe to the Act of Settlement, and submit to the church government. This caused serious problems for the universities, as the Visitation Papers show at great length. In addition to the staff, textbooks, dictation, and book-buying also came under severe scrutiny.[29] Some men resigned before the visitors had a chance to remove them, most notably the medics Sibbald, Halkett, and Pitcairne at Edinburgh. Others, like the principals of Glasgow, Edinburgh, and St Andrews, objected, claiming these were matters of individual conscience, and were subsequently outed.[30] In St Andrews, where Episcopalianism appears to have been a particular problem, the principal of St Salvator's College, Andrew Skene, protested 'for myselfe and in name of all the other Masters and Professors of the Universitie excepting Mr John Monro'.[31] The result was the removal of most Episcopalian professors and regents from the Scottish universities and the conforming of the rest to the new regime.[32]

The story of the visitation of Edinburgh has been told before.[33] Proceedings were held against the entire university staff. The principal, Dr Alexander Monro, the Professor of Divinity, Dr John Strachan, the Professor of Hebrew, Alexander Douglas, and the regents Thomas Burnet and John Drummond were outed. James Gregory, the Professor of Mathematics, survived but left for Oxford in about a year. The three remaining regents, Herbert Kennedy, Alexander Cunningham, and Andrew Massie – though temporarily removed – survived the visitation despite serious allegations of immoral and undisciplined behaviour.[34] Monro, Strachan, Burnet, and Drummond were replaced by men who were known for their Presbyterian zeal, especially the new Principal, Gilbert Rule. The newly founded medical chairs as well as the Chair of Hebrew and Oriental Languages also fell victim to the committee. Yet the move towards professionalization, which had begun two decades earlier, was continued through the establishment of a regius chair in ecclesiastical history and through plans for curricular reform, to rid the universities of 'popish' and 'prolix' teachings and to standardize the philosophy curriculum.

Politically, the largely Jacobite University's clash with the new regime had been inevitable. So too was the Town Council's assertion of its role in the University's affairs. Disappointed with the Williamite government, which cared little for Scottish Presbyterian concerns and was distracted by international affairs, the new regime's aspirations were as much intellectual as political. The Commission's dual aim was the 'Advancement of Religion and Learning'. After removing all 'Popish' elements and making new appointments, the Commission tackled the curriculum.[35] In 1692, a document entitled *Overtures for the Visitation of Colleges* was put to the Visitation Commission by the delegates of the universities, listing a number of recommendations to improve both the curriculum and teaching methods. This initiative was taken up by the Commission and three years later the idea of a 'uniform course of philosophie to be hereafter taught in all the colledges' was introduced.[36] The universities were convinced of the need for a printed course of philosophy 'for we cannot think it adviseable that any course already printed can be fitt'. In a letter to the Visitation Commission, in which the universities expressed their support, the philosophy curriculum was analysed in detail. Many of the current texts were written by 'Popish' authors, but there were a number of other problems as well with the French, Swiss, Dutch, and English writers who might be used:

The course that runs fairest is Philosophia vetus et nova, which is done by popish authors and smells rank of that religion, but therin the Logicks ar barren, and nothing of the Topicks, the Metaphysicks barren, the Ethicks erroneous, and the Physicks too prolix; for Ars cogitandi[37] tho it be a pretty book yet cannot be the standard to be taught, labouring with obscurity, fitt only for the more adult and not intelligible by youths, short in the Topicks and runs out in many digressiones idly and makes use of Protestant arguments as examples of sophisms, and his treatise De methodo is very dangerous. Derodon his large Logicks ar too prolix, his Didactics ar very defective, his Ethicks hardly deserve that name runneing only out de libero arbitrio &c. and his Physicks only some generall questiones.[38] Burgerdicks Logicks have only positive doctrine and non of the disputes which are absolutely necessary for the youth in their Logicks to fitt them to dispute, nor gives he arguments and reasons for what he says.[39]

In addition, Henry Moore's Ethicks were considered to be Arminian,[40] 'Mr Gaven' was prolix and obscure,[41] De Vries's ontology and pneumatology was too short and defective,[42] Le Clerc was 'meerely sceptical and socinian', and 'Cartesius, Rohault and others of his gang [. . .] give not sufficient account of the other hypotheses and of the old philosophy which must not be ejected, and weer never designed to be taught to students'.[43] The divinity curriculum, however, was mainly Dutch and Genevan, listing, among others, Wendelin's *Systema*

Theologiae,[44] Calvin's *Institutions*,[45] Turretin's *Institutio Theologiae Elencticae*,[46] and a work by an unidentifiable author - or perhaps a compendium - entitled *Theses Leidensis*, as well as texts by [Samuel] Maresius, [Andreas] Essenius, and [Johann Heinrich] Alting.[47] This attack against many of the foreign and some of the more modern elements in the philosophy curriculum was inspired more by 'Calvinist religiosity' than by a conscious rejection of what was modern (and Dutch). Roger Emerson has referred to the resulting arts curriculum as a 'still [...] decadent and eclectic scholasticism', which was ultimately changed by the 'largely unconscious [...] adoption of an empirical philosophy'.[48] At the same time a memorandum had been added to the *Overtures* of 1692 'for the College of Edinburgh in particular', consciously proposing the establishment of 'new professions yet wanting, as of law and physic', the expansion of the library with 'all new books that shall be published and such old ones as are wanting' and mathematical instruments, and the extension of the college buildings and grounds.[49]

The universities were led by seemingly contradictory desires.[50] On the one hand they agreed with the Commission's concern about 'popish' and 'prolix' elements, yet at the same time they were in favour of modernization. The Visitation Papers show a fascinating struggle between new and old ideas, between the universities and their decidedly reactionary Commissioners, and, later on, about financial affairs as well. It appears that the universities became decidedly unhappy with their visitors' interference, which explains in part the ultimate failure of the attempt to establish a printed course of philosophy.[51] The most far reaching reforms were submitted by the University of Glasgow. Its masters proposed 'the fixation of al the classes in Every University'. Oratory, mathematics (consisting of arithmetic), geometry, geography, astronomy and chronology, and 'experimental philosophie' should all be added to the new, standard Arts curriculum. To speed things up, Glasgow even went so far as to propose that the printed courses of logic, metaphysic, and rhetoric could be allotted to 'a universitie abroad of yr near affinitie'.[52] Lastly, teaching methods were in desperate need of reform: more disputations were required to replace dictation, especially on Aristotle, in the oriental languages, and in the humanities.[53] St Andrews, the most traditional of the Scottish universities, was very much in favour of a key place for mathematics in the new curriculum, which given the nature of the subject meant more science as well. It seems to have had a serious problem with the abolition of dictation and the introduction of disputations.[54]

For all the universities, the biggest stumbling blocks were the establishment of a fixed Professor of Greek, the place of Hebrew within the Divinity faculty, the separation of ethics and metaphysics from theology and of physics from medicine, and the availability of capable mathematicians and medics for the scientific part of the philosophy curriculum.[55] The teaching of Cartesianism posed one of the biggest problems.[56] It was agreed that both the old and the new philosophies should be understood by students. The new philosophy might therefore be taught alongside Aristotelianism, but 'Clerk & Locke should not be so commended being dangerous to be read by Students'. The authors of the printed courses were warned, by the principals of the universities, that nothing should be included which 'taught what is contrary to Scripture'.[57] Lastly, the minutes of the Visitation Commission include a book list with a number of early seventeenth-century 'historie bookes'. This suggests an interest in civil and ecclesiastical history on the part of the Commissioners. In 1692, a lecturer in both subjects was appointed in Glasgow.[58] St Andrews as well appears to have employed a lector in history.[59] Whether this was ever considered in Edinburgh is unclear. The notes on the printed course certainly do not include any references to history as a discipline in the arts curriculum, although the strong case made by Glasgow for the inclusion of oratory may have been intended to apply to history too, as a part of that discipline.[60]

Finally in 1698, a division of the writing of the printed course was agreed upon by all the universities apart from St Salvator's College, St Andrews. Glasgow was responsible for the course on general and special ethics, St Andrews for the one on logic and metaphysics, Edinburgh for pneumatology, and the Marischal and King's Colleges of Aberdeen for general and special physics respectively.[61] King's and Marischal were the only colleges that finished their printed courses, although several drafts by the other universities have been identified and described extensively by Christine King (Shepherd). Two years later an *Act of Commission anent the Greek and Philosophy Class in each College* was passed, establishing a fixed teacher of Greek, 'and not ambulatory as he now is', for the first year of the arts curriculum, although without much success.[62] In 1702, the plans for 'ane uniform course of philosophie' appear to have been abandoned. Academic disagreements, financial problems, the loss of the papers in a fire, and the constant interference of the Visitation Commission, had contributed to a climate in which co-operation between the universities became impossible. The fear of losing their autonomy ultimately caused the universities to abandon the plan for a standard, printed philosophy course.[63] One year after the failure of this 'Presbyterian experiment', William Carstares became principal of Edinburgh University. His ambitions differed greatly from those of the Visitation Commission. Despite their shared experience of exile, Carstares was driven by religious moderation and the ambition to bring Edinburgh into line with the institutions he knew intimately, the universities of the Dutch Republic.

'The good and great Mr William Carstares'[64]

William Carstares was born in 1649 in Cathcart, near Glasgow, as the son of a clergyman. After taking his MA at the University of Edinburgh in 1667, under the reform-minded principal Alexander Colville (d. 1675), he went abroad to complete his studies, first at Utrecht and later at Leiden.[65] Like many young Scots, Carstares found a safe haven in the Netherlands to avoid the problems the Restoration regime brought many Presbyterians - his father had been deprived in 1662.[66] Carstares was not alone: between 1660 and 1690 some 400 Scots lived in exile in the Netherlands, and 67 of them attended university. Carstares matriculated at the University of Utrecht in 1669.[67] It was the most orthodox of the Dutch universities, and also further removed from the watchful eye of the English ambassador at The Hague than Leiden.[68] Although little is known about his time at Utrecht, we can safely assume that, like his Scottish fellow students, he followed a curriculum of his own choice, interspersed with visits to important people and towns. Unlike many Scots of a later generation, he seems to have been in Utrecht without a tutor. He enrolled in the Faculty of Theology, but he probably also took some subjects in the Arts Faculty, almost certainly history, Greek, and Hebrew, possibly moral philosophy and one of the oriental languages. He might also have attended anatomical dissections and demonstrations in chemistry or physics and visited the medical cabinets and the botanical gardens as did so many others. According to his biographer, Robert Story, Carstares studied Hebrew under Leusden at Utrecht, and divinity under Witsius.[69] Whether this is an error or whether the latter was the Leiden Professor Wittichius, who taught divinity from 1671 until 1686, or Witsius who taught the same subject, first at Franeker from 1675 until 1680, then at Utrecht until 1698, and afterwards in Leiden until 1707, is not clear. Carstares certainly did study at Leiden in the 1680s during his exile, though most likely also in the early 1670s.[70] He may well have been one of those Scottish students who studied at more than one university, without matriculating at each. The combination of Leiden and Utrecht certainly was a very popular one. Having rounded off his studies in Utrecht, Carstares was probably also ordained there, by a Dutch *classis*.

William Carstares thus had first-hand knowledge of the two most important Dutch universities - conservative Utrecht and progressive Leiden - and their curricula. He also must have been familiar with many of their professors. In Utrecht he almost certainly would have attended lectures, colleges, and sermons by Gijsbert Voet (Voetius), Professor of Theology, minister of the church and champion of Dutch orthodox theology, and his colleagues, Andreas Essenius and Matthias Nethenus.[71] Indeed, Carstares's Library Catalogue from 1685 looks like the standard reading list of a Utrecht theology student.[72] It lists a number of works by Voetius and his supporters, yet none by his adversary Johannes Cocceius, who taught in Leiden from 1650 until his death in 1669, the same year that Carstares matriculated at Utrecht. Scottish theology students generally ignored the battle between Voetians and Cocceians, which determined the Dutch academic landscape throughout most of the second half of the seventeenth century.[73]

Apart from divinity and Hebrew, Carstares might have taken philosophy with De Vries and history with Graevius, who also taught politics. If he did study at Leiden in the 1670s, Carstares might also have studied with some of the history professors, including Jacobus Gronovius senior, whose son was a member of the academic circle of supporters of William III. So far there was nothing remarkable about Carstares's career which would single him out as the future father of religious moderatism. Upon his return to Scotland, he became involved with the radical Presbyterian resistance against the government and the crown. For that he suffered imprisonment and torture. He remained in close contact with the Scottish exile community in the Netherlands, to which he fled due to his participation in the Rye House plot in 1683.

Carstares had first met the Stadholder William III as a student in Utrecht. According to his biographer Joseph McCormick, he was introduced to the Grand Pensionary Caspar Fagel by a family friend shortly after his arrival in the United Provinces. Fagel apparently was taken with the young Scot and immediately presented him to William III and his favourite Willem Bentinck, the future Earl of Portland (1649–1709).[74] When Carstares was forced into exile in the 1680s, he returned to William's court in The Hague, where he became one of William's closest advisers and his personal chaplain. For a brief period of time, he also acted as second minister to the English Church in Leiden. Although he matriculated as a student at Leiden in 1686, taking advantage of the legal protection the universities provided, he probably never took any courses. He might have known a number of professors though, such as the Divinity Professors Witsius and Jacobus Trigland,[75] the Utrecht Philosophy Professor De Vries, and most likely the Leiden History Professor Jacobus Gronovius Jr. and his Franeker colleague Jacobus Perizonius- men whose ideas and textbooks were to feature prominently in Carstares's future reform of Edinburgh University. He almost certainly met Herman Boerhaave.[76] At the same time, Carstares also found himself in the middle of the Scottish exile community which had gathered in Utrecht. As one of William III's confidants and his personal chaplain and as a close friend to Bentinck (Portland), Carstares was at the centre of both Dutch and exile politics. His fellow exile Sir Thomas Stewart of Coltness, brother to Sir James Stewart of Goodtrees, referred to him as ' ... the good and great Mr William Carstares, high favourite of King William, and of his cabinet-councell for Scots affairs ... '.[77] He retained this position from his return to Scotland with William III in 1688 until the latter's death in 1702.

It was during his exile in the 1680s that Carstares's ideas on religion were formed. As a member of the circle surrounding the stadholder William III, he experienced and came to appreciate Dutch religious policy first hand.[78] Since the Synod of Dort, the Dutch Reformed Church had combined strict anti-Arminian principles with a degree of state involvement, the extent of which depended on the local situation. Tolerant Holland, home to the University of Leiden, stood out as the most latitudinarian as well as the wealthiest and commercially most successful of the Dutch provinces. Utrecht on the other hand, as town, province, and University, was a bulwark of Voetian orthodoxy. The difference between the two would not have escaped Carstares.

While at court, he was closely involved in the discussion between Bentinck (Portland) and Sir James Stuart Goodtrees on the eve of the Revolution concerning James II & VII's Declaration of Indulgences.[79] Goodtrees famously defended the Indulgences, while Cartstares and other exiles like Patrick Hume of Polwarth opposed them. After the

Revolution, Portland and William III relied on him in the dispute regarding Scotland's religious settlement. Subsequently, Carstares effectively became Scotland's 'regional manager' alongside Portland, who was responsible for ruling Scotland on William III's behalf for most of his reign.[80] As the country's leading clergyman and politician, Carstares was instrumental in shaping Williamite policy. In religious terms, this meant conformity and a degree of toleration which was at odds with the Presbyterian zeal of the former exiles. Carstares successfully mediated between the court and the Scottish politicians. Portland was sympathetic towards the Prebyterian demands and with his support, Carstares obtained a religious settlement which was acceptable to all but the staunchest of Presbyterians.[81]

Throughout the rest of Carstares's career, his Dutch experience remained a crucial influence on his political and religious thinking. As William of Orange's adviser on Scottish ecclesiastical affairs after 1688, his immediate concern was with religious matters. According to Joseph McCormick:

His sentiments upon ecclesiastical matters were formed upon in Holland, where, though all religions are tolerated, yet only one is established and countenanced by the legislature. His great object, therefore, was to have the same form of church government established over the whole island.[82]

McCormick did add, however, that Carstares personally favoured Presbyterianism. It has been even been suggested that Carstares, as a member of the 'Scotish-Dutch' group which returned with William of Orange in 1688 would have favoured 'the re-organisation of the Scots Kirk [...] from the model of what they had known in Holland.'[83] Whether this degree of Erastianism was ever seriously considered is highly questionable, although Carstares was undoubtedly in favour of a moderate settlement.[84] Unlike his more orthodox fellow exiles, he opposed the abolition of patronage in the Church and he sought to maintain the royal prerogative.

Carstares's interest in the Scottish universities related directly to his concern with ecclesiastical matters.[85] The persecution and expulsion after the Restoration of many Presbyterian ministers, including his own father, and James VII and II's increasingly anti-Presbyterian policies in the 1680s, had forced many Presbyterian leaders into exile, depriving the younger generation of a university education.[86] As Story put it, '[t]he younger men, who furtively entered the ministry between 1662 and 1688, set greater store by Presbyterian zeal than by liberal scholarship or theological science'.[87] Uneasy with any kind of zealousness, Carstares put the reform of the Scottish universities on his own agenda. As early as 1689, he mentioned the universities in his 'Hints to the King' concerning the Episcopal and the Presbyterian clergy, recommending that the King gave particular attention and encouragement to the universities in Scotland 'in order to their being immediately supplied with men of good learning and sound principles, as the only security for a right succession of clergy and statesmen in time to come'.[88] The question of university appointments had political significance, and in Edinburgh would have to be considered in the light of civic concerns. Carstares applied the same principles he had displayed in his religious politics, seeking to co-operate with the government, the Town Council, and the professions. He may very well have found a willing listener in William III, who took a personal interest in the affairs of the University of Leiden and involved himself with the professorial appointments.[89]

In 1691, a year after the establishment of the *Commission for Visiting Universities Colledges & Schools*, Carstares went back to the United Provinces with William of Orange.[90] His good friend, the English Dissenter Edmund Calamy, described how Carstares was looking for Dutch professors to fill the vacancies at the Scottish universities: '... one of his principal aims was to pick up some that might be fit and qualified to make masters of in the several Colleges of Scotland, which had been before either too much neglected, or filled with improper persons'.[91] In April that same year, Carstares wrote informing his brother-in-law William Dunlop, recently appointed principal of the University of Glasgow with Carstares's patronage, that he had spoken to the king 'about allowing to the universities some part of the bishop's rents, and he seems to be much more inclined to do so than to give them to particular men. I shall not fail to push the matter as far as it will go, because it is service to the King and country.'[92] Both Carstares and William III himself appear to have been keen to appoint Dutch professors: 'I think you [Dunlop] may have the allowance for an extra-ordinary professor of Divinity and another of philosophy; but I would have them from Holland where they are very good, and I suppose it will please the King best'.[93] Two years later Carstares obtained a 'Grant to the Universities of Scotland [. . .] for the maintenance of professors and bursars in Divinity'.[94] It was to cover the 'maintenance of one professor of Divinity [. . .] to be called Nominated and Presented by their Maiesties and their Royal Successors from abroad [. . .]'.[95] Moreover, it was also stipulated that the 'ten Bursers in Divinity in each Colledge' were to 'study Divinity by the direction and oversight of the Professors aforesaid by the space of two full yeares within one of the four Colledges aforesaid and the third year they are to goe abroad and study one year in a Protestant University by the direction of the Professors aforesaid whereby they may be instructed disposed and qualified to be Ministers of the Gospell as they shall have occasion to be called after their Returne and their three yeares of study in Divinity [. . .]'.[96] The resulting chair in Divinity and Ecclesiastical History was the first regius chair at Edinburgh University.[97] While Carstares clearly had Dutch theologians in mind to fill the vacancies, the Chair of Ecclesiastical History remained unoccupied until 1702, when John Cumming was appointed, probably due to Carstares's influence.[98] In 1693/4 another royal deed followed for Edinburgh and Aberdeen for the establishment of a second Chair of Divinity. This project failed, however, perhaps due to the interference of the Faculty of Advocates which attempted to transfer the king's endowment for a second chair of Divinity to a first Chair of Law.[99] Instead, the money was used for the existing Chair of Ecclesiastical History and to re-establish the Chair of Hebrew and Oriental Languages which had been left vacant after its last occupant's removal in 1688. The Faculty of Advocates obtained its first chair, in 'Civil Law in this Kingdome', in 1698 – funded by the Scottish Parliament - although its occupant, Alexander Cunningham of Block, never taught.[100]

Although knowledge of Hebrew was deemed essential for future ministers of the Kirk, the question of studying the language had always been problematic. In the *Overtures* of 1692, it had been recommended that all divinity students should be obliged to take Hebrew.[101] It was unclear who was to teach and there were obvious problems with finding acceptable Hebraists. In 1642, Justus Otto, a German Jew, had been appointed as Professor of Hebrew in the Arts Faculty at Edinburgh. Aberdeen's King's College had a similar teacher. Elsewhere Hebrew was offered but probably poorly taught. In 1692 Patrick Sinclair became Professor of Hebrew. After his death in 1694, money became available from William of Orange's deed. Alexander Rule (d. *c*.1745), the son of principal Gilbert Rule, Carstares's predecessor and possibly a 'Dutch' Scot, was appointed as Professor of Hebrew and Oriental Languages. In 1702, it was stipulated that all philosophy students should take Hebrew, and all prospective divinity students were to produce a 'testificate of his education & receiving the degree of Master of Arts from the Colledge where he was taught' and to continue their study of Hebrew once they had entered the faculty of Divinity.[102] That same year William of

Orange died. Carstares left court and the London political arena. The next year he was appointed principal of the University of Edinburgh, where he was to dedicate all his time to the project which had always been in the back of his mind, the reform of the Scottish universities, starting with Edinburgh.

The reforms of 1708

Supported by the Secretaries of State Roxburgh and Mar, Carstares set out to reform his university after the model of the Dutch civic universities. This coincided with actions taken by the the Town Council to assert its authority and to discipline its professors.[103] Carstares's reign began with a confirmation in 1703 of the 'Forme and Ordour of Teaching and Proceiding of the Students in thair Foure Yeires Course in the Colledge of Edinburgh' by the Council and Provost of Edinburgh, which dated back to 1628. Significantly, this curriculum was not based on the acts or proposals of the Visitation Commission.[104] The first two years of this programme were dedicated to the study of Latin and Greek, the New Testament, and Ramus' *Dialectics*. In the second year, rhetoric, Aristotelian philosophy, arithmetic, and logic were added. The third and fourth years essentially elaborated on this, incorporating ethics and physics as well as the study of Hebrew. A year later, Carstares, as part of 'a committie to have under ther considderatione the complaints conteaned in the memoir given in to the Counsell against the masters of philosophie and students of the Colledge' introduced a number of disciplinary measures, followed by the famous reform of the Philosophy programme in 1708.[105] The result was a completely revised 'undergraduate' curriculum, in which 'all the parts of the Philosophy be taught in two years, as they are in the most famous Universities abroad'[106] The four existing regents became professors, each fixed to a different chair, namely Greek, logic, moral philosophy, and natural philosophy.[107] The regent of humanity, who taught Latin, also obtained his own chair, and henceforth his class was required to matriculate.[108] Although a sound knowledge of Greek was considered to be the basis of the philosophy programme, it was no longer a compulsory part of the arts degree. As a result many students forewent the classes of Greek and humanity and entered the philosophy course immediately, if their Latin was good enough.[109] In 1708, Charles Morthland, Professor of Oriental Languages at Glasgow and a Dutch 'Scot', described the new situation in Edinburgh.[110] There were the four professors of philosophy, 'all Gentlemen of excellent liberal Education, who have studied Abroad as well as at home, Philosophy, Mathematicks and the Civil Law, and some of them Divinity'. Laurence Dundas was the Professor of Humanity, to whose chair the discipline of Roman history and oratory had been added, most likely after the Dutch model.[111] James Gregory, who had studied at Leiden in the 1670s, taught Mathematics. The Divinity Faculty consisted of William Carstares and George Meldrum as first and second Professors of Divinity, the aforementioned John Cumming, Professor of Ecclesiastical History, who was Carstares's protégé, and John Goodal (d. 1719), Professor of Hebrew and Oriental Languages. Goodal was succeeded in 1719 by James Crawford (c.1680–1731), who also held the Chair of Chemistry and Physic from 1713. Law and medicine were still largely in the hands of 'city gentlemen', the lawyers, surgeons, and physicians.[112] In 1707, Charles Erskine was appointed Regius Professor of Public Law and the Law of Nature and Nations, with support from Mar and some likely input by Carstares. The post was carefully defined to avoid any potential clash with Cunningham's parliamentary Chair in Civil Law, although it was in effect a sinecure to subsidize his editing project of the Digest, which he carried out in The Hague.[113] Erskine immediately left for the Netherlands, to study at Leiden, leaving Edinburgh still without a Law Professor. Civil law was taught *extra muros* by James Craig, who would be appointed as Professor of Civil Law upon Carstares's recommendation in 1710. Botany as well was taught outside the university, although in 1706 Charles Preston had been appointed Professor.[114]

Carstares's reform looked remarkably like the proposal Glasgow had put forward in the early 1690s on the one hand, and the *Memorandum for the College of Edinburgh in Particular* on the other. In line with the latter, Carstares's attempts at reform stretched beyond divinity and the philosophy curriculum. He appears to have taken an interest in the teaching of medicine very early on. Already in 1692 the Town Council recorded a 'national interest' in law and medicine in its minutes: 'The revenues of the Bishopric and Deanery of Edinburgh . . . cannot be more piously and usefully employed than for the further encouragement of the learned professions already founded in the said University [by] establishing the other professions of law and medicine, [. . .] and providing and furnishing the library'[115] Later that same year, the *Memorandum concerning Edinburgh* had expressed a similar sentiment. In 1697 an anatomical theatre had opened in Edinburgh. It is unlikely that Carstares had a direct hand in this, since anatomical dissections were performed by the College of Surgeons. Carstares's lifelong friend Archibald Pitcairne, the Jacobite physician who had resigned before the Visitation of 1690–5, had supported the idea though: 'I do propose if this be granted to make better improvements in anatomy than have been made at Leyden these thirty years. For I think most or all anatomists have neglected, or not known, what was most useful for a physician'.[116] In 1705, the Leiden educated surgeon Robert Elliot was appointed Professor of Anatomy, joined in 1708 by Adam Drummond.[117] The arguments which were made in support of Elliot's appointment were familiar. Instruction in anatomy would serve the country at home and abroad in her armies and fleets; it would save the nation money which would otherwise be spent abroad; and, lastly, it prevented her youth from going abroad and the 'many dangers and inconveniences' that came with it.[118] In 1706, Charles Preston, a well connected Leiden MD, became the first Professor of Botany.[119] Carstares was the catalyst in the establishment of the Chair of Chemistry and Physic at Edinburgh. In 1713 James Crawford was appointed: he held an MD from Leiden and had ties with both Carstares and Pitcairne. The new chair gave the University a medical professor and thus made it easier to grant MDs.The most likely reason behind this appointment, however, was to keep up with Glasgow, which had obtained such a chair only months before. Crawford indeed almost left for Glasgow to take up the chair there.[120] Chemistry and materia medica had been taught privately since 1699 by Alexander Monteith, the Surgeon's anatomist and a protégé of Archibald Pitcairne. From 1719 onwards, Crawford lectured intermittently on chemistry and physic while also occupying the Chair of Hebrew and Oriental Languages.[121] He held his two posts until 1726. Finally in 1715, only months before his death, Carstares made a bid for another medical chair. His 'Memoriall concerning the Profession of Medicine in Edinburgh', presented to the Duke of Montrose, stated the same arguments which had been used in 1705 in the request for a professorship of Anatomy: Scotland's medical students were forced to go abroad 'through want of Professions at home'.[122] The Jacobite Rebellion of that same year and Carstares's death prevented the plan from taking effect. Anatomy came in 1720 but it was not until 1726 that the university finally obtained its medical faculty.[123]

Carstares's involvement in university affairs stretched beyond curricular reform, or even his own university. His brother-in-law, William Dunlop was appointed principal of Glasgow University with his patronage and his nephew, Alexander Dunlop, was made regent in 1704. Over the years, Carstares involved himself frequently with Glasgow, even after he became Principal of Edinburgh. John Stirling, Dunlop's successor, was his friend and shared many of his ideals, but sometimes disliked his 'meddling'.[124] In 1709, Carstares appears to have supported Robert Sinclair as candidate for the Glasgow chair of Hebrew and Oriental Languages, which went to Charles Morthland instead.[125] More importantly, he tried to obtain a regius Chair of Ecclesiastical History for Alexander Dunlop.[126] At St Andrews, Carstares was involved in the filling of chairs. He supported the strict Presbyterian principal James Hadow in the creation of a what became a sinecure Chair of Divinity in 1707 and in a proposed visitation of the University.[127] He also used his position within the Scottish Church to strengthen the bonds between Scottish and English Presbyterians. His friendship with a number of English dissenters, most notably Edmund Calamy, dated back to his time in exile in the Netherlands.[128] Encouraged by the new possibilities opened up by the impending Union of 1707, both Edinburgh and Glasgow began courting the English dissenters.[129] Carstares presented his plans in 1709, in his famous 'Considerations and proposals for Encouraging of parents in sending their sons to the University of Edinburgh'. It was an elaborate plan to offer English parents and sons a viable alternative to the universities abroad and to the private dissenting academies in England.[130] It looked decidedly English: English tutors and assistants living with the students in a college offering board and lodging and a riding school for such 'manly exercises' as riding and fencing were to attract both Scots and English dissenters to Edinburgh, making the university 'one of the finest in Britain, even Europe'.[131] However, due to Carstares's untimely death in 1715, and the Jacobite Rebellion that same year, the project never got off the ground.

Carstares and the Netherlands

So to what extent were Carstares's reforms Dutch originated? In answering this question it is important to understand the different elements involved. First of all, there was a Dutch-continental influence, through the introduction and adoption of ideas and textbooks which often reached Scotland via the Netherlands but which were not all necessarily Dutch. It was some of these elements against which the Visitation Commission agitated. Secondly, there was the adoption of specifically Dutch teaching methods, for which Carstares was largely responsible during his years as principal. Thirdly, there was the model of Leiden University as an example of a successful civic university.

Although he never got his Dutch professors, Carstares did employ many Dutch-educated Scots to fill his new chairs. As the Chairs in Civil and Public Law and Medicine became established, the Faculty of Philosophy finally gained independence from Divinity, as it had in Leiden in 1657 when the States of the Province of Holland adopted an edict confirming the separation of philosophy and theology.[132] The classical and the oriental languages remained the basis for the arts curriculum, but for different reasons. Hebrew, although considered important to all arts students from a philological viewpoint, was no longer deemed crucial. The chair of Greek at last became fixed and was remodelled after the Dutch Chairs of Greek Language, History, and Eloquence.[133] The Professor of Humanity also came to teach a course in Roman history and oratory, like his Dutch counterparts Graevius, Gronovius, and Perizonius. In the now radically shortened philosophy courses, the scholastic works continued to be supplanted by Dutch textbooks, a development which the Visitation Commission had been unable to stop. In 1708 Morthland gave the following, indicative, list of 'Dutch' textbooks: '*De Vries* or *Le Clerk's Metaphysick*', '*Puffendrof* [sic] *de Officio hominis & Civis*, or *Grotius de jure belli ac pacis*', and 'Le Clerk's *Physicks*'.[134] Compared to the discussion of the philosophy curriculum in the 1690s, this was a transformation indeed.

The new Chairs in Medicine and Law were essentially established by the professions, yet Carstares should be credited with much of the groundwork. He enthusiastically lent them his support, using his influence first at court, and later with the secretaries of State: Roxburgh, Mar, and Montrose, as well as with the Town Council. The Chairs of Botany, Anatomy, Chemistry and Physic and Civil and Public Law were filled with 'Dutch' Scots and supplied with Dutch textbooks like the ones Morthland noted. Many more were imported directly from the Netherlands.[135] Boerhaave's teaching methods and students were in high demand in Edinburgh. Both the Professor for Civil Law, Alexander Cunningham of Block, and the Professor for Public Law, Law of Nature and Nations, Charles Erskine, were sent to the United Provinces to study after their appointments. Although Cunningham never taught and it is unclear whether Erskine did, their Dutch education was certainly considered an essential part of Edinburgh's reform.[136] A preparatory course in Greek and Roman antiquities was coupled with the Chair of Civil Law, after the example of Leiden where the Professors Gronovius and Perizonius had been teaching a similar course for Dutch law students since 1692.[137] From 1719 onwards, this course was taught by the newly appointed Professor of Universal Civil History, Charles Mackie, also a 'Dutch' Scot, and a relative of Carstares, who followed his Dutch teachers Gronovius, Perizonius, and especially Pieter Burman senior closely.[138]

It is an irony that the height of the Dutch influence came after Carstares's death, in the 1720s. The Faculty of Law and the Medical School were established on Dutch models; clinical teaching was introduced following the Leiden pattern. When Mackie became Professor of Universal Civil History, another subject was taught in the Dutch way. The rest of the Scottish universities followed the example of Edinburgh and were reformed along similar lines. In 1741, the *Scots Magazine* published a 'Short Account of the University of Edinburgh', according to which the professors of moral philosophy, logic, and Hebrew as well as the law professors all still taught from Dutch textbooks.[139]

The University of Leiden was the example after which the University of Edinburgh was modelled. Leiden, much more so than Utrecht or any of the other Dutch universities, was the institution where the Dutch burgers and regents traditionally received an education specifically tailored towards their future role as the country's political elite. Its part was that of a civic university, designed to train magistrates and ministers. This was translated and adapted by Carstares for the Scottish situation when he shaped Edinburgh for the same function. Scotland's future politicians, professionals, and ministers needed a polite and progressive education at home, to fit with their future role in society. Carstares seems to have been particularly concerned with Leiden's mechanics and constitution, as were his like-minded friends John Stirling and Edmund Calamy.[140] The idea of a four year 'undergraduate' course, which offered a well-rounded degree but at the same time prepared students for further study in one of the three higher Faculties of Divinity, Medicine, or Law was an idea imported from the Continent, but Edinburgh's transformation from a Presbyterian seminary into a civic university was based on the example of Leiden. So too was the solution to the problem of an independent Philosophy Faculty, with which the universities had struggled in the 1690s. This was solved by changing its purpose and shortening its duration, making it more secular, professionally oriented, and, indeed, civic in outlook. Moreover, the absence of any reform of the Divinity Faculty and its curriculum suggests a 'division of labour' similar to the one which seems to have developed between the progressive University of Leiden and the orthodox University of Utrecht in the late seventeenth century, and which Carstares had seen for himself in the 1680s.

Carstares's university reform was as much the continuation of old Scottish concerns, dating back to the seventeenth century, as a break with Scotland's and his own, Covenanting past. In the 1690s several forces had involved themselves with university reform: the conservative, even reactionary, *Commission for Visiting Universities Colledges & Schools*, run by the new Presbyterian establishment, Carstares, the professions, and the universities themselves.[141] Despite a Presbyterian backlash, a number of precedents had been created in the 1680s and 1690s - the Edinburgh *Memorandum* and the Glasgow proposals - from which Carstares benefited when the time came to reform his university. Moreover, modern continental ideas continued to be imported into Scotland. The Dutch example, as experienced by Carstares personally, provided the model for the 1708 reform. He shared with the members of the Visitation Commission profound concerns with Scotland and her Church, but unlike them he chose toleration and moderation over orthodoxy to bolster the established Church. Reform and renewal of the Scottish universities, along Dutch lines, gave Scots the option of a polite and progressive education at home which would keep the students and their money in the country, and their religion moderate. This ideal was shared by the professions and the gentry. Carstares's reforms continued in the work of others. Much as it owed the Dutch, Carstares's university reform was ultimately the continuation of old Scottish concerns, dating back to the Reformation. If his reforms were essential for the Enlightenment in Scotland, then the Scottish Enlightenment too owed something to these reforms.

Department of History
University of Reading
School of Humanities
Whiteknights
Reading RG6 6AA
United Kingdom

REFERENCES

1. The author wishes to thank the anonymous reader for their helpful comments.
2. The *St Andrews History of the Universities Project* has been ongoing since 2002. It is a major research initiative focused on the history of the Scottish Universities in their local, national, and international contexts. See S. J. Reid, 'Education in post-Reformation Scotland: Andrew Melville and the University of St Andrews' (Ph.D. thesis, St Andrews, 2008) (Not available for consultation until 2011). Cf. Roger L. Emerson, *Academic Patronage in the Scottish Enlightenment. Glasgow, Edinburgh and St Andrews Universities* (Edinburgh, 2008).
3. For a discussion of previous attempted reforms in the years 1639–43, see C. M. King, 'Philosophy and Science in the Arts Curriculum in the Seventeenth Century' (Ph.D. thesis, Edinburgh, 1974), 34–41.
4. John W. Cairns, 'The Origins of the Edinburgh Law School: the Union of 1707 and the Regius Chair', *Edinburgh Law Review*, 11 (2007), 300–48; Emerson, *Academic Patronage*, esp. ch. viii; King, 'Philosophy and Science'; M. A. Stewart, 'The Origins of the Scottish Greek Chairs', in E. M. Craik (ed.), *'Owls to Athens'. Essays on Classical Subjects Presented to Sir Kenneth Dover* (Oxford, 1990), 391–400.
5. Joseph McCormick, *State-Papers and Letters Addressed to William Carstares* (Edinburgh, 1774). McCormick was related to Carstares and apparently had met him when he was young. With thanks to Roger Emerson.
6. See for instance Grant G. Simpson (ed.), *Scotland and the Low Countries 1124–1994* (East Linton, 1996).
7. Ginny Gardner, *The Scottish Exile Community in the Netherlands, 1660–1690* (East Linton, 2004), apps 1–3, 213–32. Cf. Douglas Catterall, *Community Without Borders. Scots Migrants and the Changing Face of Power in the Dutch Republic, c. 1600–1700* (Leiden, 2002); Esther Mijers, 'Scottish Students in the Netherlands, 1680–1730', in Alexia Grosjean and Steve Murdoch (eds), *Scottish Communities Abroad* (Leiden, 2005), 301–31.
8. Notker Hammerstein, 'Relations with Authorities', in Hilde de Ridder-Symoens (ed.), *Universities in Early Modern Europe (A History of the University in Europe, Vol. II*, Cambridge, 1996), 114–54, 139; James Kirk, '"Melvillian" Reform in the Scottish Universities', in *The Renaissance in Scotland: Studies in Literature, Religion, History and Culture offered to John Durkan*, ed. A. A. MacDonald, Michael Lynch, and Ian B. Cowan (Leiden, 1994), 276–300; John Durkan and James Kirk, *The University of Glasgow, 1451–1577* (Glasgow, 1977), 262–346. Cf. Reid, 'Education in post-Reformation Scotland'.
9. Hammerstein, 'Relations with Authorities', 138.
10. For a description of teaching methods in the seventeenth century see King, 'Philosophy and Science', ch. ii.

11. The first visitation, to the University of St Andrews, took place in 1597. *Evidence, Oral and Documentary, Taken and Received by the Commissioners Appointed by his Majesty George IV. July 23, 1826; and Reappointed by His Majesty William IV. October 12th, 1830; for Visiting the Universities of Scotland*, iii: *University of St Andrews* (London, 1837), 187.
12. See for instance Hugh Trevor-Roper, 'The Scottish Enlightenment', *Studies on Voltaire and the Eighteenth Century*, 58 (1967), 1635–58. For the Presbyterian viewpoint, see the discussion below of the Visitation Papers of the 1690s.
13. Ronald G. Cant, 'Origins of the Enlightenment in Scotland: The Universities', in: R. H. Campbell and Andrew S. Skinner (eds), *The Origins of the Scottish Enlightenment* (Edinburgh, 1982) 42–64, 43.
14. Christine M. Shepherd, 'Newtonianism in Scottish Universities in the Seventeenth Century', in Alexander Campbell and R. H. Skinner (eds), *Origins and Nature of the Scottish Enlightenment* (Edinburgh, 1982), 65–86, 66–7.
15. Cant, 'Origins of the Enlightenment in Scotland', 45.
16. In the seventeenth century, the only university to offer law was King's College, Aberdeen.
17. EUL, La.II.89/147, 'Sir John Nisbits Advyse to the Earle of Perth'. Nisbit's list of mainly Dutch law books was to illustrate the importance of civil and canon law as the basis of the laws of all nations.
18. King, 'Philosophy and Science', 18–20. *Munimenta Alme Universitatis Glasguensis. Records of the University of Glasgow from its Foundation till 1727* (3 vols, Glasgow, 1854), ii. 492. NAS, Visitation Papers Glasgow, PA10/5/48. *Evidence Oral and Documentary*, ii: *University of Glasgow*, 269.
19. Hugh Ouston, 'York in Edinburgh: James VII and the Patronage of Learning in Scotland, 1679–1688', in John Dwyer, R. A. Mason, and Alexander Murdoch (eds), *New Perspectives on the Politics and Culture of Early Modern Scotland* (Edinburgh, 1982) 33–155, 133.
20. Nicolas Phillipson, 'Commerce and Culture: Edinburgh, Edinburgh University, and the Scottish Enlightenment', in T. Bender (ed.), *The University and the City. From Medieval Origins to the Present* (Oxford, 1988), 100–16, 102.
21. Roger L. Emerson, 'Scottish Universities in the Eighteenth Century, 1690–1800', *Studies on Voltaire and the Eighteenth Century*, 167 (1977), 453–74, 465–7.
22. 'Act for Visitation of Universities, Colleges and Schools', *Evidence, Oral and Documentary*, i: *University of Edinburgh*, 36–7.
23. 'Act for Visitation', i. 36.
24. The visitation of 1690–5 can be compared to that of 1642. NAS, PA10, Visitation Papers. King, 'Philosophy and Science', 41–2.
25. For example one 'List of Edinburgh Members on the Commission for Visiting Universities Colledges & Schools', dated 1699, gives sixty-two

names and identifies twenty-nine additional members who joined in 1697. NAS, PA10/2, Visitation Papers.

26. *Munimenta Alme Universitatis Glasguensis*, ii. 495–6.
27. Many exiles had also been deeply concerned about Dutch observation of the Sabbath. See for instance: *Journal of the Hon. John Erskine of Carnock 1683–1687*, ed. Walter Macleod (Edinburgh, 1893), 167.
28. The first edition of Grotius' work printed in the British Isles dated from 1650. Hugo Grotius, *De Veritate Religionis Christianæ. Editio decima additis annotationibus* (Oxford, 1650) (and other editions). NAS, PA10/3, Visitation Papers Aberdeen.
29. NAS, GD26/7/224, 'Instructions By the Commissioners Appointed for Visiting of Universities Colledges & Schools'.
30. For the story of Gregory's 'trial', see EUL, Gregory Papers, Dk1.2 and R. K. Hannay, 'The Visitation of the College of Edinburgh in 1690', in *The Book of the Old Edinburgh Club* (Edinburgh, 1916), 79–100. Pitcairne left Edinburgh and was appointed Professor of Medicine at the University of Leiden in 1692. He left a year later without notifying the Senate or officially resigning: P. C. Molhuysen (ed.), *Bronnen tot de Geschiedenis der Leidsche Universiteit*, iv: *18 februari 1682–8 februari 1725* (The Hague, 1920), 'Resoluties der Curatoren' (1692). His nomination at Leiden is somewhat of a mystery given the fact that he was a known Episcopalian and Jacobite, and William of Orange was personally involved with the appointments at Leiden. His friendship with William Carstares may have had something to do with this, although there is no evidence for this.
31. NAS, PA10/6, Visitation Papers St Andrews.
32. The Aberdeen Colleges Marischal and King's were the only universities where no one was removed. For their story, see Roger L. Emerson, *Professors, Patronage and Politics. The Aberdeen Universities in the Eighteenth Century* (Aberdeen, 1992), 10.
33. Hannay, 'The Visitation of the College of Edinburgh' and Emerson, *Academic Patronage*, 213–24.
34. It should be noted that the regent Alexander Cunningham was not the same as the tutor and book collector, Alexander Cunningham of Block.
35. The term 'Popish' was a trope which did not necessarily refer to Catholicism.
36. *Munimenta Alme Universitatis Glasguensis*, ii. 513.
37. Pierre Nicole, *Logica, Sive Ars Cogitandi, In Qua Praeter Vulgares Regulas Plura Nova Habentur ad Rationem Dirigendam Utilia. E Tertia Gallos Editione Recognita & Aucta in Latinum Versa* (London, 1677) (and other editions). This four part text contained a 'Treats [Treatise] of the Most Profitable Method for Demonstrating or Illustrating Any Truth'.
38. Derodon must have been the French author David Derodon (*c.*1600–64), the author of *Tombeau de la Messe*. Neither the ESTC nor the STCN list any philosophical works by him. David Derodon, *The Funeral of the Mass: Or, the Mass Dead and Buried, Without Hope of Resurrection. Translated out of French* (London, 1673) (and other editions).

39. Franco Burgersdijk, *Institutionum Logicarum, Sive Rudimenta Logica* (Leiden, 1632) 8° (and other editions).
40. Henry More, *Opera Philosophica, Tum Quae Latine, Tum Quae Anglice Primitus Scripta Sunt* (London, 1679).
41. Gaven may have been Antonio Gavin (d. 1726) an Italian author who published several texts on Catholic church orders.
42. Gerard de Vries, *De Natura Dei et Humanae Mentis Determinationes Pneumatologicae* (Utrecht, 1690) 8° (and other editions). This included his 'ontology'.
43. NAS, PA10/2, Visitation Papers. Reprinted in *Munimenta Alme Universitatis Glasguensis*, ii. 530–2, and *Evidence, Oral and Documentary*, i. 41–2.
44. Marcus Friedrich Wendelin, *Christianae Theologiae Libri duo* (Amsterdam, 1646) (1st Dutch edition and other editions).
45. Jean Calvin, *The Institution of Christian Religion, VVrytten in Latine by Maister Ihon Caluin, and Translated into Englysh According to the Authors Last Edition. Seen and Allowed According to the Order Appointed in the Quenes Maiesties Iniunctions* (London, 1561) (1st English edition and other editions).
46. Franciscus Turrettinus, *Institutio Theologiae Elencticae* (Leiden and Utrecht, 1696) (1st Dutch edition and other editions).
47. NAS, PA10/5/41, Visitation Papers Glasgow.
48. Emerson, 'Scottish Universities', 461, 464.
49. *Evidence, Oral and Documentary*, i. 38.
50. The Visitation Papers of Marischal College Aberdeen and especially of Glasgow show a similar internal tension.
51. King, 'Science and Philosophy', 54.
52. Glasgow meant the Dutch universities. A link between Glasgow and The Netherlands, especially the University of Utrecht, was established in the second half of the 1690s when Anne, Duchess of Hamilton created a bursary for theology students to study in the Netherlands.
53. NAS, PA10/5/41, Visitation Papers Glasgow.
54. NAS, PA10/6, Visitation Papers St Andrews.
55. Stewart, 'The Origins of the Scottish Greek Chairs', 391–6.
56. Although not so much Cartesianism as the new philosophy itself. Cf. King, 'Science and Philosophy'.
57. NAS, PA10/2, 'Remarcks on the Several Parts of Philosophy Compiled by the Universities, Made by the Principals Meet to Gather for That Effort by Order of the Commission of Parliament in the Months of May & June 1700'.
58. Emerson, *Scottish Universities*, 463.
59. NAS, Visitation Papers St. Andrews, PA10/6, 'Rentalls of St Salvator's Colledge in St Andrews'.
60. Glasgow after all obtained a chair in civil and ecclesiastical history in the same year the Overtures were composed.
61. King, 'Science and Philosophy', 45.

62. *Evidence, Oral and Documentary. I*, 45–6. Cf. Stewart, 'Origins of the Scottish Greek Chairs', 392–3.
63. King, 'Science and Philosophy', 54.
64. *Coltness Collections 1608–1840* [ed. James Dennistoun], (Edinburgh, 1842), 77–8.
65. Robert Herbert Story, *William Carstares. A Character and Career of the Revolutionary Epoch (1649–1715)* (London, 1874), 14.
66. Gardner, *The Scottish Exile Community in the Netherlands, 1660–1690*, 25.
67. *Album Studiosorum Academiae rheno-Trajectina, MDCXXXVI - MDCCCLXXXVI* (Utrecht, 1886).
68. E. Mijers, ' "For the Cause of Religion and [Academic] Liberty": Connected Political and Academic Networks in Late Seventeenth Century Utrecht', *Dutch Crossing*, 29/1 (2005), Special Issue: *Williamite Scotland*, 69–78.
69. Story, *William Carstares*, 25. Story has confused Carstares' first stay in The Netherlands with his second stay in the 1680s.
70. He matriculated on 21 October 1686, not to study but most likely for political reasons. *Album Scholasticum Academiae Lugduno-Batavae, MDLXXV-MCMXL* (Leiden, 1941).
71. K. van Berkel, 'Descartes in Debat met Voetius. De Mislukte Introductie van het Cartesianisme aan de Utrechtse Universiteit (1639–1645)', *Tijdschrift voor de Geneeskunde, Natuurkunde Wiskunde en Techniek*, 7 (1984), 4–18. For the importance of Voetius to the Scots at Utrecht, see Mijers, ' "For the Cause of Religion and [Academic] Liberty".
72. 'Catalogus Librorum Gul. Carstares. April 9. Londini 1685', in *Selections from the Family Papers preserved at Caldwell* (3 vols, Glasgow, 1854), i. 166–8.
73. E. Mijers, 'Scotland and the United Provinces: A Study in Educational and Intellectual Relations, 1680–1730' (Ph.D. Thesis, St. Andrew, 2002), ch. III.
74. McCormick, 'The life of Mr. William Carstares', in *State-Papers and Letters addressed to William Carstares*, 1–91. Cf. Gilbert Burnet, *History of His Own Time: From the Restoration of King Charles the Second to the Treaty of Peace at Utrecht, in the Reign of Queen Anne* (London, 1883), 379.
75. Trigland wrote to Carstares at least twice, once in 1698 and once in 1704. EUL Dk 1.1/12, Dk 1.1/37. According to McCormick, De Vries was one of the Dutch academics whom Carstares tried to persuade to move to Edinburgh. Incidentally, De Vries was also on good terms with Wodrow and wrote to him frequently. NLS, Wodr. Lett. Qu. I.
76. Boerhaave was almost certainly taught by Carstares's good friend Archibald Pitcairne during his brief professorship at Leiden; Boerhaave's father Jacobus and Trigland were close friends.
77. *Coltness Collections*, 77–8.
78. McCormick, 'Life of Mr. William Carstares', 43.
79. *Correspondentie van Willem III en van Hans Willem Bentinck, Eersten Graaf van Portland*, ed. N Japikse ('s- Gravenhage, 1937). *Calendar of*

State Papers. Domestic Series of the Reign of James II, iii: *June 1687-February 1689* (London, 1972), 34–7, 40–5, 68–9, 388–9, 757–61; CSP. Cf. Gardner, *The Scottish Exile Community in the Netherlands, 1660–1690*, ch. vi.

80. David Onnekink, *The Anglo-Dutch Favourite. The Career of Hans Willem Bentinck, 1st Earl of Portland (1649–1709)* (Aldershot, 2007), 121.
81. Onnekink, *The Anglo-Dutch Favourite*, 139–40.
82. McCormick, 'The life of Mr. William Carstares', 43.
83. A. Ian Dunlop, *William Carstares and the Church by Law Established* (Edinburgh, 1967), 77–8.
84. Gardner, *The Scottish Exile Community in the Netherlands, 1660–1690*, 42–3.
85. Carstares's motivation thus differed strongly from that of Andrew Fletcher of Saltoun, alleged author of a pamphlet on the need for university reform, entitled *Proposals for the Reformation of Schools & Universities. In Order for the Better Education of Youth. Humbly Offer'd to the Serious Consideration of the High Court of Parliament* (1704).
86. Dunlop, *William Carstares*, 28.
87. Story, *William Carstares*, 213.
88. 'Hints to the King', quoted in McCormick, *State-Papers and Letters*, 39–40.
89. *Correspondentie Willem-Portland*, 88: Portland to William, The Hague, 4 Feb 1690; 96: Willem aan Portland, Kensington, 17 Feb 1690. With thanks to David Onnekink.
90. Letter to Dunlop, quoted in Story, *William Carstares*, 211. Carstares would have been an obvious candidate for membership of the Visitation Commission. However, he spent the whole of the 1690s at court, in London and in the Netherlands.
91. Edmund Calamy, *An Historical Account of My Own Life, with Some Reflections on the Times I have lived in (1671–1731)*, ed. John Towill Rutt, vol. i (London, 1830, 2nd ed.), 172.
92. Quoted in Story, *William Carstares*, 213.
93. *Ibid.*, 215.
94. Peter John Anderson (ed.), *Fasti Academiae Mariscallanae Aberdonensis* (3 vols, Aberdeen, 1889), i. 346–7.
95. *Ibid.*, 346.
96. *Ibid.*, 347. It seems that Glasgow was the only university to have put this scheme into action. NLS, Wodrow Lett. Q. I. In 1694 this university was granted a bursary by Anne, Duchess of Hamilton 'for the maintenance of three students of theology [...] to study two years at Glasgow [...] and one year more at one or more Protestant Universities abroad'. 'Mortification by Anna Duchess of Hamilton', *Munimenta Alme Universitatis Glasguensis*, i. 431.
97. According to D. B. Horn, this was in effect a sinecure. EUL, Horn Mss, Ms Gen. 1824.

98. Dunlop, *William Carstares*, 105. Carstares may have known his father, Patrick Cumming, as a fellow exile in The Netherlands.

99. It should be noted that in the grants dated 1695 and 1699, the stipulations on sending students and appointing professors from abroad were eliminated. See Anderson, *Fasti Academiae Mariscallanae*, 347.

100. Cairns, 'The Origins of the Edinburgh Law School', 308, 314.

101. *Evidence, Oral and Documentary*, i. 38. Cf. EUL, Dc.1.4, Papers Illustrative of the History of the University of Edinburgh.

102. 'Laws and Regulations enacted by the Faculty and Senatus', in: *Charters, Statutes and Acts of the Town Council and the Senatus 1583–1858*, ed. Alexander Morgan (Edinburgh, 1937), 222; Town Council Minutes, 19 August 1702. According to the 'Laws and Regulations', these regulations were introduced in 1699. This may have been an important motivation for theology students to go to The Netherlands. Cf. EUL, Wodrow Lett. Q. I.

103. 'Acts of the Town Council anent the College and University, 15 February 1703, 22 October 1703', *Charters, Statutes and Acts of the Town Council*, 138–56.

104. 'Acts of the Town Council anent the College and University, 15 February 1703, 22 October 1703', in *Ibid.*, 138, 150. For the 'Forme and Ordour', see 110–16.

105. *Ibid.*, 21 June 1704; 5 September 1704, 156, 157–61.

106. i.e. in the Netherlands, where the philosophy curriculum took 2.5 years. Carstares was very well informed about the structures and constitutions of the Dutch universities. *Ibid.*, 16 June 1708, 164–6.

107. They were: William Scott for Greek, Colin Drummond for logic William Law for moral philosophy, and Robert Stewart, the nephew of the Lord Advocate Sir James Stewart for natural philosophy.

108. EUL, Ms Gen. 1824.

109. Stewart, 'Origins of the Scottish Greek Chairs', 395.

110. Charles Morthland, *An Account of the Government of the Church of Scotland* (London, 1708), 22.

111. D. B. Horn has suggested that right before his death, Carstares tried to obtain a royal endowment for a Chair in Civil History, to complement the one in Ecclesiastical History. This project failed due to Carstares's untimely death. EUL, Ms Gen. 1824, Dk.1.1/2. Already in 1693, Carstares had appointed his brother-in-law William Dunlop as Historiographer Royal. Carstares's interest in history may date back to his time in The Netherlands.

112. Morthland, *An Account of the Government of the Church of Scotland*, 22–24. Cf. Cairns 'The Origins of the Edinburgh Law School: the Union of 1707'.

113. Cairns, 'The Origins of the Edinburgh Law School', 314. Cf. John W. Cairns, 'Alexander Cunningham's Proposed Edition of the Digest: An Episode in the History of the Dutch Elegant School of Roman Law', *Tijdschrift voor Rechtsgeschiedenis* 69 (2001), 81–117, 307–59.

114. 'Acts of the Town Council anent the College and University', 29 August 1705', in *Charters, Statutes and Acts of the Town Council*, 162–4.

115. Ms Gen. 1824, Town Council Minutes, 10 February 1692.

116. George Chalmers, *The Life of Thomas Ruddiman* (Edinburgh, 1794), 30.

117. E. Ashworth Underwood, *Boerhaave's Men at Leyden and After* (Edinburgh, 1977), 90–1, 94–5, 97, 104.

118. 'Acts of the Town Council anent the College and University', 29 August 1705, in *Charters, Statutes and Acts of the Town Council*, 162–4. Moreover, it would protect the monopoly of the Edinburgh Surgeons.

119. The subject was already taught. In 1676 a man called Sutherland had been made intendant and in 1695 had been given status in the college. With thanks to Roger Emerson.

120. Both the Visitation Papers, NAS, PA10, and the Stirling Papers, GUL, Ms Gen. 204–7, show rivalry between Edinburgh and Glasgow. GUL, Stirling Papers, Ms Gen 204/135, William Carstares to John Stirling.

121. D. B. Horn has suggested that this unlikely combination might have been a way to 'weaken the connection between the chair of Hebrew and the faculty of Divinity, and give effect to recommendations that Arts students should be taught Hebrew'. EUL, Ms Gen. 1824. However, before 1709, Robert Sinclair at Glasgow combined his Chair in Mathematics with the teaching of Hebrew and the oriental languages, until Charles Morthland was appointed. EUL, La.II.577/3,12, Robert Pringle to William Carstares.

122. EUL, La.II. 676.

123. Edinburgh was already an important centre of medical learning. See Helen M. Dingwall, *Physicians, Surgeons and Apothecaries: Medicine in Seventeenth-Century Edinburgh* (East Linton, 1995). Cf. Roger L. Emerson, 'The Founding of the Edinburgh Medical School: the Real Story', *Journal of the History of Medicine and Allied Sciences*, 59 (2004), 183–218.

124. GUL, Ms Gen 204/58, Sir J.Stewart to John Stirling, Ms Gen 204/63, William Carstares to John Stirling. For Stirling's irritation with Carstares's 'meddling', see for instance Ms Gen 206/113.

125. Morthland was awarded the chair although he had not finished his studies yet. He apparently had studied Hebrew at Utrecht, with Reland. He did not matriculate. EUL, La.II. 577/3, 12. Cf. EUL, La.II. 407/13. GUL, Ms Gen 204/58, Lord Pollock to John Stirling, Ms Gen 205/67, the Earl of Sunderland to John Stirling, Ms Gen 206/64, 71, Charles Morthland to John Stirling. Carstares seems to have been irritated by this appointment. Ms Gen 204/100, William Carstares to John Stirling.

126. GUL, Ms Gen 204/130, 132, William Carstares to John Stirling. Cf. Robert Wodrow, *Analecta, or Materials for a History of Remarkable Providences Mostly Relating to Scotch Ministers and Christians* (4 vols, Edinburgh, 1842–3), 370–1. 'This seems not to be soe much desired at that University; and the Queen's presentments, except to the Principale, have ever been in use here; and it's thought it may be of ill consequence, he being Extraordinary Preofessour of Divinity, the Court may very soon send doun persons

to that post, who may be of very ill influence on this Church'. Alexander Dunlop's brother, William, became Regius Professor of Ecclesiastical History at Edinburgh in 1720.

127. EUL, La.II. 577/17, James Hadow to William Carstares. Hadow had been a fellow exile in The Netherlands. Cf. App. II. Cf. Emerson, *Academic Patronage*, 408–11.

128. Calamy, *An Historical Account of My Own Life*, 172.

129. GUL, Ms Gen 206/34, I. Bates to James Wodrow, Ms Gen 206/82, D. Williams to Stirling, Dk 1.1/50, Chr. Taylor to Carstares.

130. EUL, La.II. 407/6. Cf. EUL, Dk 1.1/50, Chr. Taylor to William Carstares.

131. EUL, Dk1.1/50, Idem.

132. J. I. Israel, *The Dutch Republic. Its Rise, Greatness and Fall 1477–1806* (Oxford, 1995), 894.

133. Graecae Linguae, Historiarum et Eloquentiae Professor. Alexander Bower, *The History of the University of Edinburgh: Chiefly Compiled from Original Papers and Records, Never Before Published* (Edinburgh, 1817–30), 85. According to Bower, a divinity student from the University of Franeker, presumably a Scot, was appointed as assistant to the Professor of Greek in 1713. *Ibid.*, 25.

134. Morthland, *An Account of the Government of the Church of Scotland*, 22.

135. Esther Mijers, 'The Scottish-Dutch Trade in Academic Books in the Early Eighteenth Century' and 'Thomas Johnson and Charles Mackie' in: Stephen Brown & Warren McDougall (eds), *The Edinburgh History of the Book in Scotland, Volume II: Enlightenment and Expansion 1707–1800* (Edinburgh, forthcoming 2011).

136. Cairns 'The Origins of the Edinburgh Law School'.

137. John Spottiswood, *A Discourse Shewing the Necessary Qualifications of a Student of the Laws: And what is Propos'd in the College of Law, History and Philology, Establish'd at Edinburgh* (Edinburgh, 1704).

138. Mijers, 'Scotland and the United Provinces', ch. VI.

139. 'A Short Account of the University of Edinburgh, the Present Professors in it, and the Several Parts of Learning Taught by Them', *The Scots Magazine* (1741), 371–4.

140. GUL, Ms Gen 204/142,143, W. Forbes to John Stirling.

141. The Town Council, despite its official position, was notably absent in all this.

'A Manly and Generous Discipline'?: Classical Studies and Generational Conflict in Eighteenth and Early Nineteenth Century Oxford

*Heather Ellis**

There have been many studies dealing with the issue of institutional and examination reform at Oxford; it is a subject touched upon in histories of the university, of the individual colleges, and of English higher education in general.[1] While much time has been spent tracing the specific nature of the changes introduced, less interest has been shown in attempting to explain why the reform process developed as it did. Despite the pioneering work of Sheldon Rothblatt over thirty years ago, many scholars continue to view such reforms as a largely predictable side-effect of nineteenth-century modernization; in this view, meritocracy and competitive examination will inevitably supersede 'arcane' forms of academic disputation and 'modern' subjects such as mathematics, science, and modern languages will replace the traditional curriculum of classical studies and divinity.[2]

This whiggish discourse of reform which historical sociologist Keith Hoskin has termed the 'predictable advance' model[3] has, for a number of years, been routinely challenged in studies which focus upon reforms primarily affecting the working classes, including franchise reform, factory reform, and legislation to improve housing and sanitation; other, less altruistic motives have been sought to explain policies which were hailed at the time (and have since been hailed) as forward-thinking, modern and progressive.[4] Moving beyond reductive notions of social control, historians have shown that governments attempted to use reformist policies as a means of negotiating with newly empowered classes, to retain influence in a changing political world.[5]

The history of the reform of elite institutions such as Oxford and Cambridge has proved much more resistant to this type of analysis as historians have perceived no social or political threat to come from the ranks of the middle class and aristocracy. There have, however, been a few significant exceptions to this trend; as long ago as 1974, Sheldon Rothblatt argued that the decision to introduce competitive examinations at Oxford in 1800 should be considered against the background of the French Revolution and the fears of senior members that undergraduates might be adversely influenced by revolutionary ideas from France.[6]

However, there have been few attempts to apply Rothblatt's analysis to other aspects of university reform. This article aims to extend his scepticism about the ability of pure reformist motives to explain developments in English higher education to an area little touched on in his own analysis, the curriculum. A study of Oxford's curriculum policy in the so-called 'Age of Revolution' is particularly interesting as the hallmark of the university's attitude in the first half of the nineteenth century (usually hailed as the most intensive period of internal reform) was a steadfast determination to preserve the traditional syllabus of classical studies and divinity. The main reason scholars have been reluctant to explore this phenomenon is clear – historical treatments of Oxford are still dominated by the assumption that the university was an inward-looking, fundamentally conservative institution whose natural desire was to maintain the status quo.[7]

This article, however, will suggest that the favouring of classical studies was an actively chosen and carefully thought-out policy, just as deliberate as Rothblatt has argued the introduction of competitive examination to have been. Although classical studies (together with divinity) formed the traditional syllabus at Oxford, it was not the university's only option; as will be seen, Cambridge, when faced with similar challenges, chose a very different policy, preferring to modernize its largely classical curriculum as early as the first quarter of the eighteenth century. In 1800, the framers of the New Examination Statute at Oxford saw compelling reasons for an almost exclusive focus not merely on classical studies as a whole, but on particular tasks and texts, which, they believed, would help undergraduates to imbibe correct moral and political ideas and to resist the unsavoury principles of revolutionaries and religious radicals.

Some years ago now, Rothblatt complained that we would probably never know precisely what motivated the heads of houses to propose the New Examination Statute of 1800, which not only introduced competitive examination but also prescribed the first uniform syllabus in classics and divinity. This was due to the frustrating fact that the minutes of the meetings of the Hebdomadal Board are almost completely lost for the crucial years immediately preceding the Statute's passage and there are almost no documents relating clearly to the motivations behind its introduction.[8] Almost as an aside, Rothblatt mentioned that 'details of the examinations themselves are plentiful'.[9] Although he spent time looking at the Statute's structural and disciplinary provisions, he did not analyse the curriculum which it prescribed for clues about the aims it was designed to achieve. If the clear focus on a narrow curriculum of classical studies and divinity is placed in the political and ideological context of the university in the decades preceding and following the introduction of the Statute, much may be gleaned about what led the Hebdomadal Board and senior members more generally to press for the new examination system and syllabus.

In particular, it will be suggested that, against the background of the French Revolution, the Statute of 1800 was designed to transfer to a university level measures previously introduced at some of the leading colleges to gain greater control over an increasingly volatile undergraduate population earlier in the eighteenth century. Initially, moves had been taken to combat the increasingly violent participation of undergraduates in Jacobite rioting, while the 1760s and 1770s saw the threat posed by religious dissenters and political radicals take centre stage against the background of the American Revolution. Important evidence confirming this interpretation may also be found in the diverse commentaries on the Statute published in the years following its introduction. One of the most striking features of texts both supportive and critical of the Statute's provisions was the assumption that it was introduced to strengthen the control of senior members over the university's older[10] and increasingly independent-minded undergraduate body.

Rioting and rising ages: Oxford in the eighteenth century

As long ago as 1973, Dame Lucy Sutherland called for a revision of the overwhelmingly negative image of eighteenth-century Oxford presented in the historiography. She questioned the oft-made claims that 'its curriculum was antiquated and sterile, making no demands upon the ability or industry of those taking its degrees', that 'its professors made little or no contribution to learning', that in the colleges 'Fellows frittered away their time in worthless pursuits' while 'neglecting their students'.[11] Yet despite the efforts of Sutherland to counter this image, both in her James Bryce Memorial Lecture of 1973 and in the later volume of the *History of the University of Oxford* which she edited with Leslie G. Mitchell,[12] the picture of eighteenth-century Oxford as a sleepy backwater cut off from the social and political turmoil of the period has persisted in the secondary literature.[13]

However, the life of dons in the eighteenth-century university was far from the 'snug and content' image which historians like Graham Midgley have presented.[14] In particular, Oxford witnessed the development of new and unprecedented tensions between junior and senior members.[15] Increasingly, we see undergraduates pushing the boundaries of what was considered acceptable behaviour by their tutors. While this could involve private and relatively inconspicuous activities such as the smuggling of local girls, often prostitutes, into student rooms, increasingly, junior members were also taking to riotous and rebellious behaviour in public. In the first half of the century, the most extreme examples of this usually took the form of demonstrations in support of the Jacobite cause. As is well known, Oxford as a whole was notoriously Jacobite in this period, and it might be thought that senior members would have supported junior expressions of Jacobite sentiment; if such opinions were voiced in private, they were usually condoned, even endorsed, but if they were expressed in public, and particularly if associated with violent behaviour, senior members were forced to denounce them and take action, as such occurrences placed the whole university under suspicion of disloyalty. Already distrusted by the Protestant House of Hannover and their Whig ministers, the governors of the university, the Hebdomadal Board, could not afford for their reputation to be tarnished further.

Beginning with a number of particularly violent riots in the period immediately following the accession of George I in 1714, Oxford undergraduates were involved in intermittent Jacobite rioting throughout the first half of the eighteenth century. The worst outbreaks of unrest, however, came in the years immediately following the failed rebellion of Charles Edward Stuart in 1745 when the university authorities were forced to intervene and take serious measures to punish those involved. On 23 February 1748, there was a serious brawl between undergraduates and townsmen and the proctors attempted to arrest the student ringleaders. The confident attitude and lack of respect for the university authorities is clear from the words of one of the most notorious participants, James Dawes, who physically assaulted a proctor trying to restrain him: 'I am the man that dare say God bless King James the 3d and tell you my Name is Dawes of St Mary Hall. I am a man of Independent Fortune and therefore am afraid of . . . no man'.[16]

Yet, it was not merely the fact that Oxford suffered from a reputation for Jacobitism which helps to explain the rising levels of tension between junior and senior members in the eighteenth century. There were a number of key social changes affecting both Oxford and Cambridge in this period which contributed significantly to the widening generational breach. The first of these was a significant increase in the overall student age. As Lawrence Stone has demonstrated, from the beginning of the eighteenth century until its close, the average age of undergraduates rose by almost two years, so that by the end of the century nearly all students reached twenty-one (and, crucially, the age of majority) before leaving university.[17] Combining to make students older was the fact that a much greater proportion was staying on to take degrees than had been the case in the previous century. The average period of residence was thus protracted, which meant that undergraduates also had more time to bond as a group and establish a sense of shared identity.[18] A third trend which exacerbated the impact of a rising student age and extended residence was that tutors themselves were, on average, becoming younger. As historians such as John Gascoigne have shown, colleges at both Oxford and Cambridge had substantially increased the number of Church of England livings in their gift over the course of the eighteenth century, which meant a much higher turnover of fellows and tutors.[19]

It should be reiterated that these changes affected Oxford and Cambridge similarly and cannot, therefore, on their own, explain the unprecedented levels of generational tension witnessed at Oxford in the course of the eighteenth century. For while Cambridge also experienced student rioting in this period,[20] in general, relations between undergraduates and the university authorities appear to have been significantly less strained; nor is it simply the relative absence of Jacobite sentiment among junior and senior members at Oxford's sister university which can account for this. Rather, it will be suggested here that Cambridge's senior members recognized the possible consequences of the rising student age and took important steps to adapt the university's institutions, examination system, and curriculum to accommodate these developments.

By 1747, the same year which saw some of the worst undergraduate rioting at Oxford, the authorities at Cambridge had introduced a system of competitive university examinations, complete with a uniform syllabus and, by 1753, an honours list.[21] These changes were justified at the time in terms of presenting the new, maturer undergraduate with an honourable system of emulation in which he could engage in manly competition with his peers. In a pamphlet of 1751, designed to promote the new examination system, the master of Corpus Christi College, John Green, pointed proudly to the fact that it encouraged 'an Ambition to excel' in undergraduates.[22] When proposing the institution of further (annual) public examinations in 1774, James Lambert, Regius Professor of Greek, looked back at the development of the BA examination and argued that Cambridge had recognized the challenge posed by the rising student age and devised a demanding, modern course, more appropriate for the new kind of student. 'We have long found', he wrote, 'that we cannot govern our Youth here *now*, as *Youth . . . were wont* to be governed. And we have so far accommodated to the times, as to relax of our boyish discipline' and 'to substitute more suitable discipline in its stead'. Taking the form of '*laws* more fitted for the man' than the boy, the university had 'endeavoured, by every *possible incentive* to study' to make students '*ambitious* of acquiring *every manly attainment* [original emphasis]'.[23]

At the same time, there was, at the university level, a remarkable shift away from the heavily classical syllabus required by the Elizabethan Statutes, which had been instituted at a time when the average student was of schoolboy age; hence the close similarities of the sixteenth and seventeenth-century syllabus to that of a typical grammar school. While Oxford, as we shall see, proved resistant to the unprecedented levels of criticism about the schoolboy nature of its curriculum which appeared in the first half of the eighteenth century, Cambridge soon came to specialize in mathematics and natural philosophy. This was in large part due to the presence of Isaac Newton, the Lucasian Professor of Mathematics, and to the active promotion of his philosophical principles by many of his latitudinarian and Whig colleagues at the university, above all, Richard Laughton,[24] Richard Bentley,[25] and William Whiston.[26] There grew up what scholars have termed a 'Holy Alliance' between Newtonian natural philosophy and Anglican apologetics at Cambridge in the first half of the eighteenth century, based on the belief that Newton's findings supported the so-called argument from design.[27] Within a decade or so, Newton's *Principia* came to dominate the undergraduate curriculum and formed a staple part of the examinations for Cambridge's newly instituted mathematical tripos, then known as the Senate House Examination. Many Cambridge dons gloried in the new curriculum and considered it a point in which their university far excelled Oxford. In particular, they stressed the extent to which a mathematical and scientific curriculum offered the older, more independent-minded student a more challenging and thought-provoking education, designed to occupy his time and secure his loyalty for the university authorities. 'In this part of Public Education', wrote William Bennet, a tutor at Emmanuel College in the 1770s and 1780s, referring to curriculum reform, 'I consider our University having by far the Superiority over Oxford'.[28] Another important factor which helped to ease generational tension at Cambridge was the much greater sympathy among senior members with many basic Enlightenment ideas such as natural rights and the Lockean social contract. Junior members at Cambridge found a considerable number of tutors who were openly sympathetic to the American, and even to the French, Revolution, causes which were popular with undergraduates at both ancient universities.[29]

The contrast with Oxford was indeed stark. Far from showing any willingness to adapt their curriculum to changing conditions, Oxford clung ever more tightly to its traditional classical syllabus. In response to the growing student involvement in Jacobite rioting, individual colleges began to take new measures to extend their control over how undergraduates spent their time. At the centre of this was a move, led by the largest and most influential college, Christ Church, to examine undergraduates far more rigorously in the texts they had been given to read in a particular term. These became known as college 'collections' and soon spread beyond Christ Church. By the end of the eighteenth century, a number of other colleges including Magdalen, Trinity, Balliol, and Hertford had instituted similar internal examinations.[30]

While these moves have received some attention in college (and occasionally university) histories, another significant and complementary policy has remained largely unnoticed. In addition to moves taken to assess students' work more rigorously, several colleges, once more led by Christ Church, urged a much more careful selection of which texts students were reading. It is not that early eighteenth-century undergraduates enjoyed a peculiar flexibility or were deliberately offered a degree of choice in the subjects they studied either at a college or a university level. Indeed, the Laudian Code of 1636 had laid down very minutely both the subjects of study and the exercises by which students' knowledge was to be tested. It was rather that by the early years of the eighteenth century, the Code's provisions for the course of study leading to the BA had, more or less, fallen into desuetude.[31] The system of university lectures which was intended to form the basis of both college study and the content of the examinations for the BA degree was extremely patchy in its provision, with many professors not lecturing at all.[32] Likewise, the quality of instruction provided at a college level, as well as the degree of relevance such instruction bore to the BA course specified in the Laudian Code, varied greatly from one society to another.[33] In such a situation, the range of texts read by undergraduates and upon which they were examined for the degree of BA was wide, particularly given the fact that candidates were allowed to choose which classical authors to read as well as which MAs were to examine them, subject only to the approval of a master of the schools which was almost never withheld.[34] The exercises themselves, although regularly held, were, for the most part, laxly administered, and seem in general to have aroused little interest on the part either of candidates or of their teachers.[35]

In the first half of the eighteenth century, the criticism that Oxford's curriculum was little more challenging than that offered at a typical grammar school attained increasing prominence.[36] While the relatively low standard of classical knowledge required at Oxford has usually been treated as evidence of the university's innate conservatism, it will be suggested here that it rather reflects the results of a deliberate policy on the part of senior members. For the beginning of the eighteenth century, the Christ Church collections books (which listed those texts set for examination in the college) reveal a wide range of classical texts.[37] After heavy student involvement in Jacobite rioting in the years following the accession of George I, there appeared a sudden and sharp decline in variety and choice. From 1717, we see the replacement of individual reading lists with standard lists, often containing the same classical texts, drawn up for whole year groups to read and be examined on. A striking feature of these reading lists is the degree to which many of the texts specified, such as the *Aeneid* and the *Iliad*, would already have been familiar from school reading. The same can be said for the way in which these texts were read by students. Individual reflection was actively discouraged by promoting what were literally schoolboy tasks: construing (or word-for-word translation), Latin verse composition, and general syntactical and grammatical exercises.

It was, however, to be the repeated threats of a Royal Visitation following the worst student rioting in the years around mid-century which caused this use of the classical curriculum to take on a new, positive dimension. Instead of trying simply to restrict student reading, the authorities made attempts to select certain texts for the moral and political lessons they were felt to teach. In particular, students were given the historians of Greece and Rome to read, above all Thucydides, Herodotus, and Xenophon, who became some of the most regularly selected authors in the Christ Church collections books in the second half of the eighteenth century. The thinking behind this is clearly demonstrated by Oriel fellow and tutor Edward Bentham in his 1748 *Letter to a Young Gentleman*. Addressing the archetypal rebellious student involved in the Jacobite riots, he declared

Methinks if you find in yourself so strong a Turn for Politicks . . . those of *Greece* or *Rome* might yet a while afford sufficient scope for your Diligence and Curiosity. For when young Persons, before they have sufficiently formed their Judgment by these and the like Models . . . enter too deeply into the Consideration of our National Concern, the wretched Spirit of Party-Zeal seldom fails to enflame their Imaginations and betray them into various Extravagancies [original emphasis].[38]

Reading the ancient historians, he wrote, would teach the young man

'Tis your Duty to reverence Authority in whatever Hands you find it placed, to avoid giving Offence to it, and to recommend yourself to its esteem and Regard by improving your Mind in useful Learning, and fitting yourself to do your Duty in that State unto which you may be called hereafter.[39]

Bentham did his best to spread this policy beyond his own college by publishing a collection of funeral speeches from Thucydides, Lysias, Xenophon, and the *Menexenus* of pseudo-Plato for use by undergraduates. The speeches, which he praised as teaching the necessity of moderation in all things, were reprinted several times with more and more extended notes between 1746 and 1768.

At the centre of this move to champion Oxford's traditional classical curriculum were a group of Oxford dons who came to be known as the Hutchinsonians. Associated with the natural philosopher John Hutchinson, these men have generally been seen as offering a conservative high-church critique of Newtonian physics and the deistic notion of God which they helped to promote.[40] However, they were also firm believers in the moral benefits of a narrow, carefully-selected classical syllabus such as Christ Church and other colleges were advocating in the 1750s. One particularly prominent member of the group, George Horne, fellow and tutor of Magdalen, declared his desire to see Oxford's traditional studies of 'languages, history [and] antiquity' made useful 'handmaids to divine knowledge'.[41] Moreover, he linked this policy clearly with a desire to promote respect for established authority among the under-graduate population. Addressing the students directly ('my younger Brethren of the University') in a pamphlet of 1756, Horne stressed the need for them to 'continu[e] steadfast and immovable, in the stations allotted' them, 'living in due subordination and humble obedience to your *tutors* and *governors* in this place [original emphasis]'.[42]

Revolution and 'reform' in Oxford: The New Examination Statute of 1800

The measures taken by senior members at a college level to regain control over a student body increasingly given to riotous behaviour were to act as a template for the university's response to the much greater threat posed by religious dissenters at home and political revo-lutionaries in America and France in the final third of the century. With junior-senior relations at such a low ebb, the various ideological chal-lenges of the final part of the century hit Oxford particularly hard. The influence of Methodism in the 1760s aroused particular anxiety, with six undergraduates being expelled from St Edmund Hall in 1768 purely on suspicion of Methodist sympathies. Cambridge, by contrast, followed a policy of increasing religious tolerance; there were many dissenters, including Unitarians such as John Jebb, among the leading examination and curriculum reformers, and in 1772 the university took the ground-breaking decision to replace the centuries-old requirement for students to subscribe the Thirty-Nine Articles of the Church of England at graduation with the simple signing of a declaration of conformity to Anglican doctrines.[43] To a certain extent, the different attitudes of the two universities may well have been self-reinforcing, with greater numbers of students from families with reservations about subscription choosing to go to Cambridge rather than Oxford.[44]

With the outbreak of the American Revolution in 1775 and the circulation of widespread reports that many college students had rallied to the rebels' cause, the fears of Oxford's senior members increased substantially. While the authorities at Cambridge were certainly concerned by events in the American colonies, Oxford had to contend with the additional fact that its undergraduates had earned a particular reputation for rebelling against established authority. The 1770s and 1780s saw the publication in Oxford of the first far-reaching plans for reforming the curriculum, examinations, and disciplinary procedures at a university level. While these plans have received some attention from historians,[45] few have commented on the strong resemblance which they bore to the measures taken to combat student involvement in the Jacobite riots in the first half of the century.

Unsurprisingly perhaps, one of the first proposals to be made was for the introduction of a far more rigorous, competitive examination system at a university level. This would have taken the measures already introduced at individual colleges such as Christ Church, Magdalen, and Trinity and applied them to all of Oxford's undergraduates.[46] In addition, however, many 'reformers' argued for a narrow classical syllabus which all students would follow, with texts carefully selected for their moral content and studied through the same schoolboy tasks of construing, translation, and composition. Until then, although increasingly restricted in the books they read in college, undergraduates remained largely free to select their own texts and examining masters at a university level. In his *Considerations on the Public Exercises*, first published in 1773, John Napleton, fellow and tutor of Brasenose College, placed great emphasis on reinvigorating the study of Aristotelian logic which, he argued, would provide students with the necessary skills to distinguish and defeat the fallacious arguments of dissenters and political radicals. 'Truth and falsehood', he wrote, 'are so often... interwoven together' in the works of such writers 'that... the True Philosopher will be the more desirous... to qualify himself, in the clearest and most decisive manner, to detect and expose error, however speciously or consciously recommended'.[47] He also argued for a return to the strict division between the disciplines studied at BA and MA level enjoined by the Laudian Statutes. The particular subjects studied, wrote Napleton, should 'rise in dignity, as [the candidate] advances in standing and knowledge'.[48] In other words, those subjects considered potentially dangerous such as the analytical study of ancient history, political philosophy, and metaphysics were to be restricted to MA students.

Many of those involved with the syllabus changes within the individual colleges now came out to argue for a similar policy at a university level. Against the background of the American Revolution, Edward Bentham urged that the works of ancient historians, in particular those of Greece, should play a dominant role in any new university syllabus. A focus on the writings of Herodotus, Thucydides, and Xenophon, he argued, was crucial to 'instill [sic] in the minds of youth a reverential awe for those who are placed in exalted stations', to help them 'imbibe the excellent precepts that no man is wiser than the laws, that none can wish for an opportunity of being emancipated from their authority, without deviating widely from the rules of virtue and losing the valuable privilege of being entitled to the advantages of civil rights'.[49]

With the outbreak of the French Revolution in 1789, the frequency and urgency of these proposals increased considerably. It was widely perceived that junior-senior relations at Oxford had reached an all-time low, with more and more students showing sympathy with the cause of the revolutionaries. One Oxford magazine, *The Loiterer*, edited by a former student of St John's College, James Austen, gave this particularly depressing picture of typical tutor-pupil relations at this time:

With [a] slender stock of knowledge, and without any acquaintance with the world or any insight into characters, [the tutor] enters on his office with more zeal than discretion, asserts his own opinions with arrogance and maintains them with obstinacy, calls *contradiction, contumacy*, and *reply, pertness*, and deals out his *jobations, impositions*, and *confinements*, to every ill-fated *junior* who is daring enough to oppose his sentiments, or doubt his opinions [original emphasis].

As *The Loiterer* concluded, 'The consequence of this is perfectly natural', 'he [the tutor] treats his pupils as boys, and they think him a brute'.[50]

In such an atmosphere, senior members redoubled their efforts to devise a university-wide curriculum and system of examinations which would allow them to regain control over the undergraduate body. Against the background of the French Revolution, there developed an unprecedented conservative coalition urging similar changes, chief among which was a uniform syllabus of carefully selected classical texts and divinity tracts. It is true that, in the second half of the eighteenth century particularly, Oxford witnessed a significant growth of interest among undergraduates and some college fellows in newly popular scientific subjects such as physics, chemistry, astronomy, and anatomy. As Dame Lucy Sutherland has shown, lecture series were organized, often outside of the official curriculum, by teachers who were unattached to the university and who charged fees for attendance.

Students were required to receive the permission of their college tutor before attending and the attitude of college authorities to such lecture series was mixed and, in some cases, directly hostile. Some feared that attendance would distract undergraduates from their college work, while others expressed concern about the potential of such lectures to spread subversive ideas.[51] Indeed, the second half of the eighteenth century witnessed comparable initiatives from men within the university who established new and compulsory lecture series in more traditional subject areas, such as Edward Bentham's lectures in conservative divinity, which began in 1764 with the support of the Bishop of Oxford, Thomas Secker.[52]

It is important to note that the university-wide coalition in favour of a restricted and carefully-selected curriculum of classical studies and divinity included not only moderate conservatives such as Napleton, but also a number of leading Oxford Whigs. Perhaps the most surprising convert was Edward Tatham, fellow of Lincoln College, and notorious supporter of modern learning at Oxford. For a brief interlude in his career, Tatham became the champion of the traditional classical syllabus. In a sermon preached before the university on 5 November 1791, he quoted at length from the *Ethics* of Aristotle (the very author whose dominance at Oxford he had earlier deplored)[53], arguing that every individual should submit himself to established authority. 'If Politics be a branch of moral law', he wrote, paraphrasing Aristotle, 'submission to civil authority is a necessary, unqualified, unstipulated duty, forming the most important part of moral virtue'.[54] Indeed, he concluded that only a 'profound' study of ancient philosophy qualified men to question the correctness of established political institutions. Such deep and important issues were 'not to be compassed by the depths of mathematics or to be conquered by the subtleties of synthetic science'.[55]

The backbone of this conservative alliance was, however, comprised of prominent Hutchinsonians, showing once again the considerable continuity between the reforms introduced at a college level earlier in the century and those now being proposed for the whole university. Indeed, those writing in the 1780s and 90s included many such as George Horne and William Jones of Nayland who had championed Oxford's classical curriculum against the Newtonian philosophy popular at Cambridge in the 1750s. In a timely sermon on 'Submission to Government' given on 25 October 1789, Horne warned of the dreadful consequences if the English clergy failed to stem the tide of revolutionary feeling in their own country.[56] In particular, he stressed the value of

Greek and Roman history in illustrating the 'seditions and commotions' which he felt to be the normal consequences of radical democracy.[57] Jones took an even more active approach, republishing a number of key Hutchinsonian texts and founding in 1792 the Society for the Reformation of Principles, which endeavoured to ensure that students at Oxford and Cambridge, particularly the majority training for the Anglican ministry, would not be seduced by the dangerous ideas of dissenters and revolutionaries. The seminal publications of the Society, a collection of tracts (including many works by leading Hutchinsonians) entitled *The Scholar Armed,* and the periodical *The British Critic,* aimed to provide an acceptable, orthodox curriculum of the sort which Jones would have liked to have seen introduced at his own university. Unsurprisingly perhaps, the emphasis was strongly on schoolboy classics and carefully selected divinity tracts.[58]

In the years leading up to the New Examination Statute of 1800, pressure was certainly building for the Hebdomadal Board to formulate a response at a university level to the growing fears of senior members. A number of commentators in Oxford traced the recent bloody events in France to a subversion of the traditional classical curriculum in French universities. Such, for example, was Ralph Churton, who declared in a university sermon of 1793 that if 'there is the remotest Tendency to similar passions in our own country and among ourselves, we should crush the growing evil in the bud'.[59] Although it is unfortunate that many of the minutes of the Hebdomadal Board meetings are missing for the key period between 1793 and 1800, much may still be learned about the motivations behind the introduction of the New Examination Statute. It will be suggested here that it was designed to function as the cornerstone of the Board's attempts to gain greater control over the activities and reading material of the university's junior members. Superficially the measures contained in the Statute (which included the introduction of competitive examination to Oxford, some sixty years after Cambridge) were sold as being more appropriate for the maturer and more experienced undergraduate of the early nineteenth century.[60] However, a closer look at the Statute's provisions, particularly regarding the curriculum, tells a rather different story.

What the Statute was essentially designed to do was to transfer to the university level the key features of the conservative classical system developed at Christ Church and some of the other leading colleges over the course of the eighteenth century. Its chief framer was none other than Cyril Jackson, dean of Christ Church, who had been responsible for extensive 'reform' of the curriculum, examinations, and internal discipline of his college in the years leading up to the passage of the Statute. Also active supporters of the Statute were John Parsons, master of Balliol, and John Eveleigh, provost of Oriel, who had both introduced similar reforms at their own colleges in the closing years of the eighteenth century. In addition to the introduction of competitive examination and a raft of measures designed to increase the powers of examiners, the Statute established the first uniform syllabus for all undergraduates, based firmly on the traditional combination of classics and divinity. This was, as we have seen, in line with the recommendations of the various over-arching schemes of reform proposed in the 1780s and 90s as well as with internal college examinations.

In the classical syllabus, there was to be absolutely no innovation. Precisely the same subjects and tasks, denounced by critics as little better than schoolboy exercises, were retained. Most importantly, students would be asked to construe passages from at least three classical authors 'of the best age and stamp'.[61] For both Greek and Latin authors this meant a fairly restricted list of possible texts, confined almost exclusively to the fourth and fifth centuries BCE for Greek authors and the first centuries BCE and CE for Latin authors.[62] In addition, they would be quizzed on various aspects of Greek and Latin grammar and asked to translate passages of English into Latin. Although not actually prescribed by name until the Statute of 1807, in practice, Aristotle remained central to the undergraduate syllabus, with questions on rhetoric, logic, and moral philosophy almost entirely limited to what could be gleaned from a study of his works.[63] Questions on the 'elements of divinity' which meant in practice the Greek New Testament and the Thirty-Nine Articles, were made a compulsory part of the examination for the first time,[64] again paralleling moves taken at the college level at Christ Church from the late seventeenth century, but increasingly also at other colleges from the early 1770s. Crucially, divinity was made the most important requirement of the Statute with a poor performance here meaning an automatic failure of the whole examination.[65]

By retaining and strengthening the traditional syllabus, the division between candidates for the BA and the MA was sharply underlined. Following once more the practice of the Laudian Statutes, those subjects which were considered more dangerous and intellectually challenging - mathematics, physics, politics, and the analytical study of ancient history, were strictly reserved for the MA degree.[66] It is instructive to note that with the exception of the so-called 'Elements of Mathematics and Physics', which essentially referred to the first ten books of Euclid, candidates for the BA had no opportunity to study those subjects which had formed the staple of the undergraduate curriculum at Cambridge since the middle years of the eighteenth century.

A Curriculum for Schoolboys? The Reception
of the 1800 Statute

Further evidence of the motivations behind the Statute of 1800 may be found by examining the reactions of commentators in the years following its introduction. Significantly, both supporters and critics interpreted it not as an attempt to modernize the examination system of the university (as the Statute itself proclaimed)[67], but rather as a means by which to increase the control of the Oxford authorities over the reading material and activities of junior members. A few months after the Statute was passed, the Whig divine Samuel Parr expressed his hope that 'amidst the rapid decay of similar institutions in foreign countries', Oxford would now constitute one of 'the main pillars, not only of the learning and perhaps the science, but of the virtue and piety... which yet remain among us'.[68] 'J.M.', the writer of an article in the *British Magazine* reviewing the changes, agreed. 'We have witnessed', he wrote, 'a *gradual* progress in the learned upon the continent towards those principles, which by being secretly and extensively disseminated, and at length by being openly avowed and acted upon, have filled the world with its present miseries [original emphasis]'. The English nation, he declared, 'in such an exigency calls with a far more earnest and authoritative voice upon her public seminaries of learning'. 'It is high time', he wrote, 'to think of laying some restraint upon the profligacy which will always be found among young men who are too much their own masters'; and 'no method', he concluded of the Examination Statute, '[could] be more effectual for the accomplishment of this end'.[69]

In 1802, William Barrow, the master of an academy in Soho Square, London and a graduate of Queen's College, Oxford, praised the Examination Statute and in particular, the decision to restrict the curriculum to a narrow range of classical texts similar to those which would have been read in school. 'When boys are treated as men', he observed, 'the vices of men are naturally encouraged'.[70] Far better that through a profound study of Aristotelian logic 'the rising generation...amidst the decay and downfall of the academical establishments on the continent, may learn to resist and refute the metaphysical subtleties which have thrown half the nations of Europe into confusion'.[71] In a crisis such as the French Revolution, it was precisely the schoolmaster's policy of carefully selecting texts for the moral and political lessons they could teach which was needed at the university level. 'The choice of books', he wrote, 'may...be directed by the circumstances of the times; by the military or political transactions, in which our own or foreign nations happen to be engaged'.[72] The particular context of the French Revolution, he suggested, made especially pertinent the reading of 'the history of Cataline's Conspiracy in Sallust, and the Orations of Cicero on the subject'.[73] Significantly, these two texts featured particularly prominently in the reading lists of the leading Oxford colleges in the last years of the eighteenth century.[74]

Even Edward Copleston, fellow and tutor of Oriel College, who took on the mantle of official apologist for the system created in 1800, found it difficult to conceal the fears of junior rebellion which had provided such a strong incentive for the Statute's framers. At numerous points in his *Reply* to attacks on Oxford's classical syllabus published in the *Edinburgh Review* in 1808 and 1809,[75] he described the course of study set down in 1800 as providing undergraduates with 'a manly and generous discipline'.[76] He praised Aristotle as the 'manly' philosopher *par excellence* and argued that the university's classical curriculum offered the perfect training of the mind and morals for the challenges of manhood.[77] 'Without directly qualifying a man for any of the employments of life', he wrote, 'it enriches and enobles all'; it is 'that complete and generous education which fits a man to perform justly, skilfully, and magnanimously, all the offices, both private and public, of peace and war'.[78] However, a closer reading of Copleston's *Reply* makes plain that the Statute was also concerned with increasing supervision of junior behaviour. 'Constant admonition, the consciousness of an overseeing eye, the fear of reproof, and the hope of praise', he wrote with reference to the Statute, 'are...necessary to overcome the desultory habits of youth, to check its wanderings, and keep it to its purpose'. Likewise, he was quite clear about the reasons for encouraging undergraduates to read particular classical texts. 'In the favourite studies of the place', he declared, students

meet with nothing but what tends to breed and foster … noble sentiments, to
make them feel what they owe to their country in a land of freedom, and what
their country expects from them. In the histories of Thucydides and Xenophon
they … read, unmixed with the prejudiced and perverse clamours of party, the
fatal consequences of misrule and anarchy, of wild democracy, of unlimited or
unjust power.[79]

In 1807, the Hebdomadal Board took the decision to introduce a revised
Examination Statute which prescribed in even more minute detail the
course of study and the texts to be preferred. Aristotle was accorded
particular prominence. He was hailed as the 'master of logic' and his
moral and ethical treatises were to become a compulsory and central
focus of the BA examination.[80] This further strengthening of the traditional syllabus received criticism not only from external commentators
but also from those within the university. Although he had supported
the original Statute against the background of the French Revolution,
Edward Tatham, now rector of Lincoln College, could not see the need
for a further restriction of the syllabus when, in his view, the danger had
receded. In the first of a series of passionate *Addresses* to Oxford's
chancellor, Lord Grenville, and to the members of convocation at
large, he declared that the revised Statute demanded such a low level
of classical knowledge that it was 'such as a country school-master
would have spurned'.[81] With a strengthening of Aristotelian philosophy
and absolutely no provision for modern learning, it was designed, he
wrote, to keep Oxford undergraduates in 'the dark ages'.[82] At times,
Tatham's language shares strong similarities with the criticisms made of
Oxford's classical syllabus in *The Edinburgh Review*. Writing in that
journal in 1809, Sydney Smith had argued likewise that 'A genuine
Oxford tutor would shudder to hear his young men disputing upon moral
and political truth, forming and pulling down theories, and indulging in
all the boldness of youthful discussion. He would augur nothing from it,
but impiety to God, and treason to kings'.[83] Another Oxford man, Henry
Home Drummond, a graduate of Corpus Christi College and a cautious
supporter of the 1800 Statute, criticized 'the officious anxiety' visible in
the revised version of 1807, in particular the way in which the Board had
'regulated every minute particular that was to be spoken or to be heard in
the whole course of Academical Discipline'.[84]

However, what Tatham was most concerned about (and what most
clearly reveals his thoughts on the motivations behind the 1800 Statute)
was that the attempt of the Board to increase their control over the

activities of junior members was failing badly. It had, he wrote, 'proved abortive in practice', for the new 'scheme of Public Education' had 'met, in the midst of so many honours it affected to confer, with... contempt from all the best qualified and most distinguished young men' among the candidates.[85] Tatham was certainly right about this. In the years after the revised Statute came into effect in 1807, public expressions of contempt for the narrow classical syllabus and the lack of recognition accorded modern learning appeared in increasing numbers from among undergraduates and bachelors. They perceived correctly that the system had from its inception been designed to increase control over them and limit the range of information to which they were exposed. These publications represent the first example of the junior body asserting a collective identity in the public domain and emerging as a separate interest group within the university.[86]

Among the first such publications, we must count a short pamphlet produced anonymously in 1811 by Percy Bysshe Shelley and his friend and fellow undergraduate, Thomas Jefferson Hogg, entitled provocatively *The Necessity of Atheism*. While not focusing explicitly on the restrictive university syllabus, the essay was widely interpreted as criticizing the stronger emphasis placed on conservative divinity since the introduction of the new Statutes of 1800 and 1807. It was considered particularly offensive, appearing just a few short months after Copleston's defence of Oxford's course of studies against the charges in the *Edinburgh Review* in which he had fought hard to defend the element of compulsory divinity introduced in 1800. As well as offering the pamphlet for sale to the public, the two friends posted copies with handwritten letters inviting criticism and discussion to all the professors and heads of houses at Oxford as well as to various bishops and senior members at Cambridge.[87] Copleston was among those to receive a copy of the essay and, as Shelley told a number of friends after the incident, it was he who went on to discover the authorship of the pamphlet and to ensure the subsequent expulsion of both Shelley and Hogg from University College.[88]

In the following years, undergraduate resentment appeared to a number of visitors to Oxford so strong as to be almost tangible. One such, 'E.P', recorded his impressions in a pamphlet entitled *A Week at Oxford* which was published in 1817. The undergraduates he encountered seemed to have no respect for their tutors, instead resenting their authority and that of the university as a whole. From talking to a number of students, he connected this attitude with the rigorous system of discipline to which they had been subject since 1800 and 1807. In a conversation with one undergraduate, 'E.P' was given the young man's contrasting opinions of Cambridge and Oxford. For him, Cambridge 'was as far superior to Oxford in many points, as it was possible'. 'The former was a gentlemanlike place where every man did as he liked, without being pestered with the daily remonstrances of the Tutors; [there]...a man might cut lecture as often as he pleased'. 'I say it', the young man continued, 'and I'll maintain it too...I wish with all my heart and soul I had gone there instead of coming to this mere school; a place where one is treated like a child; where if one does not perfectly understand his lecture, the Tutor endeavours to expose him. D–n the place, say I'.[89]

The first publication to give a distinctive voice to undergraduate grievances was *The Oxford Spy*, a series of five dialogues in verse between an undergraduate, 'P', and a senior member, 'C', which appeared between 1818 and 1819. They were written by James Shergold Boone, a second-year undergraduate at Christ Church, when he was just twenty years old. It is telling that many of the undergraduate complaints about the restricted nature of the syllabus came from junior members at Christ Church which, as we have seen, was the power house behind the changes introduced in 1800. In the *Oxford Spy*, there was a strong emphasis on the childishness of Oxford's classical studies. At one point, Boone compared the 'minute and puerile accuracy' of his university studies with the 'wide and manly spirit of inquiry' he had hoped to find there.[90] Moreover, it is clear at a number of points from the similarity of phrasing employed that Boone had closely read the criticisms published in the *Edinburgh Review* a decade earlier. Like Sydney Smith, he claimed that boys received a higher standard of classical education at country grammar schools than the young men who attended Oxford;[91] elsewhere, he echoed Smith's criticism that works of imagination, in particular the Greek poets, with Homer chief among them, were emphasized far too much at Oxford. Other subjects, which train the powers of 'reason and investigation', were needed, he wrote: above all, a critical study of ancient history, politics and moral philosophy.[92] The influence of other prominent critics of the university is also visible in *The Oxford Spy*. Boone's complaint that Aristotle exercised a 'despotic empire o'er the mind' at Oxford is strongly reminiscent of Tatham's comparison of Aristotle's relationship to Oxford with Alexander the Great's military stranglehold over much of the known world.[93]

In an appendix to *The Oxford Spy* where Boone wrote in his own voice, he articulated the grievances of a whole generation of students. 'We are not yet of an age', he declared, 'to bear all this with the philosophical indifference of our seniors; but, on the other hand, we are no longer children, and it is time that we should have, "what even slaves are free to," liberty of thought'. Exposing the true aims of the Statutes of 1800 and 1807, he remarked,

Our men in authority may display all the suspicion which accompanies the consciousness of a bad cause; all the severity which is the offspring of fear; and all the resolution which is the consequence of despair: but they will not deter us from exercising our own understandings on points which concern our own welfare and have a reference not only to ourselves, but to every generation which may succeed us in this place. Our selfish, and our disinterested feelings, shall be all equally awakened.[94]

Boone was not unjustified to depict those of his fellow undergraduates interested in reform as a sizeable group. His confident assertion that 'we are no longer children, and . . . they will not deter us from exercising our own understandings' was met with a flurry of other undergraduate publications in the months and years following the appearance of *The Oxford Spy*. Some, indeed, such as *A Letter to the Oxford Spy*, by Henry John Herbert, 3rd Earl of Carnarvon, which came out in the same year, were inspired directly by Boone's efforts.[95] Like Boone, Herbert was an undergraduate at Christ Church; while Boone had been twenty, he was just eighteen and a university freshman.

Two more undergraduates inspired by Boone to voice their own dissatisfaction with the limited curriculum were John Henry Newman and James Bowden, who were both at this time students at Trinity College. In *The Undergraduate*, which ran for six issues in 1819, the two editors made specific reference to *The Oxford Spy* and endorsed Boone's criticism of the classical curriculum prescribed by the Statutes of 1800 and 1807. In the opening number, they imagined their 'chief supporters' would be those undergraduates who were keen to see 'the cultivation of modern literature' at Oxford.[96] The dominance of Aristotle following the revised Statute of 1807 was held up to ridicule, with one issue placing the 'practical utility of Aristotle'[97] (so often argued for by Copleston in the *Replies*) on the moon along with everything else which 'had at any period been lost upon earth'.[98] They considered the motivations behind the Statutes a legitimate topic for public debate. 'Was it pride or meanness', they asked, 'ambition of respect, or the dread of degradation, that dictated the framers of academical laws, their ridiculous enactments?'[99] Just as with *The Oxford Spy*, *The Undergraduate* did not stop at mere criticism, but articulated at times an open threat of rebellion against the university authorities. 'Do they really enjoy the sulky homage of the sneering undergraduate', Newman asked,

> or suppose, that as long as they require reverence by arbitrary rule, the obedience of their temporary subjects can ever be extended into an affection for their persons?... It will be well if these and other faults be amended quickly. A stronger pen than mine may otherwise be roused against them. Its energies repressed in one direction, may burst forth with double fury in another, and sweep away with a resistless force, both the obstacles of pride, and the arguments of folly.[100]

Bachelors too became involved in the debate. In 1820, Charles William Stocker published his satirical pamphlet entitled *Reflections occasioned by the Flirtations of Alma Mater and the Stagyrite*. As is clear from the title, his main focus was upon the continued dominance of Oxford by the study of Aristotelian philosophy. Like Boone, Stocker was candid about the reforms he would like to see in order to reduce the 'puerility' of the current classical curriculum. In particular, he wanted ancient history to be taken seriously and an end to the exclusion of so-called dangerous classical texts from the syllabus. 'We would have', he asserted, 'the classical department thrown open; we would wish to see the excellent sense of Polybius and the profound maxims of Tacitus, raised to a level with writings frequently offensive by their puerility'; and 'the fire of Demosthenes, and the polish of Cicero proposed to the embryo senator, as equally improving'.[101]

Sheldon Rothblatt was right to describe the Statute of 1800 as an intriguing intervention on the part of the university authorities requiring explanation. Too often it has simply been accepted as a predictable side-effect of nineteenth-century modernization. Moreover, despite the loss of most of the minutes of the Hebdomadal Board meetings for the years immediately preceding the passage of the Statute, we can still learn much about the motivations behind its introduction. Although pressure for change at a university level grew significantly in the wake of the French Revolution, interest in reform did not begin with events in France. The fear of junior rebellion among senior members and a determination to counter it with effective measures developed considerably earlier, at least as far back as the Jacobite riots of the first half of the eighteenth century. The Statute of 1800, then, should not be seen as an emergency measure designed to combat new and unprecedented conditions, but should rather be treated as the culmination of a much longer process. As has been suggested here, it was the decision of the Hebdomadal Board (led by Cyril Jackson of Christ Church, John Eveleigh of Oriel, and John Parsons of Balliol) to institute at a university level a set of measures which had proved, to their minds, effective at combating the threat posed by older, increasingly rebellious undergraduates within their individual colleges.

While competitive examination, as focused on by Rothblatt, was one important aspect of this, the introduction of a narrow classical curriculum for all undergraduates was at least equally significant. This measure has, however, received comparatively little attention from historians because, unlike the competitive principle, it has been frequently dismissed as simply more evidence of Oxford's famed reluctance to adapt to modern conditions. However, when placed against the background of the widespread tightening of the classical syllabus at a college level to counter student involvement in Jacobite rioting, and the growing fears about undergraduate susceptibility to radical ideas in the second half of the eighteenth century, it appears as a carefully planned strategy by the Hebdomadal Board. It is surely no coincidence that the majority of commentators, both critics and supporters of the Statute, expressed the view that its restricted selection of classical texts and requirement of schoolboy tasks were designed primarily to increase the control of senior members over the reading material and ideas to which undergraduates were exposed.

Furthermore, Oxford is shown to have offered a significantly different response to the rising student age and changing social and political conditions of the second half of the eighteenth century when compared with Cambridge. Reform at Cambridge seems to have been primarily the product of a desire on the part of the university's Whig and latitudinarian dons to adapt the traditional curriculum to Enlightenment ideas and modern learning. At Oxford, by contrast, what was advertised as 'reform' has been revealed as a fundamentally conservative discourse driven by persistent conditions of generational mistrust, centred on the fears of senior members that older, more independent-minded undergraduates with a history of involvement in rioting would be unable to resist the dangerous ideas of political and religious radicals in the 'Age of Revolution'.

Centre for British Studies
Humboldt-Universität zu Berlin
Mohrenstraße 60
D-10117 Berlin
Germany

REFERENCES

* I am grateful to participants in the Life Cycles seminar at the Institute of Historical Research, University of London, for helpful comments and suggestions on an earlier version of this paper which was presented at the seminar in February 2009. I am also indebted to my doctoral supervisors Jane Garnett and Stephen Harrison, for encouraging me to examine the relationship between classical studies and generational identity at Oxford.

1. For discussions of institutional and examination reform at Oxford, see for example Vivian H. H. Green, 'Reformers and Reform in the University', in Lucy S. Sutherland and Leslie G. Mitchell (eds), *The History of the University of Oxford*, v: *The Eighteenth Century* (Oxford, 1986), 607–38; Michael C. Curthoys, 'The Examination System' in Mark G. Brock and Michael C. Curthoys (eds), *The History of the University of Oxford*, vi: *The Nineteenth Century, Part I* (Oxford, 1997), 339–74; Christopher Harvie, 'Reform and Expansion, 1854–1871' in Brock and Curthoys (eds), *The History of the University of Oxford*, vi. 697–730; John Jones, *Balliol College: A History* (Oxford, 1997), 174–201; Robert D. Anderson, *British Universities: Past and Present* (London, 2006), 35–50.

2. Nimmo, for example, has explained 'the rise of modern examinations' in nineteenth-century Oxford as part of 'a cumulative and fundamental process of reform effecting the transition from what may be called pre-industrial to modern conditions', a process affecting not merely the university but 'the nation as a whole'. See Duncan B. Nimmo, 'Mark Pattison and the Dilemma of University Examinations' in Roy MacLeod (ed.), *Days of Judgement: Science, Examinations, and the Organization of Knowledge in Late Victorian England* (Driffield, North Humberside, 1982), 153–67, 153.

3. Keith Hoskin, 'The Examination, Disciplinary Power and Rational Schooling', *History of Education*, 8/2 (1979), 135.

4. Such interpretations are usually based on the assumption that the British elite were flexible and far-sighted enough to introduce such reforms before they were demanded from below and to thus avoid the sort of revolutionary upheaval which blighted much of continental Europe in the first half of the nineteenth century. For this view, see, for example, Eric J. Evans, *The Forging of the Modern State: Early Industrial Britain, 1783–1870* (London, 1983); Ian R. Christie, *Stress and Stability in Late Eighteenth Century Britain: Reflections on the British Avoidance of Revolution* (Oxford, 1984). For a summary of the relevant historiography and an endorsement of this interpretation,

see Frank O'Gorman, 'The Recent Historiography of the Hanoverian Regime', *The Historical Journal*, 29/4 (December 1986), 1005–20.

5. See R. Arthur Burns and Joanna Innes (eds), *Rethinking the Age of Reform: Britain 1780–1850* (Cambridge, 2003), 33; for a fairly recent example of this type of analysis, see Boyd Hilton, *A Mad, Bad, and Dangerous People?: England 1783–1846* (Oxford, 2006).

6. Sheldon Rothblatt, 'The Student Sub-culture and the Examination System in Early 19th Century Oxbridge' in Lawrence Stone (ed.), *Oxford and Cambridge from the 14th to the Early 19th Century (The University in Society, Vol I,* Princeton, 1974), 284–7. This article was republished, largely unaltered, as Sheldon Rothblatt, 'The first undergraduates, recognizable as such' in ibid., *The Modern University and its Discontents: The Fate of Newman's Legacies in Britain and America* (Cambridge, 1997), 106–78. For a similar point of view, see also Lawrence Stone, 'Social Control and Intellectual Excellence: Oxbridge and Edinburgh (1560–1983)', in Gary McCulloch (ed.), *The RoutledgeFalmer Reader in History of Education* (London, 2005), 24.

7. See William R. Ward, *Victorian Oxford* (London, 1965), 13, for a tentative connection between the insistence on compulsory divinity in the Examination Statute of 1800 and fears about the religious orthodoxy of undergraduates against the background of the French Revolution. For an endorsement of this view, see also Green, 'Reformers and Reform in the University', 621–2. More recently, Jacob has argued that the quality of instruction in divinity provided at both Oxford and Cambridge in the eighteenth and early nineteenth centuries was taken more seriously in an attempt to defend the established order against the dangerous ideas of the French revolutionaries: William M. Jacob, *The Clerical Profession in the Long Eighteenth Century: 1680–1840* (Oxford, 2007), 31–63. He has suggested that a greater focus on the teaching of logic at Oxford in particular was designed to provide future members of the Anglican clergy with the rhetorical skills necessary to defeat the arguments of dissenters and secular radicals (45).

8. Rothblatt, 'The first undergraduates, recognizable as such', 148.

9. Ibid., 148.

10. For detailed figures on the rising age of students at Oxford in this period, see Lawrence Stone, 'The Size and Composition of the Oxford Student Body 1580–1909' in Stone (ed.), *Oxford and Cambridge from the 14th to the Early 19th Century,* 111–49, 97–8 (Tables 6 and 7).

11. Dame Lucy S. Sutherland, *The University of Oxford in the Eighteenth Century: A Reconsideration* (Oxford, 1973), 15.

12. Sutherland and Mitchell (eds), *History of the University of Oxford,* v.

13. See, for example, the presentation of Oxford in Graham Midgley, *University Life in Eighteenth-Century Oxford* (New Haven, Conn., 1996), where he described the typical don as 'a statutable drone' able to 'Sleep life out' in his college (57). For Midgley, the lifestyle of college fellows remained out of touch with the rest of English society, a way of life 'doomed to extinction'

once 'a new and more serious age came on' (159). For criticism of Midgley's presentation of eighteenth-century Oxford, see the review of his book
by David Spadafora in *Albion: A Quarterly Journal Concerned with British
Studies*, 30/1 (Spring 1998), 127.

14. Midgley, *University Life in Eighteenth-Century Oxford*, 159.
15. Junior members included both undergraduates and bachelors while senior
    members comprised all those who had received the MA.
16. William R. Ward, *Georgian Oxford: University Politics in the Eighteenth
    Century* (Oxford, 1958), 170; see also Paget Toynbee, 'Horace Walpole's
    Delenda est Oxonia', *English Historical Review* (January 1927), 95–108.
17. Stone, 'Size and Composition of the Oxford Student Body 1580–1909',
    97–8 (Tables 6 and 7); Stone, 'Social Control and Intellectual Excellence:
    Oxbridge and Edinburgh (1560–1983)', 24.
18. For Oxford, see Stone, 'The Size and Composition of the Oxford Student
    Body', 95; for Cambridge, see John A. Venn, *Oxford and Cambridge
    Matriculations 1544–1906* (Cambridge, 1908), 13.
19. John Gascoigne, 'Maths and Meritocracy: The Emergence of the Cambridge
    Mathematical Tripos', *Social Studies of Science,* 14 (1984), 547–84, 562–3.
20. Denys A. Winstanley, *Unreformed Cambridge: A Study of Certain Aspects
    of the University in the Eighteenth Century* (Cambridge, 1935), 212–25.
21. For the origins of the Senate House Examination at Cambridge in the first
    half of the eighteenth century, see Gascoigne, 'Maths and Meritocracy',
    547–84.
22. [John Green], *Considerations on the Expediency of Making, and the Manner
    of Conducting the Late Regulations at Cambridge* (London, 1751), 15.
23. James Lambert, *A Letter to the Author of an Observation on the Design of
    Establishing Annual Examinations at Cambridge* (Cambridge, [1774]), 21.
    This pamphlet has sometimes also been attributed to Ann Jebb.
24. Richard Laughton was a tutor at Clare College, Cambridge between 1694
    and 1723. As proctor between 1709 and 1710 he enthusiastically promoted
    Newton's works as subjects in the annual undergraduate disputations.
25. Richard Bentley was master of Trinity College, Cambridge from 1699 until
    his death in 1742. He was responsible for commissioning and distributing
    the second edition of Newton's *Principia* published by Cambridge Univer-
    sity Press in 1713. In addition, he edited other works of natural philosophy
    such as Manilius' *Astronomica* with the advice of Newton.
26. William Whiston was a cosmographer deeply influenced by Newtonian
    physics and a close friend of Newton. He succeeded Newton as Lucasian
    Professor of Mathematics at Cambridge in 1702.
27. John Gascoigne, *Cambridge in the Age of the Enlightenment: Science,
    Religion and Politics from the Restoration to the French Revolution* (Cam-
    bridge, 2002).
28. Emmanuel College, Cambridge, MS 3.1.29, f. 197 cited in Gascoigne,
    'Maths and Meritocracy', 571.

29. Christopher Stray, 'Politics, Culture and Scholarship: Classics in the *Quarterly Review*' in Jonathan Cutmore, *Conservatism and the Quarterly Review* (London, 2007), 96, 105.
30. For the origins of 'collections' at Hertford (1739), see Richard Newton, *Rules and statutes...for the government of a college intended to be incorporated by the name...Hertford College* (London, 1739), 9; for Magdalen (c. 1770), see James Hurdis, *A word or two in vindication of the University of Oxford and of Magdalen College in particular from the posthumous aspersions of Mr Gibbon* ([1796]), 14; for Trinity (1789), see Trinity College Archive *Liber Decani* I, 31–2; for Balliol (1798), see Jones, *Balliol College*, 177.
31. Dame Lucy S. Sutherland, 'The Laudian Statutes in the Eighteenth Century' in Sutherland and Mitchell (eds), *History of the University of Oxford*, v. 191–204.
32. Dame Lucy S. Sutherland, 'The Curriculum' in Sutherland and Mitchell (eds), *History of the University of Oxford*, v. 469–92, 469–70, 472.
33. Ibid., 476.
34. Sutherland, *University of Oxford in the Eighteenth Century*, 16.
35. Sutherland, 'The Curriculum', 471.
36. See, for example, Nicholas Amhurst, *Terrae-Filius* (52 nos, London, January-July 1721) no. viii (4–8 February 1721).
37. See Peter Quarrie, 'The Christ Church Collections Books' in Sutherland and Mitchell (eds), *The History of the University of Oxford*, v. 493–512.
38. Edward Bentham, *A Letter to a Young Gentleman of Oxford* (Oxford, 1748), 5.
39. Ibid., 6.
40. See John Hutchinson, *Philosophical and Theological Works*, ed. Robert Spearman and Julius Bate (12 vols, London, 1748–9).
41. George Horne, *An Apology for Certain Gentlemen in the University of Oxford, Aspersed in a late Anonymous Pamphlet* (Oxford, 1756), 20.
42. Ibid., 63.
43. Vivian H.H. Green, 'Religion in the Colleges, 1715–1800' in Sutherland and Mitchell (eds), *The History of the University of Oxford*, v. 425–68, 465.
44. It is difficult to find detailed statistical evidence regarding the religious background of students entering Oxford and Cambridge in this period. However, that the two universities were widely seen as catering for sections of the population with quite different religious views is clear. According to Brown, Cambridge had won a reputation as a 'nest of puritans' as early as the middle part of the sixteenth century, with Christ's College and Emmanuel College being particularly renowned for their Protestant views: John Brown, *Puritan Preaching in England. A Study of Past and Present* (London, 1900), 67. By contrast, in the years following the Restoration, Oxford became, in the words of Lawrence Stone 'the most zealous exponent of the doctrines of the Divine Right of Kings and Passive Obedience, and the last-ditch defender of the absolute monopoly of a persecuting Anglican state

church': 'Size and Composition of the Oxford Student Body', 54. For the probable effect which this had in terms of reducing the variety of religious backgrounds of students sent to Oxford in the late seventeenth and eighteenth centuries, see Stone, 'Size and Composition of the Oxford Student Body', 54–5.

45. See, for example, Green, 'Reformers and Reform in the University', 615–21.
46. See, for example, John Napleton, *Considerations on the Public Exercises for the First and Second Degrees in the University of Oxford* ([Oxford], 1773); Edward Tatham, *The Chart and Scale of Truth* (2 vols, Oxford, 1790–?), i.
47. Napleton, *Considerations on the Public Exercises*, 44.
48. Ibid., 50.
49. [Edward Bentham], *The Honor of the University of Oxford Defended Against the Illiberal Aspersions of E-d B-e Esq., with Pertinent Observations on the Present Rebellion in America* (London, [1776]), 4–5.
50. James Austen, *The Loiterer* (Oxford, 1790), 358.
51. Sutherland, *University of Oxford in the Eighteenth Century*, 26–7; Sutherland, 'The Curriculum', 472–3.
52. Richard Greaves, 'Religion in the University, 1715–1800' in Sutherland and Mitchell (eds), *History of the University of Oxford*, 401–24, 403–6.
53. Tatham, *The Chart and Scale of Truth*, i. 318.
54. Edward Tatham, *A Sermon preached before the University of Oxford on the 5ᵗʰ of November 1791* (London, 1791), 8. Here Tatham refers to and quotes from Aristotle, *Nichomachean Ethics* 1.1.
55. Tatham, *A Sermon preached before the University of Oxford*, 21.
56. George Horne, *Discourses on Several Subjects and Occasions* (2 vols, Oxford, 1794), ii. 360.
57. Ibid., 362.
58. William Jones (ed.), *The Scholar Armed Against the Errors of the Time* (2 vols, London, 1795), i. Despairing of any improvement until a university-wide system had been agreed upon, Jones wrote in the preface (p. vi) of the Society's determination to 'recommend to young students' only such texts 'as may furnish their minds with good principles and with such sober and strong reasons as may . . . enable them not only to retain their own ground for themselves, but also to recover to the truth those who have departed from it'.
59. Ralph Churton, *A Sermon preached before the University of Oxford at St Mary's on Friday, April 19, 1793* (Oxford, 1793), 17.
60. G.R.M. Ward and James Heywood (eds), *Oxford University Statutes* (2 vols, London, 1845–51), i. 29. The Statute's preamble claimed the primary aim was to render the examination system better 'adapted to the present times'.
61. Ibid., 33.
62. For a detailed list of the authors most frequently offered under the New Examination Statute, see [James Pycroft], *The Student's Guide to a Course of Reading Necessary for Obtaining University Honours* (Oxford, 1837).
63. Ward and Heywood (eds), *Statutes*, i. 33.

64. Ibid., 33–4.
65. Ibid., 39–40.
66. Ibid., 33.
67. Ibid., 29.
68. Samuel Parr, *A spital sermon, preached at Christ Church, upon Easter Tuesday, April 15, 1800* (London, 1800), 112.
69. 'J.M.', 'The proposed regulations in the University of Oxford', *British Magazine*, 1 (1800), 425–7.
70. William Barrow, *An Essay on Education* (2 vols, London, 1804), i. 253.
71. Ibid., 308.
72. Barrow, *An Essay on Education* , ii. 331.
73. Ibid., 332.
74. Quarrie, 'The Christ Church Collections Books', 499, 501.
75. [John Playfair], 'Traité de Méchanique Céleste. Par P.S. La Place', *Edinburgh Review*, 11/22 (January 1808), 249–84; [Richard Payne Knight], 'The Oxford Edition of Strabo', *Edinburgh Review*, 14/28 (July 1809), 429–41; [Sydney Smith], 'Essays on Professional Education. By R. L. Edgeworth, Esq.', *Edinburgh Review*, 15/29 (October 1809), 40–53.
76. [Edward Copleston], A *Reply to the Calumnies of the Edinburgh Review Against Oxford Containing an Account of Studies Pursued in that University* (Oxford, 1810), 158.
77. Ibid., 29.
78. Ibid., 112–3.
79. Ibid., 159. Such fears about the possibility of junior rebellion and the idea that stricter controls were needed to secure the obedience of undergraduates appear even more understandable at a time when there was a surfeit of well-educated men all over Europe, many of whom would become involved in violent revolution. See Leonore O'Boyle, 'The Problem of an Excess of Educated Men in Western Europe, 1800–1850', *The Journal of Modern History*, 42/4 (December 1970), 471–95.
80. Ward and Heywood (eds), *Statutes*, i. 63.
81. Edward Tatham, *An Address to the Right Hon. Lord Grenville, Chancellor of the University of Oxford upon Great and Fundamental Abuses in that University. By the Rector of Lincoln College* (Oxford, 1811), 15.
82. Edward Tatham, *An Address to the Members of Convocation at Large on the Proposed Statute of Examination, Jan. 14th 1807* (Oxford, 1807), 2.
83. [Smith], 'Essays on Professional Education, 50.
84. Henry Home Drummond, *Observations Suggested by the Strictures of the Edinburgh Review upon Oxford and by the Two Replies Containing Some Account of the Late Changes in that University* (Edinburgh, 1810), 58–9.
85. Tatham, *Address to the Members of Convocation at Large*, 4.
86. Paul Deslandes has examined student magazines produced at Oxford and Cambridge in some detail for the period 1850–1920 but has not looked at undergraduate publications produced in the first half of the nineteenth

century: Paul Deslandes, *Oxbridge Men: British Masculinity and the Under-graduate Experience, 1850–1920* (Bloomington, Ia, 2005).

87. Newman I. White, *Shelley* (New York, 1972), 111–12.
88. Ibid., 114.
89. 'E.P.', *A Week at Oxford* (Oxford, 1817), 17–18.
90. [James S. Boone], *An Appendix to the Oxford Spy* (Oxford, 1818), 15.
91. Ibid., 10. Cf. [Smith], 'Edgeworth's Professional Education', 50, where he declared that tutors at Oxford continued to 'bring up the first young men of the country as if they were all to keep grammar schools in little country towns'.
92. Ibid., 73. Cf. [Smith], 'Edgeworth's Professional Education', 48–9: 'The present state of classical education [at Oxford] cultivates the imagination a great deal too much, and other habits of mind a great deal too little; and trains up many young men to a style of elegant imbecility . . . All the solid and masculine parts of [the] understanding are left wholly without cultivation'.
93. [James S. Boone], *The Oxford Spy; In Verse; Dialogue the Fourth* (Oxford, 1818), 16. Cf. Edward Tatham, *A Letter to the Rev. the Dean of Christ-Church Respecting the New Statute Upon Public Examination to which is added a Third Address to the Members of Convocation on the Same Subject by the Rector of Lincoln College* (Oxford, 1807), 14.
94. [Boone], *Appendix to the Oxford Spy*, 28.
95. [Henry J.G. Herbert], *A Letter [in verse, in reply] to the Oxford Spy, from the Bigwig's Friend* (Oxford, 1818).
96. [John H. Newman and James Bowden], *The Undergraduate* (Oxford, 1819), 7–8.
97. Ibid., 17.
98. Ibid., 23.
99. Ibid., 37.
100. Ibid., 37–8.
101. [Charles W. Stocker], *Reflections Occasioned by the Flirtations of Alma Mater and the Stagyrite* (Oxford, 1820), 13. For attribution of this piece to Stocker, see Rupert Simms, *Bibliotheca Staffordiensis* (Lichfield, 1894), 436.

Dirk van Miert, *Humanism in an Age of Science. The Amsterdam Athenaeum in the Golden Age, 1632–1704*. Translated by Michiel Wielema, with Anthony Ossa-Richardson [Brill's Studies in Intellectual History, vol. 179] (Leiden & Boston: Brill, 2009), xiv+433 p.

Willem Frijhoff

The Dutch landscape of early modern higher education was much more complex than previous traditions in university history have suggested. Focussing mainly on learning, they privileged the stars of science and scholarship at Leiden University, without devoting much attention to teaching and to the students' role in the didactic process, as expressed in theses, disputations and lecture notes. At best they took into account some of the minor celebrities at peripheral institutions, bound to migrate sooner or later to the only university that internationally seemed to matter: that of Leiden, formally covering the academic needs of the provinces of Holland and Zeeland but with proto-'national' ambitions. However, the research of the last decades has profusely shown that early modern higher education in the Northern Netherlands has much to gain from a wider view. It cannot be understood correctly without taking into account the whole range of institutions providing higher learning, i.e., not only the five full-fledged provincial universities (Leiden, Franeker, Groningen, Utrecht, and Harderwijk) but also the ten 'illustrious schools' or 'athenaea' (including the short-lived university of Nijmegen), to be considered as semi-universities without graduation rights. Dispersed over the Dutch Republic, mainly in the major towns, they locally prepared students for an intellectual profession or a political career, got them acquainted with academic culture, or simply dispensed a lower level of learning preparing for access to a higher faculty in the provincial university. Foreign students quite naturally went to the most notable institutions and the most famous professors. The evidence they have left of academic life in the Dutch Republic is therefore biased, sometimes rather heavily. Leiden was more than Scaliger and Boerhaave, and Dutch higher education more than Leiden. In reality, the fifteen Dutch institutions of higher education functioned by and large as a fully integrated network of teaching and learning in which professors and students, just like knowledge, ideas and values, could easily circulate from one institution to another, and most of the time they actually did so. For many Dutch students, the *peregrinatio academica* was not really an international journey but much more an inter-provincial enterprise, enclosed within the frontiers of their Republic.

The illustrious schools of the Dutch Republic were founded by the authorities of province, district, territory, or town, and in the case of Breda by the local overlord. They were therefore rather different in nature and did not enjoy the institutional autonomy of the full-fledged universities. Though some of them, similar to the German *gymnasia academica*, closely resembled the formal universities, as was the case of Deventer and of the illustrious schools of Utrecht and Harderwijk which soon would be elevated to university level indeed, there was no unique model to which all had to conform. Some enjoyed a different structure; others were barely more than a rather loosely composed bundle of chairs. With the exception of the athenaeum of Deventer, that at its foundation was intended to become a full-fledged university but failed to obtain the provincial monopoly and graduation rights, virtually no matriculation registers of illustrious schools are left, and due to the uncertain legal status or the subaltern institutional position of the illustrious schools few of its archives subsist.

Until quite recently, the Amsterdam illustrious school was one of the lesser-known athenaea, in spite of its position in the commercial metropolis of the country. In 1877 it was elevated to university level as the city university of Amsterdam, but in its self-consciousness the university goes back to its foundation as an illustrious school by the city government in 1632. As Dirk van Miert rightly asserts in the book under review – the English translation of his 2004 PhD dissertation – the historiography of the Athenaeum is 'hampered not only by the scarcity of sources but also by the variability of their survival' (9). In fact, archival material reaches barely further back than the end of the eighteenth century, and most studies on the Amsterdam Athenaeum, written at one of the jubilees, focus on town and gown, and on professors and learning, rather than on teaching and students.

The originality of Van Miert's thesis is twofold: he is the first to propose a really scholarly comprehensive view of the Amsterdam Athenaeum during the first century of its existence, and he is the first to approach higher education in the early modern Dutch Republic resolutely from the perspective of the practice and the contents of teaching in student perspective. Besides the well-known sources of traditional academic historiography (the works of professors and their printed lectures), he proposes an exhaustive analysis of a rather neglected source: the academic disputations. It is true that disputations as a source of learning have resurfaced from oblivion during the last decades in the Netherlands. Margreet Ahsmann, for instance, has analysed the early Leiden disputations in jurisprudence (1990); several authors have included them in their analysis of the evolution of scholarship in philosophy, theology, medicine or science at particular institutions, whereas Ferenc Postma and Jacob van Sluis have erected an impressive monument for the practice of disputation with their *Auditorium Academiae Franekerensis* (1995), a complete bibliography of all the lectures, disputations and dissertations known of the Frisian university. But in most cases the analysis turns out to feature the professor's work, not the student's.

Dirk van Miert, in contrast, has taken another stance. Having described the Dutch academic landscape and the 'Cortege' of the Amsterdam professors, from the founders Vossius and Barlaeus in 1632 to the death of the Italian convert Gregorio Leti in 1701 and the professor of rhetoric Petrus Francius in 1704, he devotes the major part of his thesis to a very thorough analysis of the teaching practices at the Athenaeum (115–182) and to the contents of teaching in the arts (history and eloquence, and languages), philosophy (logic, physics, mathematics, and moral philosophy), law, medicine and theology as reflected in the students' disputations (185–348). Early modern teaching practices are not easy to detect, because in addition to public teaching, different forms of private teaching were the rule at the universities and illustrious schools of the Netherlands. We know that the *privatissima* were sometimes used by professors to discuss ideas and defend doctrines that could neither be taught in public nor formally announced on the *ordo lectionum,* such as Cartesianism in its early period at some of the Dutch universities. The curators appointed by the Amsterdam city council too wanted to retain full control and they probably preferred preventing disturbances in the auditorium whenever disputations went against official or traditional doctrine. But the *privatissima* have left few traces. Van Miert focuses therefore mainly on what he calls 'semi-public teaching', i.e., on the disputation as a formal and ceremonial teaching practice, on practice orations (speeches by students, e.g. prior to their graduation), and on clinical and anatomical teaching.

The disputations in particular are rather well known, because professors were eager to publish them as their own work (which often was the case) or as the work of their students (which according to Van Miert may have happened more frequently than is often assumed), using them for future teaching and for their own scholarly reputation in the Republic of Letters. Van Miert has retrieved all the printed disputations of the Amsterdam Athenaeum before 1704 he could find in libraries throughout the world. The University Library of Amsterdam and the British Library were particularly rewarding for his search, but Philadelphia figures also in a surprisingly high place on the list, thanks to the heritage of Reverend Henricus Selyns. Selyns defended in two years eight philosophical disputations under professor Arnoldus Senguerdius. He took his collection of 93 disputations, including his own, with him to New Amsterdam (New York) where he became a minister of the Reformed Church. From there it went to Philadelphia. Such small private collections of disputations by friends and fellow-students may have been rather frequent, but only few have survived. The whole corpus of disputations collected by Van Miert amounts to 411 titles, mostly dating form the 1650s and 1660s.

Through careful analysis of this corpus of texts embracing a broad range of disciplines, Van Miert exhibits not only mastery of the neo-Latin language of academic teaching with its disciplinary varieties, but above all 'that' he is able to reconstruct the intellectual background and the doctrinal scope of teaching at the Amsterdam Athenaeum during the seventeenth century. The majority of the disputations concern the faculty of arts, the backbone of the Athenaeum as a propaedeutical institution. Van Miert's general conclusion is quite straightforward: contrary to what has often been tacitly assumed, the Amsterdam Athenaeum was not the hotbed of doctrinal innovation one would probably expect in the commercial capital of the seventeenth-century world economy, but a very traditional and rather dull place of Aristotelian learning, mostly at a very basic level. Cartesianism, for instance, remained until the 1670s outside the city's illustrious school, and empirical research was rare. It was only after the 1670s that original thoughts emerged in the arts curriculum under Cartesians like De Raei, and Wolzogen, and practical scientists like De Bie and Bernagie. Only the lectures in marine navigation by Martinus Hortensius met from the start much success–unsurprisingly in the ruling port of Europe where the Admiralty and the East and West India Companies were established.

Theology came late to the Amsterdam Athenaeum, and only moderately. The Erastian attitude of the Amsterdam city council prevented the school from any involvement in the theocratic doctrines of Dutch Calvinist orthodoxy. Moreover, as early as 1634 the council allowed the competing Reformed community, the Arminians (Remonstrants) whose right to existence had formally been rejected by the Synod of Dordt in 1618–19, to establish in their city a theological seminary for its ministers. Throughout the period it maintained more or less loose ties with the Athenaeum. Toleration reigned early in Amsterdam, as disputations by Jewish students show. On the other hand, the interests of the *res publica* were constantly and strongly emphasized. The city council fostered law teaching and generally speaking it considered the Athenaeum above all as an institute of great interest for the civic community. What we know of the recruitment of the school confirms this impression: 78% of the students known by name from the disputations mentioned an Amsterdam birth, but the very high immigration rate at Amsterdam suggests that the remaining group was at least partially composed by children of immigrants, born elsewhere but settled in the city. This exceptionally high degree of local recruitment allows us certainly to call the Amsterdam Athenaeum a reflection of the local community.

It is on this point that Dirk van Miert has introduced a polemical element in his assessment of the illustrious school's historiography. In the past, it was essentially the period of the Athenaeum's origin that caught the attention of historians, in particular the famous opening lecture with its fascinating title *Mercator sapiens* (The merchant philosopher), held by Caspar Barlaeus on January 9, 1632. This beautiful text has long been interpreted as a programmatic document in favour of a new, broader academic conception of higher education. As a true critical historian Van Miert distrusts the centuries-old *Mercator sapiens* hype, just as he concludes his book with a very critical assessment of the early impact of the Radical Enlightenment, a thesis advanced among others by Jonathan Israel. He opposes him with the conviction expressed in the title of his book that humanism continued to flourish at the Amsterdam Athenaeum in its traditional outlook and Aristotelian content well into the age of science.

With regard to the founding years of the Athenaeum, Van Miert rejects on several occasions my own interpretation of the Athenaeum's foundation by the Amsterdam city council. In my view, the city council initially aimed at creating an institute essentially meant for the promotion of civic culture among the Amsterdam citizenry by teaching a suitable range of disciplines. Suggestions to attract innovating star scholars like Galileo and Grotius next to Barlaeus and Vossius reinforced this idea, but basically I had drawn my conclusion after examination of the arguments developed by the council in its legal procedure against Leiden University. When in the early 1630s throughout the Dutch Republic several illustrious schools started almost simultaneously to teach on academic level, Leiden feared for its future and tried to safeguard its teaching monopoly by preventing in particular the foundation of its most potentially powerful competitor, the Amsterdam Athenaeum. As we know, Leiden lost the case. But Amsterdam's real motivations remain a bit unclear and subject to interpretation since several diverging arguments were put forward at the same time in order to convince the court. Yet Van Miert's own arguments are strong: if the Athenaeum was founded at all as a civic academy, it must have lost this character rather quickly because as early as the 1640s teaching appears to be quite traditional, both as a teaching practice and in its essentially Aristotelian content. In other words, the Athenaeum quickly represented itself not any more as a civic academy with a new conception of teaching and learning, but as a traditional semi-university. I must confess that I would probably have chosen less pronounced formulas had I known Van Miert's masterly analysis of the Athenaeum's teaching in later years.

Yet, even if I basically agree with his conclusion, I have the impression that the two theses are not as opposite as they may seem at first sight. Van Miert recognizes that his analysis of disputation practices concerns only the regular ones, by young students, whereas witnesses tell us that quite often adult auditors, whose identity unfortunately remains unknown, attended the public lectures. Moreover, methodically there is no reason to monopolize such motivations. In booming Amsterdam the Athenaeum was a brand-new institution whose internal structure remained long rather loose and uncertain before after several decades it finally took the way of a full-fledged semi-university with regular faculties. It may well have fulfilled during a certain time several opposing or competing cultural requirements and answered a variety of motivations and expectations. I am not fully convinced by

Van Miert's repeated insistence on the essentially traditional character of the Athenaeum. Moreover, there may be room for doubt or differentiation in his own perception, given his contention that the 'Athenaeum may be seen as an instrument of local, civic culture, when it comes to its representative function for Amsterdam as an important city, the self-interest of patrician families, and their power over the Church, but this did not translate into any educational ideology. The Athenaeum's curriculum was not adjusted to the assumed emancipation of the "citizen". The public lectures at best offered citizens a means of keeping their knowledge at a basic level' (358).

This may be perfectly true, yet in few cities of Europe the university was used to play such a public function at all. On the contrary, virtually everywhere the university remained closed for non-students, and during the early modern period regulations were in many countries confirmed and even sharpened. We may assume that in the long run the Amsterdam Athenaeum has answered to the academic prototype. Yet, even in that case its difference from similar institutions would have manifested itself not so much in the teaching programme as in the margins, in the locally determined forms of interplay between schooling, culture and society. I would therefore be less categorical in evacuating the sense of novelty that could be aroused by such a key institution for cultural development in a city that daily discovered its fundamentally new and powerful role in the world. Like so many other institutions, the Amsterdam Athenaeum evolved together with the local community, its rulers and elites, and their requirements. Van Miert's book shows this interplay throughout the book. During the first half of the seventeenth century, especially in the 1620s and 1630s, Dutch society innovated profoundly in virtually all the domains of scholarship, technology and science, but its innovative power faded away after the consolidation of the Republic around 1650. It may well be this consolidation of power, riches and culture that was reflected in the more traditional stance of the Athenaeum's later teaching.

Faculty of Letters
VU-University, Amsterdam/Erasmus University, Rotterdam
The Netherlands

Lyse Roy, *L'université de Caen aux xve et xvie siècles: identité et représentation*. Education and Society in the Middle Ages and Renaissance, 24 (Brill, Leiden & Boston, 2006). 314pp.

Peter Denley

Even within the relatively narrow field of university history, monographs presenting individual universities have become unfashionable. Most scholars either choose highly specialized themes within the history of an institution–a discipline, a college, relations with power–or broader comparative approaches. But despite the scope and format of this study, Roy's is a far from traditional approach. Themes of contemporary interest are combined with the conventional concerns of the university historian in a crisp, lively, and effective treatment.

The University of Caen is unusual in that it was founded by an occupying power. At the height of English fortunes in the Hundred Years' War, the king (or more accurately his regent, the Duke of Bedford) came to see the erection of a university–something no English monarch had actually attempted on home ground–as an important step in the consolidation of royal authority in Normandy, both to ensure the provision of expertise and administrators and as a way of establishing a Norman identity that would be loyal to the occupying sovereign power. Chapter 1 traces this process and its consequences. The English foundation in 1432 was in a sense actually more 'modern' than its successor. The king approved the university's statutes, which gave him extensive rights of intervention; subjects were required not to attend other universities (a significant measure given that Normans formed the largest nation within the arts faculty at Paris); and the funds required for the establishment of the new institution were exacted from the Norman *États*. The foundation appears to have been popular and successful (despite predictable opposition from the University of Paris). On the reconquest of the duchy Charles VII accepted the legitimacy of the foundation, but since he was clearly ambivalent about taking on his enemy's achievements the *États* suggested a refoundation. When that came in 1452 it took a more liberal form, scaling down the role of the king himself and granting the university greater autonomy, along the traditional lines of the Parisian model.

Having given a full chronological account of the emergence of the university, Roy turns to details. Chapter 2 profiles the university from an institutional perspective, describing the constitution as it was established and then reformed, before surveying the position of each faculty. This is anything but dry constitutional history; the institutional elements are presented as the foundations for corporative memory, with a strong emphasis on identity (as evidenced by the proportion of time the general assembly spent on the defence of the university's privileges). The dynamics of the disciplines are highlighted. Within the treatment of each faculty there is considerable emphasis on the ceremonies for the obtention of degrees, for which the sources provide rich descriptions. The section on the arts faculty includes a discussion of other elements such as the pedagogies and colleges which grew to support the faculty by offering access and accommodation to the youngest students in particular. The same outward-looking approach is evident in the section on the faculty of medicine, with its control over apothecaries. But the most unusual and impressive aspect of the university's cultural role related to the written word. Not only did the institution create one of the earliest and best French examples of a university library (the 1515 inventory of which is edited in an appendix); it also acted as regional centre for the production and dissemination of books, playing a key role in the trade both before and after the advent of printing. Chapter 3, on 'L'espace social de l'université', is perhaps the most traditional in terms of approach, being based on the meticulous quantitative analysis of recruitment, attendance and the size of the faculties. The figures are presented with a light touch; the formidable statistical evidence is wisely relegated to appendices, and cautious judgement informs a professional and accessible account which really does demonstrate the social value of the institution to the region. This leads readily into Chapter 4 ('Des privilégiés dans la ville'), which eschews conventional 'town-gown' themes in favour of an emphasis on social dynamics seen from unusual angles. The first part of the chapter highlights the problem of the substantial number of officers who, though neither studying nor teaching at the university, by virtue of their membership of that body acquired the same privileges as their academic colleagues. This was a real issue because in a small town like Caen exemptions from taxation placed added fiscal burdens on the remainder of the population. Controversy over the number of such officials continued to eat away at relations between the *studium* and its urban hosts throughout the sixteenth century. In the second half of the chapter the author turns to an area pioneered by her former supervisor, Serge Lusignan, in a highly original treatment of public representations of the function of the university, through drama, processions, orations, and other forms of discourse. In just over twenty pages Roy gives a succinct yet wide-ranging taste of how the university conveyed its message in a variety of situations; positively, at the entry of the king (1532, 1603) or the governor of the region (1583, 1588), or critically (for example, using drama to challenge the imposition of a *decima* in 1493). The use of allegory in all these situations is both carefully crafted (even when very little notice of the event was given) and clearly spelt out to the audience. The organizers of these events had as clear a perception of the relationship between *savoir* and *pouvoir* as the intended audience, a sure sign of the strength of the university's position within the duchy.

The Wars of Religion hit Caen hard. The university was critical in the town's brief role as a protestant centre, but even after this episode it suffered through the twin crises of confessional conflict and its economic consequences. In her final chapter Roy demonstrates that the eventual outcome of these years of 'L'université dans la tourmente' was a rescue package with significant long-term consequences. As the Norman *parlement* took greater control, the university lost much of the independence accorded it by the terms of Charles VII's refoundation. Yet the creation of a salaried teaching staff for the first time solved a number of endemic problems, and was an important step towards the eventual professionalization of university teaching as an occupation. The fate of Caen shows there were many different routes to the 'modernization' of the university system. This clear and original synthesis, based on intimate understanding of the Norman sources and also extensive knowledge of the history of other universities at the time, both within and beyond France, does an excellent job in presenting these issues.

Peter Denley
School of History
Queen Mary University of London
327 Mile End Road
London E1 4NS

Patrick Ferté and Caroline Barrera (eds), *Etudiants de l'exil. Migrations internationales et universités refuges (XVI-XXe siècle)* (Toulouse, 2009)

Frank Caestecker

This volume edited by Patrick Ferté and Caroline Barrera offers a wide-ranging overview of historical research on international students at West European universities since the sixteenth century. Its fifteen contributors cross disciplinary borders, scrutinizing Europe from the early modern to the contemporary era. They include specialists in European university history, but also in colonial and migration history, and analyze the subject from very different angles. The earlier period is covered by international historians whose specializations match the scope of the volume, but for the twentieth century only French historians, focusing on the French sphere of influence, collaborated in this endeavour.

This volume presents international student migration as a response to the attractiveness of Western European universities as places of learning in a dynamic economic, social, and political environment. However, as the title suggests, the volume does not limit its explanation of student mobility to supply and demand in the international educational market. The major cause of mobility presented here is the lack of opportunity for particular students to study in their own countries. In early modern Europe, there were restricted opportunities for religious dissenters to pursue higher education. Thus Irish Catholics went to France; and French Protestants crossed the Channel or travelled to the Netherlands or Switzerland for university studies. The early modern period is very well represented in this volume, with contributions including Hilde de Ridder-Symoens's examination of the Sephardic Jews in the Low Countries and Willem Frijhoff's work on Catholics in seventeenth-century Holland. In the nineteenth and twentieth centuries, would-be students sought university places in

Western Europe due to discrimination on the grounds of gender (examined by Natalia Tikhonov), ethnicity, and religion. They were sometimes prompted to leave for foreign universities by the unmeritocratic admission procedures characterizing corrupt states, or by the simple lack of provision for higher education, as in interwar North Africa (Mohamed Dhifallah). Victor Karady, in his excellent article on the late nineteenth-century boom in Eastern European migration to Western European universities points out the functional need for these degrees in changing East European societies, but also the high social status of degree holders in these societies.

Student international mobility did not depend only on push factors. Western European states were willing to train international students because they saw them as the future elites of their home countries. The ties created by this period of study abroad could be mobilized for the economic, cultural, and political benefit of the state. Receiving large numbers of foreign students was also a symbol of a state's soft power. Whether these presumed national interests were indeed served by the student migration is hardly examined in the volume, but the article by Jean-François Berdah, who focuses on students leaving Spain for university studies, shows the potential of a transnational approach. He underlines the importance of Western Europe for the modernization of the Spanish educational system in the first decades of the twentieth century. The Spanish authorities granted about a hundred scholarships to enable promising young scholars to pursue their studies in Germany, France or Britain. Most importantly the article demonstrates by reconstructing the careers of some of these students that these grant-holders had considerable influence on the future organization of Spanish universities, at least until the Spanish civil war. In considering the motives of departure and further careers of these alumni of the West European universities, the article provides a useful basis on which to assess the significance of the West European market for international students. Of course this state-organized student mobility which Jean-François Berdah analyses is easier to study than the informal international student migration which comprises the majority of cases.

The attractiveness of Western European universities diminished in the interwar period as the states where they operated curtailed immigration. Pierre Moulinier gives due attention to the protectionism which characterized the medical profession already at the end of the nineteenth century. Caroline Barrera shows how attacks on foreign students by their French counterparts and by the liberal professions increased and resulted in legislative changes in the interwar period. After the Second World War, the nature of international student migration changed. André Cabanis offers a quantitative approach to the influx of foreign students into French universities over the century from 1880 to 1980. Until 1940, almost all foreign students in France were European, but after 1945 they came from all over the French Empire. André Cabanis attributes the pattern and extent of this migration primarily to France's international relations.

Students from Asia and Sub-Saharan Africa receive scant attention in this volume. The articles by Pierre Vermeren and Guy Pervillé on North African students have the merit of being strongly transnational in approach, with a strong focus on the students' political activities. Both authors synthesize their recent doctoral research in this field, having analyzed the social and political origins and the politicization of North African students at French universities. These students were not necessarily part of the traditional North African elite. They studied mostly in Paris, and became involved in nationalist struggles. The authors outline the organizational life of these students and the attempts by the French authorities to depoliticize them by funnelling them into smaller universities outside Paris. These graduates of the French universities became, in the 1960s, the administrative and political elites of independent Morocco, Tunisia, and Algeria. Intellectuals trained in Arabic were less successful in securing occupational positions (and power) after independence.

This impressive volume gives a very good overview of research on European student migration from the sixteenth to the nineteenth century. For the twentieth century the contributions are centred on France and are less wide-ranging. We have seen an upsurge in student mobility since the turn of the twentieth century, founded on the twentieth-century experience. "The early 21st century is seeing an upsurge in student mobility and this contemporary experience makes historians look back", which closes with a sixty-page bibliography on student migration to Western Europe since the sixteenth century.[1] Research on this subject would benefit from a more intensive and systematic global or transnational approach. The essays in this volume on North African and Spanish students highlight the potential of such a perspective.

Frank Caestecker
University of Ghent

History of Universities

REFERENCES

1. Recent publications related to this area include for the Belgian case Frank Caestecker and Andrea Rea, *Migreren voor een diploma, studenten van buiten de Europese Unie aan het Belgisch Hoger Onderwijs* (Louvain, 2009). A French edition will be published in 2011; Pieter Dhondt, 'Foreign students at Belgian universities. A statistical and bibliographical approach', in *Belgisch Tijdschrift voor Nieuwste Geschiedenis*, 38/1–2 (2008), 5–44.

Rainer Christoph Schwinges (ed.), *Examen, Titel, Promotionen. Akademisches und staatliches Qualifikationswesen vom 13. bis zum 21. Jahrhundert.* (Veröffentlichungen der Gesellschaft für Universitäts- und Wissenschaftsgeschichte 7, Basel, 2007); Rainer A. Müller, *Bilder—Daten— Promotionen. Studien zum Promotionswesen an deutschen Universitäten der frühen Neuzeit,* ed. Hans-Christoph Liess and Rüdiger von Bruch (Stuttgart, 2007)

Joseph S. Freedman

The conferral of academic degrees has been a basic function of universities throughout their history. However, it is a subject-matter that has received relatively little scholarly attention. These two volumes of collected articles, which also touch upon a number of related topics pertaining to academic degrees, will be helpful to a wide range of scholars, including those who wish to pursue further research pertaining thereto.

Bilder—Daten—Promotionen is the smaller volume of the two; it consists of ten articles as well as a biography and bibliography that serve to highlight the career and publications of Rainer A. Müller (1944–2004), whose untimely death occurred while this volume was in preparation. Articles by Wolfgang Smolka, Wolfgang Weber, and Sibylle Appuhn-Radtke focus on the use of illustrations in ceremonies where degrees were awarded, within published disputations or dissertations, and in a wide range of other published academic writings. Manfred Komorowski's two articles in this collection discuss academic degrees—and published writings pertaining thereto—at the Universities of Königsberg and Duisburg and at the University of Heidelberg, respectively.

Kurt Mühlberger's contribution to this volume examines the *Collegium poetarum (et mathematicorum)* as well as ceremonies honouring poets at the University of Vienna during the sixteenth century. Michael Maaser's brief article highlights the large quantity of disputations held at the University of Helmstedt during the decades following its foundation in 1576 and discusses ceremonies held there for recipients of doctoral degrees. Ulrich Rasche's extensive and very well documented contribution-focusing mainly on the University of Jena during the seventeenth, eighteenth, and early nineteenth centuries-examines the institutional and social contexts of academic degrees as well as of published writings that accompanied those degrees.

Michael Philipp's article discusses the career perspectives of students who studied politics during the seventeenth century. Focusing on students from the city of Nördlingen, he presents extant information concerning their studies, shows that many of those same students went on to study jurisprudence as well, and provides evidence concerning their subsequent professional careers. The contribution by Reiner Flik is devoted to discussion of the doctorate in economics (*Staatswissenschaft/ Staatswirtschaft*) at the University of Tübingen during the nineteenth and early twentieth centuries; he places this discussion into the broader context of the general tension between university autonomy, state oversight of education, and economic factors that has continually impacted universities.

Examen—Titel—Promotionen contains an introduction by Rainer Christoph Schwinges, a short conclusion by Peter Moraw, twenty articles, and an index of persons and places mentioned therein. The first article in this volume is Laetitia Boehm's general survey of the history of academic degrees—with primary emphasis on Central Europe—from the thirteenth to the beginning of the twenty-first century. The final article, by Walter Höflechner, examines the history of the Austrian *Promotio sub auspiciis Imperatoris* from 1624 through to 1918; this doctoral degree, awarded for the purpose of recognizing excellence, was reconstituted as the *Promotio sub auspiciis Praesidentis rei publicae* in the year 1952.

Martin Kintzinger's article is devoted to the prehistory and early history of academic degrees during the middle ages and places his discussion in contemporary contexts. Rainer Christoph Schwinges addresses the central questions of where, when, and why academic degree documents were created during the middle ages. Christian Hesse uses quantitative data to discuss academic degrees awarded at medieval Central European universities. Wolfram Kändler and Frank Wagner provide comparative analysis of academic degrees awarded at the

Universities of Erfurt, Leipzig, and Rostock during the first half of the fifteenth century together with discussion of (1) the time required to earn these degrees and (2) the extent to which degree candidates visited or studied at more than one university. Suse Baeriswyl-Andresen focuses on the question, utilizing relevant quantitative information, of the extent to which employers recognized European academic degrees during the fifteenth century. Marian Füssel discusses graduation ceremonies and the accompanying rituals held for the awarding of academic degrees during the early modern period.

Manfred Komorowski's contribution is a very well researched bio-graphical and bibliographical essay on those students from the Duchy of Kleve and the County of Moers who received degrees in theology, jurisprudence, medicine, and philosophy at universities in France (Or-léans), Germany (Duisburg, Erfurt, Frankfurt an der Oder, Heidelberg, Marburg, and Rinteln), Italy (Bologna, Padua, and Siena), the Nether-lands (Franeker, Groningen, Harderwijk, Leiden, and Utrecht), and Switzerland (Basel) between 1575 and 1700. The article by Hanspeter Marti addresses the complex question of the authorship of academic disputations held in Central Europe during the seventeenth, eighteenth, and nineteenth centuries; during this period, the author—generally speaking—ceased to be the presider (*praeses*) and increasingly became the respondent (*respondens*) in disputations. Kurt Mühlberger examines the practice at the University of Vienna's Philosophy Faculty of award-ing its students not only academic degrees, but titles of nobility as well; Mühlberger traces this development during the late seventeenth and early eighteenth centuries and also documents the awarding of titles of nobility to individual students.

Ulrich Rasche discusses academic degrees awarded *in absentia* dur-ing the eighteenth and nineteenth centuries in light of efforts to modern-ize universities on the one hand and in the context of economic and social considerations on the other. Notker Hammerstein's article focuses on the evolving relationship between the *Promotion* and the *Habilitation* at German universities during the course of the nineteenth century. The lengthy contribution by Harm-Hinrich Brandt (pages 625–706) places the practice of awarding doctoral degrees in German universities in the eighteenth and early nineteenth century into social contexts; the stan-dards for these degrees were continually subject to compromise due to the large number of candidates, many of whom were motivated largely by economic and social considerations.

Alois Kernbauer's lengthy article is devoted to the evolution of doctoral degrees in the Habsburg territories from the late eighteenth century to the early twentieth century; this article discusses doctoral degrees in theology, jurisprudence, medicine, and philosophy as well as in newer, technical fields of specialization such as engineering. Kernbauer also notes (130–1) the introduction, beginning in 1784, of German in lieu of Latin as the language of instruction in individual Habsburg university faculties. Peter Lundgren's brief but well-documented contribution discusses the role of academic examinations both in pre-doctoral studies and as opposed to the doctorate itself. His study covers German universities during the eighteenth, nineteenth, and twentieth centuries, and concludes by making some international comparisons.

Ingo von Münch's brief article discusses regulations governing the granting of doctoral degrees in Germany during the twentieth century and then proceeds to present a number of individual cases where those regulations have not been followed. Rüdiger von Bruch's contribution surveys the evolution of academic degrees in Germany during the twentieth century; it concludes with discussion of the introduction of Bachelors and Masters degrees in German universities during the first decade of the twenty-first century. Annette Vogt examines the careers of women academics in German universities between 1900 and 1945; her research indicates that the National Socialist government forced most of these women academics out of their positions there from 1933 onwards.

Taken together, these thirty articles, almost all of which are based on extensive and detailed research utilizing relevant source materials spanning nine centuries, serve as a basis for two general conclusions. First, as noted by Alois Kernbauer (*Examen—Titel—Promotionen,* 89), academic degrees cannot be separated from the broader context of the history of universities. And second, as implied by Peter Moraw (*Examen—Titel—Promotionen,*752), the study of the multi-faceted and complex history of academic degrees over the course of many centuries requires the collective efforts of many individual experts. And the collective efforts that have resulted in these two published volumes constitute a notable contribution to our knowledge concerning the history of academic degrees as well as to our understanding of the broad range of historical contexts that pertain thereto.

Joseph S. Freedman
Alabama State University
Montgomery, Alabama/USA

Bibliography

Publications on University History since 1977: A Continuing Bibliography

Edited by Marc Nelissen

Produced with the co-operation of the International Commission for the History of Universities

Preface

This issue contains 1105 references to books and articles on the history of universities in the world. We offer bibliographical lists for Austria, Belgium and The Netherlands, The British Isles, The Czech Republic, Germany, Italy, Romania, Scandinavia, Spain and The United States, together with some additional references for France, New Zealand, Russia, Switzerland and Ukraine.

The reports group publications about the universities in a given country, and often also publications on other universities that have appeared in the same country. The editor is most grateful to all contributors for their continuing help. Many thanks to Jeroen Nilis for his help in processing the files.

The following have contributed reports for this issue (membership of the International Commission for the History of Universities is indicated by an asterisk):

Kurt Mühlberger* (Austria–154 items)
Pieter Dhondt (Belgium and The Netherlands–152)
Robert D. Anderson* (The British Isles–76)
Jiřina Urbanová and Petr Svobodný* (Czech Republic–46)
Hans-Christoph Liess (Germany–105)
Maria Teresa Guerrini and Maria Grazia Suriano (Italy–220)
Veronika Kiku (Poland–8)
Ana-Maria Stan (Romania–26)
Pieter Dhondt (Scandinavia–67)
Juan Luis Polo Rodríguez and Luis E. Rodríguez-San Pedro* (Spain–113)

Marcia Synnott (The United States–95)

Individual contributions were received from Suse Andresen (1), Marie-Luise Bott* (13), Sylvie Mazzella (1), Norbert Moermans (3), Pierre Moulinier (4) and Natalia Tikhonov (15).

Anyone who wishes to contribute (or to renew their former co-operation in this project) by supplying bibliographical references about a specific university or a broader geographic region, is welcome to contact Marc Nelissen at the address below.

Apart from this, contributions from individuals are truly welcome, and should be addressed to Drs. Marc Nelissen, Bibliography editor–History of Universities, University Archives K.U.Leuven, Mgr. Ladeuzeplein 21, B-3000 Leuven, Belgium, e-mail marc.nelissen@bib.kuleuven.be

Austria

Additions to Earlier Lists

For 1996

Riedl-Dorn, Christa, 'Ignaz von Born (1742–1791) - ein siebenbürgischer Naturforscher', *Stapfia*, 45, 1996: 345–355 [Vienna].

—— 'Die Sammlungen Friedrich Simonys am NHMW', in *Ein Leben für den Dachstein Friedrich Simony zum 100. Todestag*, special issue of *Stapfia*, 1996: 199–266 [Vienna - zugleich Kataloge des OÖ Landesmuseums NF 103].

For 1999

Riedl-Dorn, Christa, 'Österreichische naturforschende Reisende des 19. Jahrhunderts', *Philosophia Scientiae.Travaux d'histoire et de philosophie des sciences. Cahier Spécial*.2, 1998–1999: 155–180 [Vienna].

For 2000

Bolognese-Leuchtenmüller, Birgit and Sonia Horn (eds.), *Töchter des Hippokrates. 100 Jahre akademische Ärztinnen in Österreich*, Vienna, 2000, 172 p. [Vienna].

For 2002

Salvini-Plawen, Luitfried, 'Zur wissenschaftlichen Laufbahn von Univ.-Prof. Dr. F. Starmühlner', in K. Edlinger, V. Stagl and H. Sattmann (eds.), *Festschrift 75. Geburttag von Universitätsprofessor Dr. Ferdinand Starmühlner*, Vienna, 2002, 33–34 [Vienna].

Urban, Otto H., ' " . . . und der deutschnationale Antisemit Dr. Matthäus Much"– der Nestor der Urgeschichte Österreichs? Mit einem Anhang zur Urgeschichte in Wien während der NS-Zeit, 2. Teil', *Archäologia Austriaca*, 86, 2002: 7–43 [Vienna].

For 2003

Pichler, Franz (ed.), *Der Harmoniegedanke gestern und heute. Peuerbachsymposium 2002*, Linz, 2003, 215 p. [Vienna].

Salvini-Plawen, Luitfried, 'Gregor Johann Mendel (1822–1884) - ein biographischer Streifzug', in Daniela Angetter and Johannes Seidl (eds.), *Glücklich, wer den Grund der Dinge zu erkennen vermag. Österreichische Mediziner, Naturwissenschafter und Techniker im 19. und 20. Jahrhundert*, Frankfurt am Main, 2003, 73–98 [Vienna].

For 2004

Fettweis, Günter B., *Zur Geschichte und Bedeutung von Bergbau und Bergbauwissenschaft. 21 Texte eines Professors für Bergbaukunde zur Entwicklung des Montanwesens in Europa und speziell in Österreich* (Österreichische Akademie der Wissenschaften, Veröffentlichungen der Kommission für Geschichte der Naturwissenschaften, Mathematik und Medizin, 54), Vienna, 2004, 543 p.

Schübl, Elmar, Christine Dollinger, Sandra Kowald and Andreas Pawlitschek, *Chancen kultureller Netzwerke. Konferenz zur Standortbestimmung der Österreich-Bibliotheken im Ausland und ihrer Perspektiven–Österreich in einem Europa der Kultur. Auslandskulturtagung 2003*, Vienna, 2004, 66 p.

For 2005

Balder, Hans-Georg, *Die deutschen Burschenschaften. Ihre Darstellung in Einzelchroniken*, Hilden, 2005, 435 p.

Berger, Harald, 'Die anonymen Quästionen zur Ars vetus im Cod. 5461 der ÖNB Wien, Bl. 90ra-119vb (geschr. um 1370). Kritische Transkription von 13 der 50 Quästionen (I.1–3, 8; II.1–2, 7, 12; III.1, 3, 15–17)', in special issue of *Studia Antyczne i Mediewistyczne*, 3 [38], 2005: 163–212 [Vienna/Prague].

Ottner, Christine, 'Jenes urkundliche Material ist Quelle der Erkenntniß in allen Richtungen. Zur Geschichte der Projekte der Regesten Friedrichs III. und Maximilians I.' *Anzeiger der phil.-hist. Klasse der Österreichischen Akademie der Wissenschaften*, 140.2, 2005: 113–129 [Vienna].

——, Joseph Chmel and Johann Friedrich Böhmer, 'Die Anfänge der Regesta Imperii im Spannungsfeld von Freundschaft und Wissenschaft', in Karel Hruza and Paul Herold (eds.), *Wege zur Urkunde–Wege der Urkunde–Wege der Forschung. Beiträge zur europäischen Diplomatik des Mittelalters* (Forschungen zur Kaiser- und Papstgeschichte des Mittelalters. Beihefte zu J.F. Böhmer, Regesta Imperii, 24), Vienna - Cologne, 2005, 259–293 [Vienna].

For 2006

Berger, Harald, 'Berichtigungen und Ergänzungen zur Bio-Bibliographie des Wiener Professors Petrus de Treysa. Ende 14. und Anfang 15. Jahrhundert', *Mensch–Wissenschaft–Magie. Mitteilungen der Österreichischen Gesellschaft für Wissenschaftsgeschichte*, 24, 2006: 195–200 [Vienna].

Ebner, Paulus, 'Auswirkungen der politischen Umwälzungen 1918/19 auf die Hochschule für Bodenkultur Wien', in Christoph Haidacher and Richard Schober (eds.), *Von Stadtstaaten und Imperien* (Veröffentlichungen des Tiroler Landesarchivs, 3), Innsbruck, 2006, 445–453 [Vienna, Agriculture] *(henceforth* Haidacher and Schober (eds.), *Von Stadtstaaten und Imperien).*

Mikoletzky, Juliane, 'Innovationen - Weiblich. Inhaberinnen von Erfindungsprivilegien in der Habsburgermonarchie während der 1. Hälfte des 19. Jahrhunderts', in Thomas Brandstetter, Dirk Rupnow and Christina Wessely (eds.), *Mensch - Region - Unternehmen. Festschrift für Franz Mathis zum 60. Geburtstag*, Innsbruck, Innsbruck University Press, 2006, 157–174 [Vienna, Technical University].

——'Zum Verhältnis von Stadt und Universität am Beispiel der TU Wien', in Haidacher and Schober (eds.), *Von Stadtstaaten und Imperien*, 454–463 [Vienna, Technical University].

For 2007

Badelt, Christoph, Wolfhard Wegscheider and Heribert Wulz (eds.), *Hochschulzugang in Österreich* (Allgemeine Wissenschaftliche Reihe, 3), Graz, 2007, 599 p.

Berger, Harald, 'Ein bemerkenswerter spätmittelalterlicher Codex zur Philosophie, Astronomie und Medizin: Mainz, Stadtbibliothek, Hs I 613', *Traditio*, 62, 2007: 237–258 [Prague].

——'Martinus Anglicus (dictus Bilond?), Tractatus de suppositione. Einleitung und Text', *Bochumer Philosophisches Jahrbuch für Antike und Mittelalter*, 12, 2007: 157–173 [Vienna, Prague].

Kernbauer, Alois, ' "Eine Universität für die Provinzen im Südosten des Reichs". Die Karl-Franzens-Universität Graz und ihr Lehr- und Forschungsauftrag', in Mathias Beer, Harald Heppner, Gerhard Seewann and Stefan Sienerth (eds.), *Danubiana Carpathica. Jahrbuch für Geschichte und Kultur in den deutschen Siedlungsgebieten Südosteuropas*, Munich, 2007, 1 (48), 113–141 [Graz].

For 2008

Bösche, Andreas, *Zwischen Kaiser Franz Joseph I. und Schönerer. Die Innsbrucker Universität und ihre Studentenverbindungen 1859–1918*, Innsbruck, 2008, 305 p. [Innsbruck].

Brezinka, Wolfgang, *Beiträge zur österreichischen Bildungspolitik 1957–1969* (Retrospektiven in Sachen Bildung, R. 10, Übersehene Quellen, 30.1–3), Klagenfurt, 2008, 103, XXXV p.

——*Pädagogik in Österreich. Die Geschichte des Faches an den Universitäten vom 18. bis zum 21. Jahrhundert. Band 3: Pädagogik an den Universitäten Czernowitz, Salzburg und Linz* (Österreichische Akademie der Wissenschaften phil.-hist. Klasse, Vienna, 2008, XV, 758 p. [Czernowitz/Salzburg/Linz].

Gastgeber, Christian, 'Liebe zwischen Tradition und Innovation. Epithalamien auf Wiener Humanisten des 16. Jahrhunderts', *Biblos*, 57, 2008: 31–44 [Vienna - Georg Tanner, Wolfgang Lazius, Johannes Sambucus].

Gröger, Helmut, 'Das Syndrom des "Autistischen Psychopathen"–Hans Asperger. Zwischen Pädiatrie, Kinderpsychiatrie und Heilpädagogik', *Schriftenreihe der Deutschen Gesellschaft für Geschichte der Nervenheilkunde*, 14, 2008: 199–213 [Vienna].

Hayer, Leopold, 'Das Paul F. Lazarsfeld Archiv an der Universität Wien [Institut für Soziologie]', *Mitteilungen der VÖB*, 61.4, 2008: 91–95 [Vienna].

Höflechner, Walter, 'Bemerkungen zum Thema Wissenschaftsfreiheit in Österreich', *Veröffentlichungen der Gesellschaft für Universitäts- und Wissenschaftsgeschichte*, 9, 2008: 263–275.

——'Die "Historischen Wissenschaften" an der Universität Wien im ausgehenden 19. Jahrhundert. In Hinblick auf Alois Riegl', in *Alois Riegl (1858–1905). Un secolo dopo (Atti dei Convegni Lincei, Rom 2008)*, Rome, 2008, 25–37 [Vienna - Alois Riegl (1858–1905)].

——'Nachholende Eigenentwicklung? Der Umbau des Habsburgischen Universitätssystems nach der Mitte des 19. Jahrhunderts', in Rüdiger vom Bruch (ed.), *Die Berliner Universität im Kontext der deutschen Universitätslandschaft nach 1800, um 1860 und um 1910*, Berlin, 2008, in print.

——'Universität, Religion und Kirchen. Ein Tagungsbericht', *Jahrbuch für Universitätsgeschichte*, 11, 2008: 264–268.

——'Wissenschaftsorganisation und Wissenschaftspolitik im Kaiserreich Österreich', in Bernhard vom Brocke (ed.), *Wissenschaftsorganisation und Wissenschaftspolitik um 1900 im Deutschen Reich und im internationalen Vergleich aus Anlaß des 100. Todestages von Friedrich Althoff (19.2.1839 - 20.10.1908)* (Dahlemer Archivgespräch, 73), Berlin, 2008.

Horn, Sonia, ' "... eine Akademie in Absicht der Erweiterung der medizinisch–chirurgischen Wissenschaft..."–Hintergründe für die Entstehung der medizinisch-chrirurgischen Akademie "Josephinum" ', in Wolfgang Schmale, Renate Zedinger and Jean Mondot (eds.), *Josephinism—eine Bilanz/Échecs et réussites du Joséphisme* (Jahrbuch der Österreichischen Gesellschaft zur Erforschung des achtzehnten Jahrhunderts, 22), Bochum, 2008, 215–244 [Vienna].

Hruza, Karel, 'Heinz Zatschek (1901–1965). "Radikales Ordnungsdenken" und "gründliche, zielgesteuerte Forschungsarbeit" ', in Karel Hruza (ed.), *Österreichische Historiker 1900–1945. Lebensläufe und Karrieren in Österreich, Deutschland und der Tschechoslowakei in wissenschaftsgeschichtlichen*

Porträts, Vienna - Cologne - Weimar, 2008, 677–792 [Vienna] (henceforth Hruza (ed.), *Österreichische Historiker 1900–1945*).

Jiří, Němec, 'Eduard Winter (1896–1982). "Eine der bedeutendsten Persönlichkeiten der österreichischen Geistesgeschichte unseres Jahrhunderts ist in Österreich nahezu unbekannt" ', in Hruza (ed.), *Österreichische Historiker 1900–1945*, 619–675 [Vienna].

Just, Thomas, 'Ludwig Bittner (1877–1945). Ein politischer Archivar', in Hruza (ed.), *Österreichische Historiker 1900–1945*, 283–305 [Vienna].

Kernbauer, Alois, 'Hans Pirchegger (1875–1973). "Der" Landeshistoriker', in Hruza (ed.), *Österreichische Historiker 1900–1945*, 225–246.

Kiehn, Michael and Monika Kiehn, 'Gerard van Swieten–Reformer und Visionär', *Biblos*, 57, 2008: 119–126 [Vienna].

Kniefacz, Katharina, *Zeitungswissenschaft in Wien 1900–1945. Die Institutionalisierung im Kontext der deutschsprachigen Fachentwicklung*, s.l., 2008 [Vienna - Univ.Vienna, Diploma Thesis].

Koger, Friedrich, *Die Anfänge der Ethnologie in Wien. Ein Beitrag zur Wissenschaftsgeschichte* (Austria: Universitätsgeschichte, 2), Vienna, 2008, 159 p. [Vienna].

Kolář, Pavel, *Geschichtswissenschaft in Zentraleuropa. Die Universitäten Prag, Wien und Berlin um 1900* (Geschichtswissenschaft und Geschichtskultur im 20. Jahrhundert, 9), Berlin, 2008, 2 vols., 580 p. [Vienna, Prague].

Mikoletzky, Juliane, 'Historische Entwicklung der Stellung von AusländerInnen und Frauen an österreichischen Hochschulen', in Martin Scheutz and Vlasta Vales (eds.), *Gleichbehandlung im Hochschulbereich* (Schriften zum Bildungsrecht und zur Bildungspolitik, 12), Vienna, 2008, 55–80.

—— 'Prechtls Brille', in Thomas Brandstetter, Dirk Rupnow and Christina Wessely (eds.), *Sachunterricht. Fundstücke aus der Wissenschaftsgeschichte*, Vienna, 2008, 67–73 [Vienna, Technical University].

Neugebauer, Wolfgang, Kurt Scholz and Peter Schwarz (eds.), *Julius Wagner-Jauregg im Spannungsfeld politischer Ideen und Interessen–eine Bestandsaufnahme. Beiträge des Workshops vom 6./7. November 2006 im Wiener Rathaus* (Wiener Vorlesungen: Forschungen, 3), Frankfurt am Main, 2008, 91 p. [Vienna].

Ogris, Werner, 'Zum Erscheinen von Band 125 der Zeitschrift der Savigny-Stiftung für Rechtsgeschichte', *Zeitschrift der Savigny-Stiftung für Rechtsgeschichte (ZRG), Germanistische Abteilung (GA)*, 125, 2008: 31–48 [Vienna - Zweitabdruck: ebenda Romanistische Abteilung (RA) 125 (2008) 1–24].

Ottner, Christine, 'Zwischen Wiener Localanstalt und Centralpunct der Monarchie: Einzugsbereich und erste Geschichtsforschungsunternehmen der kaiserlichen Akademie der Wissenschaften', *Anzeiger der phil.-hist. Klasse der Österreichischen Akademie der Wissenschaften*, 143.1, 2008: 171–196 [Vienna].

Reif-Acherman, Simón, 'Otto Redlich. Chemist and Gentleman from the "Old School"', *Quimica Nova*, 31, 2008: 1901–1908 [Vienna].

Rentetzi, Maria, *Trafficking Materials and Gendered Experiments Practices. Radium Research in Early 20th Century Vienna*, New York, 2008 [Vienna].

Riedl-Dorn, Christa, *Hohes Tier. Die Geschichte der ersten Giraffe in Schönbrunn* (Tiergarten Schönbrunn - Geschichte, 4), Vienna, 2008 [Vienna].

——'Von Leermeldungen zu achtzehn Dossiers–Zehn Jahre Provenienzforschung am Naturhistorischen Museum', in Gabriele Anderl, Christoph Bazil, Eva Bliminger and others (eds.), '... *wesentlich mehr Fälle als angenommen'. 10 Jahre Kommission für Provenienzforschung* (Schriftenreihe der Kommission für Provenienzforschung, 1), Vienna - Cologne - Weimar, Böhlau, 2008, 176–194 [Vienna].

——'Österreichs Goldenes Zeitalter der Blumenliebhaberei', in *Franz Xaver Gruber 1801–1862*, ed. Galerie Szaal, Vienna, 2008, 11–15 [Vienna].

——*Schätze des Archivs–Treasures from the Archives. Naturhistorisches Museum Wien*, Vienna, 2008 [Vienna].

Salvini-Plawen, Luitfried and Matthias Svojtka, *Fische, Petrefakten und Gedichte: Rudolf Kner (1810–1869)–ein Streifzug durch sein Leben und Werk* (Denisia, 24), Linz, 2008, 132 p. [Vienna].

Scheutz, Martin, 'Wilhelm Bauer (1877–1953). Ein Wiener Neuzeithistoriker mit vielen Gesichtern. "Deutschland ist kein ganzes Deutschland, wenn es nicht die Donau, wenn es Wien nicht besitzt"', in Hruza (ed.), *Österreichische Historiker 1900–1945*, 247–281 [Vienna].

Schmutzer-Hollensteiner, Eva (ed.), *Universitätsbericht 2008*, 2. Auflage, Vienna, 2008, 336 p. [Vienna].

Strohmaier, Brigitte, 'Berta Karlik (1904–1990). Kernphysikerin, Wissenschaftsmanagerin, erste Ordinaria an einer philosophischen Fakultät in Österreich', *Strahlenschutz aktuell. Mitteilungen des Österreichischen Verbandes für Strahlenschutz*, 42.1, 2008: 20–29 [Vienna].

Stumpf, Robert, 'Bausteine der Wissensvermehrung: Alois Jesinger und die NS-Opposition an der Universitätsbibliothek Wien, 1938–1945', *Mitteilungen der VÖB*, 61.4, 2008: 7–41 [Vienna].

Wanek, Nina-Maria, 'Die Briefe Egon Wellesz' im Fonds der Österreichischen Nationalbibliothek: Inhaltliche Erschließung und Aufbau eines Regestkataloges. Abschlussbericht', *Biblos*, 57, 2008: 89–96 [Vienna].

Zajic, Andreas H., 'Hans Hirsch (1878–1940). Historiker und Wissenschaftsorganisator zwischen Urkunden- und Volkstumsforschung', in Hruza (ed.), *Österreichische Historiker 1900–1945*, 307–417 [Vienna].

Publications 2009

Acham, Karl (ed.), *Kunst und Geisteswissenschaften aus Graz. Werk und Wirken überregional bedeutsamer Künstler und Gelehrter: vom 15. Jahrhundert bis zur Jahrtausendwende*, Vienna - Cologne - Weimar, 2009, 785 p. [Graz].

Angetter, Daniela, 'Joseph Grailich (1829–1859) und seine Anschauungsweise über den naturwissenschaftlichen Unterricht', in Seidl (ed.), *Eduard Suess*, 245–254 [Vienna].

——'Die österreichische Dermatologie 1918–1945', in Albrecht Scholz, Karl Holubar, Günter Burg, Walter Burgdorf and Harald Gollnick (eds.), *Geschichte der deutschsprachigen Dermatologie*, Weinheim, 2009, 287–297 [Vienna].

——and Nora Pärr, *Blick zurück ins Universum. Die Geschichte der österreichischen Astronomie in Biografien*, ed. Generaldirektion des Österreichischen Staatsarchivs, Vienna, 2009, 321 p. [Vienna].

Baierl, Rudolf and Wolfgang Volk, 'Ernst Max Mohr. Dokumente', *Forum der Berliner mathematischen Gesellschaft*, 8, 2009: 16–75 [Prague].

Berger, Harald, 'Leben und Werk des Prager Professors und Rektors Wikbold Stutte aus Osnabrück (14. Jahrhundert)', *Sudhoffs Archiv*, 93, 2009: 96–113 [Prague].

Bessudnova, Zoya, 'Russian geologists' contribution to Eduard Suess' global compilation', in Seidl (ed.), *Eduard Suess*, 401–412 [Vienna].

Bihl, Wolfdieter, *Orientalistik an der Universität Wien. Forschungen zwischen Maghreb und Ost-Südasien. Die Professoren und Dozenten*, Vienna - Cologne - Weimar, 2009, 263 p. [Vienna].

Camilleri, Carla and Edith Leisch-Prost, 'Das Archiv des Technischen Museums Wien', *Scrinium*, 63, 2009: 47–52 [Vienna, Technical Museum].

Cernajsek, Tillfried and Johannes Seidl, '100 Jahre Österreichische Geologische Gesellschaft, vormals Geologische Gesellschaft in Wien. Zur Problematik einer Vereinsgeschichtsschreibung und ihrer Methoden', *Geohistorische Blätter*, 12.1, 2009: 47–52 [Vienna].

Csendes, Peter, 'Wien in der liberalen Ära', in Seidl (ed.), *Eduard Suess*, 13–22 [Vienna].

Durand-Delga, Michel, 'Les confiantes et fructueuses relations entre Eduard Suess et les géologues français', in Seidl (ed.), *Eduard Suess*, 343–394 [Vienna].

Egglmaier, Herbert H., 'Der Literat und Ästhetiker Ludwig Eckardt–seine vergeblichen Bemühungen im Jahre 1868 im akademischen Leben Fuß zu fassen. Ein Beitrag zum Selbstverständnis der österreichischen Universitäten zwei Jahrzehnte nach der Reform des Bildungswesens 1848/49', *Mitteilungen der Österreichischen Gesellschaft für Wissenschaftsgeschichte. Mensch–Wissenschaft–Magie*, 26, 2009: 107–122 [Vienna].

Flügel, Helmut, 'Benedikt Hermanns Briefe an seinen Verleger Nicolai', *Mitteilungen der Österreichischen Gesellschaft für Wissenschaftsgeschichte. Mensch–Wissenschaft–Magie*, 26, 2009: 75–92 [Vienna].

Flügel, Helmut W. (ed.), *Briefe im Netzwerk österreichischer 'Mineralogen' zwischen Aufklärung und Restauration* (Scripta geo-historica. Grazer

Schriften zur Geschichte der Erdwissenschaften, 1), Graz, 2009, 328 p. [Graz, Vienna].

Franz, Inge, 'Eduard Suess- Biedermeier oder Vormärzler?' in Seidl (ed.), *Eduard Suess*, 105–144 [Vienna].

Goller, Peter, 'Universitätsarchiv der Universität Innsbruck', *Scrinium*, 63, 2009: 32–34 [Innsbruck].

Grössing, Helmuth and Hans Ullmann (eds.), *Ruder Boskovic (Boscovich) und sein Modell der Materie. Zur 250. Wiederkehr des Jahres der Erstveröffentlichung der Philosophia Naturalis Theoria, Wien 1758* (Österr. Akademie der Wissenschaften, mat.-nat. Kl., 59), Vienna, 2009, 197 p. [Vienna].

Hasenbichler, Elisabeth, 'Archiv der Alpen-Adria-Universität Klagenfurt', *Scrinium*, 63, 2009: 36–40 [Klagenfurt].

Häusler, Wolfgang, 'Adalbert Stifter und Friedrich Simony entdecken die Alpen. Die geologische Grundlegung der Geographie in Österreich', *Österreich in Geschichte und Literatur*, 53, 2009: 113–140 [Vienna].

Heller, Lynne, 'Archiv der Universität für Musik und darstellende Kunst', *Scrinium*, 63, 2009: 53–57 [Vienna, Music and performing arts].

Herbert, Edlinger, 'Das Archiv der Johannes Kepler-Universität Linz, AJKU', *Scrinium*, 63, 2009: 41–46 [Linz].

Hlobil, Tomáš, 'Die Frühzeit der Ästhetik an der Wiener Universität', *Mitteilungen der Österreichischen Gesellschaft für Wissenschaftsgeschichte. Mensch–Wissenschaft–Magie*, 26, 2009: 15–44 [Vienna].

Hoffrath, Christiane, *Bücherspuren. Das Schicksal von Elise und Helene Richter und ihrer Bibliothek im "Dritten Reich"* (Schriften der Universitäts- und Stadtbibliothek Köln, 19), Cologne - Vienna - Weimar, 2009, 224 p. [Vienna].

Höflechner, Walter, *Geschichte der Karl-Franzens-Universität Graz. Von den Anfängen bis in das Jahr 2008*, Graz, 2009 [Graz].

——'Wissenschaftsgeschichte als Instrument der Reflexion. Zur "Geschichte der Pädagogik in Österreich" von Wolfgang Brezinka, Band 3, 2008', *Mitteilungen der Österreichischen Gesellschaft für Wissenschaftsgeschichte. Mensch–Wissenschaft–Magie*, 26, 2009: 181–186 [Czernowitz/Salzburg/Linz].

Huber, Andreas, *Studenten im Schatten der NS-Zeit. Entnazifizierung und politische Unruhen an der Universität Wien 1945–1950*, s.l., 2009, 256 p. [Vienna - Ungedr. Diplomarbeit, Univ. Wien].

Kaudel, Helga, 'Archiv der Universität für Musik und darstellende Kunst Graz. KUG-Archiv', *Scrinium*, 63, 2009: 11–17 [Graz, Music and performing arts].

Kernbauer, Alois, 'Grazer Geschichtsforscher von europäischem Rang', in Acham (ed.), *Kunst und Geisteswissenschaften aus Graz*, 559–576 [Graz].

——'Universitätsarchiv der Karls-Franzens-Universität Graz', *Scrinium*, 63, 2009: 18–25 [Graz].

Klemun, Marianne, ' "Da bekommen wir auf einmal wieder zwei Etagen mehr! Wohin soll das noch führen!"–Geologische Wissenskommunikation zwischen

Wien und Zürich: Arnold Escher von der Linths Einfluss auf Eduard Suess' alpines Deckenkonzept, diskutiert anhand seiner Ego-Dokumente (1854–1856) und seiner Autobiografie', in Seidl (ed.), *Eduard Suess*, 295–318 [Vienna].

Knierzinger, Wolfgang, *Das Gasteiner Forschungsinstitut in der Forschungslandschaft des "Ständestaates" und des "Dritten Reichs"*, s.l., 2009 [Vienna - Wien, Diploma Thesis].

Lobitzer, Harald, 'Eduard Suess und die geologische Erforschung des Salzkammergutes', in Seidl (ed.), *Eduard Suess*, 319–332 [Vienna].

Malakhova, Irena G., 'Eduard Suess (1831–1914)–the foreign member of the Russian Academy of Sciences', in Seidl (ed.), *Eduard Suess*, 395–400 [Vienna].

Matschinegg, Ingrid, 'Aspekte der Alltagsorganisation in studentischen Lebensumgebungen am Beginn der Frühen Neuzeit', in Barbara Krug-Richter and Ruth-E. Morhmann (eds.), *Frühneuzeitliche Universitätskulturen. Kulturhistorische Perspektiven auf die Hochschulen in Europa* (Beihefte zum Archiv für Kulturgeschichte, 65), Vienna - Cologne - Weimar, 2009, 97–108 [Vienna].

Mikoletzky, Juliane, 'Die Fachgruppe "Archive an österreichischen Universitäten und wissenschaftlichen Einrichtungen"', *Scrinium*, 63, 2009: 7–10.

—— 'Das Universitätsarchiv der Technischen Universität Wien', *Scrinium*, 63, 2009: 58–66 [Vienna, Technical University].

Minina, Elena L., 'Eduard Suess and V. A. Obruchev: A creative correspondence', in Seidl (ed.), *Eduard Suess*, 413–428 [Vienna].

Mühlberger, Kurt, 'Das "Antlitz" der Wiener Philosophischen Fakultät in der zweiten Hälfte des 19. Jahrhunderts. Struktur und personelle Erneuerung', in Seidl (ed.), *Eduard Suess*, 67–102 [Vienna].

—— and Thomas Maisel, 'Archiv der Universität Wien', *Scrinium*, 63, 2009: 67–74 [Vienna].

Obermaier, Walter and Hermann Böhm (eds.), *Johann Nestroy Dokumente* (Johann Nestroy sämtliche Werke, Vienna, 2009, 822 p. [Vienna].

Obručev, Vladimir A. and M. Zotina, *Eduard Sueß*, eds. Tillfried Cernajsek and Johannes Seidl (Berichte der Geologischen Bundesanstalt, 63), Vienna, 2009 [Vienna - Aus dem Russischen übersetzt von Barbara Steininger mit einem Geleitwort von A. M. Celâl Şengör].

Ogris, Werner, 'Die Savigny-Stiftung 1863 bis ??' *Zeitschrift der Savigny-Stiftung für Rechtsgeschichte (ZRG), Germanistische Abteilung (GA)*, 126, 2009: 36–46 [Vienna].

Reininghaus, Alexandra (ed.), *Recollecting. Raub und Restitution. MAK Wien, 3.12.2008–15.2.2009*, Vienna, 2009, 349 p. [Vienna, Applied Arts].

Renner, Gerhard, Wendelin Schmidt-Dengler and Christian Gastgeber (eds.), *Buch- und Provenienzforschung. FS für Murray G. Hall zum 60. Geb.*, Vienna, 2009, 201 p.

Riedl-Dorn, Christa, 'Abteilung Archiv und Wissenschaftsgeschichte am Natur-historischen Museum', *Scrinium*, 63, 2009: 75–82 [Vienna, Museum of Natural History].

—— 'Zu Freibeutern und Piraten im Auftrag des Kaisers. Forschungsreisen im 18. Jahrhundert', in R. Zedinger and W. Schmale (eds.), *Franz Stefan von Lothringen und sein Kreis* (Jahrbuch der österreichischen Gesellschaft zur Erforschung des 18. Jhs, 23), Bochum, 2009, 269–291; 502–505 [Vienna].

—— ' "Die Zeit meiner ersten wissenschaftlichen Schulung" - Eduard Suess und das Naturhistorische Museum', in Seidl (ed.), *Eduard Suess*, 23–66 [Vienna].

Riess, Marta and Johannes Seidl, 'Die Universität Wien im Blick. Das Bildarchiv des Archivs der Universität Wien wird digitalisiert - ein Werkstattbericht', *Mitteilungen der Vereinigung österreichischer Bibliothekarinnen und Bibliothekare*, 62.1, 2009: 7–17 [Vienna].

Ruggendorfer, Peter and Hubert D. Szemethy (eds.), *Felix von Luschan (1854–1924). Leben und Wirken eines Universalgelehrten*, Vienna - Cologne - Weimar, 2009, 339 p. [Vienna].

Schober, Eva, 'Das Universitätsarchiv der Akademie der bildenden Künste', *Scrinium*, 63, 2009: 83–85 [Vienna, Visual arts].

Schrittesser, Ilse (ed.), *University goes Bologna: Trends in der Hochschullehre. Entwicklungen, Herausforderungen, Erfahrungen*, Vienna, 2009, 232 p.

Schroll, Erich, 'Eduard Suess und der Bergbau in Bleiberg', in Seidl (ed.), *Eduard Suess*, 333–342 [Vienna].

Schweizer, Claudia, 'Naturforschung im Spielfeld der Wissenschaftspolitik im Vormärz: die Beziehungen der k. k. Hofnaturalienkabinette in Wien zur Gesellschaft des Vaterländischen Museums in Böhmen', in Seidl (ed.), *Eduard Suess*, 145–210 [Vienna].

Seidl, Johannes (ed.), *Eduard Suess und die Entwicklung der Erdwissenschaften zwischen Biedermeier und Sezession* (Schriften des Archivs der Universität Wien, 14), Göttingen, 2009 [Vienna].

——, Franz Pertlik and Matthias Svoijtka, 'Franz Xaver Maximilian Zippe (1791–1863)–Ein böhmischer Erdwissenschafter als Inhaber des ersten Lehr-stuhls für Mineralogie an der Philosophischen Fakultät der Universität Wien', in Seidl (ed.), *Eduard Suess*, 161–209 [Vienna].

—— 'Von der Geognosie zur Geologie. Eduard Sueß (1831–1914) und die Entwicklung der Erdwissenschaften an den österreichischen Universitäten in der zweiten Hälfte des 19. Jahrhunderts', in *Festschrift für HR Dr. Tillfried Cernajsek, Bibliotheksdirektor i. R. der Geologischen Bundesanstalt zum 66. Geburtstag* (Jahrbuch der Geologischen Bundesanstalt, 149.2–3), Vienna, 2009, 375–390 [Vienna] (henceforth *Festschrift für HR Dr. Tillfried Cernajsek*).

Sengör, A. M. Celal, *Globale Geologie und ihr Einfluss auf das Denken von Eduard Suess. Der Katastrophismus-Uniformitarianismus-Streit* (Scripta geo-historica. Grazer Schriften zur Geschichte der Erdwissenschaften, 2), Graz, 2009, 179 p. [Vienna].

Sienell, Stefan, 'Das Archiv der Österreichischen Akademie der Wissenschaften', *Scrinium*, 63, 2009: 86–91 [Vienna, Academy of Sciences].

Stadler, Isabella and Rudolf Werner Soukup, 'Das Gästebuch der Familie Lieben als Dokument der Kontakte dieser Wissenschaftlerfamilie zu in- und ausländischen Gelehrten vor und nach dem 1. Weltkrieg', *Mitteilungen der Österreichischen Gesellschaft für Wissenschaftsgeschichte. Mensch–Wissenschaft–Magie*, 26, 2009: 161–180 [Vienna].

Stuchlik, Jakob, *Der arische Ansatz. Erich Frauwallner und der Nationalsozialismus* (Sitzungsberichte der Österreichischen Akademie der Wissenschaften, ph.-Kl., 797), Vienna, 2009, 202 p. [Vienna].

Stumpf, Markus, ' "Aus einer liquidierten jüdischen Buchhandlung". Provenienzforschung an der Universitätsbibliothek Wien: Kontinuitäten und Brüche', in Gerhard Renner, Wendelin Schmidt-Dengler and Christian Gastgeber (eds.), *Buch- und Provenienzforschung. FS für Murray G. Hall zum 60. Geb.*, Vienna, 2009, 171–186 [Vienna].

Svatek, Petra, 'Die Institutionalisierung der Raumforschung in Österreich. Kontinuitäten und Wandlungen von der NS-Zeit bis zur Zweiten Republik am Beispiel der Universität Wien', in Heinrich Mäding and Wendelin Strubelt (eds.), *Vom Dritten Reich zur Bundesrepublik. Beiträge einer Tagung zur Geschichte von Raumforschung und Raumplanung am 12. und 13. Juni 2008 in Leipzig*, Hannover, 2009, 226–240 [Vienna].

Svoijtka, Matthias, Johannes Seidl and Michel Coster Heller, 'Frühe Evolutionsgedanken in der Paläontologie–Materialien zur Korrespondenz zwischen Charles Robert Darwin und Melchior Neumayr', in *Festschrift für HR Dr. Tillfried Cernajsek*, 357–374 [Vienna].

——, Johannes Seidl and Barbara Steininger, 'Von Neuroanatomie, Paläontologie und slawischem Patriotismus: Leben und Werk des Josef Victor Rohon (1845–1923)', *Mensch–Wissenschaft–Magie. Mitteilungen der Österreichischen Gesellschaft für Wissenschaftsgeschichte*, 26, 2009: 123–159 [Vienna].

Szögi, Laszlo, 'Der Ausbau des modernen Universitätsnetzes in der bürgerlichen Gesellschaft Ungarns 1848–1918', *Mitteilungen der Österreichischen Gesellschaft für Wissenschaftsgeschichte. Mensch–Wissenschaft–Magie*, 26, 2009: 93–106 [Austria, Hungary].

Vávra, Norbert, 'Mediziner, Wissenschaftler und Künstler aus zwei Jahrhunderten–die Familie des August Emanuel Reuss', in Seidl (ed.), *Eduard Suess*, 211–228 [Vienna].

Vesulak, Marieluise, 'Archiv und Dokumentation der Technischen Universität Graz', *Scrinium*, 63, 2009: 26–31 [Graz, Technical University].

Wiltsche, Peter, 'Das Archiv der Universität für Bodenkultur', *Scrinium*, 63, 2009: 92–96 [Vienna, Agriculture].

Winkelbauer, Thomas, 'Oswald Redlich und die Geschichte der Habsburgermonarchie', *Mitteilungen des Instituts für Österreichische Geschichtsforschung*,
117, 2009: 399–417 [Vienna].

Publications 2010

Angetter, Daniela, 'Die Geschichte österreichischer Astronomie in Biographien.
Zu Ausstellung und Buch "Blick zurück ins Universum"', *Der Sternenbote*,
53, 2010: 26–34 [Vienna].

Berger, Harald, 'Personen, Lehrveranstaltungen und Handschriften aus der
Frühzeit der Universität Wien', in Mühlberger and Niederkorn-Bruck (eds.),
Die Universität Wien im Konzert europäischer Bildungszentren, 27–36
[Vienna].

Csendes, Peter, 'Universität und Stadt: Universitätsangehörige im Spiegel städ-
tischer Quellen', in Mühlberger and Niederkorn-Bruck (eds.), *Die Universität
Wien im Konzert europäischer Bildungszentren*, 161–168 [Vienna].

Denk, Ulrike, 'Studentische Armut an der Universität Wien in der Frühen
Neuzeit im Spiegel der Verfügungen der landesfürstlichen Behörden', in
Mühlberger and Niederkorn-Bruck (eds.), *Die Universität Wien im Konzert
europäischer Bildungszentren*, 141–158 [Vienna].

Glassner, Christine, 'Wiener Universitätshandschriften in Melk. Bemerkungen
zum Lehrbetrieb an der Artistenfakultät', in Mühlberger and Niederkorn-
Bruck (eds.), *Die Universität Wien im Konzert europäischer Bildungszentren*,
87–100 [Vienna].

Grössing, Helmuth, 'Die Lehrtätigkeit des Konrad Celtis in Wien. Ein Rekon-
struktionsversuch', in Mühlberger and Niederkorn-Bruck (eds.), *Die Universität Wien im Konzert europäischer Bildungszentren*, 223–234 [Vienna].

Heiss, Gernot, 'Die Wiener Jesuiten und das Studium der Theologie und der Artes
an der Universität und im Kolleg im ersten Jahrzehnt nach ihrer Berufung,
1551', in Mühlberger and Niederkorn-Bruck (eds.), *Die Universität Wien im
Konzert europäischer Bildungszentren*, 245–268 [Vienna].

Hesse, Christian, 'Der Blick von außen. Die Anziehungskraft der spätmittelal-
terlichen Universität Wien auf Studenten und Gelehrte', in Mühlberger and
Niederkorn-Bruck (eds.), *Die Universität Wien im Konzert europäischer
Bildungszentren*, 101–112 [Vienna].

Kern, Anita and Bernadette Reinhold, *Grafikdesign von der Wiener Moderne bis
heute. Von Kolo Moser bis Stefan Sagmeister. Aus der Sammlung der Universität für angewandte Kunst Wien*, ed. Patrick Werkner, Vienna, Edition Angewandte im Verlag Springer, 2010 [Vienna, Applied Arts].

Kühtreiber, Thomas, 'Universitätsgeschichte aus Schutt und Scherben–Die
Wiener Universität bis zur Errichung der Jesuitenuniversität 1623–1654
aus archäologischer Sicht', in Mühlberger and Niederkorn-Bruck (eds.),
Die Universität Wien im Konzert europäischer Bildungszentren, 169–206
[Vienna].

Lackner, Christian, 'Wissen für den Hof. Die Universität Wien und der Hof der österreichischen Herzoge im späten 14. und frühen 15. Jahrhundert', in Mühlberger and Niederkorn-Bruck (eds.), *Die Universität Wien im Konzert europäischer Bildungszentren*, 37–52 [Vienna].

Lechner, Elmar (ed.), *Zwischen Verklärung und Verdammung. Vorarbeiten (1966 ff.), Gründungsgesetz (1970) und Emeritierungsrede des Gründungsrektors (1988) als dokumentarische Eckpunkte der Geschichte der Universität Klagenfurt* (Retrospektiven in Sachen Bildung, R. 10, 39), Klagenfurt, 2010, V, 77, LXIX p. [Klagenfurt].

Mühlberger, Kurt, 'Universität und Stadt im 14. und 15. Jahrhundert am Beispiel Wiens. Wesentliche Grundlagen und ausgewählte Szenen einer "konfliktbeladenen Harmonie" ', in Mühlberger and Niederkorn-Bruck (eds.), *Die Universität Wien im Konzert europäischer Bildungszentren*, 53–85 [Vienna].

———, Kurt and Meta Niederkorn-Bruck (eds.), *Die Universität Wien im Konzert europäischer Bildungszentren, 14.-16. Jahrhundert* (Veröffentlichungen des Instituts für Österreichische Geschichtsforschung, 56), Vienna - Munich, 2010, 278 p. [Vienna].

Niederkorn-Bruck, Meta, 'Die Stimme der Universität Wien im mehrstimmigen Satz des Wissenskonzertes im ausgehenden 15. und beginnenden 16. Jahrhundert', in Mühlberger and Niederkorn-Bruck (eds.), *Die Universität Wien im Konzert europäischer Bildungszentren*, 113–140 [Vienna].

———'Die Universität und die Verschriftlichung ihrer Identität. Überlegungen zu den Acta Universitatis Vindobonensis', in Mühlberger and Niederkorn-Bruck (eds.), *Die Universität Wien im Konzert europäischer Bildungszentren*, 207–212 [Vienna].

Salvini-Plawen, Luitfried, 'Die Zoologie in der Habsburger-Monarchie', *Mitteilungen der Österreichischen Gesellschaft für wissenschaftsgeschichte*, 27, 2010: 63–80 [Vienna].

Seidl, Johannes, 'Der Nachlass Paul Uibleins–eine bedeutende Quelle zur Erforschung der Frühgeschichte der Universität Wien. Ein Werkstattbericht', in Mühlberger and Niederkorn-Bruck (eds.), *Die Universität Wien im Konzert europäischer Bildungszentren*, 213–219 [Vienna].

Ubl, Karl, 'Die Universität als Pfaffenstadt. Über ein gescheitertes Projekt Rudolfs IV', in Mühlberger and Niederkorn-Bruck (eds.), *Die Universität Wien im Konzert europäischer Bildungszentren*, 17–26 [Vienna].

Wakounig, Marija, 'Lukas Drinak alias iz Dobrepolj alias Gutenfelder alias Bonicampus alias Agathopedius', in Mühlberger and Niederkorn-Bruck (eds.), *Die Universität Wien im Konzert europäischer Bildungszentren*, Vienna - Munich, 2010, 235–244 [Vienna].

Belgium and The Netherlands

Additions to Earlier Lists

For 2002

Albarello, Luc, 'Etre étudiant à l'UCL en l'an 2002', in Hiraux, Honnoré and Mirguet (eds.), *La vie étudiante à Louvain. 1425–2000*, 107–124 [Louvain-la-Neuve].

Courtois, Luc, 'L'admission des étudiantes à l'Université de Louvain en 1920', in Hiraux, Honnoré and Mirguet (eds.), *La vie étudiante à Louvain. 1425–2000*, 19–34 [Leuven].

Dekimpe, Quentin, 'Les visages de l'étudiant. Quelques figures littéraires', in Hiraux, Honnoré and Mirguet (eds.), *La vie étudiante à Louvain. 1425–2000*, 125–137.

Fachinat, Anne and Anne Vancauwenberghe, 'Le foyer catholique chinois 1926–1974. Un demi-siècle de présence chinoise à Louvain', in Hiraux, Honnoré and Mirguet (eds.), *La vie étudiante à Louvain. 1425–2000*, 75–84 [Leuven].

Hiraux, Françoise, Laurent Honnoré and Françoise Mirguet (eds.), *La vie étudiante à Louvain. 1425–2000* (Publications des Archives de l'Université catholique de Louvain, 4), Louvain-la-Neuve, Academia-Bruylant, 2002 [Leuven, Louvain-la-Neuve].

Ledent, Michel, 'Le Placet: "Un lieu dans le monde..." ', in Hiraux, Honnoré and Mirguet (eds.), *La vie étudiante à Louvain. 1425–2000*, 161–172 [Leuven].

Mormont, Marinette, 'L'UCL, lieu de transit des conceptions chrétiennes du développement. L'exemple du Chili', in Hiraux, Honnoré and Mirguet (eds.), *La vie étudiante à Louvain. 1425–2000*, 75–84 [Louvain-la-Neuve].

Mourad, Georges, 'Quelques souvenirs et réflexions d'un étudiant syrien à Louvain 1954–1958', in Hiraux, Honnoré and Mirguet (eds.), *La vie étudiante à Louvain. 1425–2000*, 149–154 [Leuven].

Rezsohazy, Rudolf, 'Lignes de force de cinquante ans de transformations: Le regard de l'Association des amis et anciens de l'Université catholique de Louivain de 1946 à 1996', in Hiraux, Honnoré and Mirguet (eds.), *La vie étudiante à Louvain. 1425–2000*, 35–46 [Leuven].

Rosart, Françoise, 'La Jeunesse universitaire catholique 1929–1940. Essai éphémère d'action catholique en milieu universitaire', in Hiraux, Honnoré and Mirguet (eds.), *La vie étudiante à Louvain. 1425–2000*, 85–106 [Leuven].

Servais, Paul, 'Les étudiants non européens à Louvain 1920–1970', in Hiraux, Honnoré and Mirguet (eds.), *La vie étudiante à Louvain. 1425–2000*, 47–60 [Leuven].

Sturbois, Xavier, 'Le sport universitaire, berceau de l'Institut d'éducation physique et de réadaptation', in Hiraux, Honnoré and Mirguet (eds.), *La vie étudiante à Louvain. 1425–2000*, 155–160 [Leuven].

Swartenbroekx, Bernard, 'Y a-t-il une identité étudiante?' in Hiraux, Honnoré and Mirguet (eds.), *La vie étudiante à Louvain. 1425–2000*, 15–18 [Leuven].

Wallemacq, Claude, 'Un étudiant de l'ULB accueilli à l'UCL 1941–1944', in Hiraux, Honnoré and Mirguet (eds.), *La vie étudiante à Louvain. 1425–2000*, 141–148 [Leuven].

For 2003

Knoll, Stefanie A., *Creating Academic Communities. Funeral monuments to professors at Oxford, Leiden and Tübingen 1580–1700*, Haren, Equilibris, 2003 [Leiden, Oxford, Tübingen].

For 2005

Haye, Thomas, 'Briefe aus der Studentenzeit. Die Pariser Korrespondenz des Adrian de But (1437–1488)', *Analecta cisterciensia*, 2005, 269 ff.

Laconte, Pierre, 'Planification d'une ville universitaire nouvelle et adaptation au changement d'échelle: le cas de Louvain-la-Neuve', *Les Cahiers de l'urbanisme*, 57, 2005, 46–50.

Thielen, Paul and André Tihon, 'La paroisse universitaire de Louvain à Louvain-la-Neuve. Une histoire à construire, *Revue d'histoire religieuse du Brabant wallon*, 19.4, 2005, 254–257.

Wils, Kaat, 'Le génie s'abritant sous un crâne féminin? La carrière belge de la physiologiste et pédologue Iosefa Ioteyko', in Jacqueline Carroy and others (eds.), *Les femmes dans les sciences de l'homme (XIXe-XXe siècles). Inspiratrices, collaboratrices ou créatrices?*, Paris, Seli Arslan, 2005.

For 2006

Art, Jan, 'De Nieuwste Geschiedenis aan de Rijksuniversiteit Gent tussen 1815 en 1945', *Handelingen van de Maatschappij voor Geschiedenis en Oudheidkunde te Gent*, 60, 2006: 63–74 [Ghent].

Blok, F. F. and C. S. M. Rademaker, 'Isaac Vossius' Grand Tour, 1641–1644. The correspondence between Vossius and his parents. Part I', *Lias*, 33, 2006: 151–216.

Boone, Marc, 'De "Gentse historische school". Colloquium n.a.v. 75 jaar V.G.K. - 28 november 2006', *Handelingen van de Maatschappij voor Geschiedenis en Oudheidkunde te Gent*, 60, 2006: 1–2 [Ghent].

——'Henri Pirenne (1862–1935): godfather van de Gentse historische school?' *Handelingen van de Maatschappij voor Geschiedenis en Oudheidkunde te Gent*, 60, 2006: 3–20 [Ghent].

Caenegem, R. C. van, 'Professor herdacht', *Handelingen van de Maatschappij voor Geschiedenis en Oudheidkunde te Gent*, 60, 2006: 21–30 [Ghent].

Deroover, J. and F. Leroy, 'L'organisation de l'enseignement et de la pratique de l'obstétrique dans nos contrées (en particulier à Bruxelles) au XIXe siècle', *Revue Médicale de Bruxelles*, 27.1, 2006: 54–60 [Brussels].

Gompel, C., 'L'Institut J. Bordet: son histoire et son avenir', *Revue Médicale de Bruxelles*, 27.3, 2006: 191–197 [Brussels].

Soly, Hugo, 'Honderd jaar geschiedenis van de Nieuwe Tijd aan de Universiteit Gent: de dynamiek van een selectief en kritisch eclectisme', *Handelingen van de Maatschappij voor Geschiedenis en Oudheidkunde te Gent*, 60, 2006: 49–62 [Ghent].

Thoen, Erik, 'Adriaan Verhulst (1929–2002) en de Gentse historische school. Een subjectieve visie op een groot historicus', *Handelingen van de Maatschappij voor Geschiedenis en Oudheidkunde te Gent*, 60, 2006: 31–48 [Ghent].

For 2007

Allart, Barbara, 'Utrechtse universitaire historische collecties in onderwijs en onderzoek. Een pilot van gebruik van de praktijk', *Gewina. Tijdschrift voor de geschiedenis der Geneeskunde, Natuurwetenschappen, Wiskunde en Techniek*, 30.3, 2007: 182–193 [Utrecht].

Calff, Josje, 'Voor onderwijs en onderzoek. Bijzondere documenten en documentaire verzamelingen van de Leidse universiteitsbibliotheek', *Gewina. Tijdschrift voor de geschiedenis der Geneeskunde, Natuurwetenschappen, Wiskunde en Techniek*, 30, 2007: 127–137 [Leiden].

Delft, Dirk van, 'Facilitating Leiden's Cold. The International Association of Refrigeration and the Internationalisation of Heike Kamerlingh Onnes 's Cryogenic Laboratory', *Centaurus*, 49, 2007: 227–245 [Leiden].

——'Tegen de roof: het Kamerlingh Onnes Laboratorium in oorlogstijd', *Gewina. Tijdschrift voor de geschiedenis der Geneeskunde, Natuurwetenschappen, Wiskunde en Techniek*, 30, 2007: 247–264 [Leiden].

Koolmees, Peter A., 'Over koetjes en kalfjes? De collectie diergeneeskunde van het Universiteitsmuseum Utrecht', *Gewina. Tijdschrift voor de geschiedenis der Geneeskunde, Natuurwetenschappen, Wiskunde en Techniek*, 30, 2007: 162–174 [Utrecht].

Leroy, F. and J. Deroover, 'L'évolution des institutions hospitalières bruxelloises et l'individualisation progressive des services d'obstétrique', *Revue Médicale de Bruxelles*, 28.1, 2007: 61–67 [Brussels].

Mantels, Ruben, *Geleerd in de tropen. Leuven, Congo & de wetenschap, 1885–1960* (Lovaniensia, 28), Leuven, Universitaire Pers, 2007 [Leuven, Lovanium].

Monquil-Broersen, Tiny, 'Actueel verzamelen van academisch erfgoed. Een verkenning vanuit interuniversitaire collectieprojecten', *Gewina. Tijdschrift voor de geschiedenis der Geneeskunde, Natuurwetenschappen, Wiskunde en Techniek*, 30, 2007: 194–202.

—— (ed.), *Universitaire collecties in Nederland. Nieuw licht op het academisch erfgoed*, Zwolle, Waanders, 2007.

Polak, Menno, 'Universiteitsarchieven, onderzoeksarchieven en onderzoeks-data', *Gewina. Tijdschrift voor de geschiedenis der Geneeskunde, Natuurwetenschappen, Wiskunde en Techniek*, 30, 2007: 138–152.

Stamhuis, Ida H. and Arve Monsen, 'Kristine Bonnevie, Tine Tammes and Elisabeth Schiemann in Early Genetics. Emerging Chances for a University Career for Women', *Journal of the History of Biology*, 40, 2007: 427–466.

Tollebeek, Jo and Ruben Mantels, 'Highly educated mission: the University of Leuven, the Missionary congregations and Congo, 1885–1960', *Exchange. Journal of Missiological and Ecumenical Research*, 36, 2007: 359–385 [Leuven, Lovanium].

—— 'Een stormachtige familie. Paul Fredericq en de vorming van een academische historische gemeenschap in de negentiende eeuw', *Tijdschrift voor geschiedenis*, 120.1, 2007: 60–73.

—— 'L'Université de Leuven depuis 1968: bilan', *Revue générale*, 142.2, 2007: 21–36 [Leuven].

Zuidervaart, Huib J., 'Academische schouwplaatsen en hun collecties. Het begin van de Nederlandse universitaire verzamelingen', in T. Monquil (ed.), *Universitaire collecties in Nederland. Nieuw licht op het academisch erfgoed*, Zwolle, Waanders, 2007, 11–27.

—— ' "Een schat van alderleij natuurelijke vreemdigheden". Over de relatie tussen academisch erfgoed en wetenschapsgeschiedenis', *Gewina. Tijdschrift voor de geschiedenis der Geneeskunde, Natuurwetenschappen, Wiskunde en Techniek*, 30, 2007: 107–126.

For 2008

Amersfoort, Jacobus van, 'S. D. van Veen (1856–1924). Een kerkhistoricus wars van idealisering van het verleden', in G. J. Schutte (ed.), *De geschiedenis aan het volk verteld. Populaire protestants-christelijke geschiedschrijving in de negentiende en twintigste eeuw*, Hilversum, Verloren, 2008, 139–160 [Utrecht].

Asso, Cecilia, 'The campaign against biblical humanists at the University of Leuven. Martin Dorp and Eward Lee', in Erika Rummel (ed.), *Biblical Humanism and Scholasticism in the Age of Erasmus* (Companions to the Christian Tradition, 9), Leiden, Brill, 2008 [Leuven] (henceforth Rummel (ed.), *Biblical Humanism and Scholasticism*).

Baneke, David, *Synthetisch denken. Natuurwetenschappers en hun rol in een moderne maatschappij, 1900–1940*, Hilversum, Verloren, 2008.

Bedouelle, Guy and James Farge, 'The faculty of theology at Paris and the "theologizing humanists" ', in Rummel (ed.), *Biblical Humanism and Scholasticism* [Paris].

Bervoets, Jan, 'Het Nijmeegse studentenleven, een spagaat tussen twee culturen', in Dorsman and Knegtmans (eds.), *Keurige wereldbestormers*, 91–104 [Nijmegen].

Blankesteijn, Annemarieke, 'The Peregrinatio Academica and what is left of it. A case study: Dutch students at german universities, 1750–1850', in Maria Teresa Guerrini et al. (eds.), *La storia delle università alle soglie del XXI secolo*. *Atti del Convegno internazionale di studi. Aosta, 18–20 dicembre 2006*, Bologna, CLUEB, 2008, 233–244 (henceforth Guerrini et al. (eds.), *La storia delle università alle soglie del XXI secolo*).

Blok, F. F. and C. S. M. Rademaker, 'Isaac Vossius' Grand Tour, 1641–1644. The correspondence between Vossius and his parents. Part II: Isaac Vossius in Italy', *Lias*, 35.1–2, 2008: 209–280.

Broeyer, Frits G. M., 'Calvijnjaar 1909. Valeton en Einstein eredoctor in Genève', *Tijdschrift voor Nederlandse Kerkgeschiedenis*, 11.4, 2008: 112–121.

——'De kwestie Nethenus: ontslag van een hoogleraar (1662)', *Oud-Utrecht. Tijdschrift voor geschiedenis van stad en provincie Utrecht*, 81.1, 2008: 22–25 [Utrecht].

Caljé, Pieter A. J., 'Studentencultuur in de negentiende eeuw: professionalisering en aristocratisering tegelijkertijd', in Dorsman and Knegtmans (eds.), *Keurige wereldbestormers*, 9–18.

Claes, Dirk, 'The study of Church history at the Catholic University of Leuven: 1834–1968', in Guerrini et al. (eds.), *La storia delle università alle soglie del XXI secolo*, 125–137 [Leuven].

Collin, Mathilde, *L'illusion identitaire des étudiants francophones. Le mouvement des étudiants universitaires belges d'expression française (MUBEF) 1961–1974* (Publications des Archives de l'Université catholique de Louvain, 19), Louvain-la-Neuve, Academia-Bruylant, 2008.

—— *L'Université catholique de Louvain et la coopération au développement. Entre microcosme des relations internationales et laboratoires d'innovations sociales 1908–1981* (Publications des Archives de l'Université catholique de Louvain, 20), Louvain-la-Neuve, Academia-Bruylant, 2008 [Leuven].

Coster, Anuschka de, 'Foreign and Citizen Teachers at Bologna University in the 15th and 16th centuries. Statutes, statistics and student teachers', *Annali di Storia delle Università italiane*, 12, 2008: 329–356 [Bologna].

Deelstra, Hendrik and Michel Péters, 'L'Ecole sucrière Belge de Glons', *Studium. Tijdschrift voor Wetenschaps- en Universiteitsgeschiedenis/Revue d'Histoire des Sciences et des Universités*, 1.3, 2008: 226–242 [Liège (Glons)].

Delft, Dirk van, 'Zero-Point Energy: The Case of the Leiden Low-Temperature Laboratory of Heike Kamerlingh Onnes', *Annals of Science*, 65, 2008: 339–362 [Leiden].

Dorsman, Leen J., 'Oorlog en wetenschap: de Utrechtse universiteit in de periode 1914–1918', *Oud-Utrecht. Tijdschrift voor geschiedenis van stad en provincie Utrecht*, 81.6, 2008: 172–175 [Utrecht].

—— and Annemarieke Blankesteijn, *'Work with universities' The 1948 Utrecht conference and the birth of the IAU*, Utrecht, Matrijs, 2008 [Utrecht].

—— and Peter Jan Knegtmans (eds.), *Keurige wereldbestormers. Over studenten en hun rol in de Nederlandse samenleving sedert 1876* Hilversum, Verloren, 2008.

Faasse, Patricia, *In splendid isolation. A history of the Willie Commelin Scholten Phytopathology Laboratory 1894–1992* (History of science and scholarship in the Netherlands, 11), Amsterdam, Koninklijke Nederlandse Academie van Wetenschappen, 2008 [Amsterdam].

Faber, Sjoerd, 'De vacante leerstoel strafrecht aan de Gemeente Universiteit Amsterdam (1927–1932). De kandidaten: F.W. Goudsmit, D. Hazewinkel-Suringa, J.P. Hooykaas, B.J. Stokvis, M.P., D. Hazewinkel-Suringa', *Pro Memorie*, 10.2, 2008: 131–148 [Amsterdam (UvA)].

Feenstra, Robert, 'Bibliotheca Frisica Juridica II. Bio-bibliografische notities over enkele weinig bekende Friese juristen', *Tijdschrift voor Rechtsgeschiedenis*, 76.3–4, 2008: 329–351.

Flipse, Abraham C., 'Against the Science-Religion Conflict: the Genesis of a Calvinist Science Faculty in the Netherlands in the Early Twentieth Century', *Annals of Science*, 65, 2008: 363–392 [Amsterdam (VU)].

Geelhoed, Alex, ' "De volkeren der aarde. Zij wachten op ons". Sociaal en politiek engagement van de eerste studentengeneratie aan de Politiek Sociale Faculteit van de Universiteit van Amsterdam', in Dorsman and Knegtmans (eds.), *Keurige wereldbestormers*, 73–90 [Amsterdam (UvA)].

Gielis, Marcel, 'The campaign against biblical humanists at the University of Leuven. Leuven theologians as opponents of Erasmus and of humanistic theology', in Rummel (ed.), *Biblical Humanism and Scholasticism* [Leuven].

Görts, Coen, ' "Oproerig en allerinfaamst gedrag": predikant en Patriot Ysbrand van Hamelsveld', *Oud-Utrecht. Tijdschrift voor geschiedenis van stad en provincie Utrecht*, 81.4, 2008: 96–102 [Utrecht].

Haxhe, Jean-Jacques, '50 ans de médecine à l'U.C.L. 1950–2000', *Bulletin et Mémoires de l'Académie Royale de Médecine*, 163.5, 2008: 247–253 [Louvain-la-Neuve].

Helvoort, Ton van, *De chemie van de universitaire wetenschapsbeoefening. Een halve eeuw Scheikunde in Groningen 1945–1995* (Studies over de Geschiedenis van de Groningse Universiteit, 4), Hilversum, Verloren, 2008 [Groningen].

Hiraux, Françoise (ed.), *Les engagements étudiants. Des pratiques et des horizons dans un monde globalisé* (Publications des Archives de l'Université catholique de Louvain, 18), Louvain-la-Neuve, Academia-Bruylant, 2008.

Hiraux, Françoise, 'La part de l'image dans la construction d'une histoire de l'université', in Guerrini et al. (eds.), *La storia delle università alle soglie del XXI secolo*, 75–90.

Hoeven, Diederik van der, *Verschil maken*. *Twintig jaar NW&S in Utrecht*, Utrecht, 2008 [Utrecht].

Hulscher, Han, 'Studenten in het Amsterdamse muziekleven sinds 1878', in Dorsman and Knegtmans (eds.), *Keurige wereldbestormers*, 19–38 [Amsterdam (UvA)].

Jacopssen, André and Sabine Verhulst, *Itinéraires d'un Brugeois en Italie et en Sicile (1821–1823)*, Geneva, Droz, 2008.

Kempen, Ronald van (ed.), *Honderd jaar geografie in Utrecht: over gebieden, actoren en stromen*, Utrecht, Faculteit Geowetenschappen, Universiteit Utrecht, 2008 [Utrecht].

Knegtmans, Peter Jan, 'Voor wetenschap en maatschappij. Het zelfbeeld van studenten in de Sociaal-Democratische Studentenclubs', in Dorsman and Knegtmans (eds.), *Keurige wereldbestormers*, 39–51.

Levi, Marcel M., 'De status quo van de Amsterdamse Internistenschool', in Van Lieburg (ed.), *De Amsterdamse Internistenschool 1828–2008* [Amsterdam (UvA)].

Lieburg, Mart J. van (ed.), *De Amsterdamse Internistenschool 1828–2008. De traditie van de inwendige geneeskunde aan het Atheneum en de Universiteit van Amsterdam weerspiegeld in de academische redes van hoogleraren en lectoren*, Amsterdam, Erasmus Publishing, 2008 [Amsterdam (UvA)].

—— 'In de traditie van de Amsterdamse Internistenschool', in Van Lieburg (ed.), *De Amsterdamse Internistenschool 1828–2008* [Amsterdam (UvA)].

Louryan, S., 'Scolastique, médecine et université', *Revue Médicale de Bruxelles*, 29.2, 2008: 211–215 [Brussels].

—— 'Un portrait des enseignants d'anatomie humaine à l'ULB entre 1834 et 1905', *Revue Médicale de Bruxelles*, 29.1, 2008: 63–69 [Brussels].

Maar, Rimko van der, 'De deeltjesversneller. Ton Regtien en de studentenbeweging in de jaren zestig', in Dorsman and Knegtmans (eds.), *Keurige wereldbestormers*, 105–131.

Mirguet, Françoise and Françoise Hiraux, *L'institut supérieur de philosophie de Louvain (1889–1968). Inventaire des archives. Introduction historique* (Publications des Archives de l'Université catholique de Louvain, 21), Louvain-la-Neuve, Academia-Bruylant, 2008 [Leuven].

Pien, Armand and Ronny Martens, *100 jaar sterrenkundig observatorium te Gent. Van Willem I tot de UGent Volkssterrenwacht*, Ghent, Volkssterrenwacht UGent, 2008 [Ghent].

Porcu, Ornella, 'Hoe internationaal is het university college?' *Transfer. Onafhankelijk vakblad voor internationale samenwerking in hoger onderwijs en onderzoek*, 15.4, 2008: 12–15 [Utrecht, Maastricht, Middelburg].

Randeraad, Nico, 'De statistische reizen van Jan Ackersdijck', *De negentiende eeuw*, 32.1, 2008: 15–27 [Utrecht].

Reiding, Jurrie, Ernst Homburg, Klaas Van Berkel, Leen J. Dorsman and others, 'Discussiedossier naar aanleiding van: "Martijn Eickhoff, In naam der wetenschap? P.J.W. Debye en zijn carrière in Nazi-Duitsland (Amsterdam 2007)" ', *Studium. Tijdschrift voor Wetenschaps- en Universiteitsgeschiedenis/Revue d'Histoire des Sciences et des Universités*, 1.4, 2008: 269–286.

Ridder-Symoens, Hilde de, 'Intellectual freedom under strain in the Low Countries during the long 16th century', in R. A. Muller and R. C. Schwinges (eds.), *Wissenschaftsfreiheit in Vergangenheit und Gegenwart* (Veröffentlichungen der Gesellschaft für Universitäts- und Wissenschaftsgeschichte, 9), Basle, Schwabe Verlag, 2008, 229–248.

Rubens, Robert, 'De artsen-rectoren in Gent en prof. dr. J.J. Bouckaert, rector 1961–1969', *Tijdschrift voor Geneeskunde*, 64.9, 2008: 477–480 [Ghent].

Sartori, Paolo, 'The campaign against biblical humanists at the University of Leuven. Frans Titelmans, the Congregation of Montaigu and Biblical Scholarship', in Rummel (ed.), *Biblical Humanism and Scholasticism* [Leuven].

Schepers, L. W., *Van pand naar klant? Het veranderingsproces van de vastgoedorganisatie binnen de Universiteit Utrecht*, Rotterdam, Erasmus Universiteit, 2008 [Utrecht].

Snippe, Harm (ed.), *Catharijnesingel 59: een bijzonder gebouw met bijzondere bewoners. Impressies ter gelegenheid van het 100ste geboortejaar van Prof. Dr. K.C. Winkler*, Utrecht, Eijkman-Winkler Center for Microbiology, Infectious Diseases and Inflammation, University Medical Center Utrecht, 2008 [Utrecht].

Stamhuis, Ida H. and Brigitte Hertz, "Wij namen alles vreselijk serieus'. De eerste meisjesstudenten in de exacte vakken aan de gereformeerde Vrije Universiteit (1930–1960)', in Dorsman and Knegtmans (eds.), *Keurige wereldbestormers*, 53–71 [Amsterdam (VU)].

Tollebeek, Jo, 'Leuven/Louvain-la-Neuve: de universiteitsbibliotheek: verdeeldheid in de wereld van de geest', in Jo Tollebeek, Geert Buelens, Gita Deneckere and Chantal Kesteloot and others (eds.), *België, een parcours van herinnering: 2. Plaatsen van tweedracht, crisis en nostalgie*, Amsterdam, Bakker, 2008, 138–151 [Leuven, Louvain-la-Neuve].

——'A stormy family, Paul Fredericq and the formation of an Academic historical community in the nineteenth-century', *Storia della storiografia*, 53, 2008: 58–72.

Trommelen, Mieke, *Buitenkrachten, binnenkrachten: de Utrechtse taalkunde, 1979–1989*, Utrecht, Matrijs, 2008 [Utrecht].

Verbaeys, A. and P. Van Cauwenberge, 'De activiteiten van de Gentse studenten geneeskunde in de tweede helft van de 20ste eeuw', *Tijdschrift voor Geneeskunde*, 64.9, 2008: 481–483 [Ghent].

Vermij, Rienk, *David de Wied. Toponderzoeker in polderland*, Utrecht, Matrijs, 2008 [Utrecht].

Wesseling, H. L., *Zoon en vader. Vader en zoon*, Amsterdam, Prometheus/Bert Bakker, 2008 [Leiden].

Witte-Rang, Margarita Etje, *Geen recht de moed te verliezen. Leven en werken van dr. H.M. de Lange 1919–2001*, Zoetermeer, Boekencentrum, 2008 [Utrecht].

Publications 2009

Abma, Ruud, Jaap Bos, Willem Koops and Henk van Rinsum, 'Ontmoeting over de grenzen. Internationale contacten van de Utrechtse school', in Dorsman and Knegtmans (eds.), *Over de grens*, 141–166 [Utrecht].

Baetens, Roland, 'Het Prins Leopold Instituut voor Tropische Geneeskunde te Antwerpen: een overzicht', in Leo Van Bergen and Stephen Snelders (eds.), *Van piratendokters tot wetenschappelijke instituten. Drie eeuwen Nederlandse en Belgische tropische geneeskunde*, special issue of *Studium. Tijdschrift voor Wetenschaps- en Universiteitsgeschiedenis/Revue d'Histoire des Sciences et des Universités*, 2.2, 2009: 116–129 [Antwerpen (Instituut voor Tropische Geneeskunde)].

Caljé, Pieter A. J., *Student, universiteit en samenleving. De Groningse universiteit in de negentiende eeuw* (Studies over de Geschiedenis van de Groningse Universiteit, 3), Hilversum, Verloren, 2009 [Groningen].

Caluwe, Rita De, *Vijftig jaar rekencentrum aan de Universiteit Gent: 1952–2002*, Ghent, Academia press, 2009 [Ghent].

Corens, Kjell, *Inventaris van het archief van rector Honoré van Waeyenbergh (1891–1971)* (Fasti Academici, 3), Leuven, Acco, 2009 [Leuven].

Damme, Mascha van, 'Serene monumentaliteit. De universiteitsbibliotheek in de binnenstad', *Post Planjer. Utrechts Bulletin voor Architectuur en Stedenbouw*, 57, 2009: 14–22 [Utrecht].

Delft, Dirk van, 'Koude drukte. Het laboratorium van Heike Kamerlingh Onnes als internationaal centrum van lagetemperaturenonderzoek', in Dorsman and Knegtmans (eds.), *Over de grens*, 31–52 [Leiden].

Dorsman, Leen J., 'Academisch internationalisme', in Dorsman and Knegtmans (eds.), *Over de grens*, 11–29.

——'Wetenschap en wereld. Het leven van de professor in brieven', in Van Egmond, Jaski and Mulder (eds.), *Bijzonder onderzoek*, 66–71 [Utrecht].

—— and Peter Jan Knegtmans (eds.), *Over de grens. Internationale contacten aan Nederlandse universiteiten sedert 1876* (Universiteit & Samenleving, 5), Hilversum, Verloren, 2009.

Egmond, Marco van, Bart Jaski and Hans Mulder (eds.), *Bijzonder onderzoek. Een ontdekkingsreis door de Bijzondere Collecties van de Universiteitsbibliotheek*, Zwolle, Waanders, 2009 [Utrecht].

Harinck, George, ' "Uwe komst in Amerika zou ten rijken zegen kunnen zijn". Hoe de Vrije Universiteit in de negentiende eeuw internationale betekenis kreeg', in Dorsman and Knegtmans (eds.), *Over de grens*, 101–120 [Amsterdam (VU)].

Hollestelle, Marijn, 'Paul Ehrenfests internationalisme. Bloei en verval van de Leidse theoretische fysica', in Dorsman and Knegtmans (eds.), *Over de grens*, 69–87 [Leiden].

Knegtmans, Peter Jan, 'Professor Ernst Laqueur en de grenzen aan het internationalisme in de wetenschap in het interbellum', in Dorsman and Knegtmans (eds.), *Over de grens*, 89–100 [Amsterdam (UvA)].

Korf, Lindie, 'Afrikaner nationalisten als product van het Nederlandse hoger onderwijs? Het voorbeeld van D.F. Malan', in Dorsman and Knegtmans (eds.), *Over de grens*, 121–140.

Ledegang-Keegstra, Jeltine L. R., 'La présence de Théodore de Bèze dans les Albums Amicorum (1559–1605)', *Bulletin de la Société de l'Histoire du Protestantisme français*, 155, 2009: 421–446.

Naaijkens, Ton, 'Zum Geleit', in Ton Naaijkens (ed.), *Rückblicke, Ausblicke. Zur Geschichte der Germanistik in den Niederlanden*, special issue of *Utrechter Blätter*, 1, 2009: 7–9.

Netten, Djoeke van, 'Uniek Utrechts drukwerk. Disputaties uit de eerste halve eeuw van de universiteit', in Van Egmond, Jaski and Mulder (eds.), *Bijzonder onderzoek*, 56–61 [Utrecht].

Onghena, Sofie, 'Altruïstisch ambtenaar of heroïsch genie? Het gepropageerde beeld van provinciale en academische directeurs van bacteriologische laboratoria in België (ca. 1900–1940)', *Studium. Tijdschrift voor Wetenschaps- en Universiteitsgeschiedenis/Revue d'Histoire des Sciences et des Universités*, 2.4, 2009: 191–210.

Roegiers, Jan, *Collegium Veteranorum Aedes Sacrae Facultatis*, Leuven, Peeters Publishers, 2009 [Leuven].

Tollebeek, Jo, 'Een labyrint van herinneringen: de aula van de Gentse universiteit', in Jo Tollebeek and Henk Te Velde (eds.), *Het geheugen van De Lage Landen*, Rekkem, Ons erfdeel, 2009, 34–43 [Ghent].

Vandersteene, Liesbeth, *De geschiedenis van de Rechtsfaculteit van de Universiteit Gent: van haar ontstaan tot aan de Tweede Wereldoorlog (1817–1940)* (Verhandelingen der Maatschappij voor geschiedenis en oudheidkunde te Gent, 33), Ghent, 2009 [Ghent].

Velden, Bastiaan Van der, *Van Praktizijnsopleiding tot Juridische Faculteit: 140 jaar juridisch onderwijs op Curaçao*, Den Haag, Boom Juridische Uitgevers, 2009.

Publications 2010

Boute, Bruno, 'Saint, Scholar, Exorcist? About Jacobus Jansonius, Professor at Louvain (1547–1625)', in Delsaerdt, Delville, Schwall and Vanysacker (eds.), *The Quintessence of Lives*, 83–110 [Leuven].

Collier, Mel, 'The University Library of Leuven today', in Lamberigts and Kenis (eds.), *Omnia autem probate, quod bonum est tenete*, 45–64 [Leuven].

Courtois, Luc, 'Aux origines de la crise moderniste en Belgique: Une dénonciation anonyme de l'exégète Paulin Ladeuze (février 1903)', in Delsaerdt, Delville, Schwall and Vanysacker (eds.), *The Quintessence of Lives*, 485–504 [Leuven].

Delsaerdt, Pierre, Katharina Smeyers and Marc Derez (eds.), *Anima Academiae Bibliotheca. Dertig jaar aanwinsten voor de Leuvense Universiteitsbibliotheek 1980–2010*, Leuven, Universiteitsbibliotheek K.U.Leuven, 2010, 159 p. (Huldeboek Jan Roegiers) [Leuven].

——, Jean-Pierre Delville, Hedwig Schwall and Dries Vanysacker (eds.), *The Quintessence of Lives. Intellectual Biographies in the Low Countries presented to Jan Roegiers* (Bibliothèque de la Revue d'Histoire ecclésiastique, 91), Turnhout, Brepols Publishers, 2010.

Dorsman, Leen J., 'Digital sources to the history of Utrecht University. "The Digital Album Promotorum"', in Ulf Morgenstern and Thomas Riechtert (eds.), *Catalogus Professorum Lipsiensis. Konzeption, technische Umsetzung und Anwendungen fur Professorenkataloge im Semantic Web* (Leipziger Beiträge zur Informatik, 21), Leipzig, 2010, 151–159 [Utrecht].

Falek, Pascale, 'A Multifaceted Image of Jewish Women at Belgian Universities during the Interwar Period', *Journal of Jewish Identities*, 3.1, 2010: 25–40.

François, Wim and Albert van Roey, 'Andreas Masius (1514–73). Löwener Alumnus, Gelehter der syrischen Studien und biblischer Humanist', in Delsaerdt, Delville, Schwall and Vanysacker (eds.), *The Quintessence of Lives*, 7–28 [Leuven].

Frijhoff, Willem, 'Johannes Lomejer (1636–1699), un historien du livre en route vers l'histoire culturelle', in Delsaerdt, Delville, Schwall and Vanysacker (eds.), *The Quintessence of Lives*, 2010, 205–226.

Gevers, Lieve, ' "One Day the World will be what we want it to be". Albrecht Rodenbach and the Flemish Catholic Student Movement', in Delsaerdt, Delville, Schwall and Vanysacker (eds.), *The Quintessence of Lives*, 469–484 [Leuven].

Gispen, Willem Hendrik, 'David de Wied. Eminent scientist and academic leader: a personal note', *European Journal of Pharmacology*, 626, 2010: 4–8 [Utrecht].

Hendrix, Guido, 'Les livres du recteur P.F.X. De Ram à la bibliothèque de l'abbaye des trappistes à Westmalle', in Delsaerdt, Delville, Schwall and Vanysacker (eds.), *The Quintessence of Lives*, 347–358 [Leuven].

Holans, Ludo, 'Kanttekeningen van een campusbibliothecaris Wetenschap en Technologie', in Lamberigts and Kenis (eds.), *Omnia autem probate, quod bonum est tenete*, 39–44 [Leuven].

Janssens, Gustaaf, 'Joachim Hopperus en Willem van Oranje, 1566–1576', in Delsaerdt, Delville, Schwall and Vanysacker (eds.), *The Quintessence of Lives*, 29–42 [Leuven].

Lamberigts, Mathijs and Leo Kenis, 'De Maurits Sabbebibliotheek van de Faculteit Godgeleerdheid', in Lamberigts and Kenis (eds.), *Omnia autem probate, quod bonum est tenete*, 1–20 [Leuven].

—— and Leo Kenis (eds.), *Omnia autem probate, quod bonum est tenete. Opstellen aangeboden aan Etienne D'hondt, bibliothecaris van de Maurits Sabbebibliotheek*, Leuven, Peeters Publishers, 2010 [Leuven].

Louchez, Eddy, 'La congrégation des Oblats de Marie Immaculée et les universités', in Delsaerdt, Delville, Schwall and Vanysacker (eds.), *The Quintessence of Lives*, 397–424.

Meerbeeck, Michel Van, 'De Louvain à Senez en Provence: l'ordination sacerdotale d'un future archevêque', in Delsaerdt, Delville, Schwall and Vanysacker (eds.), *The Quintessence of Lives*, 269–282 [Leuven, Paris - Corneille-Jean Barchman Wuytiers].

Nilis, Jeroen, 'Bibliography Jan Roegiers', in Delsaerdt, Delville, Schwall and Vanysacker (eds.), *The Quintessence of Lives*, xxi–xxxvii.

——*Irish students at Leuven University, 1548–1797. A Prosopography* (Fasti Academici, 4), Leuven, Acco, 2010 [Leuven].

Persoons, Ernest, 'Betrekkingen van de kapucijn Antonius-Maria van Reita met de Nederlanden', in Delsaerdt, Delville, Schwall and Vanysacker (eds.), *The Quintessence of Lives*, 161–184 [Leuven].

Put, Eddy, 'Mal du siècle des archives? Jacques Wellens et le classement des archives de l'Université de Louvain en 1757–1766', in Delsaerdt, Delville, Schwall and Vanysacker (eds.), *The Quintessence of Lives*, 283–292 [Leuven].

Quaghebeur, Toon, 'Damen, an anti-Jansenist in the Service of the Archbishops of Mechlin 1690–1730', in Delsaerdt, Delville, Schwall and Vanysacker (eds.), *The Quintessence of Lives*, 249–268 [Leuven].

Roegiers, Jan, 'De Leuvense Bibliotheek Godgeleerdheid 1445–2010', in Lamberigts and Kenis (eds.), *Omnia autem probate, quod bonum est tenete*, 21–38 [Leuven].

——'Universitaire heemkunde?' in Delsaerdt, Smeyers and Derez (eds.), *Anima Academiae Bibliotheca*, 145–154 [Leuven].

Soen, Violet, 'The Loyal Opposition of Jean Vendeville (1572–1592): Contributions to a Contextualized Biography', in Delsaerdt, Delville, Schwall and Vanysacker (eds.), *The Quintessence of Lives*, 43–62 [Leuven].

Tournoy, Gilbert, 'À la recherche de la bibliothèque du juriste liégeois Gerardus Corselius (1568–1636), professeur à l'Université de Louvain', in Delsaerdt, Delville, Schwall and Vanysacker (eds.), *The Quintessence of Lives*, 127–150 [Leuven].

Verberckmoes, Johan, 'Juan de Palafox y Mendoza (1600–1659) and the Politics of God's Grace', in Delsaerdt, Delville, Schwall and Vanysacker (eds.), *The Quintessence of Lives*, 151–160.

Welkenhuysen, Andries, ' "Dien Pater capucyn, die hier van Wenen gekomen is". Reita en de kring rond Puteanus, 1642–1645', in Delsaerdt, Delville, Schwall and Vanysacker (eds.), *The Quintessence of Lives*, 185–204 [Leuven].
Wils, Kaat, 'Un parfum de sainteté laïque. Hector Denis, Political Economy and Sociology in the late 19th Century Belgium', in Delsaerdt, Delville, Schwall and Vanysacker (eds.), *The Quintessence of Lives*, 425–444 [Brussels].

The British Isles

Additions to Earlier Lists

For 2004
Murphy, A. B. and D. Raftery (eds.), *Emily Davies: collected letters, 1861–1875*, London, 2004 [Cambridge - women].
Pagnamenta, P., *The hidden Hall: portrait of a Cambridge college*, London, 2004 [Cambridge, Trinity Hall].

For 2005
Horsler, V., *Girton: thirty years in the life of a Cambridge college*, London, 2005 [Cambridge].

For 2006
Butler, C., *Christ Church, Oxford: a portrait of the House*, London, 2006 [Oxford].
Feingold, M. and V. Navarro-Brotons (eds.), *Universities and science in the early modern period*, Dordrecht, 2006.
Leonard, A. (ed.), *The magnificent McDowell: Trinity in the golden era*, London, 2006 [Dublin - 20th cent.].
McCord, N., *Newcastle University: past, present and future*, London, 2006 [Newcastle-upon-Tyne].
Prest, W. R. (ed.), *The letters of Sir William Blackstone, 1744–80*, London, 2006 [Oxford].

For 2007
Baker, H. and C. Tripp, *SOAS, a celebration in many voices*, London, 2007 [London, School of Oriental and African Studies].
Gilbraith, C. and C. Walston, *Pembroke in our time: a portrait of Pembroke College*, London, 2007 [Cambridge].
Knox, R. B., *Westminster College, Cambridge: its background and history*, Cambridge, 2007 [Cambridge].

McAnallen, D., P. Mossey and S. Moore, 'The "temporary diaspora" at play: the development of Gaelic games in British universities', *Sport in Society*, 10, 2007: 402–424.

Morphet, D., *St John's College, Cambridge: excellence and diversity*, London, 2007 [Cambridge].

Parkes, S. M. and D. Raftery, *Female education in Ireland, 1700–1900*, Dublin, 2007.

Procter, I., *Sociology at the University of Warwick: a history*, Coventry, 2007 [Warwick].

Pullan, B. and others, *A portrait of the University of Manchester*, London, 2007 [Manchester].

Rivière, P. (ed.), *A history of Oxford anthropology*, Oxford, 2007 [Oxford].

Silver, H., 'Higher education and social change: purpose in pursuit?' *History of Education*, 36, 2007: 535–550.

Stray, C. (ed.), *Oxford classics: teaching and learning, 1800–2000*, London, 2007 [Oxford].

Watson, N., *The Durham difference: the story of Durham University*, London, 2007 [Durham].

Watts, R., *Women in science: a cultural and social history*, London, 2007.

For 2008

Adelman, J., 'The agriculture diploma in Queen's College, Belfast, 1845–1863, and science education in nineteenth-century Ireland', *Irish Economic and Social History*, 35, 2008: 51–67 [Belfast].

Anderson, R., 'Elite education and the British university model, 1945–1970', in D. Menozzi and M. Rosa (eds.), *La storia della Scuola Normale Superiore di Pisa in una prospettiva comparativa*, Pisa, 2008, 23–30.

Archer, I. and A. Cameron, *Keble past and present*, London, 2008 [Oxford, Keble College].

Brookes, B., 'A corresponding community: Dr Agnes Bennett and her friends from the Edinburgh Medical College for Women of the 1890s', *Medical History*, 52, 2008: 237–256 [Edinburgh].

A century of scholarship: travelling students of the National University of Ireland, ed. National University of Ireland, Dublin, 2008.

Darwall-Smith, R., *A history of University College, Oxford*, Oxford, 2008 [Oxford].

Fiddes, J., *The Scott Sutherland School of Architecture and Built Environment: a commemorative history*, Aberdeen, 2008 [Aberdeen].

Glanzer, P. L., 'Searching for the soul of English universities: an exploration and analysis of Christian higher education in England', *British Journal of Educational Studies*, 56, 2008: 163–183.

Hall, C., 'The early fellows of Gonville Hall and their books', *Transactions of the Cambridge Bibliographical Society*, 13, 2008: 233–252 [Cambridge].

Harford, J., *The opening of university education to women in Ireland*, Dublin, 2008.

Henry, J., 'Historical and other studies of science, technology and medicine in the University of Edinburgh', *Notes and Records of the Royal Society (of London)*, 62, 2008: 223–235 [Edinburgh - 20th cent.].

Hutchins, R., *British university observatories, 1772–1939*, Aldershot, 2008.

Janin, H., *The university in medieval life, 1179–1499*, Jefferson NC, 2008.

Kirby, J., 'Alice M. Cooke and the beginnings of medieval history in the University of Leeds, 1907–1921', *Northern History*, 45, 2008: 351–359 [Leeds].

Liang, W. Y. and C. Brooke, *A portrait of Gonville and Caius College*, London, 2008 [Cambridge].

Lubenow, W. C., 'Roman Catholicism in the University of Cambridge: St Edmund's House in 1898', *Journal of Ecclesiastical History*, 59, 2008: 697–713 [Cambridge].

Mathers, H., 'Scientific women in a co-educational university: Sheffield, 1879–1939', *History of Education Researcher*, 81, 2008: 3–19 [Sheffield].

McGuinness, B. (ed.), *Wittgenstein in Cambridge: letters and documents, 1911–51*, Oxford, 2008 [Cambridge].

Neild, R., *Riches and responsibility: the financial history of Trinity College, Cambridge*, Cambridge, 2008 [Cambridge].

Newton, G., 'The history of Dutch at Sheffield', *Dutch Crossing*, 32, 2008: 145–153 [Sheffield].

Prest, W. R., *William Blackstone: law and letters in the eighteenth century*, Oxford, 2008 [Oxford].

Raban, S. (ed.), *Examining the world: a history of the University of Cambridge Examinations Syndicate*, Cambridge, 2008 [Cambridge].

Roberts, A., *The Welsh National School of Medicine, 1893–1931: the Cardiff years*, Cardiff, 2008 [Cardiff].

Sandell, M., ' "Truly international?" The International Federation of University Women's quest for expansion in the interwar period', *History of Education Researcher*, 82, 2008: 74–83.

Simpson, A. D. C., 'Thomas and John Donaldson and the Edinburgh medical class cards', *Book of the Old Edinburgh Club, new series*, 7, 2008: 71–86 [Edinburgh].

Stray, C. (ed.), *An American in Victorian Cambridge: Charles Astor Bristed's 'Five years in an English university'*, Exeter, 2008 [Cambridge].

Thompson, D. M., *Cambridge theology in the nineteenth century: enquiry, controversy and truth*, Aldershot, 2008 [Cambridge].

Wintersgill, D., *The rectors of the University of St Andrews 1859–2005*, Edinburgh, 2008 [St Andrews].

Withers, C. W. J., 'Edinburgh's geographical centenary - but an intellectual and a departmental history?' *Scottish Geographical Journal*, 124, 2008: 103–116.

Publications 2009

Anderson, R., 'The idea of a university', in K. Withers (ed.), *First class? Challenges and opportunities for the UK's university sector*, London, 2009, 37–45.

Andersson, D. C., 'Humanism and natural philosophy in Renaissance Cambridge: Bodley MS 616', *History of Universities*, 24, 2009: 69–116 [Cambridge].

Berlin, I., *Enlightening: letters 1946–1960*, ed. H. Hardy and J. Holmes, London, 2009 [Oxford"].

Brockliss, L., *Magdalen College Oxford: a history*, Oxford, 2009 [Oxford].

Cheeseright, P., *The phoenix rises: a portrait of Coventry University in its city*, London, 2009 [Coventry].

Craig, A. (ed.), *Fides Nostra Victoria. A portrait of St John's College, Durham*, London, 2009 [Durham].

Craik, A. D. D. and A. D. Roberts, 'Mathematics teaching, teachers and students at St Andrews University, 1765–1858', *History of Universities*, 24, 2009: 206–279 [St Andrews].

Crook, J. M., *Brasenose: the biography of an Oxford college*, Oxford, 2009 [Oxford].

Davies, C. and J. Garnett, *Wadham College, 1610–2010*, London, 2009 [Oxford].

Eddy, M. D., *The language of mineralogy: John Walker, chemistry and the Edinburgh Medical School, 1750–1800*, Farnham, 2009 [Edinburgh].

Evans, G., *The University of Cambridge: a new history*, London, 2009 [Cambridge].

Leach, C. and A. Jacobs, ' "More men would have been more fun": the University of Winchester alumni voices project', *History of Education Researcher*, 83, 2009: 12–20 [Winchester].

Lubenow, W. C., 'The Cambridge ritualists, 1876–1924: a study of commensurability in the history of scholarship', *History of Universities*, 24, 2009: 280–308 [Cambridge - classical studies].

Macdonald, C. M. M., ' "To form citizens": Scottish students, governance and politics, 1884–1948', *History of Education*, 38, 2009: 383–402.

MacQueen, H., 'Scotland's first women law graduates: an Edinburgh centenary', in *Stair Society, Miscellany VI*, Edinburgh, 2009, 221–265 [Edinburgh].

Mitchell, L., *Maurice Bowra: a life*, Oxford, 2009 [Oxford - 20th cent.].

Muldowney, M., *Trinity and its neighbours: an oral history*, Dublin, 2009 [Dublin].

O'Brien, G. and P. Roebuck (eds.), *The University of Ulster: genesis and growth*, Dublin, 2009 [Ulster].

Pagnamenta, P. (ed.), *The University of Cambridge: an 800th anniversary portrait*, London, 2009 [Cambridge].

Ralston, I., 'Gordon Childe and Scottish archaeology: the Edinburgh years, 1927–1946', *European Journal of Archaeology*, 12, 2009: 47–90 [Edinburgh].

Roberts, D., *Bangor University, 1884–2009*, Cardiff, 2009 [Bangor].

Robinson, J., *Bluestockings: the remarkable story of the first women to fight for an education*, New York, 2009.

Simpson, R., *The development of the PhD degree in Britain, 1917–1959 and since: an evolutionary and statistical history in higher education*, Lampeter, 2009.

Tight, M., *Higher education in the United Kingdom since 1945*, Buckingham, 2009.

Publications 2010

Evans, G. R., *Creating a system of higher education in Britain, 1850–2010: state regulation vs academic autonomy*, Lampeter, 2010.

Manning, A., 'Twentieth century science in Edinburgh: a brief personal selection', *Book of the Old Edinburgh Club, new series*, 8, 2010: 55–62 [Edinburgh].

Czech Republic

Additions to Earlier Lists

For 1998

Čornejová, Ivana, 'Karolinum a Klementinum: zápas o výchovu mládeže na počátku 17. století', *Acta Universitatis Carolinae. Historia Universitatis Pragensis*, 36–38.1–2, 1996–1998: 41–47 (publ. 2004, summary in German) [Das Karolinum und das Klementinum–ein Wettstreit um die Erziehung der Jugend zu Beginn des 17. Jahrhunderts].

Hlaváček, Ivan, 'Knihy a knihovny na pražské univerzitě ve středověku (stručný nástin)', *Acta Universitatis Carolinae. Historia Universitatis Pragensis*, 36–38.1–2, 1996–1998: 23–29 (publ. 2004, summary in German) [Bücher und Bibliotheken an der Prager Universität im Mittelalter. Knapper Abriss].

Míšková, Alena, 'Německá (Karlova-) Univerzita v Praze v letech druhé světové války', *Acta Universitatis Carolinae. Historia Universitatis Pragensis*, 36–38.1–2, 1996–1998: 55–60 (publ. 2004, summary in German) [Die Deutsche (Karls-) Universität in Prag während des Zweiten Weltkrieg].

Pešek, Jiří, 'Pražská utrakvistická univerzita a náboženské poměry 16. století', *Acta Universitatis Carolinae. Historia Universitatis Pragensis*, 36–38.1–2, 1996–1998: 31–40 (publ. 2004, summary in German) [Die Prager utraquistische Universität und die religiösen Umstände des 16. Jahrhunderts].

Pousta, Zdeněk, 'Studijní prověrky na českých vysokých školách', *Acta Universitatis Carolinae. Historia Universitatis Pragensis*, 36–38.1–2, 1996–1998: 87–93 (publ. 2004, summary in German) [Studienüberprüfungen an den tschechischen Hochschulen].

Svatoš, Michal, 'Pražská univerzita a její vzory', *Acta Universitatis Carolinae. Historia Universitatis Pragensis*, 36–38.1–2, 1996–1998: 11–21 (publ. 2004, summary in German) [Die Prager Universität und ihre Vorbilder].

Svobodný, Petr, 'Rasová hygiena na lékařské fakultě Německé Karlovy univerzity v Praze (1938–1945)', *Acta Universitatis Carolinae. Historia Universitatis Pragensis*, 36–38.1–2, 1996–1998: 61–71 (publ. 2004, summary in German) [Rassenhygiene an der medizinischen Fakultät der Deutschen Karls-Universität in Prag (1938–1945)].

Zilynská, Blanka, 'Cesta k ovládnutí českých univerzit komunistickou stranou (1945–1948)', *Acta Universitatis Carolinae. Historia Universitatis Pragensis*, 36–38.1–2, 1996–1998: 73–86 (publ. 2004, summary in German) [Der Weg zur Beherrschung der tschechischen Universitäten durch die kommunistische Partei (1945–1948)].

For 2002

Beránek, Karel, 'Triumf jezuitských bakalářů v Praze roku 1602', *Miscellanea oddělení rukopisů a starých tisků*, 17, 2001–2002 (publ. 2003): 217–233 (summary in German) [Triumph der im Jahre 1602 in Prag graduierten jesuitischen Baccalaurei].

Kašparová, Jaroslava, *Utilitas Matheseos: jezuitská matematika v Klementinum (1602–1773)*, Prague, 2002 [Jesuit mathematics in the Clementinum (1602–1773)].

For 2003

Devátá, Markéta, 'Profesoři jmenovaní v letech 1948–1950 na českých vysokých školách', *Acta Universitatis Carolinae. Historia Universitatis Pragensis*, 43.1–2, 2003: 193–251 (publ. 2004, summary in German) [Von 1848–1950 an den tschechischen Hochschulen ernannte Professoren].

Konrád, Ota, 'Eine lange Feindschaft, Die Prager Professoren Erich Gierach und Gerhard Gesemann in der Tschechoslowakischen Republik und im Nationalsozialismus', *Acta Universitatis Carolinae. Historia Universitatis Pragensis*, 43.1–2, 2003: 173–192 (publ. 2004).

Mačák, Karel, 'Matematika v pražském Klementinu v letech 1600–1740', *Acta Universitatis Carolinae. Historia Universitatis Pragensis*, 43.1–2, 2003: 83–105 (publ. 2004, summary in German) [Matematik im Prager Klementinum in den Jahren 1600–1740].

Štemberková, Marie, 'Výuka románských jazyků na Univerzitě Karlově za první republiky', *Acta Universitatis Carolinae. Historia Universitatis Pragensis*, 43.1–2, 2003: 135–172 (publ. 2004, summary in German) [Römische Sprachhunterricht an der Karlsuniversität während der 1. Republik].

Publications 2004

Čornejová, Ivana, 'Barokní vzdělanost', in Olga Fejtová et al. (eds.), *Barokní Praha – Barokní Čechie 1620–1740: sborník příspěvků z vědecké konference o fenoménu baroka v Čechách, Praha, Anežský klášter a Clam-Gallasův palác, 24.-27. září 2001*, Prague, Scriptorium, 2004, 575–582 (summary in English) [Baroque scholarship].

Čornejová, Ivana, 'Pražská univerzita a absolutismus', in Petr Kreutz and Vojtěch Šustek (eds.), *Seminář a jeho hosté II. Sborník příspěvků k nedožitým 70. narozeninám doc. Rostislava Nového*, Prague, Skriptorium, 2004, 175–186 (summary in German) [Die Prager Universität und der Absolutismus].

Devátá, Markéta, 'Russische und ukrainische Emigranten an tschechischen Hochschulen nach dem Februar 1948', in Antonín Kostlán and Alice Velková (eds.), *Wissenschaft im Exil: Die Tschechoslowakei als Kreuzweg 1918–1989*, Prague, Výzkumné centrum pro dějiny vědy, 2004, 289–306 (henceforth Kostlán and Velková (eds.), *Wissenschaft im Exil*).

Havránek, Jan, 'Akademická mládež mezi křesťanstvím a atheismem a Rádlova profesura na universitě', in Tomáš Hermann and Anton Markoš (eds.), *Emanuel Rádl – vědec a filosof*, Prague, Oikoymenh, 2004, 523–531 (summary in German) [Die akademische Jugend zwischen Christentum und Atheismus. Rádls Professur an der Karlsuniversität].

―――'František Graus a Filozofická fakulta Univerzity Karlovy', in Zdeněk Beneš, Bohumil Jiroušek and Antonín Kostlán (eds.), *František Graus – člověk a historik*, Prague, Výzkumné centrum pro dějiny vědy, 2004, 39–47 [František Graus and Faculty of Arts of Charles University].

Hlaváčková, Ludmila, 'Proměny speciálního školství–pražské lékařské fakulty v 19. století', in Kateřina Bláhová and Václav Petrbok (eds.), *Vzdělání a osvěta v české kultuře 19. století: sborník příspěvků z 24. ročníku sympozia k problematice l9. století Plzeň, 4.-6. března 2004*, Prague, Ústav pro českou literaturu AV ČR, 2004, 401–409 (summary in German) [Die Wandel der medizinischen Bildung–Prager medizinischen Fakultät im 19. Jahrhundert] (henceforth Bláhová and Petrbok (eds.), *Vzdělání a osvěta v české kultuře 19. Století*).

Hlobil, Tomáš, 'Pražské univerzitní přednášky z estetiky a poetiky Augusta Gottlieba Meissnera podle zápisků Josefa Jungmanna', *Česká literatura*, 52.4, 2004: 466–484 (summary in English) [The Lectures of August Gottlieb Meissner–Professor of Aesthetics and Classical Literature at Prague–based on Josef Jungmann´s notes].

Koucká, Ivana, 'Pedagogická kariéra a působení doc. PhDr. Stanislava Sedláčka na Univerzitě Palackého v Olomouci v letech 1959–1995', in Ivana Koucká (ed.), *Laudatio Brevis: sborník věnovaný Stanislavu Sedláčkovi*, Olomouc, Univerzita Palackého v Olomouci, 2004, 21–38 [Pedagogical career and activity of Doc. PhDr. Stanislav Sedláček at Palacky University in Olomouc in 1959–1995].

Kuchařová, Hedvika, 'Řádové koleje a domácí studia premonstrátů a cisterciáků: nárys jedné z forem mimo univerzitního vyššího církevního školství doby baroka', in Olga Fejtová et al. (eds.), *Barokní Praha – Barokní Čechie*

1620–1740: sborník příspěvků z vědecké konference o fenoménu baroka v Čechách, Praha, Anežský klášter a Clam-Gallasův palác, 24.-27. září 2001, Prague, Scriptorium, 2004, 589–599 (summary in English) [Order colleges and Premonstratensian and Cistercian own study facilities].

Lach, Jiří, 'Josef Borovička na univerzitách v Bratislavě a v Brně', *Časopis Matice moravské*, 123.2, 2004: 395–420 (summary in English) [Josef Borovička at universities in Bratislava and Brno].

Litsch, Karel, 'Proměny právnického studia 1945–1989', in Karel Malý and Ladislav Soukup (eds.), *Vývoj práva v Československu v letech 1945–1989*, Prague, Karolinum, 2004, 84–131 (summary in English) [Transformations of the study of law in the period 1945–1989].

Lorenzová, Helena, 'Bolzano a jeho žáci (zejména Robert Zimmermann)', in Bláhová and Petrbok (eds.), *Vzdělání a osvěta v české kultuře 19. století*, 32–38 (summary in German) [Bernard Bolzano und sein Schüler Robert Zimmermann].

Loužil, Jaromír, 'Bernard Bolzano–učitel a vychovatel', in Bláhová and Petrbok (eds.), *Vzdělání a osvěta v české kultuře 19. století*, 21–31 (summary in German) [Bernard Bolzano als Lehrer und Erzieher].

Makovcová, Alena, 'Phenomenon "Woman" at the Faculties of Forestry in the Czech Lands in the 20th Century', in Štrbáňová, Stamhuis and Mojsejová (eds.), *Women scholars and institutions*, 509–534.

Malina, Jaroslav et al., *Antropologie. Brněnská antropologie v českém a mezinárodním kontextu (se zaměřením na Katedru antropologie Přírodovědecké fakulty Masarykovy univerzity v Brně*, ed. Rudolf Musil (Folia Historica, 73), Brno, Masarykova univerzita, rd, 185–219 p. [Antropology in Brno. An Overal Historical Review with Respect to National and International Kontext].

Mikovcová, Alena (ed.), *Historie Mendlovy zemědělské a lesnické univerzity v Brně v datech a obrazech 1919–2004*, Brno, Mendlova zemědělská a lesnická univerzita, 2004, 165 p. [History of the Mendel University of Agriculture and Forestry].

——'Russische und ukrainische Wissenschaft an der Hochschule für Landwirtschaft in Brünn', in Kostlán and Velková (eds.), *Wissenschaft im Exil*, 180–221 (Práce z dějin vědy; sv. 17).

——'Die "Arisierung" an der Deutschen Universität Prag', in Antonín Kostlán (ed.), *Wissenschaft in den böhmischen Ländern 1939–1945*, Prague, KLP, 2004, 97–106 (Práce z dějin vědy; s. 9) (henceforth Kostlán (ed.), *Wissenschaft in den böhmischen Ländern*).

——'Das Schicksal der Professoren der Prager Deutschen Universität in der Nachkriegszeit', in Kostlán and Velková (eds.), *Wissenschaft im Exil*, 136–153 (Práce z dějin vědy; sv. 17).

Pešek, Jiří and David Šaman, 'Die Chemie an der Deutschen Universität Prag in den Jahren 1938–1945', in Kostlán (ed.), *Wissenschaft in den böhmischen Ländern*, 136–142 (Práce z dějin vědy; sv. 9).

Pokorná, Lenka and Arnošt Vilém Kraus, 'Der erste Literaturwissenschaftler am Lehrstuhl für Germanistik an der tschechischen Karl-Ferdinands-Universität in Prag nach 1882', in Kostlán (ed.), *Wissenschaft in den böhmischen Ländern*, 37–67.

Prucek, Josef, 'Diáře rektorů olomoucké koleje a univerzity', *Střední Morava*, 18; 19, 2004: 72–78; 126–132 [Diaries of the Rectors of the Olomouc College and University].

Schwarz, Karl, 'Prager Professoren Gustav Adolf Skalský und Ludwig Wahrmund und die Reform des Eherechts', in Zdeněk Kučera and Jan B. Lášek (eds.), *Docete omnes gentes* (Fontes Pragenses, 35), Brno, L. Marek, 2004, 94–104 (henceforth Kučera and Lášek (eds.), *Docete omnes gentes*).

Šimůnek, Michal, 'Ein neues Fach. Die Erb- und Rassenhygiene an der Medizinischen Fakultät der Deutschen Karls-Universität Prag 1939–1945', in Kostlán (ed.), *Wissenschaft in den böhmischen Ländern*, 190–316.

Šišma, Pavel, *Učitelé na německé technice v Brně 1849–1945* (Práce z dějin techniky a přírodních věd, 2), Prague, Společnost pro dějiny věd a techniky, 2004, 205 p. (summary in English) [Teachers at the German Technical University in Brno, 1849–1945].

Soukup, Pavel, 'Rytíři ducha na pražské univerzitě. Jakoubkovo kázání Abiciamus opera tenebrarum', in Eva Doležalová, Robert Novotný and Pavel Soukup (eds.), *Evropa a Čechy na konci středověku: sborník příspěvků věnovaných Františku Šmahelovi*, Prague, Filosofia, 2004, 413–431 (summary in English) [The Knights of the Spirit at the Prague University. Jakoubek´s sermon Abiciamus opera tenebrarum] (henceforth Doležalová, Novotný and Soukup (eds.), *Evropa a Čechy na konci středověku*).

Sršeň, Lubomír, 'Oslavné portréty profesora Vincence Julia Krombholze', in Jaroslav Pánek (ed.), *Vlast a rodný kraj v díle historika: sborník prací žáků a přátel věnovaný profesoru Josefu Petráňovi* (Práce Historického ústavu AV ČR. Řada C, 15), Prague, Historický ústav Akademie věd České republiky, 2004, 495–529 (summary in German) [Glorifizierende Porträts des Prof. Vincenz Julius Krombholz].

Stočes, Jiří, 'Rostocký doklad o činnosti konzervátora práv pražského obecného učení', in Doležalová, Novotný and Soukup (eds.), *Evropa a Čechy na konci středověku*, 395–411 (summary in English) [Rostock´s Proof of Activity by the Prague General Teaching Conservator of Law].

Štrbáňová, Soňa, Ida H. Stamhuis and Kateřina Mojsejová (eds.), *Women scholars and institutions. Proceedings of the international conference (Prague, June 8–11, 2003)*, Prague, Výzkumné centrum pro dějiny vědy, 2004, 861 p.

226 Bibliography

Svobodný, Petr, 'Neue Menschen, neue Disziplinen. Die deutsche Medizinische Fakultät in Prag 1939–1945', in Kostlán (ed.), *Wissenschaft in den böhmischen Ländern*, 143–163.

—— 'Women Docents and Professors at Medical Faculties in Czechoslovakia, 1918–1939', in Štrbáňová, Stamhuis and Mojsejová (eds.), *Women scholars and institutions*, 375–399.

Vaňáč, Martin, 'Katolická teologická fakulta Univerzity Karlovy v letech 1891–1939', in Kučera and Lášek (eds.), *Docete omnes gentes*, 125–136 (summary in German p. 173) [Die Katholische Theologische Fakultät der Karls-Universität in den Jahren 1891–1939].

Zilynská, Blanka, 'Karl Adolf Konstantin Ritter von Höfler jako univerzitní učitel', in Pavel Soukup and František Šmahel (eds.), *Německá medievistika v českých zemích do roku 1945* (Práce z dějin vědy, 18), Prague, Výzkumné centrum pro dějiny vědy, 2004, 193–224 [Karl Adolf Konstantin Ritter von Höfler als Universitätslehrer].

France

Additions to Earlier Lists

For 1999

Charle, Christophe, 'Les femmes dans l'enseignement supérieur. Dynamiques et freins d'une présence, 1946–1992', in Vincent Duclert, Rémi Fabre and Patrick Fridenson (eds.), *Avenirs et avant-gardes en France, XIXe-XXe siècles. Hommage à Madeleine Rebérioux*, Paris, La Découverte, 1999.

For 2005

Alice, Gérard, 'L'enseignement supérieur de l'histoire en France de 1800 à 1914', in Christian Amalvi and others (eds.), *Les lieux de l'histoire*, Paris, 2005, 242–302.

Stoskopf, Nicolas, *Université de Haute Alsace. La longue histoire d'une jeune Université*, Strasbourg, La Nuée bleue, 2005, 93 p.

For 2007

Caron, Jean-Claude, 'Former des élites au XIXe siècle: entre modèles nationaux et normalisation européenne (Allemagne, France, Grande Bretagne, 1815–1914)', *Administration et éducation*, 116, 2007: 25–38.

Condette, Jean-François, *Histoire de la formation des enseignants en France (XIXe-XXe siècles)*, Paris, L'Harmattan, 2007, 354 p.

For 2009

Mazzella, Sylvie, *La mondialisation étudiante. Le Maghreb entre Nord et Sud*, s.l., Karthala-IRMC, 2009, 408 p.

Moulinier, Pierre, 'Naître hors de la métropole et se former à Paris: le cas des docteurs reçus à la Faculté de médecine de Paris au XIXe siècle', *Outre-Mers*, 97, 2009: 362–363.

Tikhonov Sigrist, Natalia, 'Les femmes et l'université en France, 1860–1914. Pour une historiographie comparée', in *L'enseignement supérieur: bilan et perspectives historiographiques*, special issue of *Histoire de l'éducation*, 122, 2009.

Germany

Additions to Earlier Lists

For 2003
Spengler, Dietmar, *Spiritualia et pictura: die Graphische Sammlung des ehemaligen Jesuitenkollegs in Köln*, Cologne, 2003.

For 2005
Vogt, Annette, 'Le rôle des femmes scientifiques dans les universities et les institutions académiques en Allemagne de 1919 à 1945', in Jacqueline Carroy and others (eds.), *Les femmes dans les sciences de l'homme (XIXe-XXe siècles). Inspiratrices, collaboratrices ou créatrices?*, Paris, Seli Arslan, 2005.

Publications 2009
Acham, Karl (ed.), *Kunst und Geisteswissenschaften aus Graz. Werk und Wirken überregional bedeutsamer Künstler und Gelehrter: Vom 15 Jahrhundert bis zur Jahrtausendwende*, Cologne - Weimar, 2009.

Adam, Thomas, Simone Lässig and Gabriele Lingelbach (eds.), *Stifter, Spender und Mäzene. USA und Deutschland im historischen Vergleich* (Transatlantische Historische Studien, 38), Frankfurt am Main, 2009.

Altermatt, Urs, 'Die Universität Freiburg in der Schweiz: von der "katholischen Staatsuniversität" zur Universität mit katholischer Tradition', *Jahrbuch für Universitätsgeschichte*, 12, 2009: 75–86.

Asche, Matthias, 'Jena als Typus einer protestantischen Universitätsgründung im Zeichen des Humanismus', *Zeitschrift für Thüringische Geschichte*, 63, 2009: 117–142.

Baur, Sebastian, *Vor vier Höllenrichtern... Die Lizentiats- und Doktorpromotionen an der Juristischen Fakultät der Universität Heidelberg*, Frankfurt am Main, 2009.

Bihl, Wolfdieter, *Orientalistik an der Universität Wien. Forschungen zwischen Maghreb und Ost- und Südostasien: Die Professoren und Dozenten*, Vienna, 2009.

Blanke, Horst Walter, *Historie und Historik. 200 Jahre Johann Gustav Droysen. Festschrift für Jorn Rösen*, Cologne - Weimar, 2009.

Böhm, Steffen, Alexander Krex Philip Jaeger and others, 'Verdrängte Ursprünge. Skizze einer langen Liaison zwischen Hypnose, Okkultismus und Psychoanalyse', *Jahrbuch für Universitätsgeschichte*, 12, 2009: 13–39.

Bott, Marie-Luise, 'Rückschau 1948. Max Vasmers Rede "Die Haltung der Berliner Universität" im Nationalsozialismus', *Jahrbuch für Universitätsgeschichte*, 12, 2009: 189–255.

Brockmann, Christian and others (eds.), *Antike Medizin im Schnittpunkt von Geistes- und Naturwissenschaften. Internationale Fachtagung aus Anlass des 100-jährigen Bestehens des Akademievorhabens Corpus Medicorum Graecorum, Latinorum* (Beiträge zur Altertumskunde, 255), Berlin, 2009.

Brunner, Richard, *Johann Andreas Schmeller und die Ludwig-Maximilians-Universität München. Dokumente und Erläuterungen* (Ludovico Maximilianea. Quellen, 4), Berlin, 2009.

Bruns, Florian, *Medizinethik im Nationalsozialismus. Entwicklungen und Protagonisten in Berlin (1939–1945)*, Stuttgart, 2009.

Bünz, Enno, 'Schulen im Umfeld der spätmittelalterlichen Universität Leipzig', in *Erleuchtung der Welt. Essays*, Dresden, 2009, 16–23.

Bürgel, Matthias and Andreas Umland (eds.), *Geistes- und sozialwissenschaftliche Hochschullehre in Osteuropa IV. Chancen und Hindernisse internationaler Bildungskooperation*, Frankfurt am Main, 2009.

Cholet, Julia, *Die Finanzen der Universität Leipzig im Ersten Weltkrieg und in der frühen Weimarer Republik. Eine Untersuchung zur Inflationszeit 1914 bis 1925* (Beiträge zur Leipziger Universitäts- und Wissenschaftsgeschichte, 12), Leipzig, 2009.

Coulin, Christian-Karl, *Karl August Heinsheimer (1869–1929). Vom badischen Richter zum Lehrer an der Universität Heidelberg*, Frankfurt am Main, 2009.

Daniels, Mario, *Geschichtswissenschaft im 20. Jahrhundert. Institutionalisierungsprozesse und Entwicklung des Personenverbandes an der Universität Tübingen 1918–1964* (Contubernium, 71), Stuttgart, 2009.

Döring, Detlef, Cecilie Hollberg and Tobias Müller (eds.), *Erleuchtung der Welt. Sachsen und der Beginn der modernen Wissenschaften. (600 Jahre Universität Leipzig. Erschienen aus Anlaß der Jubiläumsausstellung der Universität Leipzig; Stadtgeschichtliches Museum Leipzig, Altes Rathaus, 9. Juli - 6. Dezember 2009)*, Dresden, 2009.

Dotzler, Bernhard, ' " . . . die richtige Art wissenschaftlicher Objekte . . . ": Ein Epilog mit Warren McCullochs "Embodiments of Mind" ', *Berichte zur Wissenschaftsgeschichte*, 32.1, 2009: 100–108.

Fischer, Stephan, 'Geschichte als Theorie der Gelegenheiten oder der Simulationsnexus geschichtswissenschaftlicher Erklärungen', *Österreichische Zeitschrift für Geschichtswissenschaften*, 20.1, 2009: 131–157.

Füssel, Marian, 'Talar und Doktorhut. Die akademische Kleiderordnung als Medium sozialer Distinktion', in *Frühneuzeitliche Universitätskulturen. Kulturhistorische Perspektiven auf die Hochschulen in Europa*, Cologne, 2009, 245–272.

Gangl, Manfred, Gilbert Merlio and Markus Ophälders (eds.), *Spengler–ein Denker der Zeitenwende*, Frankfurt am Main u.a., 2009.

Gerhardt, Uta, *Soziologie im zwanzigsten Jahrhundert. Studien zu ihrer Geschichte in Deutschland*, Stuttgart, 2009.

Graevenitz, Karoline, 'Die Abenduniversität der Prager Bohemisten. Hochschulbildung im Untergrund am Ende der kommunistischen Diktatur', *Jahrbuch für Universitätsgeschichte*, 12, 2009: 157–188.

Graf, Friedrich-Wilhelm (ed.), *Intellektuellen-Götter. Das religiöse Laboratorium der klassischen Moderne*, Munich, 2009.

Haas, Renate and Albert Hamm, *Die Universität Straßburg und die Etablierung der Anglistik auf dem Kontinent. Ein Beitrag zu einer europäischen Geschichte der Anglistik*, Frankfurt am Main, 2009.

Haedrich, Martina, Gerhard Lingelbach and Olaf Werner (eds.), *Rechtswissenschaft in Jena. Der Neuanfang 1989*, Vienna, 2009.

Hahn, Reinhard, '"Sein Einflußpotential bestand in seinen Schülern". Gerhard Scholz und sein Kreis. Zur Schulenbildung in der Germanistik in der DDR', *Jahrbuch für Universitätsgeschichte*, 12, 2009: 133–156.

Hanssen-Decker, Ulrike, 'Geschichtswissenschaft für den Ostseeraum? Der Conventus primus historicorum Balticorum 1937 in Riga', *NORDEUROPAforum*, 1, 2009: 65–82.

Hempfer, Klaus and Philipp Antony (eds.), *Zur Situation der Geisteswissenschaften in Forschung und Lehre. Eine Bestandsaufnahme aus der universitären Praxis*, Stuttgart, 2009.

Hettling, Manfred, 'Gibt es noch eine Einheit der Geschichtswissenschaft? Epochale Vielfalt und disziplinäre Gemeinsamkeit', *Geschichte in Wissenschaft und Unterricht*, 60.3, 2009: 140–147.

Huber, Heinz, *Geschichte der medizinischen Fakultät Innsbruck und der medizinisch-chirurgischen Studienanstalt (1673–1938)*, Vienna, 2009.

Kändler, Wolfram, *Anpassung und Abgrenzung. Zur Sozialgeschichte der Lehrstuhlinhaber der Technischen Hochschule Berlin-Charlottenburg und ihrer Vorgängerakademien 1851 bis 1945* (Pallas Athene, 31), Stuttgart, 2009.

Kieselstein, Jana, *Eduard Gans und das Völkerrecht. Die Vorlesung zum Positiven Völkerrecht*, Frankfurt am Main, 2009.

Kippenberg, Hans, 'Joachim Wachs Bild vom George-Kreis und seine Revision von Max Webers Soziologie religiöser Gemeinschaften', *Zeitschrift für Religions- und Geistesgeschichte*, 61.4, 2009: 313–331.

Kirschstein, Corinna, *Theater Wissenschaft Historiographie. Studien zu den Anfängen theaterwissenschaftlicher Forschung in Leipzig* (Leipziger Beiträge zur Theatergeschichtsforschung, 1), Leipzig, 2009.

230 Bibliography

Kißener, Michael and Friedrich Moll (eds.), *Ut omnes unum sint. Teil 3: Gründungsprofessoren der Chemie und Pharmazie* (Beiträge zur Geschichte der Johannes Gutenberg-Universität Mainz–Neue Folgen, 7), Stuttgart, 2009.

Klöppel, Ulrike, 'Das historische Krankenakten-Archiv der Nervenklinik der Charité', *Jahrbuch für Universitätsgeschichte*, 12, 2009: 267–270.

Klose, Jürgen (ed.), *Die Belter-Gruppe. Studentischer Widerstand gegen das SED-Regime an der Universität Leipzig* (Belter Dialoge. Impulse zu Zivilcourage und Widerstand, 1), Leipzig, 2009.

Kohler, Alfred, 'Die Gründung der Universität Jena in der Perspektive des Wiener Hofes', *Zeitschrift für Thüringische Geschichte*, 63, 2009: 99–116.

Krebs, Stefan, *Technikwissenschaft als soziale Praxis. Über Macht und Autonomie der Aachener Eisenhüttenkunde 1870–1914*, Stuttgart, 2009.

Krüger, Kersten (ed.), *Die Universität Rostock zwischen Sozialismus und Hochschulerneuerung. Zeitzeugen berichten, Teil 3*, Rostock, 2009 (http:// rosdok.uni-rostock.de/file/rosdok_derivate_000000003946/Studien3.pdf).

Krug-Richter, Barbara and Ruth E. Mohrmann (eds.), *Frühneuzeitliche Universitätskulturen. Kulturhistorische Perspektiven auf die Hochschulen in Europa* (Archiv für Kulturgeschichte, Beiheft, 65), Cologne, 2009.

Kudraß, Eva, 'Zwischen Natur- und Geisteswissenschaft: Der Streit um Felix von Luschan an der Berliner Universität', in Ruggendorfer and Szemethy (eds.), *Felix von Luschan*, 99–113.

Langewiesche, Dieter, 'Zum Selbstbild der Universität. Leipziger Rektoratsreden im Kaiserreich und in der Weimarer Republik', *Leipziger Universitätsreden, NF.*, 108, 2009: 15–26.

Lehnardt, Andreas, *Die Jüdische Bibliothek an der Johannes Gutenberg-Universität Mainz 1938–2008* (Beiträge zur Geschichte der Johannes Gutenberg-Universität Mainz–Neue Folgen, 8), Stuttgart, 2009.

Lenger, Friedrich, *Sozialwissenschaft um 1900. Studien zu Werner Sombart und einigen seiner Zeitgenossen*, Frankfurt am Main, 2009.

Liess, Hans-Christoph, 'Nationalökonomische Visionen. Historisch-epistemologische Überlegungen zur aktuellen Schumpeter-Renaissance', *Jahrbuch für Universitätsgeschichte*, 12, 2009: 41–55.

Lipphardt, Veronika, 'Wenn Forscher Rassen am Geruch erkennen. Intuitive Erkenntniswege der deutschen Rassenbiologie', *Jahrbuch für Universitätsgeschichte*, 12, 2009: 57–73.

Lochbrunner, Birgit, 'Zum Diskurs zwischen universitärer Medizin und Homöopathie. Ein Selbstversuch zur Homöopathie an der Universität Gießen 1997', *Jahrbuch für Universitätsgeschichte*, 12, 2009: 257–265.

Lorenz, Sönke, 'Johannes Reuchlin und die Universität Tübingen', *Zeitschrift für Württembergische Landesgeschichte*, 68, 2009: 139–156.

Markschies, Christoph, 'Carl Schmidt und kein Ende. Aus großer Zeit der Koptologie an der Berliner Akademie und der Theologischen Fakultät der Universität', *Zeitschrift für antikes Christentum*, 13, 2009: 5–28.

Morat, Daniel, 'Esoteriker des Mainstreams. Martin Heidegger in der Öffentlichkeit der frühen Bundesrepublik', *Zeitschrift für Geschichtswissenschaft*, 57.9, 2009: 723–738.

Moritz, Werner and Klaus-Peter Schroeder (eds.), *Carl Joseph Anton Mittermaier (1787–1867). Ein Heidelberger Professor zwischen nationaler Politik und globalem Rechtsdenken im 19. Jahrhundert*, Ubstadt-Weiher, 2009.

Neef, Katharina, 'Rudolf Goldscheid - Soziologe oder Sozialpolitiker? Zur wissenschaftshistorischen Exklusion konstitutiver Diskursteilnehmer der frühen deutschsprachigen Soziologie', in Pirmin Stekeler-Weithofer and others (eds.), *Ein Netz der Wissenschaften? Wilhelm Ostwalds "Annalen der Naturphilosophie" und die Durchsetzung wissenschaftlicher Paradigmen. Vorträge des Kolloquiums, veranstaltet von der Sächsischen Akademie der Wissenschaften zu Leipzig und dem Institut für Philosophie der Universität Leipzig im Oktober 2007*, Stuttgart, 2009, 23–45.

Niedhart, Gottfried (ed.), *Gustav Mayer. Als deutsch-jüdischer Historiker in Krieg und Revolution 1914–1920. Tagebücher, Aufzeichnungen, Briefe*, Munich, 2009.

Oberkrone, Willi, *Ordnung und Autarkie. Die Geschichte der deutschen Landbauforschung, Agrarökonomie und ländlichen Sozialwissenschaft im Spiegel von Forschungsdienst und DFG (1920–1970)*, Stuttgart, 2009.

Osterhammel, Jürgen, 'Die Einheit der Geschichtswissenschaft: vertikal, horizontal, diagonal', *Geschichte in Wissenschaft und Unterricht*, 60.3, 2009: 166–172.

Pawelletz, Jörg, *Die Geschichte des Marburger Universitätsbundes 1920–1954*, Marburg, 2009 (Dissertation, http://nbn-resolving.de/urn:nbn:de:hebis:04-z2009-01588).

Pawliczek, Aleksandra, ' "Überrepräsentierung" versus "Zurücksetzung": Juden an der Friedrich-Wilhelms-Universität zu Berlin 1871–1933', *Jahrbuch für Universitätsgeschichte*, 12, 2009: 113–131.

Peter, Hartmut, 'Jüdische Studenten aus Russland an der Universität Halle 1900–1914', in *Jüdische Bildung und Kultur in Sachsen-Anhalt von der Aufklärung bis zum Nationalsozialismus*, Berlin, 2009, 317–346.

Pieper, Christine, *Hochschulinformatik in der Bundesrepublik und der DDR bis 1989/1990* (Wissenschaft, Politik und Gesellschaft, 4), Stuttgart, 2009.

Pinwinkler, Alexander, ' "Bevölkerungssoziologie" und Ethnizität: Historisch-demografische Minderheitenforschung in Österreich, ca. 1918–1938', *Zeitschrift für Geschichtswissenschaft*, 57.2, 2009: 101–133.

Ratajszczak, Theresa, *Landesherrliche Bildungspolitik und bürgerliches Mäzenatentum. Das Stipendienwesen an der Universität Leipzig 1539–1580* (Beiträge zur Leipziger Universitäts- und Wissenschaftsgeschichte, 14), Leipzig, 2009.

Rauh, Hans-Christoph and Hans-Martin Gerlach (eds.), *Ausgänge. Zur DDR-Philosophie in den 70er und 80er Jahren*, Berlin, 2009.

Reydon, Thomas A.C., Helmut Heit and Paul Hoyningen-Huene, *Der universale Leibniz. Denker, Forscher, Erfinder*, Stuttgart, 2009.

Roesler, Jörg, 'Die Transformation der Geschichtswissenschaft in Ostdeutschland nach 1990', *Jahrbuch für Forschungen zur Geschichte der Arbeiterbewegung*, 8.2, 2009: 175–177.

Ruggendorfer, Peter and Hubert D. Szemethy, *Felix von Luschan (1854–1924). Leben und Wirken eines Universalgelehrten*, Cologne - Weimar, 2009.

Schäfer-Hartmann, Günther, *Literaturgeschichte als wahre Geschichte. Mittelalterrezeption in der deutschen Literaturgeschichtsschreibung des 19. Jahrhunderts und politische Instrumentalisierung des Mittelalters durch Preußen*, Frankfurt am Main, 2009.

Schaich, Eberhard, *Dr. rer. pol. 175 Jahre Promotion an der Wirtschaftswissenschaftlichen Fakultät der Eberhard Karls Universität Tübingen*, Stuttgart, 2009.

Schaller, Helmut Wilhelm, *Geschichte der Slawischen und Baltischen Philologie an der Universität Königsberg*, Frankfurt am Main u.a., 2009.

Schleiermacher, Sabine and Norman Pohl, *Medizin, Wissenschaft und Technik in der SBZ und DDR. Organisationsformen, Inhalte, Realitäten* (Abhandlungen zur Geschichte der Medizin und der Naturwissenschaften, 107), Husum, 2009.

——and Udo Schagen (eds.), *Wissenschaft macht Politik. Hochschule in den politischen Systembrüchen 1933 und 1945* (Wissenschaft, Politik und Gesellschaft, 3), Stuttgart, 2009.

Schmoll, Friedemann, *Die Vermessung der Kultur. Der 'Atlas der deutschen Volkskunde' und die Deutsche Forschungsgemeinschaft 1928–1980*, Stuttgart, 2009.

Sebald, Andrea Elisabeth, *Der Kriminalbiologe Franz Exner (1881–1947). Gratwanderung eines Wissenschaftlers durch die Zeit des Nationalsozialismus*, Frankfurt am Main, 2009.

Siebe, Daniela, *'Germania docet'. Ausländische Studierende, auswärtige Kulturpolitik und deutsche Universitäten 1870–1933* (Historische Studien, 495), Husum, 2009.

Sollbach, Gerhard, '350 Jahre bis zur Universität', *Heimat Dortmund - Stadtgeschichte in Bildern und Berichten*, 2009.1, 2009: 10–16.

——'Der Studentenprotest bei der Eröffnung der Universität Dortmund am 16. Dezember 1968 aus historischer Sicht', *Heimat Dortmund - Stadtgeschichte in Bildern und Berichten*, 2009.1, 2009: 41–43.

Spix, Boris, *Abschied vom Elfenbeinturm? Politisches Verhalten Studierender 1957 bis 1967–Berlin und Nordrhein-Westfalen im Vergleich*, Essen, 2009.

Stambolis, Barbara, *Leben mit und in der Geschichte. Westdeutsche Historiker Jahrgang 1943*, Essen, 2009.

Stöckel, Sigrid, Wiebke Lisner and Gerlind Rüve, *Das Medium Wissenschaftszeitschrift seit dem 19. Jahrhundert. Verwissenschaftlichung der Gesellschaft–*

Vergesellschaftung von Wissenschaft (Wissenschaft, Politik und Gesellschaft, 5), Stuttgart, 2009.

Strack, Georg, ' "De Germania parcissime locuti sunt…" ' Die deutsche Universitätsnation und das "Lob der Deutschen" im späten Mittelalter', in Gerhard Krieger (ed.), *Verwandtschaft, Freundschaft, Bruderschaft. Soziale Lebens- und Kommunikationsformen im Mittelalter*, Berlin, Akademie Verlag, 2009, 472–490.

Troebst, Stefan, 'Geschichtswissenschaft im post-kommunistischen Ost(mittel)europa', *Deutschland Archiv*, 42.1, 2009: 87–95.

Vogt, Helmut, 'Mittelpunkt des geistigen Lebens in der Bundeshaupt- und Universitätsstadt. Planungen zur neuen Bonner Universitätsbibliothek (1949–1955) im Kontext der Hauptstadtpolitik des Landes Nordrhein-Westfalen', *Rheinische Vierteljahrsblätter*, 73, 2009: 226–236.

Wallentin, Stefan, *Fürstliche Normen und akademische 'Observanzen'. Die Verfassung der Universität Jena 1630–1730*, Vienna, 2009.

Wallnig, Thomas and Thomas Stockinger, *Die gelehrte Korrespondenz der Brüder Pez. Text, Regesten, Kommentare. Band 1: 1709–1715*, Vienna, 2009.

Walter, Rudolf, 'Professor Heinrich Polloczek, ein außergewöhnlicher schlesischer Musikerzieher. Ein Beitrag zur deutschen Musikpädagogik', *Jahrbuch der Schlesischen Friedrich-Wilhelms-Universität zu Breslau*, 49, 2009: 221–248.

Walther, Helmut, 'Die Grundlagen der Universitäten im europäischen Mittelalter', *Zeitschrift für Thüringische Geschichte*, 63, 2009: 75–98.

Wilke, Carsten, 'Rabbinerpromotionen an der Philosophischen Fakultät der Universität Halle-Wittenberg, 1845–1895', in *Jüdische Bildung und Kultur in Sachsen-Anhalt von der Aufklärung bis zum Nationalsozialismus*, Berlin, 2009, 261–316.

Wirth, Günther, 'Paul Hofmann, die Berliner Universität und seine neue Humanitätsphilosophie', *Zeitschrift für Religions- und Geistesgeschichte*, 61.4, 2009: 356–371.

Woelki, Thomas, 'Zwei Brüder machen Karriere. Lodovico und Francesco Pontano an den Universitäten von Bologna, Florenz und Siena (ca. 1426–1436)', *Jahrbuch für Universitätsgeschichte*, 12, 2009: 87–112.

Zöllner, Reinhard, 'Frühe Neuzeit und Frühmoderne als Konzept der ostasiatischen Geschichtswissenschaft', in Helmut Neuhaus (ed.), *Die frühe Neuzeit als Epoche* (Historische Zeitschrift. Beihefte, 49), Munich, 2009, 479–490.

Publications 2010

Bruch, Rüdiger vom and Rainer C. Schwinges (eds.), *Universitätsreformen vom Mittelalter bis zur Gegenwart*, special issue of *Jahrbuch für Universitätsgeschichte*, 13, 2010.

Bungert, Heike, 'Globaler Informationsaustausch und globale Zusammenarbeit: Die International Association of Universities, 1950–1968', *Jahrbuch für Universitätsgeschichte*, 13, 2010: 177–191.

Burg, Peter, 'Das Projekt einer Europäischen Universität des Saarlandes (1948–1957) im Spiegel eines 'saar-französischen' Memorandums', *Jahrbuch für Universitätsgeschichte*, 13, 2010: 155–175.

Fure, Jorunn Sem, 'Die Universität Oslo während der Besatzungszeit. Neuordnung, Anpassung, Kollaboration und Widerstand', *Jahrbuch für Universitätsgeschichte*, 13, 2010: 139–154.

Jeskow, Jan, 'Die Universitätsfinanzierung in Preußen und Thüringen in der Zwischenkriegszeit', *Jahrbuch für Universitätsgeschichte*, 13, 2010: 111–137.

John, Jürgen, 'Geistiger Neubeginn? Eine Jenaer Denkschrift 1945 über die Rolle der deutschen Intelligenz', *Jahrbuch für Universitätsgeschichte*, 13, 2010: 193–239.

Kusche, Sebastian, 'Konfessionalisierung und Hochschulverfassung. Zu den lutherischen Universitätsreformen in der zweiten Hälfte des 16. Jahrhunderts', *Jahrbuch für Universitätsgeschichte*, 13, 2010: 27–44.

Mälzer, Moritz, ' "Die große Chance, wie einstens die Berliner Universität so heute eine Modell-Universität zu schaffen". Die frühen 1960er Jahre als Universitätsgründerzeiten', *Jahrbuch für Universitätsgeschichte*, 13, 2010: 73–92.

Maurer, Tina, 'Universitätsrefom im Mittelalter. Wesen und Inhalt anhand französischer und deutscher Beispiele', *Jahrbuch für Universitätsgeschichte*, 13, 2010: 11–25.

Pelger, Gregor, ' "Eine einzige ununterbrochene und noch nicht abgeschlossene Tragödie". Über die Durchsetzung der Wissenschaft des Judentums im 19. Jahrhundert', *Jahrbuch für Universitätsgeschichte*, 13, 2010: 93–109.

Röhn, Hartmut, ' "…Damals waren hier andre Zustände". Julius Hoffory an der Friedrich-Wilhelms-Universität zu Berlin (1883–1892)', *Jahrbuch für Universitätsgeschichte*, 13, 2010: 241–251.

Wirbelauer, Eckhard and Norbert Schappacher, 'Zwei Siegeruniversitäten: Die Straßburger Universitätsgründungen von 1872 und 1919', *Jahrbuch für Universitätsgeschichte*, 13, 2010: 45–72.

Zschaler, Frank E. W., 'Das Eichstätter Universitätsarchiv–neue Institution in einer alten Wissenschaftslandschaft', *Jahrbuch für Universitätsgeschichte*, 13, 2010: 253–256.

Italy

Additions to Earlier Lists

For 1986

Ulivieri, S., 'La donna et gli studi universitari nell'Italia postunitaria', in F. De Vivo and G. Genovesi (eds.), *Cento anni di Università–L'instruzione superiore in Italia dall'unità ai giorni nostri*, Naples, 1986.

For 2003

Negri, Antonio, *Luciano Ferrari Bravo: ritratto di un cattivo maestro. Con alcuni cenni suslla sua epoca*, Rome, Manifesto libri, 2003.

For 2004

Alberoni, Francesco, 'Che cosa mi ha insegnato Trento', in Cambi, Quaglioni and Rutigliano (eds.), *L'Università a Trento*, 177–178 [Trent].

Andreolli, Tarcisio, 'Il passaggio dal libero Istituto alla libera Università', in Cambi, Quaglioni and Rutigliano (eds.), *L'Università a Trento*, Trent, Università degli Studi di Trento, 2004, 171–176 [Trent].

Armanini, Aronne, 'Nascita e sviluppo della Facoltà di Ingegneria', in Cambi, Quaglioni and Rutigliano (eds.), *L'Università a Trento*, Trent, Università degli Studi di Trento, 2004, 217–220 [Trent].

Aversa, Giovanni, 'Studenti a Sociologia tra gli anni Settanta e gli Ottanta', in Cambi, Quaglioni and Rutigliano (eds.), *L'Università a Trento*, 193–198 [Trent].

Barbano, Filippo, 'La sociologia di Trento. Il mio coinvolgimento', in Cambi, Quaglioni and Rutigliano (eds.), *L'Università a Trento*, 139–159 [Trent].

Boato, Marco, 'L'esperienza di Sociologia prima e dopo il Sessantotto', in Cambi, Quaglioni and Rutigliano (eds.), *L'Università a Trento*, 179–187 [Trent].

Bobbio, Norberto, 'A trento ho imparato molte cose', in Cambi, Quaglioni and Rutigliano (eds.), *L'Università a Trento*, 165–169 [Trent].

Cambi, Fabrizio, Massimo Egidi and Diego Quaglioni, 'Alcune questioni aperte dell'università di oggi', in Cambi, Quaglioni and Rutigliano (eds.), *L'Università a Trento*, 49–67 [Trent].

——, Diego Quaglioni and Enzo Rutigliano (eds.), *L'Università a Trento. 1962–2002*, Trent, Università degli Studi di Trento, 2004 [Trent].

Capuozzo, Tony, 'Il volto di Sociologia', in Cambi, Quaglioni and Rutigliano (eds.), *L'Università a Trento*, 189–192 [Trent].

Egidi, Massimo, 'Verso la creazione di uno spazio comune europeo per l'alta formazione: rischi e opportunità', in Cambi, Quaglioni and Rutigliano (eds.), *L'Università a Trento*, 111–128 [Trent].

Ferrari, Fabio, 'L'Ateneo trentino nel contesto universitario italiano', in Cambi, Quaglioni and Rutigliano (eds.), *L'Università a Trento*, 83–103 [Trent].

Gatta, Giampiero, 'Sessanta foto per quaranta anni. Breve "Storia" per immagini', in Cambi, Quaglioni and Rutigliano (eds.), *L'Università a Trento*, 221–280 [Trent].

Kessler, Bruno, 'A vent'anni dal sessantotto', in Cambi, Quaglioni and Rutigliano (eds.), *L'Università a Trento*, 161–164 [Trent].

Miranda, Mario, 'I primi anni di vita della Facoltà di Scienze', in Cambi, Quaglioni and Rutigliano (eds.), *L'Università a Trento*, 209–216 [Trent].

Paganelli, Arturo, ' "Un patrimonio culturale mondiale da conservare e tramandare": l'Orto botanico dell'Università degli studi di Padova', *Atti e memorie dell'Accademia di agricoltura, scienze e lettere di Verona*, 180, 2003–2004: 185–208 [Padua].

Prodi, Paolo, 'Ipotesi per un sistema universitario regionale', in Cambi, Quaglioni and Rutigliano (eds.), *L'Università a Trento*, 71–81 [Trent].

Quaglioni, Diego, 'Universita e "Spirito Pubblico" ', in Cambi, Quaglioni and Rutigliano (eds.), *L'Università a Trento*, 11–47 [Trent].

Sacco, Rodolfo, 'Come è nata Giurisprudenza a Trento', in Cambi, Quaglioni and Rutigliano (eds.), *L'Università a Trento*, 199–202 [Trent].

Tomasi, Marco, 'L'evoluzione della struttura amministrativa', in Cambi, Quaglioni and Rutigliano (eds.), *L'Università a Trento*, 129–136 [Trent].

Toniatti, Roberto, 'Come è cresciuta Giurisprudenza a Trento', in Cambi, Quaglioni and Rutigliano (eds.), *L'Università a Trento*, 203–207 [Trent].

Zuelli, Fulvio, 'Alcune riflessioni e un'interpretazione', in Cambi, Quaglioni and Rutigliano (eds.), *L'Università a Trento*, 105–110 [Trent].

For 2006

Galoppini, Annamaria, 'Le studentesse dell'Università di Pisa (1875–1940)', in Elena Fasano Guarini, Annamaria Galoppini and Alessandra Peretti (eds.), *Fuori dall'ombra. Studi di storia delle donne nella provincia di Pisa (secoli XIX e XX)* (Studi Pisani Cultura e societa, 14), Pisa, Plus, 2006.

Mazzarello, Paolo, *Il Nobel dimenticato. La vita e la scienza di Camillo Golgi*, Turin, Bollati Boringhieri, 2006.

For 2007

Cappelletti, Elsa M., 'L'Orto Botanico di Padova e l'introduzione di piante esotiche: "Rheum rhponticum" e "Oenothera biennis" ', *AMAG*, 119, 2006–2007: 115–125.

Denley, Peter, *Teachers and Schools in Siena. 1357–1500* (Documenti di storia, 78), Siena, Betti Editrice, 2007.

Spagnol, Christian, 'Il veronese Francesco Pona e le accademie letterarie del '600', *Archivio veneto*, 169, 2007: 135–150.

For 2008

Barnabei, Franco, 'Introduzione ai testi', in Nezzo (ed.), *Il miraggio della concordia*, 41–90 [Padua].

Bellomo, Manlio, *'Quaestiones in iure civilis disputate'. Didattica e prassi colta nel sistema del diritto comune fra Duecento e Trecento (Contributi codicologici di Livia Martinoli, in Appendice)* (Fonti per la storia dell'Italia medievale, Antiquitates, 31), Rome, Istituto storico italiano per il medio evo, 2008.

Berti, Giampietro, 'Note sulla Facoltà filosofico-matematica dell'Università di Padova tra il 1805 e il 1849', *Quaderni per la storia dell'Università di Padova*, 41, 2008: 207–211 [Padua].

Bibliography 237

Carletti, Christian, 'Spazi e costi della cultura sperimentale a Padova a metà Ottocento', *Quaderni per la storia dell'Università di Padova*, 41, 2008: 212–259.

Casellato, Sandra, *Per la storia della Facoltà di Scienze in Italia: le Scienze naturali a Padova (1734–1964), con la collaborazione di Cinzio Gibin* (Collana per la storia della Facoltà di scienze matematiche, fisiche, naturali dell'Università di Padova, 1), Padua, CLEUP, 2008.

Favaretto, Irene, 'Percorso di un progetto: "Il Novecento al Bo" ', in Nezzo (ed.), *Il miraggio della concordia*, 19–28 [Padua].

Forlivesi, Marco, ' "Nationes" universitarie e identità nazionale. Il caso della "natio Germanica" nello Studio di Padova', in Gregorio Piaia and Riccardo Pozzo (eds.), *Identità nazionale e valori universali nella moderna storiografia filosofica*, Padua, CLUEP, 2008, 19–33 [Padua].

Maggiolo, Paolo, 'I quattro secoli della Biblioteca Universitaria', *Padova e il suo territorio*, 136, 2008: 36–38 [Padua].

Massignan, Luigi, 'Psichiatria padovana', *Padova e il suo territorio*, 135, 2008: 26–30 [Padua].

Minnaja, Carlo, Enrico Giusti and Francesco Baldassarri (eds.), *I matematici nell'Università di Padova dal suo nascere al XX secolo*, Padua, Esedra, 2008 [Padua].

Nezzo, Marta, 'Il gioco delle parti nel teatro artistico universitario', in Nezzo (ed.), *Il miraggio della concordia*, 205–270 [Padua].

—— (ed.), *Il miraggio della concordia. Documenti sull'architettura e la decorazione del Bo e del Liviano: Padova 1933–1943*, Padua, Canova, 2008 [Padua].

Ongaro, Giuseppe, *Storie di medici e di medicina*, Padua, Il poligrafo, 2008.

Penzo Doria, Gianni, 'Il cantiere e i documenti: l'Archivio dei Consorzi edilizi (1903–1973)', in Nezzo (ed.), *Il miraggio della concordia*, 29–40 [Padua].

Piaia, Gregorio, 'Le origini della Facoltà di Magistero a Padova', *Quaderni per la storia dell'Università di Padova*, 41, 2008: 173–189 [Padua].

Piaz, Vittorio Dal, 'Storia e storie del Cantiere', in Nezzo (ed.), *Il miraggio della concordia*, 91–204 [Padua].

Prete, Ivano Dal, *Scienza e società nel Settecento Veneto. Il caso veronese 1680–1796* (Filosofia e scienza nell'età moderna. Stud), Milan, Franco Angeli, 2008 (prefazione di Gian Paolo Romagnani).

Vecchiato, Francesco, 'L'Università a Verona. Un'attesa durata seicento anni (1339–1959)', in *Università degli Studi di Verona. 25 anni per Verona*, Verona, Universita di Verona, 2008, 26–42 [Verona].

Zucchini, Stefania, *Università e dottori nell'economia del Comune di Perugia. I registri dei Conservatori della Moneta (scoli XIV-XV)* (Fonti per la storia dello Studium Perusinum, 2), Perugia, Deputazione di Storia Patria per l'Umbria, 2008 [Perugia].

Publications 2009

Adorni, Daniela, Paola Furlan and Stefano Magagnoli, 'Il potere locale', in Malatesta (ed.), *Atlante delle Professioni*, 238–252.

Alpini, Prospero, *Le piante dell'Egitto. Il balsamo (Venezia, 1592)*, Treviso, Antilia, 2009.

Álvarez Sánchez, Adriana, 'La Real Universidada de San Carlos de Guatemala, siglos XVII y XVIII. Historiografía y documentos', in Polo Rodríguez and Rodríguez-San Pedro Bezares (eds.), *Universidades Hispánicas: Colegios y Conventos Universitarios en la edad Moderna (I)*, 359–384 [San Carlos, Guatemala].

Angelozzi, Giancarlo, 'Alle origini del manuale di storia: la Epitome di Orazio Torsellini', in Brizzi and Tavoni (eds.), *Dalla pecia all'e-book*, 239–249.

Baldelli, Raffaella and Luigi Marvasi, 'Le riviste di veterinaria', in Malatesta (ed.), *Atlante delle Professioni*, 72–74.

Barbanera, Marcello, 'Contributo a una genealogia degli archeologi italiani tra Ottocento e Novecento: il caso di Pavia', in Mazzoli (ed.), *Anniversari dell'antichistica pavese*, 41–60.

Battelli, Giorgio, Adriano Mantovani and Luigi Marvasi, 'I veterinari', in Malatesta (ed.), *Atlante delle Professioni*, 163–166.

Beck Varela, Laura, 'Itinerarios de lectura para el jurista hispano (siglos XV-XVIII)', in Brizzi and Tavoni (eds.), *Dalla pecia all'e-book*, 351–360.

Bellassai, Sandro, 'La misoginia professionale', in Malatesta (ed.), *Atlante delle Professioni*, Bologna, 285–288.

——'Un trauma che si chiama desiderio. Per una storia del Sessantasette a Bologna', in De Bernardi, Romitelli and Cretella (eds.), *Gli anni Settanta*, 213–234.

Bernardi, Alberto De, 'I movimenti di protesta e la lunga depressione dell'economia italiana', in De Bernardi, Romitelli and Cretella (eds.), *Gli anni Settanta*, 119–135.

——, Valerio Romitelli and Chiara Cretella (eds.), *Gli anni Settanta. Tra crisi mondiale e movimenti collettivi*, Bologna, Archetipolibri-Gedit Edizioni, 2009.

Berti Arnoaldi Veli, Giuliano, 'Una pioniera del diritto', in Malatesta (ed.), *Atlante delle Professioni*, 261.

Betri, Maria Luisa, 'Gli epistolari: un medico cremonese del primo Ottocento', in Malatesta (ed.), *Atlante delle Professioni*, 47–49.

Bettazzi, Maria Beatrice, 'Le case editrici per architetti e ingegneri', in Malatesta (ed.), *Atlante delle Professioni*, 82–86.

Birocchi, Italo, 'I manuali di insegnamento della storia del diritto nel XIX secolo in Italia', in Brizzi and Tavoni (eds.), *Dalla pecia all'e-book*, 377–391.

Bordini, Simone, 'Tra professione legale e prassi didattica: il libro del giurista medievale. Annotazioni introduttive e spunti di riflessione', in Brizzi and Tavoni (eds.), *Dalla pecia all'e-book*, 77–90.

Brambilla, Elena, 'Bricolage didattico: l'uso della dettatura nelle Università e i repertori di luoghi comuni scritti dagli scolari', in Brizzi and Tavoni (eds.), *Dalla pecia all'e-book*, 205–215.

——'Ceti e professioni in antico regime', in Malatesta (ed.), *Atlante delle Professioni*, 91–94.

——'La mobilità studentesca nelle università italiane (XVI-XVIII secolo)', in Malatesta (ed.), *Atlante delle Professioni*, 10–16.

Brizzi, Gian Paolo, 'L'orbis academicus', in Malatesta (ed.), *Atlante delle Professioni*, 1–9.

——and Maria Gioia Tavoni (eds.), *Dalla pecia all'e-book. Libri per l'Università: stampa, editoria, circolazione e lettura. Atti el convegno internazionale di studi (Bologna, 21–25 ottobre 2008)*, Bologna, CLUEB, 2009.

——'I "Quaderni": un'esperienza esemplare di storiografia universitaria', *Quaderni per la storia dell'Università di Padova*, 42, 2009: 376–382.

Burrieza Sánchez, Javier, 'Los colegios de jesuitas en la Corona de Castilla', in Polo Rodríguez and Rodríguez-San Pedro Bezares (eds.), *Universidades Hispánicas: Colegios y Conventos Universitarios en la edad Moderna (I)*, 109–158.

Calcagno, Giancarlo and Stefano Pinotti, 'Le riviste di ingegneria', in Malatesta (ed.), *Atlante delle Professioni*, 75–79.

Callegari, Marco, 'Produzione libraria dei professori dello studio di Padova: 1550–1771', in Brizzi and Tavoni (eds.), *Dalla pecia all'e-book*, 275–281.

Calvi, Antonella, 'Il fondo Malcovati della Biblioteca Civica "Carlo Bonetta" di Pavia', in Mazzoli (ed.), *Anniversari dell'antichistica pavese*, [Pavia].

Cammarano, Fulvio and Maria Serena Piretti, 'Governo e professioni', in Malatesta (ed.), *Atlante delle Professioni*, 228–237.

Cammelli, Andrea and Angelo di Francia, 'La geografia delle professioni', in Malatesta (ed.), *Atlante delle Professioni*, 133–136.

—— and Angelo di Francia, 'Il processo di universitarizzazione ieri e oggi', in Malatesta (ed.), *Atlante delle Professioni*, 17–21.

—— and Angelo di Francia, 'L'universitarizzazione femminile più recente', in Malatesta (ed.), *Atlante delle Professioni*, 255–256.

Canella, Maria, 'La biblioteca di un architetto contemporaneo', in Malatesta (ed.), *Atlante delle Professioni*, 55–57.

——'La città come cantiere', in Malatesta (ed.), *Atlante delle Professioni*, 186–187.

——'Il designer: l'affermazione di una nuova figura professionale tra 1940 e 1980', in Malatesta (ed.), *Atlante delle Professioni*, 177–180.

——'Il Politecnico di Milano', in Malatesta (ed.), *Atlante delle Professioni*, 22–25.

Cantagalli, Alessandra, 'Le collezioni librarie: medici e ingegneri dell'Ottocento', in Malatesta (ed.), *Atlante delle Professioni*, 58–60.

——'Ragionieri e dottori commercialisti', in Malatesta (ed.), *Atlante delle Professioni*, 173–176.

——'Le riviste di ragioneria', in Malatesta (ed.), *Atlante delle Professioni*, 87–89.

Capecchi, Vittorio, 'La ricerca sociologica negli anni Settanta dentro e fuori l'Università', in De Bernardi, Romitelli and Cretella (eds.), *Gli anni Settanta*, 24–54.

Carrubba, Onofrio, 'Piero Meriggi', in Mazzoli (ed.), *Anniversari dell'antichistica*, 77–80 [Pavia].

Casalena, Maria Pia, 'Le accademie militari', in Malatesta (ed.), *Atlante delle Professioni*, 42–43.

——'Le professioni nel Risorgimento', in Malatesta (ed.), *Atlante delle Professioni*, 205–213.

Casali, Luciano and Alberto Preti, 'Sovversivi, antifascisti, partigiani', in Malatesta (ed.), *Atlante delle Professioni*, 216–227.

Casanova, Cesarina, 'Gli avvocati dei poveri', in Malatesta (ed.), *Atlante delle Professioni*, 121–123.

Casanova, Angelo, 'Gli studi di filologia greca a Pavia nel XX secolo', in Mazzoli (ed.), *Anniversari dell'antichistica pavese*, 87–96 [Pavia].

Castillo Gomez, Antonio, 'Maestros, estudiantes y copistas varios: escribir a mano en los primeros tiempos de la Universidad de Alcalá', in Brizzi and Tavoni (eds.), *Dalla pecia all'e-book*, 177–189 [Alcalá].

Catturi, Giuseppe, 'Le inserzioni pubblicitarie riguardanti scuole e libri sul metodo italiano di contabilità apparse sui giornali inglesi all'inizio del XVIII secolo', in Brizzi and Tavoni (eds.), *Dalla pecia all'e-book*, 465–479.

Cracolici, Stefano, 'Il testo medico universitario dentro e fuori l'accademia: considerazioni sul caso quattrocentesco', in Brizzi and Tavoni (eds.), *Dalla pecia all'e-book*, 103–110.

Cresci, Serena, 'Le riviste giuridiche ottocentesche', in Malatesta (ed.), *Atlante delle Professioni*, 63.

Cretella, Chiara, 'L'ala creativa bolognese. Il caso del Collettivo A/traverso', in De Bernardi, Romitelli and Cretella (eds.), *Gli anni Settanta*, 353–370 [Bologna].

Cuart Moner, Baltasar, 'Papeles de colegiales. Los expedientes de vita et moribus de los colegiales mayores salmantinos del siglo XVI', in Polo Rodríguez and Rodríguez-San Pedro Bezares (eds.), *Universidades Hispánicas: Colegios y Conventos Universitarios en la edad Moderna (I)*, 15–74 [Salamanca].

Daltri, Andrea, Paola Errani, Marco Palma and Paolo Zanfini, 'Peciae Malatestiane in rete', in Brizzi and Tavoni (eds.), *Dalla pecia all'e-book*, 111–129.

Demidov, Serguei, 'L'influence de Leonhard Euler sur les premiers manuels mathématiques de l'Empire Russe', in Brizzi and Tavoni (eds.), *Dalla pecia all'e-book*, 455–463.

Dröscher, Ariane, 'I medici universitari', in Malatesta (ed.), *Atlante delle Professioni*, 155–162.

Erba, Luisa, 'La produzione libraria per l'Università nel Seicento: il caso di Pavia', in Brizzi and Tavoni (eds.), *Dalla pecia all'e-book*, 191–204 [Pavia].

Fata, Ilaria La, 'L'assalto al muro. Immagini e graffiti sui muri del Sessantasette bolognese', in De Bernardi, Romitelli and Cretella (eds.), *Gli anni Settanta*, 338–352 [Bologna].

Ferrante, Riccardo, 'Fare lezione secondo l'ordine del codice: scienza, didattica ed editoria nelle facoltà giuridiche napoleoniche dopo la legge del 22 ventoso XII (1804)', in Brizzi and Tavoni (eds.), *Dalla pecia all'e-book*, 369–375.

Ferraresi, Alessandra and Lucio Fregonese, 'Costruire le scienze e le discipline: manuali reali e manuali virtuali all'Università di Pavia nella seconda metà del Settecento', in Brizzi and Tavoni (eds.), *Dalla pecia all'e-book*, 481–497.

Focardi, Giovanni, 'Il quartiere giudiziario', in Malatesta (ed.), *Atlante delle Professioni*, 190–193.

Forti Messina, Anna Lucia, 'I medici condotti nello stato unitario', in Malatesta (ed.), *Atlante delle Professioni*, 151–154.

Francescangeli, Eros, 'Sorvegliare con lentezza. I gruppi della sinistra extraparlamentare bolognese nelle carte di polizia', in De Bernardi, Romitelli and Cretella (eds.), *Gli anni Settanta*, 322–337.

Frova, Carla, Ferinando Treggiari and Alessandra Panzanelli Fratoni (eds.), *Maestri Insegnamenti e Libri a Perugia. Contributi per la storia dell'Università 1308–2008*, Geneva - Milan, Skira, 2009.

Gabba, Emilio, 'Gli studi di storia antica', in Mazzoli (ed.), *Anniversari dell'antichistica pavese*, 5–12 [Pavia].

Gargan, Luciano, 'Un nuovo elenco di note 'conduixit': la circolazione del libro universitario a Padova nel Tre e Quattrocento', in Brizzi and Tavoni (eds.), *Dalla pecia all'e-book*, 69–77.

——'I "Quaderni per la storia dell'Università di Padova" "strumento utilissimo per la storia dell'umanesimo" nel XL anniversario di fondazione', *Quaderni per la storia dell'Università di Padova*, 42, 2009: 366–375.

Ghisella Pieve, Maria, Giuliana Sacchi and Carla Mazzoleni, 'Enrica Malcovati filologa nella Biblioteca Universitaria di Pavia (1937–1938)', in Mazzoli (ed.), *Anniversari dell'antichistica pavese*, 177–212 [Pavia].

Giannini, Mirella, 'Le ingegnere', in Malatesta (ed.), *Atlante delle Professioni*, 272–278.

Gibbs, Robert, 'The 13th century development of illumination in Bolognese copies of the Decretals of Gregory IX', in Brizzi and Tavoni (eds.), *Dalla pecia all'e-book*, 49–67.

Gillién de Iriarte, María Clara, 'El Colegio Mayor de Nuestra Señora del Rosario (Bogotá) en la Edada Moddderna. Panorámica, fuentes y líneas de investigación', in Polo Rodríguez and Rodríguez-San Pedro Bezares (eds.),

Universidades Hispánicas: Colegios y Conventos Universitarios en la edad Moderna (I), 189–214 [Bogotá].

Giorgi, Chiara, 'I professionisti d'Oltremare', in Malatesta (ed.), *Atlante delle Professioni*, 196–199.

Gispert, Hélène, 'Les traités d'analyse et la riguer en France dans la deuxième moitié du XIXe siècle, des questions, des choix et des contextes', in Brizzi and Tavoni (eds.), *Dalla pecia all'e-book*, 415–430.

Gonzalez Gonzalez, Enrique and Victor Gutiérrez Rodríguez, 'Entre Reforma y Contrarreforma: Juan Luis Vives y sus manuales escolares en la imprenta', in Brizzi and Tavoni (eds.), *Dalla pecia all'e-book*, 163–175.

Grattan-Guinness, Ivor, 'Instruction in the calculus and differential equations in Britain, 1820s-1900s', in Brizzi and Tavoni (eds.), *Dalla pecia all'e-book*, 443–453.

Greci, Roberto, 'Il libro universitario nel Medioevo tra interessi economici e significati simbolici', in Brizzi and Tavoni (eds.), *Dalla pecia all'e-book*, 91–101.

——and Andrea Morpurgo, 'Gli atelier degli architetti', in Malatesta (ed.), *Atlante delle Professioni*, 194–195.

Gresleri, Giuliano and Andrea Morpurgo, 'Ingegneri e architetti nel Mediterraneo (1870–1950)', in Malatesta (ed.), *Atlante delle Professioni*, 200–202.

Guereña, Jean-Louis, 'La historia de la enseñanza superior en Francia. Una aproximación historiográfica', in Polo Rodríguez and Rodríguez-San Pedro Bezares (eds.), *Universidades Hispánicas: Colegios y Conventos Universitarios en la edad Moderna (I)*, 257–280.

——'La política de regulación de los manuales para la enseñanza superior en España: el caso de los manuales de literatura en la Facultad de Filosofia (1846–1867)', in Brizzi and Tavoni (eds.), *Dalla pecia all'e-book*, 499–512.

Guerrini, Maria Teresa, 'Carriere e destini profesionali dei giuristi bolognesi', in Malatesta (ed.), *Atlante delle Professioni*, 114–120 [Bologna].

Hidalgo Pego, Mónica, 'El Colegio de San Ildefonso de México. Fuentes documentales y estado de la investigación', in Polo Rodríguez and Rodríguez-San Pedro Bezares (eds.), *Universidades Hispánicas: Colegios y Conventos Universitarios en la edad Moderna (I)*, 237–255.

Hiraux, Françoise, 'Le rapport au texte, miroir du projet universitaire d'enseignement: le cas de l'Université de Louvain, XV-XVIIIe siècles', in Brizzi and Tavoni (eds.), *Dalla pecia all'e-book*, 153–162 [Leuven].

Iglesias, J. Antoni, 'Exemplaria y peciae en la España tardomedieval:¿realidad o ficción?' in Brizzi and Tavoni (eds.), *Dalla pecia all'e-book*, 33–47.

Kiene, Micheal, 'Ein halbes Jahrtausend Bibliotheken in Italiens Universitäten', *Bibliothek und Wissenschaft*, 42, 2009: 201–222.

Lipparini, Francesca, 'Ragioniere e commercialiste', in Malatesta (ed.), *Atlante delle Professioni*, 279–284.

Liva, Alberto, 'I notai milanesi tra Sette e Ottocento', in Malatesta (ed.), *Atlante delle Professioni*, 109.

Malatesta, Maria (ed.), *Atlante delle Professioni*, Bologna, Bononia University Press, 2009.

——'Le trasformazioni culturali dell'avvocatura italiana', in Malatesta (ed.), *Atlante delle Professioni*, 144–146.

Mantovani, Andrea and Luigi Marvasi, 'Le scuole di veterinaria', in Malatesta (ed.), *Atlante delle Professioni*, 37–40.

Martelli, Fabio, 'I manueli di diritto costituzionale germanico nel XVIII secolo tra conservatorismo didattico ed innovazione contenutistica', in Brizzi and Tavoni (eds.), *Dalla pecia all'e-book*, 361–368.

Martínez Hernández, Gerardo, 'Juan de la Fuente y los inicios de la Medicina académica en Mexico', in Polo Rodríguez and Rodríguez-San Pedro Bezares (eds.), *Universidades Hispánicas: Colegios y Conventos Universitarios en la edad Moderna (I)*, 385–399 [Mexico].

Martínez Neira, Manuel, 'Irma Naso-Paolo Rosso, Insignia doctoralia. Lauree e laureati all'Università di Torino tra Quattro e Cinquecento', *Cuadernos del Instituto Antonio de Nebrija*, 12.2, 2009: 320.

Massaretti, Pier Giorgio, 'Le accademie di belle arti', in Malatesta (ed.), *Atlante delle Professioni*, 44–45.

——' "Casabella" e "Domus" ', in Malatesta (ed.), *Atlante delle Professioni*, 80–81.

Mattone, Antonello and Tiziana Olivari, 'Il manuale nelle università italiane del Cinquecento: diritto e medicina. Primi appunti', in Brizzi and Tavoni (eds.), *Dalla pecia all'e-book*, 217–237.

Mazzoli, Giancarlo (ed.), *Anniversari dell'antichistica pavese* (Fonti e studi per la storia dell'Università di Pavia, 55), Milan, Cisalpino, 2009.

——'Ricordo di Enrica Malcovati', in Mazzoli (ed.), *Anniversari dell'antichistica pavese*, 163–172 [Pavia].

Mecacci, Enzo, 'Peter Denley, Commune and Studio in Late Medieval and Renaissance Siena', *Studi senesi*, I.CXXI (III Serie, LVIII), 2009: 175–178.

Menant, François, 'I notai medievali e il credito', in Malatesta (ed.), *Atlante delle Professioni*, 108.

Menozzi, Daniele, *Chiesa, pace e guerra nel Novecento*, Bologna, il Mulino, 2009.

Milani, Felice, 'Camillo Beccalli, insegnante di Enrica Malcovati al Liceo "Ugo Foscolo" di Pavia', in Mazzoli (ed.), *Anniversari dell'antichistica pavese*, 173–177 [Pavia].

Montecchi, Giorgio, 'Il passaggio dalla produzione del libro manoscritto a quella del libro a stampa nel XV e nel XVI secolo', in Brizzi and Tavoni (eds.), *Dalla pecia all'e-book*, 141–151.

Murano, Giovanna, 'Paolo di Iacopino Avvocati (fl. 1252–1297)', in Brizzi and Tavoni (eds.), *Dalla pecia all'e-book*, 13–31.

Nagliati, Iolanda, *La corrispondenza scientifica di Vittorio Fossombroni 1773–1818*, Bologna, CLUEB, 2009.

Negro, Piero Del, 'I libri di testo e la didattica universitaria nella riforma padovana 1771', in Brizzi and Tavoni (eds.), *Dalla pecia all'e-book*, 283–295.

——'I libri di testo e la didattica universitaria nella riforma padovana del 1771', *Quaderni per la storia dell'Università di Padova*, 42, 2009: 93–133.

Nuovo, Angela, 'Produzione e circolazione di libri giuridici tra Italia e Francia (sec. XVI): la via commerciale Lione-Trino-Venezia', in Brizzi and Tavoni (eds.), *Dalla pecia all'e-book*, 341–349.

Orlandi, Franca, 'Medici e mutue', in Malatesta (ed.), *Atlante delle Professioni*, 163–166.

——'L'Ospedale di Santa Maria Nuova e le sue scuole', in Malatesta (ed.), *Atlante delle Professioni*, 33–36.

——'Le riviste mediche', in Malatesta (ed.), *Atlante delle Professioni*, 69–71.

Palao Gil, Javier, 'Los jesuitas y las universidades de la Corona de Aragón', in Polo Rodríguez and Rodríguez-San Pedro Bezares (eds.), *Universidades Hispánicas: Colegios y Conventos Universitarios en la edad Moderna (I)*, 159–188 [Aragón].

Pancino, Claudia, 'La bottega dello speziale', in Malatesta (ed.), *Atlante delle Professioni*, 183.

——'Medici e chirurghi', in Malatesta (ed.), *Atlante delle Professioni*, 124–129.

——'I teatri anatomici', in Malatesta (ed.), *Atlante delle Professioni*, 31–32.

Penuti, Carla, 'I collegi professionali, fabbriche di doctores', in Malatesta (ed.), *Atlante delle Professioni*, 111–113.

Pepe, Luigi, 'Sulla via del rigore. I manuali di calcolo differenziale e integrale nell'Ottocento in Italia', in Brizzi and Tavoni (eds.), *Dalla pecia all'e-book*, 393–413.

Pesenti, Tiziana, 'Il Mantegnismo dei medici: influenze, derivazioni e citazioni mantegnesche nelle illustrazioni del Fasciculus medicinae', *Quaderni per la storia dell'Università di Padova*, 42, 2009: 3–25.

Piccinno, Lucia, 'Gli speziali', in Malatesta (ed.), *Atlante delle Professioni*, 130.

Piovan, Francesco, 'Guillame Philandrier, la natio Burgunda e le " pratiche" per il rettorato giurista padovano del 1538', *Quaderni per la storia dell'Università di Padova*, 42, 2009: 27–61 [Padua].

Polara, Giovanni, 'Gli studi di filologia latina', in Mazzoli (ed.), *Anniversari dell'antichistica pavese*, 121–142 [Pavia].

Polo Rodríguez, Juan Luis and Luis E. Rodríguez-San Pedro Bezares (eds.), *Universidades Hispánicas: Colegios y Conventos Universitarios en la edad Moderna (I) Miscelánea Alfonso IX, 2008* (Aquilafuente, 154), Salamanca, Ediciones Universidad de Salamanca, 2009.

Preti, Alberto, 'Bologna 1977: l'Università', in De Bernardi, Romitelli and Cretella (eds.), *Gli anni Settanta*, 235–248 [Bologna].

Renzo Villata, Maria Gigliola Di, 'Diritto, didattica e riforme nella Pavia settecentesca tra tradizione manoscritta e testi a stampa', in Brizzi and Tavoni (eds.), *Dalla pecia all'e-book*, 297–329.

Romitelli, Valerio, 'Politiche e "movimenti" negli anni Settanta. Problematiche, categorie d'analisi e giudizi storiografici', in De Bernardi, Romitelli and Cretella (eds.), *Gli anni Settanta*, 136–152.

Salustri, Simona, 'La fine del movimento del '77. Bologna punto e a capo?' in De Bernardi, Romitelli and Cretella (eds.), *Gli anni Settanta*, 266–284.

Sanesi, Ireneo, *Memorie di un uomo oscuro*, ed. Federica Marinoni (Fonti e studi per la storia dell'Università di Pavia, 57), Milan, Cisalpino, 2009.

Schubring, Gert, 'The way from the combinatorial school to the reception of Weierstrassian analysis', in Brizzi and Tavoni (eds.), *Dalla pecia all'e-book*, 431–442.

Selvafolta, Ornella, 'Testi, manuali e disegni per l'insegnamento dell'Architettura pratica al Politecnico di Milano nella seconda metà dell'Ottocento: il ruolo di Archimede Sacchi', in Brizzi and Tavoni (eds.), *Dalla pecia all'e-book*, 513–528.

Silvestri, Andrea, 'La rivista "Il Politecnico" da Francesco Brioschi a Cesare Saldini, e altro', in Brizzi and Tavoni (eds.), *Dalla pecia all'e-book*, 541–558.

Sofia, Francesca, 'Ordini e collegi professionali', in Malatesta (ed.), *Atlante delle Professioni*, 137–141.

Solcà, Nicoletta, *Ticinesi all'Università di Pavia* (Fonti e studi per la storia dell'Università di Pavia, 56), Milan, Cisalpino, 2009.

Tacchi, Francesca, 'Le avvocate', in Malatesta (ed.), *Atlante delle Professioni*, 257–260.

—— 'Gli avvocati nell'Italia unita', in Malatesta (ed.), *Atlante delle Professioni*, 142–143.

—— 'I circoli giuridici', in Malatesta (ed.), *Atlante delle Professioni*, 61–62.

—— 'La proliferazione delle testate giuridico-forensi', in Malatesta (ed.), *Atlante delle Professioni*, 64–66.

Tamba, Giorgio, 'I notai dall'impero romano al XVIII secolo', in Malatesta (ed.), *Atlante delle Professioni*, 95–98.

Tarozzi, Fiorenza, 'Il "Bullettino delle scienze mediche"', in Malatesta (ed.), *Atlante delle Professioni*, 67–68.

—— 'Gli esuli', in Malatesta (ed.), *Atlante delle Professioni*, 214–215.

Tavoni, Maria Gioia, 'Le collezioni librarie: medici e ingegneri dell'Ottocento', in Malatesta (ed.), *Atlante delle Professioni*, 50–54.

—— 'Docenti-editori nella prima tipografia parigina', in Brizzi and Tavoni (eds.), *Dalla pecia all'e-book*, 131–140.

Tikhonov Sigrist, Natalia, 'Les femmes et l'université en France, 1860–1914: pour une historiographie comparée', *Histoire de l'education*, 122, 2009: 53–70.

Tinti, Paolo, 'Gesuiti sotto il torchio. stampa, collegi e Università nell'Italia del Settecento', in Brizzi and Tavoni (eds.), *Dalla pecia all'e-book*, 261–274.

Todeschini, Alessandro, 'I notai dal 1860 a oggi: storia e distribuzioni', in Malatesta (ed.), *Atlante delle Professioni*, 147–150.

Tolomelli, Marica, 'Militanza e violenza politicamente motivata negli anni Settanta', in De Bernardi, Romitelli and Cretella (eds.), *Gli anni Settanta*, 192–210.

Trombetta, Vincenzo, 'I libri per la 'gioventù studiosa': manuali e testi universitari a Napoli dall'Unità al Novecento', in Brizzi and Tavoni (eds.), *Dalla pecia all'e-book*, 529–540.

Tura, Diana, 'I notai bolognesi', in Malatesta (ed.), *Atlante delle Professioni*, 99–107.

Valenti, Sandra, 'Le farmaciste', in Malatesta (ed.), *Atlante delle Professioni*, 267–271.

Varanini, Gian Maria, 'I "Quaderni per la storia dell'Università di Padova" e le riviste italiane di storia e di erudizione negli anni Sessanta del Novecento', *Quaderni per la storia dell'Università di Padova*, 42, 2009: 353–365 [Padua].

Ventura, Domenico, *Cultura e formazione economica in una realtà meridionale. La Facoltà di Economia di Catania (1920–1999)*, Catania, Università degli Studi, 2009.

Venturoli, Cinzia, 'L'Università e la protesta giovanile: gli studenti a Bologna', in De Bernardi, Romitelli and Cretella (eds.), *Gli anni Settanta*, 249–265.

Vera de Flachs, María Cristina, 'Universidad de Córdoba (Argentina), de los orígenes a la nacionalización. Fuentes documentales y líneas historiográficas', in Polo Rodríguez and Rodríguez-San Pedro Bezares (eds.), *Universidades Hispánicas: Colegios y Conventos Universitarios en la edad Moderna (I)*, 215–237 [Córdoba (Argentina)].

Veronese Ceseracciu, Emilia, 'Busti di rettori universitari del Seicento nel Palazzo del Bo', *Quaderni per la storia dell'Università di Padova*, 42, 2009: 63–91 [Padua].

Verzella, Manuela, 'Alla base della formazione giuridica: morale e diritti dell'uomo all'Università di Pavia nelle Lezioni di Pietro Tamburini', in Brizzi and Tavoni (eds.), *Dalla pecia all'e-book*, 331–340 [Pavia].

Vicarelli, Giovanna, 'Le medichesse', in Malatesta (ed.), *Atlante delle Professioni*, 262–266.

Weruaga Prieto, Ángel, 'Libros y lecturas académicas en la Salamanca del Barroco y la Ilustración', in Polo Rodríguez and Rodríguez-San Pedro Bezares (eds.), *Universidades Hispánicas: Colegios y Conventos Universitarios en la edad Moderna (I)*, 281–302 [Salamanca].

Zaragoza y Pascual, Ernesto, 'El monasterrio benedectino de San Vincente de Salamanca. Un estado de la cuestión', in Polo Rodríguez and Rodríguez-San Pedro Bezares (eds.), *Universidades Hispánicas: Colegios y Conventos Universitarios en la edad Moderna (I)*, 75–108 [Salamanca].

—— 'Profesores benedectinos del Colegio y Universitdad de Irache (siglos XVI–XIX)', in Polo Rodríguez and Rodríguez-San Pedro Bezares (eds.), *Universidades Hispánicas: Colegios y Conventos Universitarios en la edad Moderna (I)*, 303–358 [Irache].

Zocchi, Paola, 'L'Ospedale maggiore di Milano', in Malatesta (ed.), *Atlante delle Professioni*, 184–185.

Publications 2010

Bagno, Ileana Del, 'Università e studenti nella Napoli spagnola', in Brizzi and Mattone (eds.), *Dai Collegi Medievali alle Residenze Universitarie*, 55–68.

Barretta D., Antonio and Anja Gepponi, 'La casa del Porriore dell'Opera Universitaria di Siena (1933–1981)', in Brizzi and Mattone (eds.), *Dai Collegi Medievali alle Residenze Universitarie*, 181–193.

Bianchi, Angelo, 'Educandati, collegi e conservatori per l'educazione femminile tra Sette e Ottocento', in Brizzi and Mattone (eds.), *Dai Collegi Medievali alle Residenze Universitarie*, 99–112.

Brizzi, Gian Paolo, 'Dai collegi medievali alle residenze universitarie. Introduzione al convegno', in Brizzi and Mattone (eds.), *Dai Collegi Medievali alle Residenze Universitarie*, 9–15.

—— and Antonello Mattone (eds.), *Dai Collegi Medievali alle Residenze Universitarie* (Studi, 12), Bologna, CLUEB, 2010.

Calabrò, Vittoria, 'L'Università di Messina e delle Calabrie: la questione delle residenze e la fondazione della Casa dello studente', in Brizzi and Mattone (eds.), *Dai Collegi Medievali alle Residenze Universitarie*, 113–129.

Esposito, Anna, 'I Collegi universitari di Roma nel '400 e nel primo '500', in Brizzi and Mattone (eds.), *Dai Collegi Medievali alle Residenze Universitarie*, 35–41 [Rome].

Ferrante, Carla and Antonello Mattone, 'Il Collegio dei Nobili di Cagliari e la formazione della classe dirigente del Regno di Sardegna (XVIII-XIX secolo)', in Brizzi and Mattone (eds.), *Dai Collegi Medievali alle Residenze Universitarie*, 69–97.

Fois, Giuseppina, 'Le provvidenze per gli studenti e la questione della residenza universitaria a Sassari nel '900', in Brizzi and Mattone (eds.), *Dai Collegi Medievali alle Residenze Universitarie*, 159–163.

Gaudio, Angelo, 'Le provvidenze per gli studenti nell'età del Fascismo', in Brizzi and Mattone (eds.), *Dai Collegi Medievali alle Residenze Universitarie*, 153–157.

Negro, Piero Del, 'Collegi per studenti: il caso padovano', in Brizzi and Mattone (eds.), *Dai Collegi Medievali alle Residenze Universitarie*, 17–23 [Padua].

Negruzzo, Simona, 'Collegi della Riforma cattolica: il caso pavese', in Brizzi and Mattone (eds.), *Dai Collegi Medievali alle Residenze Universitarie*, 43–54 [Pavia].

Nonnoi, Giancarlo, 'Dallo Studium intramoenia all'Ateneo metropolitano. Edifici e accoglienza della gioventù studiosa nell'Università di Cagliari', in Brizzi and Mattone (eds.), *Dai Collegi Medievali alle Residenze Universitarie*, 131–152 [Cagliari].

Pérez Martín, Antonio, 'Peculiaridades del Colegio de España en Bolonia', in Brizzi and Mattone (eds.), *Dai Collegi Medievali alle Residenze Universitarie*, 25–34.

Scuttari, Alberto, 'La residenzialità universitaria quale fattore critico di successo nella società della conoscenza: prospettive e modelli', in Brizzi and Mattone (eds.), *Dai Collegi Medievali alle Residenze Universitarie*, 165–180.

New Zealand

Collins, Francis Leo, 'Bridges to learning: international student mobilities, education agencies and inter-personal networks', *Global Networks*, 9.2, 2009 [Korea; New Zealand].

Poland

Additions to Earlier Lists

For 2007

Ambrożewicz, Danuta and Grażyna Fallowa (eds.), *Kolegia uniwersyteckie średniowiecznej Europy: katalog wystawy Muzeum Uniwersytetu Jagiellońskiego*, Kraków, 2007 [University Colleges of Medieval Europe: catalogue of the exhibition at the Jagiellonian University Museum].

Skuratowicz, Jan, *Akademia Lubrańskiego: pomnik wielkopolskiej kultury i nauki*, Poznań, 2007 [Lubrański Academy: Great Poland's monument of culture and science].

Publications 2009

Szpet, Jan (ed.), *Od Akademii Lubrańskiego do Wydziału Teologicznego Uniwersytetu im. Adama Mickiewicza: tradycja wyższych studiów teologicznych w Poznaniu*, Poznań, 2009 [From Lubrański Academy to the Theology Department of Adam Mickiewicz University: the tradition of higher theological studies in Poznań].

Taczewski, Tomasz, *Architektura szkoły wyższej*, Gliwice, 2009 [The Architecture of Higher Education Schools].

Romania

Additions to Earlier Lists

For 2005

Cătană, Speranţa-Doina, Marius Cîrnu and Dan Băcilă, *Contribuţii la istoricul învăţământului muzical timişoarean*, Timişoara, Ed. Mirton, 2005, 55 p. [Contributions to the history of Timişoara musical education].

Cotea, Lidia (ed.), *Catedra de limba şi literatura franceză. Scurt istoric*, Bucharest, Editura Universităţii, 2005, 127 p. [The chair of French Language and literature. A short history].

Georgescu, Nicolae and Anca Şipoş, *Facultatea de Ştiinţe Agricole, industrie alimentară şi protecţia mediului*, Sibiu, Editura Alma Mater, 2005, 149 p. [The Faculty of Agricultural Sciences, Food Industry and Environment protection].

Grigoroviţă, Mircea, *Universitatea din Cernăuţi în perioada interbelică*, Suceava, Editura Muşatinii, 2005, 290 p. [The University of Chernivtsi/Cernăuţi during the interwar period].

Iucu, Oana, *Învăţământul juridic în România: abordare istorică şi metodică*, Bucharest, Editura Universităţii, 2005, 168 p. [Judicial education in Romania: historical and methodical approach].

Monografia Facultăţii de Mecanică din Timişoara (1920–1948–2003), Timişoara, Ed. Politenică, 2005, 288 p. [Monograph of the Faculty of Mechanics in Timişoara 1920–1948–2003].

Otiman, Păun Ioan, *Agronomia Banatica. La răspântie de drumuri şi vremuri 1989–2005. Evocările şi reflecţiile unui rector*, Timişoara, Editura Orizonturi Universitare, 2005, 486 p. [Agronomia Banatica. At the crossroads of directions and times 1989–2005. A rector's evocations and thoughts].

Pálfy, Zoltán, 'The Cluj/Kolozsvár University. Cultural politics during the war 1940–1944. An assessment of students recruitment patterns', *Studia Universitatis Babe-Bolyai Politica*, 50.1, 2005: 41–60.

Pop, Dana, *Şcoala economică clujeană interbelică*, Cluj-Napoca, Editura EFES, 2005, 427 p. [The Economy School of Cluj in the interwar period].

Rus, Vasile, *Pro Scientiarum Academia. Calvaria şi şcolile iezuite din Cluj (sec. XVI–XVIII)*, Cluj-Napoca, Editura Ecco, 2005, 273 p. [Pro Scientiarum Academia. Calvaria and the Jesuit Schools in Cluj 16th-18th centuries].

Rusu, Anca Maria (coord.), *Şcoala ieşeană de teatru – istorie şi actualitate*, Jassy, Editura Artes, 2005, 304 p. [Iassy School of drama–history and present].

Sebestyén, Kálmán, 'Kolozsváry egyetemek küldöttsége Debrecenben 1956-ban', *Művelődés*, 59.10, 2005: 4–7 [The delegation of the Universities from Cluj at Debrecen in 1956].

Stoica, Alina Mihaela, *Istoricul activității de educație fizică și sport în Universitatea București 1994–2004*, Bucharest, Editura Bren, 2005, 138 p. [The history of sports training at the University of Bucharest].

Szábo, Miklos, *Erdélyek magyarországy egyetemeken 1848 előtt*, Târgu Mureș, Mentor Kiádo, 2005, 239 p. [People form Transylvania at Universities from Hungary before 1848].

Universitatea de Științe Agricole și Medicină Veterinară a Banatului, Timișoara. 60 de ani 1945–2005, Timișoara, Editura Agroprint, 2005, 311 p. [The University of Agricultural Sciences and Veterinary Medicine of Banat from Timișoara. 60 years].

For 2006

Bişoc, Iosif, 'La riforma dell'insegnamento universitario rumeno: Le nuove sfide per la communità accademica francescana', *Studia Universitatis Babeş-Bolyai. Theologia catholica*, 51.1, 2006: 111–116.

Bodrogi, Enikö M., 'A kolozsváry Finn lektorátus három évtizede', *Korunk*, 17.1, 2006: 68–73 [Three decades of Finnish lectorate at the University of Cluj].

Boia, Stelean-Ioan, 'Rolul universităților din Europa în formarea intelectualității românești din Banat (secolele al XIX - începutul secolului al XX-lea)', *Studii de Știință și cultură*, 2.3–4, 2006: 145–154 [The role of European universities in the formation of the intellectual classes of Romanian population from Banat (the 19th century- beginning of the 20th century].

Făgăraş, Sabin, 'L'insegnamento teologico clandestino a Cluj-Napoca tragli anni 1969–1990', *Studia Universitatis Babeş-Bolyai. Theologia catholica*, 51.1, 2006: 51–60.

Gaspár, Zsófia, 'Înființarea Universității din Cluj (1872) reflectată în jurnalul Parlamentului', *Anuarul Şcolii doctorale*, 2, 2006: 449–458 [The foundation of the Cluj University, reflected in the Hungarian Parliament newspaper].

Mândruţ, Stelian, 'Bemerkungen hinsichtlich die griechisch-katolische rumänische Studierende aus Siebenbürgen an der Budapester teologischen Fakultät (1895/1896–1918/1919)', *Studia Universitatis Babeş-Bolyai. Theologia catholica*, 51.1, 2006: 7–20.

Munteanu, Simona and Ioan Toşa, 'Din activitatea catedrei de etnografie și folclor 1926–1951', *Anuarul Muzeului Etnografic al Transilvaniei*, 20, 2006: 179–206 [The activity of the ethnography and folklore Department 1926–1951].

Păcurariu, Mircea, '220 de ani de învățământ teologic sibian', *Revista Teologica*, 16.3, 2006: 13–18 [220 years of Theological education from Sibiu].

Rados, Leonidas, 'Bursierii români de la Universitatea din Atena în secolul XIX: portretul unui grup', *Anuarul Institutului de Istorie Cluj-Napoca*, 45, 2006: 119–148 [Romanian scholars at the Athens University in the XIX-th century: the portrait of a group].

Tat, Alin, 'Esquisse d'une histoire de la Faculté de théologie grecque-catholique de l'Université Babeş-Bolyai (Cluj)', *Studia Universitatis Babeş-Bolyai. Theologia catholica*, 51.1, 2006: 81–84.

Publications 2008

Stan, Ana-Maria, 'Messages intergénérationnels dans l'espace public. Le cas de l'Université de Cluj après 1919', *Studia Universitatis Babeş-Bolyai. Philologica*, 4, 2008: 57–68.

Russia

Sirotkina, Irina and Roger Smith, 'Le savoir vécu comme une passion: le combat des femmes pour l'enseignement supérieur au XIXe siècle en Russie', in Jacqueline Carroy and others (ed.), *Les femmes dans les sciences de l'homme (XIXe-XXe siècles. Inspiratrices, collaboratrices ou créatrices?*, Paris, Seli Arslan, 2005.

Tikhonov Sigrist, Natalia (ed.), *Les étudiantes de l'Empire des tsars en Europe occidentale, des exilées politiques?*, special issue of *Sextant. Revue du Groupe interdisciplinaire d'études sur les femmes de l'Université libre de Bruxelles*, 26, 2009.

—— 'Les étudiantes étrangères dans les universités occidentales, des discriminations à l'exil universitaire (1870–1914)', in Caroline Barrera and Patrick Ferté (eds.), *Etudiants de l'exil. Universités, refuges et migrations étudiantes (XVIe-XXe siècles)*, Toulouse, Presses universitaires du Mirail, 2009, 105–118.

Scandinavia

Additions to Earlier Lists

For 1992

Lykke, Palle, *Billeder af Aarhus Universitets historie*, Aarhus, University Press, 1992 [Aarhus - A Pictorial History of Aarhus University].

For 1995

Lykke, Palle, *Det lrde Selskab I Aarhus 1945–1995*, Aarhus, University Press, 1995 [Aarhus - The Aarhus Society of Science and Letters 1945–1995].

For 1996

Lykke, Palle, *By og universitet. Universitets-Samvirket, Aarhus 1921–1996*, Aarhus, University Press, 1996 [Aarhus - City and University. Aarhus University Association, 1921–1996].

——' "Det store formaal" - Om de ved Statsbiblioteket ansatte akademikeres engagement i kampen for et universitet i Århus 1906–1928 samt deres virke ved dette i årene 1928–1945', *Rotunden*, 7, 1996: 7–53 [Aarhus - 'The grand aim' - about the role of the scientific staff of the State and University Library in Aarhus participating in the fight to have the second Danish university located in the city of Aarhus 1906–1928 and their subsequent engagement in the development of the university 1928–1945].

Silvonen, Jussi, ' "Nopeammin, nopeammin..." opiskelu ja korkeakoulupolitiikka', in B. Helenius, E. Hämäläinen and J. Tuunainen (eds.), *Kohti McDonalds yliopistoa?*, Helsinki, Tammi, 1996, 73–118 ["Faster, faster..." studies and higher education policy].

For 1997

Hansen, Else, *En koral i tidens strøm. RUC 1972–1997*, Roskilde, Universitetsforlag, 1997 [Roskilde].

Kaiserfeld, Thomas, *Vetenskap och karriär: Svenska fysiker som lektorer, akademiker och industriforskare under 1900-talets första hälft* (Arkiv avhandlingsserie 46, Stockholm Papers in the History and Philosophy of Technology, TRITA-HOT, 2033), Lund, 1997.

Nielsen, Jens Chr., Niels Hasselgaard Jensenius and Henning Salling Olesen (eds.), *Utopien der slog rod. RUC - radikalitet og realisme*, Roskilde, Studenterrådet ved Roskilde Universitetscenter, 1997 [Roskilde].

For 1998

Hansen, Else, 'RUC: et barn af 68?' in *Universitetet og studenterne. Opprør og identitet* (Forum for universitetshistorie. Skriftserie, 4), Oslo, Forum for universitetshistorie, 1998, 87–105 [Roskilde].

Lykke, Palle, *Min ånd er frisk og ubedrvet... Erindringer fra studieårene i Århus. Dagbog og regnskabsbog 1930–1931 samt interview 1993*, Aarhus, University Press, 1998 [Aarhus - My spirit is ready for experience... memories from the student days at Aarhus. Diary 1930–1931 and interview 1993].

For 1999

Kaiserfeld, Thomas, 'Laboratoriets didaktik: Fysiken på läroverken i början av 1900-talet', in Sven Widmalm (ed.), *Vetenskapsbärarna: Naturvetenskapen i det svenska samhället, 1880–1950*, Hedemora, 1999, 188–231.

For 2000

Lykke, Palle, *Medicinsk Lsestue i Aarhus. Om biblioteksmssige foranstaltninger i tilknytning til etableringen af et lgevidenskabeligt miljø i Aarhus fra slutningen af det 19. århundrede og frem til tiden omkring Aarhus Universitets grundlggelse og overlge Victor Albecks død*, Aarhus, Statsbiblioteket, 2000 [Aarhus - The medical library in Aarhus. About establishing book collections in connection with the forming of a scientific medical environment from the end of the 19th century and until the opening of Aarhus University and the death of Victor Albeck].

For 2001

Hansen, Else, 'Staff structure in Danish and Swedish Mass Universities', in *Öresundsunduniversitetet: Sjælland och Skåne - före, under och efter bron*, Lund, 2001, 137–144.

For 2002

Hansen, Else, 'Universitetslærer og -forsker i Danmark og Sverige', in Harald Gustafsson (ed.), *På jakt efter Öresundsregionen*, Lund, 2002, 29–40.

For 2003

Lykke, Palle, *Et galt spektakel. Professor, dr. jur. Stig Jørgensens erindringer og betragtninger efter et halvt århundrede ved Aarhus Universitet*, Aarhus, University Press, 2003 [Aarhus - A strange kind of person. Memories and reflections of professor in jurisprudence Stig Jørgensen after half a century at Aarhus University].

For 2005

Hansen, Else, 'Frihed eller effektivitet? Diskussionen om universitetsstudier 1957–1960', *Uddannelseshistorie. Årbog fra Selskabet for Skole- og Uddannelseshistorie*, 39, 2005: 77–100.

Lykke, Palle, 'Aarhus', in Jos M. M. Hermans and Marc Nelissen (eds.), *Charters of Foundation and Early Documents of the Universities of the Coimbra Group*, Leuven, University Press, 2005, 22–23 and 97 [Aarhus].

——'Aarhus Universitet 1928–1978', in Ingeborg Christensen (ed.), *Aarhus Universitet 1978–2003*, Aarhus, University Press, 2005, 359–405 [Aarhus].

For 2006

Burman, Lars, 'Universitetets museer och det historiska kapitalet', in *Ledarskap i förändring. Rektorsperiode 1997–2006. Festskrift till Bo Sundqvist*, eds. Mattias Bolkéus Blom, Lena Marcusson, Mats Ola Ottosson and Per Ström (Acta universitatis upsaliensis. Skrifter rörande Uppsala universitet: C. Organisation och Historia, 77), Uppsala, Universitet, 2006, 183–188 [Uppsala].

Hansen, Else, 'Elektronisk registrering af studenter ved Københavns Universitet', in Else Hansen and others (eds.), *Ny viden–gamle ideer. Elektroniske registres indførelse i centraladministrationen*, Odense, Syddansk Universitetsforlag, 2006, 114–148 [Copenhagen].

——*Histories of RUC–Roskilde University Centre* (Working Papers on University Reform, 3), Copenhagen, Danmarks Paedagogiske Universitetsskole, 2006 [Roskilde].

254 Bibliography

For 2007

Kaiserfeld, Thomas, 'Den envetna differentieringen: Uppfostringskommissionens reformarbete 1724–1778', *Lychnos. Årsbok för idé- och lärdomshistoria*, 55, 2007: 199–217.

Larsen, Jesper Eckhardt, *'Ikke af brød alene...' Argumenter for humaniora og universitetet i Norge, Danmark, Tyskland og USA 1945–2005*, Copenhagen, Danmarks Pædagogiske Universitetsforlag, 2007 ['Not on bread alone...' Argumentation for the Humanities and the University in Norway, Denmark, Germany and the United States 1945–2005].

Lilja, Johanna, *Kansallisten tieteiden kansainväliset verkostot. Suomalaisen Krxirjallisuuden Seuran ja Suomen Muinaismuistoyhdistyksen julkaisuvaihto 1831–1914*, Tampere, Yliopisto, 2007 [National science in an international network. The exchange of publications by the Finnish Literature Society and the Finnish Antiquarian Society 1831–1914].

Ørberg, Jakob Williams, *Who Speaks for the University? Legislative frameworks for Danish university leadership 1970–2003* (Working Papers on University Reform, 5), Copenhagen, Danmarks Paedagogiske Universitetsskole, 2007.

For 2008

Ammert, Niklas, *Det osamtidigas samtidighet. Historiemedvetande i svenska historieläroböcker under hundra år*, Lund, 2008.

Anderson, Terry H., '1968: The American and Scandinavian experiences', in Tor Egil Førland (ed.), *1968*, special issue of *Scandinavian Journal of History*, 33.4, 2008: 491–499.

Beretta, Marco, Karl Grandin and Svante Lindqvist (eds.), *Aurora Torealis. Studies in the History of Science and Ideas in Honor of Tore Frängsmyr*, Sagamore Beach, Watson Publishing International LLC, 2008.

Burman, Lars, *Att förvalta sitt pund. Om kulturarv och kulturarvsstrategier vid Uppsala universitet*, Uppsala, Universitet, 2008 [Uppsala].

Førland, Tor Egil, ' "1968" in Norway: piecemeal, peaceful and postmodern', in Tor Egil Førland (ed.), *1968*, special issue of *Scandinavian Journal of History*, 33.4, 2008: 382–394.

——'Introduction to the special issue on 1968', in Tor Egil Førland (ed.), *1968*, special issue of *Scandinavian Journal of History*, 33.4, 2008: 317–325.

Hansen, Else, 'Styrelsesloven: den glemte alliance', *Uddannelseshistorie. Årbog fra Selskabet for Skole- og Uddannelseshistorie*, 42, 2008: 107–124.

Heilbron, John L., 'Solomon's Houses: Francesco Bianchini's Academic Places', in Beretta, Grandin and Lindqvist (eds.), *Aurora Torealis*, 51–70.

Jørgensen, Thomas Ekman, 'The Scandinavian 1968 in a European perspective', in Tor Egil Førland (ed.), *1968*, special issue of *Scandinavian Journal of History*, 33.4, 2008: 326–338.

Kolbe, Laura, 'From memory to history: year 1968 in Finland', in Tor Egil Førland (ed.), *1968*, special issue of *Scandinavian Journal of History*, 33.4, 2008: 366–381.

Larsson, Esbjörn (ed.), *Ny utbildningshistorisk forskning. Tio bidrag från Nationella forskarskolan i utbildningshistoria*, Uppsala, 2008.

Lehtonen, Eeva-Liisa, *Pohjoismaiden ensimmäinen kauppatieteiden tohtori Vilho Paavo Nurmilahti 1899–1943* (Helsingin kauppakorkeakoulun julkaisuja, B 97), Helsinki, Kauppakorkeakoulu, 2008 [Helsinki (Kauppakorkeakoulu) - The first Nordic Doctor of Economics Vilho Paavo Nurmilahti 1899–1943].

Lundin, Sverker, *Skolans matematik. En kritisk analys av den svenska skolmatematikens förhistoria, uppkomst och utveckling* (Studier i utbildnings- och kultursociologi, 2), Uppsala, Acta Universitatis Upsaliensis, 2008.

Nybom, Thorsten, 'The Persistent Use and Abuse of Wilhelm von Humboldt in History and Politics - noch einmal', in Beretta, Grandin and Lindqvist (eds.), *Aurora Torealis*, 111–128.

Rothblatt, Sheldon, 'A Note on the "Integrity" of the University', in Beretta, Grandin and Lindqvist (eds.), *Aurora Torealis*, 277–298.

Tellgren, Britt, *Från samhällsmoder till forskarbehörig lärare: Kontinuitet och förändring i en lokal förskollärarutbildning* (Örebro Studies in Education, 24), Örebro, Örebro universitetsbibliotek, 2008 [From Mother of Society to a Teacher Qualified for Post-graduate Studies–Continuity and Change in a Local Pre-school Education].

Publications 2009

Bekker-Nielsen, Tønnes, 'Koldings lange vej til universitetet', *Koldingbogen*, 2009: 5–22 [Kolding].

Berg, Anne and Hanna Enefalk (eds.), *Det mångsidiga verktyget. Elva utbildningshistoriska uppsatser* (Opuscula Historica Upsaliensia, 39), Uppsala, 2009 [The versatile tool. Eleven essays on the history of education].

Bjørgo, Narve, 'Kunnskapspolitikk i plan og i praksis. Frå etableringa av historie som universitetsfag i Tromsø', in Collett, Myhre and Skeie (eds.), *Kunnskapens betingelser*, 56–76 [Tromsø].

Collett, John Peter, 'Universitetet i staten. Striden om fundasen for Det Kongelige Frederiks Universitet 1813–1824', in Collett, Myhre and Skeie (eds.), *Kunnskapens betingelser*, 97–123 [Oslo].

——, Jan Eivind Myhre and Jon Skeie (eds.), *Kunnskapens betingelser. Festskrift til Edgeir Benum*, Oslo, Vidarforlaget, 2009 [The Conditions of Knowledge].

Fulsås, Narve, 'Litteraturen, universitetet og det moderne gjennombrotet', in Collett, Myhre and Skeie (eds.), *Kunnskapens betingelser*, 168–192.

Fure, Jorunn Sem, 'Forskningsuniversitetet– retorisk ideal eller realitet?' in Collett, Myhre and Skeie (eds.), *Kunnskapens betingelser*, 193–217.

256 Bibliography

Haave, Per, 'Fra fritt til lukket medisinstudium. Myndighet og kyndighet i konflikt (1923–1940)', in Collett, Myhre and Skeie (eds.), *Kunnskapens betingelser*, 238–261.

Hakala, Johanna, *Academic Cultures in the Finnish Mass Research University: Change and continuity* (Acta Universitatis Tamperensis, 1400), Tampere, University Press, 2009.

Halvarsson, Berit and Ingrid Holmbäck Rolander (eds.), *Från seminarieklass till akademi. Förskollärarutbildningen i Uppsala under nio decennier*, Uppsala, Universitet, 2009 [Uppsala].

Hansen, Else, 'Masseuniversiteter på tegnebrættet? 1950'ernes universitetsplanlægning i kommissioner og udvalg', in Else Hansen and Leon Jespersen (eds.), *Samfundsplanlægning i 1950'erne. Tradition eller tilløb?*, Copenhagen, Museum Tusculanum Press, 2009, 227–294.

Huusko, Mira, *Yliopistojen itsearviointi on tärkeä kehittämisen väline* (Suomen kasvatustieteellisen seuran Kasvatusalan tutkimuksia, 46), Jyväskylä, Suomen kasvatustieteellinen seura, 2009 [Self-evaluation at Finnish universities: constructing values, development work and image].

Kaataja, Sampsa, *Tieteen rinnalla tekniikkaa. Suomalaiset korkeakoulututkijat kaupallisten sovellusten kehittäjinä 1900-luvulla*, Tampere, 2009 [Technology alongside the science. Finnish academic scientists as developers of commercial technology during the 20th century].

Kallo, Johanna, *OECD education policy. A comparative and historical study focusing on the thematic reviews of tertiary education* (Kasvatusalan tutkimuksia, Jyväskylä, Koulutuksen tutkimuslaitos, 2009.

Kangas, Sini, Marjatta Hietala and Heikki Ylikangas (eds.), *Historia eilen ja tänään. Historiantutkimuksen ja arkeologian suunnat Suomessa 1908–2008* (Bidrag till kännedom av Finlands natur och folk, 179), Helsinki, Suomen Tiedeseura, 2009 [History in past and future. Avenues of research in history and archeology in Finland 1908–2008].

Kohvakka, Mikko, *Kasvukertomus. 40-vuotiaan Lappeenrannan teknillisen yliopiston elämäkerta*, Lappeenranta, 2009 (Lappeenranta (TKK)).

Kotro, Arto, Heikki Tilander and Juhani Haapala (eds.), *Sotakorkeakoulu suomalaisen sotataidon kehittäjänä*, Helsinki, Kustannusosakeyhtiö Siltala, 2009.

Lehikoinen, Esa, Risto Lemmetyinen, Timo Vuorisalo and Sari Kivistö (eds.), *Suomen lintutieteen synty - Turun Akatemian aika*, Turku, Faros-kustannus Oy, 2009 [Åbo/Turku].

Löytönen, Markku (ed.), *Suomalaiset tutkimusmatkat*, Helsinki, Suomalaisen Kirjallisuuden Seura, 2009 [Finnish scientific expeditions].

Muir, Simo, 'Anti-Semitism in the Finnish Academe: rejection of Israel-Jakob Schur's PhD dissertation at the University of Helsinki (1937) and Åbo Akademi University (1938)', *Scandinavian Journal of History*, 34.2, 2009: 135–161 [Helsinki, Åbo/Turku].

Salo, Matti (ed.), *Pohjoisen puolesta, pohjoista varten. Lapin yliopisto 1979–2008*, Rovaniemi, Lapin Yliopisto, 2009 [Lapin yliopisto].

Thue, Fredrik W., 'Masseuniversitetet som stedstap? Fysisk og sosialt rom ved det nye universitetsanlegget på Blindern, 1945–1965', in Collett, Myhre and Skeie (eds.), *Kunnskapens betingelser*, 345–372 [Oslo].

Unemar Öst, Ingrid, *Kampen om den högre utbildningens syften och mål: en studie av svensk utbildningspolitik*, Örebro, Universitet, 2009.

Publications 2010

Aalto, Sari, 'Lääkärien yhteisöllisyydestä ja opinnoista', in Samu Nyström (ed.), *Vapaus, terveys, toveruus - Lääkärit Suomessa 1910–2010*, Helsinki, Suomen Lääkäriliitto & Fennomed, 2010 [The communality and studies of physicians].

Dhondt, Pieter, 'The echo of the quartercentenary of Uppsala University in 1877. Nordic universities as examples in Europe?' *Scandinavian Journal of History*, 35.1, 2010: 21–43 [Uppsala].

Halonen, Tero, *Maaseutuopistoista yliopistoon. Maatalous- ja metsätieteiden tutkimus- ja opetustoiminnan akatemisoitumisprosessi Helsingin Yliopistossa vuoteen 1945*, Helsinki, 2010 [Helsinki - From Provincial Institutes to the University. The Academisation Process of the Research and Teaching of Agricultural and Forest Sciences at the University of Helsinki before 1945].

Spain

Additions to Earlier Lists

For 2005

Aranda Pérez, Francisco (ed.), *Letrados, juristas y burócratas en la España Moderna*, Cuenca, Ediciones Universidad Castilla-La Mancha, 2005.

Clásicos Salamanca, Salamanca, Ediciones Universidad de Salamanca, 2005, 2 vols. [Salamanca].

Gisbert Terol, Ana and M.ª Lutgarda Ortells, *Catálogo de obras impresas en el siglo XVII de la Biblioteca Histórica de la Universitat de València*, València, Servei de Publicacions de la Universitat de València, Patronat Cinc Segles, 2005, 2 vols. [Valencia].

Gragera Rodríguez, M.ª del Mar, 'La Plaza Mayor, un espacio cívico y festivo', in Alberto Estella Goytre, Ángel Vaca Lorenzo and M.ª Nieves Rupérez Almajano (eds.), *Antecedentes medievales y modernos de la Plaza Mayor de Salamanca*, Salamanca, Caja Duero, 2005, 334–361 [Salamanca].

Lahoz Finestres, José M.ª, 'Un estudio sobre los graduados de la Universidad de Huesca', *Argensola. Revista de Ciencias Sociales del Instituto de Estudios Altoaragoneses*, 115, 2005: 245–281 [Huesca].

López Yepes, José (ed.), *Diccionario enciclopédico de Ciencias de la Documentación*, Madrid, Síntesis, 2005, 2 vols.

Ollero Pina, José Antonio, 'La Universidad de Sevilla en los siglos XVI y XVII', in Ramón María Serrera Contreras and Rafael Sánchez Mantero (eds.), *Quinto Centenario. La Universidad de Sevilla, 1505–2005*, Sevilla, Universidad de Sevilla, Fundación El Monte, 2005, 135–203 [Sevilla].

Torremocha Hernández, Margarita, 'El rector de Valladolid en la Edad Moderna. Los límites de la autoridad académica', in Enrique González González and Leticia Pérez Puente (eds.), *Permanencia y cambio. Universidades Hispánicas, 1551–2001*, México, CESU, UNAM, Facultad de Derecho, 2005, 217–247 [Valladolid].

Varela Orol, Concepción, *A Biblioteca Universitaria de Santiago, 1768–1835*, s.l., 2005 [Santiago - Tesis doctoral, Santiago de Compostela].

Vones-Liebenstein, Úrsula, 'El método prosopográfico como punto de partida de la historiografía eclesiástica', *Anuario de Historia Eclesiástica*, 14, 2005: 351–364.

For 2006

Alonso Romero, M.ª Paz, 'Derecho patrio y derecho común en la Castilla moderna', in Italo Birocchi and Antonello Mattone (eds.), *Il diritto patrio tra diritto comune e codificazione (secoli XVI-XIX)*, Roma, Viella, 2006, 101–126.

——, 'Las reglas de juego: herencia procesal y constitucionalismo', *Cuadernos de Derecho Judicial*, 6, 2006: 211–242.

Ballesteros Torres, Pedro, 'Entradas y salidas de libros en bibliotecas de colegios de la Universidad de Alcalá (ss. XVI-XVIII)', in *Libro de actas. X Encuentro de historiadores del Valle del Henares*, Alcalá de Henares, Institución de Estudios Complutenses, 2006, 203–234 [Alcalá].

Borobio García, Dionisio, 'El sacramento de la penitencia en Domingo de Soto', *Salmanticensis*, 53.3, 2006: 421–486 [Salamanca].

Cano, Melchor, *De locis theologicis*, introducción y edición Juan Belda Plans, Madrid, BAC, 2006 [Salamanca].

Chabás, José, 'The University of Salamanca and Renaissance of Astronomy During the Second Half of the 15th Century', in Mordechai Feingold and Victor Navarro Brotons (eds.), *Universities and Science in the Early Modern Period*, Dordrecht, Springer, 2006, 29–36 [Salamanca] (henceforth Feingold and Navarro Brotons (eds.), *Universities and Science*).

Fuertes Herreros, José Luis, 'La escolástica del Barroco: presencia del "Cursus Conimbricensis" en el "Pharus Scientiarum" (1659) de Sebastián Izquierdo', in M. C. Pacheco and J. F. Meirinhos (eds.), *Intellect et imagination dans la Philosophie Médiévale/Intellect and imagination in Medieval Philosophy/ Intelecto e imaginaçã na Filosofia Medieval*, Turnhout, Brepols Publishers, 2006, 159–201.

García Ballester, Luis, 'Medical Science and Medical Teaching at the University of Salamanca in the 15th Century', in Feingold and Navarro Brotons (eds.), *Universities and Science*, 37–64 [Salamanca].

Lilao Franca, Óscar and Margarita Becedas González, 'La Biblioteca General Universitaria: evolución histórica y fondos', in Luis E. Rodríguez-San Pedro Bezares (ed.), *Historia de la Universidad de Salamanca. 3.2: Saberes y confluencias*, Salamanca, Ediciones Universidad de Salamanca, 2006, 879–953 [Salamanca] (henceforth Rodríguez-San Pedro Bezares (ed.), *Historia de la Universidad de Salamanca. 3.2: Saberes y confluencias*).

López, Miguel A., *Los rectores y cancilleres de la Universidad de Granada (1532–2004)*, Granada, Universidad de Granada, 2006 [Granada].

Marcos de Dios, Ángel, 'Portugueses en la Universidad de Salamanca de la Edad Moderna', in Rodríguez-San Pedro Bezares (ed.), *Historia de la Universidad de Salamanca. 3.2. Saberes y confluencias*, 1101–1128 [Salamanca].

Martín Martínez, Félix, Roberto Martínez del Río, Raimundo Gómez Blasi and Antonio Luis Morán Saus, *El arte de tunar*, Valladolid, Fundación Joaquín Díaz, 2006.

Peláez, Manuel J. (ed.), *Diccionario crítico de juristas españoles, portugueses y latinoamericanos*, Málaga et al., Universidad de Málaga et al., 2005–2006, 2 vols.

Ramírez González, Clara Inés, 'Proyección en América: una perspectiva americana', in Rodríguez-San Pedro Bezares (ed.), *Historia de la Universidad de Salamanca. 3.2: Saberes y confluencias*, 1327–1350.

Rodríguez-San Pedro Bezares, Luis E. and Águeda Rodríguez Cruz, 'Salamanca: la fascinación de un nombre', in Rodríguez-San Pedro Bezares (ed.), *Historia de la Universidad de Salamanca. 3.2: Saberes y confluencias*, 1009–1027 [Salamanca].

For 2007

Ballesteros Torres, Pedro, 'Ramillete de nuevos impresos de Alcalá de Henares entre 1701 y 1800', *Anales Complutenses*, 19, 2007: 297–324 [Alcalá].

Coronas, Santos M., 'Los estatutos de la Universidad de Oviedo (siglos XVII–XVIII)', in *Derecho, historia y universidades. Estudios dedicados a Mariano Peset*, Valencia, Universidad de Valencia, 2007, 453–477 [Oviedo] (henceforth *Derecho, historia y universidades*).

Eamon, William and Víctor Navarro Brotóns (eds.), *Más allá de la leyenda negra: España y la revolución científica. Congreso Internacional, Santander, 21–25 de septiembre de 2005*, Valencia, Servei de Publicacions de la Universitat de València, 2007.

Fuertes Herreros, José Luis, 'La ciencia del verdadero conocimiento y del verdadero amor en el Liber creaturarum (Libro de las criaturas) de Ramón Sibiuda († 1436)', *Revista Española de Filosofía Medieval*, 14, 2007: 63–78.

García Oro, José and María José Portela Silva, 'Visitas ordinarias a la Universidad de Alcalá de Henares en el siglo XVI', *Liceo Franciscano*, 59, 2007: 7–701 [Alcalá].

González González, Enrique, *Una república de lectores. Difusión y recepción de la obra de Juan Luis Vives*, coll. Víctor Gutiérrez Rodríguez, México, Universidad Nacional Autónoma de México, Instituto de Investigaciones sobre la Universidad y la Educación, Plaza y Valdés, 2007.

González Navarro, Ramón, 'Alcalá de Henares. Los nobles en la Universidad: los Mendoza', in *Derecho, historia y universidades*, 733–743 [Alcalá].

Gutiérrez Millán, María Eva, *Imágenes de la ciudad de Salamanca (1500–1620), a través de los papeles del legado Ricardo Espinosa Maeso*, Salamanca, Centro de Estudios Salmantinos, 2007 [Salamanca].

Hiniesta Martín, Rosa María, *La antigua bóveda astrológica de Fernando Gallego. Nuevas aportaciones y evolución de su estado de conservación*, Salamanca, Centro de Estudios Salmantinos, 2007 [Salamanca].

López Piñero, José María, *Medicina e Historia natural en la sociedad española de los siglos XVI y XVII*, Valencia, Universidad de Valencia, 2007.

Navarro Brotons, Víctor and William Eamon, *Más allá de la Leyenda Negra. España y la Revolución científica*, Valencia, Instituto de Historia de la Ciencia y Documentación «López Piñero», 2007.

Nieto González, José Ramrxón (ed.), *La Escuela de Nobles y Bellas Artes de San Eloy de Salamanca. Las artes plásticas*, Salamanca, Caja Duero, 2007 [Salamanca].

Pérez Jiménez, Mauricio, *Inventario del patrimonio artístico de la Universidad de La Laguna: artes plásticas y fotografía*, La Laguna, Universidad de La Laguna, 2007 [La Laguna].

Renoux-Caron, Pauline, *Figures de Saint Jérôme dans l'Espagne du XVIe siècle*, s.l., 2007 [Tesis de doctorado, Université Paris III].

Rupérez Almajano, M.ª Nieves and Ana Castro Santamaría, 'The Real Colegio de San Patricio de Nobles Irlandeses of Salamanca', *Acta Comeniana*, 20–21, 2007: 183–200 [Salamanca].

Sánchez Rivera, José Ignacio, *Aedificavit. Los edificios históricos de la Universidad de Valladolid*, Valladolid, Universidad de Valladolid, 2007 [Valladolid].

Sánchez-Blanco, Francisco, *La Ilustración goyesca. La cultura en España durante el reinado de Carlos IV (1788–1808)*, Madrid, Consejo Superior de Investigaciones Científicas, Centro de Estudios Políticos y Constitucionales, 2007.

Torremocha Hernández, Margarita, *El grado de doctor. Una concesión académica tan antigua como la Universidad de Valladolid*, Valladolid, Secretaría General de la Universidad de Valladolid, 2007 [Valladolid].

——'El proceso de creación de la Biblioteca en la Universidad de Valladolid. Otro capítulo de la reforma ilustrada', in *Derecho, historia y universidades*, 741–750 [Valladolid].

Viñas Román, Teófilo, *Agustinos en Toledo*, San Lorenzo de El Escorial, Ediciones Escurialenses, 2007 [Toledo].

For 2008

Albiñana, Salvador (ed.), *Libros en el infierno. La Biblioteca de la Universidad de Valencia, 1939*, València, Publicacions de la Universitat de València, 2008 [Valencia].

Alonso Romero, M.ª Paz, 'Catedráticos salmantinos de Leyes y Cánones en las chancillerías y audiencias regias durante el siglo XVII', in *Ciencia y academia. IX Congreso Internacional de Historia de las Universidades Hispánicas (Valencia, septiembre 2005)*, València, Servei de Publicacions de la Universitat de València, 2008, 87–104 [Salamanca] (henceforth *Ciencia y academia*).

Borobio García, Dionisio, 'El sacramento de la unción de enfermos en Francisco de Vitoria y Domingo de Soto', *Salmanticensis*, 55.2, 2008: 283–320 [Salamanca].

—— *Unción de enfermos, orden y matrimonio en Francisco de Vitoria y Domingo de Soto*, Salamanca, Publicaciones Universidad Pontificia de Salamanca, 2008 [Salamanca].

Borrero Cabal, Alfonso, *La Universidad. Estudios sobre sus orígenes, dinámicas y tendencias*, Bogotá, Compañía de Jesús, Pontificia Universidad Javeriana, 2008, 7 vols.

Ciencia y academia. IX Congreso Internacional de Historia de las Universidades Hispánicas (Valencia, septiembre 2005), València, Servei de Publicacions de la Universitat de València, 2008, 2 vols.

Coronas, Santos M., *Jovellanos y la Universidad*, Gijón, Universidad de Oviedo, Fundación Foro Jovellanos del Principado de Asturias, 2008.

Cruz Cruz, Juan (ed.), *Ley y dominio en Francisco de Vitoria*, Pamplona, Eunsa, 2008 [Salamanca].

Cuadernos del Instituto Antonio de Nebrija de Estudios sobre la Universidad, 11, 2008.

Cubas Martín, Noemí, 'Metodología aplicada al estudio de las universidades renacentistas ibéricas. El caso de los grados académicos en Salamanca', in Javier San José Lera (ed.), *La fractura historiográfica. Los investigadores de Edad Media y Renacimiento desde el Tercer Milenio*, Salamanca, Seminario de Estudios Medievales y Renacentistas (SEMYR), 2008, 555–565 [Salamanca].

Ferrer Benimeli, José Antonio, *El Colegio de la Compañía de Jesús en Huesca (1605–1905)*, Huesca, Insituto de Estudios Alto Aragoneses, 2008 [Huesca].

Fuente Noriega, Margarita (ed.), *1608–2008. Tradición de futuro. Exposición cuatro siglos de historia de la Universidad*, Oviedo, Universidad de Oviedo, 2008 [Oviedo].

García Fraile, Dámaso, *Salamanca en la historia de la Música europea*, Salamanca, Centro de Estudios Salmantinos, 2008 [Salamanca].

García Guadilla, Carmen (ed.), *Pensamiento universitario latinoamericano*. *Pensadores y forjadores de la universidad latinoamericana*, Caracas, IESALC-UNESCO, CENDES, bid & co. editor, 2008.

García Sánchez, Justo, *Los albaceas de la Universidad de Oviedo, 1566–1661*, Oviedo, Real Instituto de Estudios Asturianos, 2008 [Oviedo].

—— (ed.), *Plan de estudios de la Real Universidad de Oviedo, 1774. Reales órdenes. Edición facsímil*, Oviedo, Ediciones Universidad de Oviedo, 2008 [Oviedo].

González González, Enrique, 'Fame and Oblivion', in Charles Fantazzi (ed.), *A Companion to Juan Luis Vives*, Leiden, Brill, 2008, 359–413.

——'Juan Luis Vives. Works and Days', in Fantazzi (ed.), *A Companion to Juan Luis Vives*, 15–64.

González Novalín, José Luis, *El inquisidor general Fernando de Valdés (1483–1568). Su vida y su obra*, Oviedo, Universidad de Oviedo, 2008 [Oviedo - Reedición de la primera edición de 1968].

Gracia Noriega, Ignacio, *El arzobispo Fernando de Valdés: la mitra, la Universidad y la hoguera*, Oviedo, Universidad de Oviedo, 2008 [Oviedo].

Hernández Díaz, José María (ed.), *Influencias francesas en la educación española e iberoamericana (1808–2008). Actas de las III Conversaciones Pedagógicas de Salamanca, 15, 16, 17 y 18 de octubre de 2008*, Salamanca, Globalia Ediciones Anthema y José Luis Hernández Huerta, 2008.

Luzuriaga Sánchez, Gerardo, 'Análisis del fondo bibliográfico de la Universidad de Oñati: por años, por lugares, y por lenguas de publicación', *Boletín de la Real Sociedad Bascongada de los Amigos del País*, 64.1, 2008: 321–368 [Oñate].

—— 'Las huellas de la Inquisición en la Biblioteca de la Universidad de Oñati', *Boletín de la Real Sociedad Bascongada de los Amigos del País*, 64.2, 2008: 751–765 [Oñate].

Madrigal, Alfonso de, el Tostado, *Introducción al evangelio según San Mateo*, texto, traducción, introducción y notas José Manuel Sánchez Caro, Rosa María Herrera García and M.ª Inmaculada Delgado Jara, Salamanca, Servicio de Publicaciones de la Universidad Pontificia de Salamanca, 2008 [Salamanca - edición bilingüe].

Molas Ribalta, Pere, *Los gobernantes de la España Moderna*, Madrid, Actas, 2008.

Pena González, Miguel Anxo, 'Derecho natural y ley natural en las Indias. La propuesta de Vitoria', *Laurentianum*, 49, 2008: 121–139 [Salamanca].

Peset, Mariano, 'Enseñanza en la Facultad de Leyes de Valencia: explicaciones de Mateu Rejaule a inicios del XVII', in *Ciencia y academia*, 2, 261–321 [Valencia].

—— 'Prólogo', in *Ciencia y academia*, 1, 13–23.

Polo Rodríguez, Juan Luis, 'Inclumplimientos docentes de Torres Villarroel', in *Ciencia y academia*, 2, 323–344 [Salamanca].

Ramis Barceló, Rafael, 'El claustro de la Facultad de Leyes y Cánones de la Universidad Luliana y Literaria de Mallorca', *Cuadernos del Insitituto Antonio de Nebrija (CIAN)*, 11, 2008: 287–305 [Mallorca].

Rodríguez Cruz, Águeda, 'Protagonismo de la Universidad de Salamanca en los pensadores y forjadores de las universidades hispanoamericanas', in Carmen García Guadilla (ed.), *Pensamiento universitario latinoamericano. Pensadores y forjadores de la Universidad latinoamericana*, Caracas, CENDES, IESALC-UNESCO, bid & co. editor, 2008, 57–102 [Salamanca].

Rodríguez-San Pedro Bezares, Luis E., 'Disciplinas y saberes universitarios en "El Quijote" cervantino', in *Ciencia y academia*, 2, 469–490.

—— 'Historia e historiografía de las Universidades Hispánicas. Horizonte 2018', *Revista de História das Ideias*, 29, 2008: 715–745.

—— 'Tras las huellas de San Juan de la Cruz. Los contextos de una biografía', *Revista de Espiritualidad*, 67, 2008: 481–500 [Salamanca].

—— and Juan Luis Polo Rodríguez (eds.), *Líneas de investigación sobre Universidades Hispánicas. Miscelánea Alfonso IX, 1999*, Salamanca, Ediciones Universidad de Salamanca, 2008.

—— and Juan Luis Polo Rodríguez (eds.), *Vida estudiantil en el Antiguo Régimen. Miscelánea Alfonso IX, 2001*, Salamanca, Ediciones Universidad de Salamanca, 2008.

—— and Juan Luis Polo Rodríguez (eds.), *La Universidad contemporánea. Miscelánea Alfonso IX, 2000*, Salamanca, Ediciones Universidad de Salamanca, 2008.

—— and Juan Luis Polo Rodríguez (eds.), *La Universidad de Salamanca y sus confluencias americanas. Miscelánea Alfonso IX, 2002*, Salamanca, Ediciones Universidad de Salamanca, 2008.

Ruiz Asencio, José Manuel, Enrique Montero Cartelle, Miguel Ángel González Manjarrés and Salvador Andrés Ordax (eds.), *El documento fundacional del Colegio de Santa Cruz de la Universidad de Valladolid (1483)*, Valladolid, Universidad de Valladolid, 2008 [Valladolid - Edición facsímil].

Universidad de Oviedo. Imágenes del IV Centenario (octubre 2007-marzo 2008), Oviedo, Universidad de Oviedo, 2008 [Oviedo].

Uría, Jorge, Carmen García and Aída Terrón (eds.), *Historia de la Universidad de Oviedo. Vol. I: De la fundación a la crisis del Antiguo Régimen (1608–1808)*, Oviedo, Ediciones de la Universidad de Oviedo, 2008 [Oviedo].

Vicente Baz, Raúl, *Los libros de actas capitulares de la catedral de Salamanca (1298–1489)*, Salamanca, Cabildo Catedral de Salamanca, 2008 [Salamanca].

Vivas Moreno, Agustín and Aitana Martos García, 'Lectura y cultura escrita en "El Quijote"', *Boletín de la ANABAD*, 59.2, 2008: 189–201.

Weruaga Prieto, Ángel, *Lectores y bibliotecas en la Salamanca Moderna, 1600–1789*, Valladolid, Junta de Castilla y León, 2008 [Salamanca].

Publications 2009

Alejo Montes, Francisco Javier, 'Aproximación histórica a la formación institucional de maestros en España', *Campo Abierto. Revista de Educación*, 28.1, 2009: 131–141.

—— 'La Universidad de Salamanca bajo Felipe II en estadísticas', *Historia de la Educación. Revista Interuniversitaria*, 28, 2009: 187–206 [Salamanca].

Alejo Montes, Francisco Javier, 'La vida estudiantil en la Universidad de Salamanca en la época de Felipe II', in *Doctor Buenaventura Delgado Criado. Pedagogo e historiador*, Barcelona, Publicacions i Edicions de la Universitat de Barcelona, 2009, 271–284 [Salamanca].

Barrientos García, José, 'Francisco Cornejo, catedrátido de Filosofía Moral de la Universidad de Salamanca (23-VI-1607/25-I-1621)', *La Ciudad de Dios*, 222.1, 2009: 205–237 [Salamanca].

Borobio García, Dionisio, 'De sacramentis in genere en los salmanticenses (s. XVII). Un comentario al Cursus theologicus', *Salmanticensis*, 56.2, 2009: 237–313 [Salamanca].

Burrieza Sánchez, Javier, 'Los colegios de jesuitas en la Corona de Castilla', in Rodríguez-San Pedro Bezares and Polo Rodríguez (eds.), *Universidades Hispánicas*, 109–157.

Cuadernos del Instituto Antonio de Nebrija de Estudios sobre la Universidad, 12, 2009.

Cuart Moner, Baltasar, 'Papeles de colegiales. Los expedientes de vita et moribus de los colegiales mayores salmantinos del siglo XVI', in Rodríguez-San Pedro Bezares and Polo Rodríguez (eds.), *Universidades Hispánicas*, 15–73 [Salamanca].

Dios, Salustiano de, Javier Infante and Eugenia Torijano (eds.), *Juristas de Salamanca, siglos XV-XX*, Salamanca, Ediciones Universidad de Salamanca, 2009 [Salamanca].

Fuertes Herreros, José Luis, 'La ciencia del verdadero conocimiento y del verdadero amor en el Libro de las criaturas de Ramón Sibiuda', in Giannina Burlando (ed.), *De las pasiones en la Filosofía medieval*, Santiago de Chile, SIEMPM, Universidad Católica de Chile, 2009, 1, 371–390.

García Martín, Javier, 'En los orígenes del derecho comparado. Pierre Rebuffi (1487?-1557) y la creación de una tradición jurisprudencial salmantina en el comentario del derecho regio', in Salustiano de Dios, Javier Infante and Eugenia Torijano (eds.), *Juristas en Salamanca, siglos XV-XX*, Salamanca, Ediciones Universidad de Salamanca, 2009, 13–79 [Salamanca] (henceforth Salustiano de Dios and Torijano (eds.), *Juristas en Salamanca*).

González Calleja, Eduardo, *Rebelión en las aulas. Movilización y protesta estudiantil en la España contemporánea, 1865–2008*, Madrid, Alianza Editorial, 2009.

Hernández Díaz, José María (ed.), *Influencias alemanas en la educación española e iberoamericana (1809–2009)*, Salamanca, Globalia Ediciones Anthema y José Luis Hernández Huerta, 2009.

Hernández Sánchez-Barba, Mario, *Francisco de Vitoria*, Madrid, Universidad Francisco de Vitoria, 2009 [Salamanca].

Malho Fernández, José Luis and Diego Malho Galán, *El Palacio Maldonado*, Salamanca, Ediciones Universidad de Salamanca, 2009 [Salamanca].

Marchamalo Sánchez, Antonio, *Simbolismo, tradiciones y ceremonial histórico en la Universidad Cisneriana Complutense*, Alcalá de Henares, Excmo. Ayuntamiento de Alcalá de Henares, 2009 [Alcalá].

Marcos de Dios, Ángel, *Portugueses na Universidade de Salamanca (1550–1580)*, Salamanca, Luso-Española de Ediciones, 2009 [Salamanca].

Maté Sadornil, Lorenzo (ed.), *Actas y constituciones de los capítulos de la Congregación de San Benito de Valladolid (1497–1610)*, Santo Domingo de Silos, Studia Silentia, 2009.

Mercadier, Guy, *Diego de Torres Villarroel. Máscaras y espejos*, ed. Manuel María Pérez López, Salamanca, Ediciones de la Fundación Salamanca Ciudad de Cultura, 2009 [Salamanca].

Millán Martínez, Juan Manuel and Carlos Julián Martínez Soria (eds.), *Diego Ramírez de Villaescusa: obispo y mecenas*, Cuenca, Ediciones de la Universidad de Castilla-La Mancha, Ayuntamiento de Villaescusa de Haro, 2009.

Palao Gil, Javier, 'Los jesuitas y las universidades de la Corona de Aragón', in Rodríguez-San Pedro Bezares and Polo Rodríguez (eds.), *Universidades Hispánicas*, 159–188.

Pena González, Miguel Anxo, 'Derechos humanos en la Escuela de Salamanca', in José Ramón Flecha Andrés (ed.), *Derechos humanos en Europa*, Salamanca, Universidad Pontificia de Salamanca, 2009, 51–78 [Salamanca].

—— *La Escuela de Salamanca. De la Monarquía hispánica al Orbe católico*, Madrid, Biblioteca de Autores Cristianos, 2009 [Salamanca].

Pena González, Miguel Anxo, 'Influjo de la "Escuela de Salamanca" en las independencias americanas', *Ometeca. Science & Humanities*, 13, 2009: 27–68 [Salamanca].

—— 'La Universidad de Salamanca y el juramento inmaculista: una revisión', in Aleksander Horowski (ed.), *Religoni et doctrinae. Miscellanea de studi offerti a Bernardino de Amellada*, Roma, Istituto Storico dei Cappuccini, 2009, 451–487 [Salamanca].

Perales Birlanga, Germán, *El estudiante liberal. Sociología y vida de la comunidad escolar universitaria de Valencia, 1875–1939*, Madrid - Valencia, Getafe - Instituto Antonio de Nebrija de Estudios sobre la Universidad, 2009 [Valencia].

Peset, Mariano and Pilar García Trobat, 'Historiografía de la Universidad de Salamanca, siglos XIX–XX', in Rodríguez-San Pedro Bezares and Polo

Rodríguez (eds.), *Historia de la Universidad de Salamanca. Vol. IV: Vestigios y entramados*, 389–434 [Salamanca].

Polo Rodríguez, Juan Luis and Jacinto de Vega Domínguez, 'Fuentes impresas para el estudio de las Universidades Hispánicas de Antiguo Régimen', in Rodríguez-San Pedro Bezares and Polo Rodríguez (eds.), *Historia de la Universidad de Salamanca. Vol. IV: Vestigios y entramados*, 127–147.

Rabaté, Colette and Jean-Claude Rabaté, *Miguel de Unamuno. Biografía*, Madrid, Taurus, 2009 [Salamanca].

Ramírez González, Clara Inés and Armando Pavón Romero, 'Historiografía de las universidades iberoamericanas', in Rodríguez-San Pedro Bezares and Polo Rodríguez (eds.), *Historia de la Universidad de Salamanca. Vol. IV: Vestigios y entramados*, 501–533.

Ramos Ruiz, Isabel, *Profesores, alumnos y saberes en la Universidad de Salamanca en el rectorado de D. Antonio Tovar (1951–1956)*, Salamanca, Ediciones Universidad de Salamanca, 2009 [Salamanca].

Rodríguez-San Pedro Bezares, Luis E. and Juan Luis Polo Rodríguez, 'Bibliografía sobre la Universidad de Salamanca (1800–2007)', in Rodríguez-San Pedro Bezares and Polo Rodríguez (eds.), *Historia de la Universidad de Salamanca. Vol. IV: Vestigios y entramados*, 639–836 [Salamanca].

—— and Juan Luis Polo Rodríguez (eds.), *Historia de la Universidad de Salamanca. Vol. IV: Vestigios y entramados*, Salamanca, Ediciones Universidad de Salamanca, 2009 [Salamanca].

—— 'Salamanca y las Universidades Hispánicas. Etapa clásica, siglos XV–XVIII', in Rodríguez-San Pedro Bezares and Polo Rodríguez (eds.), *Historia de la Universidad de Salamanca. Vol. IV: Vestigios y entramados*, 329–387.

—— 'La Universidad de Salamanca en la Edad Moderna: valoración historiográfica, 1990–2007', in Salustiano de Dios and Torijano (eds.), *Juristas de Salamanca*, 441–457 [Salamanca].

—— and Juan Luis Polo Rodríguez (eds.), *Universidades Hispánicas: colegios y conventos universitarios en la Edad Moderna (I). Miscelánea Alfonso IX, 2008*, Salamanca, Ediciones Universidad de Salamanca, 2009.

Rojo Fernández, Daniel, *Religiosidad barroca en la Universidad de Salamanca. La real capilla de San Jerónimo, 1600–1625*, s.l., 2009 [Salamanca - Memoria de grado, Salamanca, Universidad de Salamanca, Facultad de Geografía e Historia].

Santander Rodríguez, Teresa, 'El Archivo Histórico de la Universidad de Salamanca hasta los procesos de informatización', in Rodríguez-San Pedro Bezares and Polo Rodríguez (eds.), *Historia de la Universidad de Salamanca. Vol. IV: Vestigios y entramados*, 51–81 [Salamanca].

Torremocha Hernández, Margarita, 'Nuevos enfoques en la historia de las universidades: la vida cotidiana de los universitarios en la Península Ibérica durante la Edad Moderna', *Chronica Nova*, 35, 2009, 193–219.

Vivas Moreno, Agustín, 'La Archivística universitaria y la función informativa', in Rodríguez-San Pedro Bezares and Polo Rodríguez (eds.), *Historia de la Universidad de Salamanca. Vol. IV: Vestigios y entramados*, 547–635.

Weruaga Prieto, Ángel, 'Libros y lecturas académicas en la Salamanca del Barroco y la Ilustración', in Rodríguez-San Pedro Bezares and Polo Rodríguez (eds.), *Universidades Hispánicas*, 281–302 [Salamanca].

Zaragoza y Pascual, Ernesto, 'Impresiones de los libros oficiales de los benedictinos españoles (siglos XV-XIX)', *Memoria Ecclesiae*, 32, 2009: 365–371.

—— 'El monasterio benedictino de San Vicente de Salamanca. Un estado de la cuestión', in Rodríguez-San Pedro Bezares and Polo Rodríguez (eds.), *Universidades Hispánicas: colegios y conventos universitarios en la Edad Moderna (I)*, 75–108 [Salamanca].

Switzerland

Additions to Earlier Lists

For 2009

Tikhonov Sigrist, Natalia, 'Academic migrations to Switzerland, 1870–1914. The networks behind the numbers', in Jürgen Barkhoff and Helmut Eberhart (eds.), *Networking across Borders and Frontiers*, Frankfurt am Main, Peter Lang, 2009.

—— 'Etrangères dans leur propre pays. Le difficile accès des femmes suisses au savoir académique', in Beatrix Mesmer (ed.), *Der Kampf um gleiche Rechte. Le combat pour les droits égaux*, ed. Association suisse pour les droits de la femme, Basle, Schwabe, 2009.

Unsere Universität–der Comic zur Gründung der Universität Basel 1460, ed. Universität Basel, Basle, Friedrich Reinhardt Verlag, 2009 [Basle].

Ukraine

Shval'b, M. H. ta (red.), *Istorija Kharhivs'koho universytetu za dvisti rokiv: systematychnyj bibliografichnyj pokazhchik*, Kharkiv, 2007 [The History of Kharkiv University over two hundred years: a systematic bibliography].

The United States

Additions to Earlier Lists

For 2005

Karabel, Jerome, *The Chosen. The hidden history of admission and exclusion at Princeton, Yale, Harvard, 1900–2005*, Boston, Houghton Mifflin, 2005.

Levy, Daniel C., *To Export Progress: The Golden Age of University Assistance in the Americas*, Bloomington, Indiana University Press, 2005.

For 2006

Pugh-Bassett, Lovell, *A Meeting of Their Minds to Control Ours: An Analysis of the 1890 and 1891 Mohonk Conferences on the Negro Question and the Creation of Selected Historically Black Colleges and Universities*, s.l., Ann Arbor, 2006 (Thesis, Ph.D., Temple University, UMI #3247302).

Ringenberg, William C., *The Christian College: A History of Protestant Higher Education in America*, 2nd ed., Grand Rapids, MI, Baker Book House Company, 2006.

Ritz, Robert L., *The Roles of Prayer, Petition and Power in Funding Pennsylvania Higher Education: The Response of Colleges and the General Assembly to the Constitutional Convention of 1872–1873*, s.l., Ann Arbor, 2006 (Thesis, Ph.D., Rice University, UMI #3227408).

Schunann, Michael Shawn, *A Historical Examination of the University of Kentucky College of Law and its Affirmative Action Policies and Programs on Admissions Relating to Major Legal Decisions in Higher Education: From 1908 through 2004*, s.l., Ann Arbor, 2006 (Thesis, Ph.D., University of Kentucky, UMI #3231204).

Sumner, Margaret, *Reason, Revelation, and Romance: The Social and Intellectual Construction of Early American College Communities, 1782–1860*, Ann Arbor, s.l., 2006 (Thesis, Ph.D., Rutgers, The State University of New Jersey, UMI #3249354).

Wooten, Melissa, *The Evolution of the Black Higher Education Field, 1854–1996*, s.l., Ann Arbor, 2006 (Thesis, Ph.D., University of Michigan, UMI #3238116).

For 2007

Anderson, Christian K., *The Creation of the Faculty Senates in American research Universities*, s.l., Ann Arbor, 2007 (Thesis, Ph.D., Pennsylvania State University, UMI #3284898).

Eichsteadt, James Eric, *"Shut It Down": The May 1970 National Student Strike at the University of California at Berkeley, Syracuse University, and the University of Wisconsin-Madison*, s.l., Ann Arbor, 2007 (Thesis, Ph.D., Syracuse University, UMI #3266291).

Hudson, Bradford Taylor, *The Historical Origins of American Higher Education for Business*, s.l., Ann Arbor, 2007 (Thesis, Ph.D., Boston University, UMI #3254461).

Kohn, Sheldon Scott, *The Literary and Intellectual Impact of Mississippi's Industrial Institute and College, 1884–1920*, s.l., Ann Arbor, 2007 (Thesis, Ph.D., Georgia State University, UMI #3260565).

Lynch, Mary Lee, *The Impact of Organizational Culture, Feminist Theory and Leadership on the First Seven Presidents on the Development of Mercyhurst College (1926–1972)*, s.l., Ann Arbor, 2007 (Thesis, Ed.D., Duquesne University, UMI #3257420).

Mettler, Suzanne, *Soldiers to Citizens: The G.I. Bill and the Making of the Greatest Generation*, New York, Oxford University Press, 2007.

Miller, Glenn T., *Piety and Profession: American Protestant Theological Education, 1870–1970*, Grand Rapids, MI: William B. Eerdmans Publishing Company, 2007.

Weber, Thomas, *Our Friend 'The Enemy': Elite Education in Britain and Germany before World War I*, Stanford, CA: Stanford University Press, 2007.

For 2008

Alleman, Nathan F., *Faculty Ritual, Solidarity, and Cohesion: Thirty-Five Years of Change at Eastern Mennonite University*, s.l., Ann Arbor, 2008 (Thesis, Ph.D., College of William and Mary, UMI #3319774).

Bahan, Benjamin and Hansel Bauman, 'The Power of Place: The Evolution of Kendall Green', in Greenwald and Vickrey Van Cleve (eds.), *A Fair Chance in the Race of Life*, 154–169.

Drezner, Noah D., 'Building Kendall Green: Alumni Support for Gallaudet University', in Greenwald and Vickrey Van Cleve (eds.), *A Fair Chance in the Race of Life*, 140–153.

Geiger, Roger L., ' "Postwar American Higher Education: Documenting Recent History", Review Essay', *Perspectives on the History of Higher Education*, 27, 2008: 141–151.

Greenwald, Brian H. and John Vickrey Van Cleve (eds.), *A Fair Chance in the Race of Life: The Role of Gallaudet University in Deaf History*, Washington, Gallaudet University Press, 2008.

Hartley, James E. (ed.), *Mary Lyon: Documents and Writings*, South Hadley, MA, Doorlight, 2008.

Hauptman, Laurence M. and Heriberto Dixon, 'Cadet David Moniac: A Creek Indian's Schooling at West Point, 1817–1822', *Proceedings of the American Philosophical Society*, 152, 2008: 322–348.

Herdlein, Richard, 'Deans of Women at Historically Black Colleges and Universities: A Story Left Untold', *Journal of Negro Education*, 77, 2008: 291–305.

Johnson-Bailey, Juanita and others, 'Lean on Me: The Support Experiences of Black Graduate Students', *Journal of Negro Education*, 77, 2008: 365–381.

Jones, Ida, 'Coming of the Race: Kelly Miller and Two Historically Black Colleges and Universities in the Niagara Movement Era', *Afro-Americans in New York Life and History*, 32, 2008: 51–64.

Jowers-Barber, Sandra, 'The Struggle to Educate Black Deaf Schoolchildren in Washington, D.C.' in Greenwald and Vickrey Van Cleve (eds.), *A Fair Chance in the Race of Life*, 113–131.

Joyner, Marieta, 'Douglas Craig, 186?–1936', in Greenwald and Vickrey Van Cleve (eds.), *A Fair Chance in the Race of Life*, 65–84.

Krause, Monika, Mary Nolan, Michael Palm and Andrew Ross (eds.), *The University Against Itself: The NYU Strike and the Future of the Academic Workplace*, Philadelphia, Temple University Press, 2008.

Krentz, Christopher, 'John Carlin and Deaf Double-Consciousness', in Greenwald and Vickrey Van Cleve (eds.), *A Fair Chance in the Race of Life*, 12–21.

Kurz, Christopher A. N., 'Two Views on Mathematics Education for Deaf Students: Edward Miner Gallaudet and Amos G. Draper', in Greenwald and Vickrey Van Cleve (eds.), *A Fair Chance in the Race of Life*, 50–64.

Leslie, W. Bruce, 'The Liberal Pan-Protestant Movement and the Emergence of the University', *Perspectives on the History of Higher Education*, 27, 2008: 127–139.

Lorenzo, David de, 'A Legacy of Leadership: Edward Miner Gallaudet and the Columbia Institution, 1857–1864', Greenwald and Vickrey Van Cleve (eds.), *A Fair Chance in the Race of Life*, 22–32.

McPherson, James M., 'A Fair Chance in the Race of Life: Thoughts on the 150th Anniversary of the Founding of the Columbia Institution', in Greenwald and Vickrey Van Cleve (eds.), *A Fair Chance in the Race of Life*, 1–11.

Miller, Rebecca L., 'Raised for Activism: Henrie Monteith and the Desegregation of the University of South Carolina', *South Carolina Historical Magazine*, 109, 2008: 121–147.

Olson, Michael J., 'The Thomas Hopkins Callaude and Alice Cogswell Statute: Controversies and Celebrations', in Greenwald and Vickrey Van Cleve (eds.), *A Fair Chance in the Race of Life*, 33–49.

Parker, Lindsey M., 'The Women of Kendall Green: Coeducation at Gallaudet, 1860–1910', in Greenwald and Vickrey Van Cleve (eds.), *A Fair Chance in the Race of Life*, 85–112.

Reimold, Daniel R., *'Sex and the University': Celebrity, Controversy, and a Student Journalism Revolution, 1997–2008*, s.l., Ann Arbor, 2008 (Thesis, Ph. D., Ohio University, UMI #3320798).

Reynolds Chaddock, Katherine and James M. Wallace, 'Shaping a Century of Criticism: H.L. Mencken on "Pedagogues" and "Obergogues" in the Rolling Mills of Higher Education', in Roger L. Geiger (ed.), *Curriculum,*

Accreditation, and Coming of Age of Higher Education (Perspectives on the History of Higher Education, 27), New Brunswick NJ, 2008, 105–126.

Sedgwick, Katherine, 'An Ambiguous Purpose: Religion and Academics in the Bryn Mawr Curriculum, 1886–1915', *Perspectives on the History of Higher Education*, 27, 2008: 65–104.

Seniors, Paula Marie, 'Cole and Johnson's The Red Moon, 1908–1910: Reimagining African American and Native American Female Education at Hampton Institute', *Journal of African American History*, 93, 2008: 21–35.

VanOverbeke, Marc A., 'Linking Secondary and Higher Education through the University of Michigan's Accreditation Program, 1870–1890', *Perspectives on the History of Higher Education*, 27, 2008: 33–63.

Wermedal, Douglas R., *It Was Once So: Gender and Generation in College Yearbook Photos*, s.l., Ann Arbor, 2008 (Thesis, Ph.D., South Dakota State University, UMI #3322420).

Williams, Timothy J., 'Confronting a "Wilderness of Sin": Student Writing, Sex, and Manhood in the Antebellum South', *Perspectives on the History of Higher Education*, 27, 2008: 1–31.

Zbrojewska, Monika, 'Dartmouth College v. Woodward: Freedom of Contracts and Private Education', *Krakowskie Studia Miedzynardowe*, 5, 2008: 397–403.

For 2009

Abdulrahim, Masoud A., Ali A. J. Al-Kandari and Mohammed Hasanen, 'The Influence of American Television Programs on University Students in Kuwait: A Synthesis', *European Journal of American Culture*, 28, 2009: 57–74.

Bastedo, Michael N., 'Conflicts, Commitments, and Cliques in the University: Moral Seduction as a Threat to Trustee Independence', *American Educational Research Journal*, 46, 2009: 354–386.

Behrens, Richard K., 'From the Connecticut Valley to the West Coast: The Role of Dartmouth College in the Building of the Nation', *Historical New Hampshire*, 63, 2009: 45–68.

Bishirjian, Richard J., 'Difficult Labor: The Perils of Birthing a New College', *Academic Questions*, 22, 2009: 284–297.

Bradley, Stefan M., *Harlem vs. Columbia University: Black Student Power in the Late 1960s*, Urbana, University of Illinois Press, 2009.

Byrd, Joseph, 'Whitewashing Blackface Minstrelsy in American College Textbooks', *Popular Music and Society*, 32, 2009: 77–86.

Candal, Cara Stillings (ed.), *Partnering for Progress: Boston University, the Chelsea Public Schools, and Twenty Years of Urban Education Reform*, Charlotte, N.C., Information Age Publishing Inc., 2009.

Christopher, Renny, *A Carpenter's Daughter: A Working-Class Woman in Higher Education*, Rotterdam, SensePublishers, 2009.

Clancy, Patrick and David D. Dill (eds.), *The Research Mission of the University: Policy Reforms and Institutional Response*, Rotterdam, SensePublishers, 2009.

Cleave, Kendra, 'Fashioning the College Woman: Dress, Gender, and Sexuality at Smith College in the 1920s', *Journal of American Culture*, 32, 2009: 4–15.

Coen, Ross, 'Not Old Enough to Vote but Able to Support Statehood: University of Alaska Students and the Statehood Movement, 1955–1957', *Alaska History*, 24, 2009: 1–14.

Cohen, Robert, *Freedom's Orator: Mario Savio and the Radical Legacy of the 1960s*, New York, Oxford University Press, 2009.

Damgaard, Marshall, 'Closing Time: A Twenty-Five-Year Retrospective on the Life and Death of the University of South Dakota at Springfield', *South Dakota History*, 39, 2009: 189–267.

Dosen, Anthony J., *Catholic Higher Education in the 1960s: Issues of Identity, Issues of Governance*, Charlotte, N.C., IAP-Information Age Publishing, Inc., 2009.

Downs, Gregory P., 'University Men, Social Science, and White Supremacy in North Carolina', *Journal of Southern History*, 75, 2009: 267–304.

Edirisooriya, Gunapala, 'A Market Analysis of the Latter Half of the Nineteenth-Century American Higher Education Sector', *History of Education*, 38, 2009: 115–132.

Gasman, Marybeth and Noah D. Drezner, 'A Maverick in the Field: The Oram Group and Fundraising in the Black College Community during the 1970s', *History of Education Quarterly*, 49, 2009: 465–506.

Gershenhorn, Jerry, ' "Not an Academic Affair": African Studies Scholars and the Development of African American Programs in the United States, 1942–1960', *Journal of African American History*, 94, 2009: 44–68.

Grubiak, Margaret M., 'Reassessing Yale's Cathedral Orgy: The Ecclesiastical Metaphor and the Sterling Memorial Library', *Winterthur Portfolio*, 43, 2009: 159–184.

Ingrassia, Brian M., *A Department of the Modern University: Discipline, Manliness, and Football in American Intellectual Culture, 1869–1929*, s.l., Ann Arbor, 2009 (Thesis, Ph.D., University of Illinois, Urbana-Champaign, UMI # DA3337801).

Kaskowitz, Sheryl, 'All in the Family: Brandeis University and Leonard Bernstein's "Jewish Boston" ', *Journal of the Society for American Music*, 3, 2009: 85–100.

Kimball, Bruce A., *The Inception of Modern Professional Education: C. C. Langdell, 1826–1906*, Chapel Hill, University of North Carolina Press, 2009.
—— ' "This Pitiable Rejection of a Great Opportunity": W. E. B. Du Bois, Clement G. Morgan, and the Harvard University Graduation of 1890', *Journal of African American History*, 94, 2009: 5–20.

King, William E., 'The Discovery of an Architect: Duke University and Julian F. Abele', *Southern Cultures*, 15, 2009: 6–21.

Knight, Jane (ed.), *Financing Access and Equity in Higher Education*, Rotterdam, SensePublishers, 2009.

Lawton, Christopher R., 'Constructing the Cause, Bridging the Divide: Lee's Tomb at Washington's College', *Southern Cultures*, 15, 2009: 5–39.

Massey, Drew, 'Leonard Bernstein and the Harvard Student Union: In Search of Political Origins', *Journal of the Society for American Music*, 3, 2009: 67–84.

Mata, Tiago, 'Migrations and Boundary Work: Harvard, Radical Economists, and the Committee on Political Discrimination', *Science in Context*, 22, 2009: 115–143.

McNulty Eitle, Tamela and Matthew Steffens, 'Religious Affiliation and Beliefs about Racial Inequality: White College Students' Attitudes about Black-White and Native American–White Inequality', *Social Science Journal*, 46, 2009: 506–520.

Minor, James T., 'A Contemporary Perspective on Public HBCUs: Perspicacity from Mississippi', *Journal of Negro Education*, 77, 2009: 323–335.

Nye, Robert A., 'The Legacy of Masculine Codes of Honor and the Admission of Women to the Medical Profession in the Nineteenth Century', in Ellen S. More, Elizabeth Fee and Manon Parry (eds.), *Women Physicians and the Cultures of Medicine*, Baltimore, Johns Hopkins University Press, 2009, 141–159 (henceforth More, Fee and Parry (eds.), *Women Physicians and the Cultures of Medicine*).

Prescott, Heather Munro, 'Women Physicians and a New Agenda for College Health, 1920–1970', in More, Fee and Parry (eds.), *Women Physicians and the Cultures of Medicine*, 294–318.

Rogers, Naomi, 'Feminists Fight the Culture of Exclusion in Medical Education, 1970–1990', in More, Fee and Parry (eds.), *Women Physicians and the Cultures of Medicine*, 205–241.

Sakamoto, Tatsuro, '1920 Nedai no Amerika Josei Daigakujin Kyokai(aauw) no akuredideshon: Fakaruti niokeru jenda no byodo o chushin ni' (Integrating gender into accreditation: The American Assocation of University Women's effort to achieve gender equity in university faculty in the 1920s)', *Amerika-shi-Kenkyu*, 32, 2009: 36–53 (In Japanese).

Shiell, Timothy C., *Campus Hate Speech on Trial*, Expanded second edition, Lawrence, University Press of Kansas, 2009.

Solberg, Winton U., 'A Struggle for Control and a Moral Scandal: President Edmund J. James and the Powers of the President at the University of Illinois, 1911–14', *History of Education Quarterly*, 49, 2009: 39–67.

Urbanski, Michael T., 'Polite Avoidance: The Story behind the Closing of Alliance College', *Polish American Studies*, 66, 2009: 25–42.

Wechsler, Harold S., 'How Getting into College Led Me to Study the History of Getting into College', *History of Education Quarterly*, 49, 2009: 1–38.

Winkle-Wagner, Rachelle, *The Unchosen Me: Race, Gender, and Identity among Black Women in College*, Baltimore, Johns Hopkins University Press, 2009.

Publications 2010

Abelmann, Nancy, *The Intimate University: Korean-American Students and the Problems of Segregation*, Durham, Duke University Press, 2010.

Baumann, Roland M., *Constructing Black Education at Oberlin College: A Documentary History*, Athens, Ohio University Press, 2010.

Clark, John B., W. Bruce Leslie and Kenneth P. O'Brien (eds.), *Suny at Sixty: The Promise of the State University of New York*, Albany, State University of New York Press, 2010.

Demas, Lane, *Integrating the Gridiron: Black Civil Rights and American College Football*, New Brunswick, Rutgers University Press, 2010.

Estes, Steve, 'The Long Gay Line: Gender and Sexual Orientation at the Citadel', *Southern Cultures*, 16, 2010: 46–64.

Lambert, Frank, *The Battle of Ole Miss: Civil Rights v. States' Rights*, New York, Oxford University Press, 2010.

Nelson, Cary, *No University is An Island: Saving Academic Freedom*, New York, New York University Press, 2010.

Smith, Brett H., *Labor's Millennium: Christianity, Industrial Education, and the Founding of the University of Illinois*, Eugene, Ore., Pickwick, 2010.